de Gruyter Studies in Organization 1

McMillan: The Japanese Industrial System

de Gruyter Studies in Organization

An international series by internationally known authors presenting current fields of research in organization.

Organizing and organizations are substantial pre-requisites for the viability and future developments of society. Their study and comprehension are indispensable to the quality of human life. Therefore, the series aims to:

- offer to the specialist work material in form of the most important and current problems, methods and results;
- give interested readers access to different subject areas;
- provide aids for decisions on contemporary problems and stimulate ideas.

The series will include monographs, collections of contributed papers, and handbooks.

Charles J. McMillan

The Japanese Industrial System

Second Revised Edition

Walter de Gruyter · Berlin · New York 1985

Dr. Charles J. McMillan
Professor of Business Policy and International Business at the Faculty of Administrative Studies of
the York University Toronto, Canada

to Kazuyo, with affection and appreciation

Library of Congress Cataloging in Publication Data

McMillan, Charles J.
  The Japanese industrial system.
  (De Gruyter studies in organization ; 1)
  Bibliography: p.
  Includes indexes.
  1. Industrial management--Japan. 2. Industry and state--Japan. I. Title. II. Series.
HD70.J3M4 1985   658'.00952   84-23270
ISBN 0-89925-005-X (U.S.)

CIP-Kurztitelaufnahme der Deutschen Bibliothek

McMillan, Charles J.:
The Japanese industrial system / Charles J. McMillan. – 2., rev. ed.
– Berlin ; New York : de Gruyter, 1985. –
  (De Gruyter studies in organization ; 1)
  ISBN 3-11-010410-5
NE: GT

---

3 11 010410 5 Walter de Gruyter · Berlin · New York
0 89 925 005 X Walter de Gruyter, Inc., New York

Preface

This book is the result of more than 15 years of study, long periods of observing the Japanese, and extensive research into Japanese companies and government, enriched during my continuous studies at American, European and Japanese universities.

The work started as an empirical study of management practices in Japanese industrial firms. Having taken a year's sabbatical in Japan in 1980, and an extensive period in France in 1981, I decided to widen the book's focus. The idea was to study the institutional framework of the entire Japanese economy and the evolving management strategies in the 1980's. This book examines the Japanese "model" at three levels that I suggest are fundamental, if the Japanese success – and their competitive threat – are to be fully understood.

The first level is government. National industrial policy has become the fashionable issue in North America, where industrial strategy is seen as the choice and use of selective policy instruments that shape a country's comparative advantage. Japan's use of information and application of global competitive analysis is crucial to this exercise. But it does not follow that government itself is as central as many writers, especially U.S. academics, have suggested, particularly in the last 15 years when Japan has reached its competitive zenith.

To this first level is added a second, namely microeconomic sector analysis within a framework of growing, maturing, and declining industries. Like all other Western countries, Japan uses traditional levers of aggregate economic policy. To them Japan has, however, developed an enormous information infrastructure for each major industrial sector with comparisons of domestic preformance to international standards of productivity, technology, and market share.

At the third level, that of the corporation, Japan differs not so much in quantity of planning as in quality. Japanese corporations can tap the munificient information systems not just of government, but also, of trading firms, consultants, commerical banks, not to mention their own planning departments. These inter-organizational networks are not unique to Japan, but the thoroughness of information gathering and strategic assessment of industrial intelligence has hardly any parallel in Western firms.

The most common question foreigners ask of books about Japan is straightforward: what can we learn from that country? In a most fundamental way, this is the wrong question. Japan's strategic thrust in industrial policy, technology, and new products reflect Japans's interest in and payoffs from the global economy. Japan will be guided by certain policies and aporoaches involving a careful assessments of their own results – car quotas in North America, protection in Europe, tax and exchange policy at home, tariff policies and import penetration from Third World countries. The fact is, Japan has its own ideas of where it should go in this and future decades. The Japanese even communicate to Westerners about these ideas, in various native languages, especially English. In reality, it is not a matter of learning the Japanese way and of applying it to western practice. Rather, the real questions are why the Japanese see the world as they do, what they intend to do about it, and how their institutional arrangements fit their strategies. Japan can serve as an effective mirror for Western countries in a broad spectrum of management functions and across the the three levels mentioned earlier. Contrary to conventional opinion, the Japanese did not and do not copy and imitate foreign management and technology; they study and learn from foreign techniques, selectively apply foreign ideas, and adapt them to the domestic environment. Foreigners themselves would do well to "copy" or "imitate" this approach.

In the course of carrying out this study, I have been the beneficiary of wise counsel, thoughtful patience, and discreet criticisms. At York University, I acknowledge the grateful assistance of numerous graduate students who indulged my learning in the guise of teaching. I am also grateful to several colleagues in the Faculty of Administrative Studies: Wallace Crowston, Vic Murray, L. S. Rosen, Rein Peterson, Dezso Horvath, Don Daly, Don Thompson, Todd Jick, Rob Lucas, Tillo Kuhn, Wade Cook and Ron Burke.

Within the academic fraternity I also thank my old friend and collaborator Koya Azumi, who introduced me to Japan and has been invaluable over the years; Professor Keith Hay, Carleton University, Ottawa; Dr. Randy Ross, McMaster University, Hamilton, Ontario; Dr. Richard Wright, McGill University, Montreal, P. Q.; David Hickson, my thesis chairman, friend and mentor at the Management Center, University of Bradford; Bob Hinings, formerly of University of Birmingham, now University of Alberta; Professor Derek Pugh, formerly of London Business School, now at the Open University, England; Charles Perrow, Stoneybrook, U.S.A.; Michael Bicheron and Daniel Rouach, Ecole Superière de Commerce, Lyon, France; Phillip Albert, Director, Institute de Recherche de L'Enterprise, Lyon, France; Dr. Rodney Schneck, School of Busuness, University of Alberta; Professor J. Ballon, Sophia University, Tokyo; Dr. Derek Channon, University of Manchester Business School; and Dr. William Evan, Wharton School, Pennsylvania.

In the course of preparing the book, I have had the opportunity to discuss and debate certain points with several hundred various industrial leaders in Europe, Japan, the U.S., Canada and elsewhere. I have benefitted from such a dialogue and especially acknowledge the help of Shotaro Nagata, D. Nagata, Tokyo and Kobe, Japan: Dr. Regis Duffy, Diagnostic Chemicals, Charlottetown, P. E. I.; Greg Guthrie, Canada-Japan Trade Council, Ottawa;

Dr. James Abegglen, Boston Consulting Group, Tokyo; Al Saipe of Thorne, Stevenson and Kellogg, Toronto; Mr. Rollie Frakes, Nova Chemicals, Calgary; Mr. Brian Mulroney, Iron Ore Company of Canada, Montreal; Mr. Pierre Hueber, Wilma International, Antwerp, Belgium; Dr. Aodh O'Dochartaigh, ICL Limited, London, England; William J. Weisz, Chief Operating Officer, Motorola Inc.; and Jacques Lagarde, PDG, Gillette France, Annecy, France.

The above mentioned individuals have generously shared with me their knowledge and insights without which this book would not have been possible. But I must not cause them to share also the blame for any of its shortcomings. That blame is mine alone.

Funding for this study has come from several sources. I thank, in particular, the following groups: Social Science and Humanities Research Council, Ottawa, Canada; York University – University of Toronto Joint Center on South East Asia; Japanese Society for the Promotion of Sciences; the Faculty of Administrative Studies Research Committee; the University of Waterloo Innovation Center; the University of Western Ontario Business School; and the Social and Humanities Research Council, London, England.

Werner Schuder has been particularly supportive in all matters relating to publication. The following journals have allowed me to reprint previously published material: California Management Review, Business Quarterly, Cost and Management, Journal of General Management, Organizational Studies, International Studies of Management and Organization.

A book requires many things, among them sufficient conceit on the part of the author to deem the work worthy of a dedication. The canons of academe suggest that a book be dedicated to one's children. Aya Chantal and Mari Christine will forgive me, however, for dedicating this work instead to my collaborator, my teacher and my first love – to Kazuyo, my wife.

Toronto, Canada   Charles McMillan
June 1983

Contents

Chapter 1
Samurai Management in a World Economy

"When looking at the West from outside the Western Hemisphere, one
attitude stands out. It is just how anx-
ious Americans and Europeans are
to *teach* the rest of the world."

Robert J. Ballon

1.1 Introduction

The area is not large – a few city blocks only minutes away from central Tokyo
by subway. By any standard the buildings are not impressive – they include five
and six storey structures covered with flashing lights and perpetually glowing
neon signs, and some old wooden buildings almost on the verge of collapse.
The stores are not exactly typical of Japan's super modern department stores.
The merchandise is piled high. The sales clerks are anything but hospitable.
The sales dialogue has more in common with a bazaar in Morocco than a retail
outlet in a country where no tipping, politeness and cleanliness are universal
watchwords.

The electronic goods on display in Tokyo's Akihabara district clearly demonstrates Japan's enormous capacity to churn out quality products of all descriptions. The list seems endless – household appliances like microwave ovens,
fridges, televisions, video recorders, stereo equipment, cooking appliances and
Kotatsu – eating tables with built-in heating elements; battery driven products
of the conventional or zany kind – from calculators, tape recorders, musical
instruments, miniature TV sets, to electrical pencil erasers, radar detection
devices, electrocution resistant wet diaper alarms and battery operated cork-
screws. There are also the products of the computer age – integrated circuits,
semi-conductors, circuit boards, memory chips, kits for small robots, random
access memory devices and video displays.

To the casual visitor, the crowded Akihabara is a natural outgrowth of the
country's inefficient distribution system; its overcrowded cities; its real life
contrast to the conventional tourist attractions such as shrines, temples, and
natural ports. Akihabara also might seem a good discount area where prices
are subject to negotiation and haggling, where language barriers mean little if
sales prices can be written on slips of paper.

Beneath this picture of the Akihabara electronics bazaar is a considerably more
complex phenomenon, and one which helps to explain why Japan may lead the

world in the twentieth century industrial revolution – the world of electronics
and the chip. Akihabara is a daily demonstration of Japanese learning and
social adaptability. It is a living display for housewives and citizens far removed
from company laboratories to see and experience new products. It is an out-
of-school classroom for very young high school students to match wits with
products described in the numerous science magazines sold at every subway
station. It is a test market for the scores of electronic engineers touring the area
to search out new applications and processes for Japan's enlightened electronics consumers. Akihabara, in short, is a window on technology for Japan's
highly literate population – a window which even encompasses introducing
English terms to the Japanese language as household words – robotics, mechatronics, semi-conductors, software, hardware, fiber optics, integrated circuits.
This area of Tokyo, and smaller replicas all over the country serve, in other
words, an educational function to the technologies of tomorrow, to describe,
analyze and demonstrate to the average citizen what the micro electronics
revolution means for everyday life – work and leisure, the factory and the
home, the car and the computer. Behind this function is a host of managerial
ideas for industry and government which give vision and direction to Japan's
managerial strategies for the 1980's and beyond.

1.2 Japan as Industrial Superpower

In 1980, Japan overtook the United States as the leading producer of automobiles. In 1981, the Japanese government launched a ten year programme to
build a fifth generation computer system, thereby becoming the world's leading
supplier of advanced computer systems. In these two developments, i.e., mas-
tering the two major industries of the nineteenth and twentieth century, Japan
has mapped out profound changes in the competitive world of the global economy, a shift in the center of gravity for technology and production away from
the North Atlantic to the Pacific. Moreover, of equally profound consequences, Japan is challenging many of the accepted cannons of management
itself – the techniques of production, marketing, and marriage of human assets
and technology.

In business and government circles in Western countries, there is uncommon
unity in one subject – Japanese economic success. The business traveller flying
Air France or British Airways to Europe can flip through the pages of the
airline magazine only to see page after page of beautiful coloured ads – all for
Japanese products. The government bureaucrat attends conferences on joint
policy initiatives – to take some action on Japanese market penetration. The
student of business administration in Europe, raised for a generation to cast an
eye across the Atlantic for American management techniques, is now likely to
ask, "but how do the Japanese do it?"

At a time when Japanese economic growth and productivity are the envy of the world, when health indicators like low infant mortality and life longevity are of Scandinavian proportions while crime rates have halved in a generation, thoughts inevitably turn to a rationalization for such success. Three views are popular, and each has a certain validity. First, there is the cultural argument about the pattern of social values and institutions which give rise to consensus and group collectivism. In this perspective, the Japanese are unique and while various management practices may work well in Osaka and Tokyo, they aren't likely to be very successful in Cleveland, Leeds, or Milan. Second, there is the superman theory of the Japanese who, with very low defense expenditures and an overwhelming commitment to economic success, are creating an industrial superstate, egged on by a desire to be number one. Steel, autos and shipbuilding are the examples from the past; computers, banking, and biotechnology are the new targets for the next decade. A third view, and the one developed in this study, is that the Japanese "system" of management is neither unique nor theoretically novel in itself – what is different is that the Japanese are applying textbook management principals in everyday work life. Such principals are economically sound, managerially rational, and equally applicable to any industrial society, including the United States, Europe and Canada.

By almost any set of forecasts, Japan stands in the vanguard of economic growth during the 1980's. This fact alone makes this resource poor, people-crowded country the focus of comparative study. While the United States is experiencing almost a decade of no real productivity improvements overall, Japanese projections see annual growth improvements of five per cent or more, with inflation at a much lower rate. While Britain and Europe suffered higher unemployment in 1981–1982 than during the worst years of the depression, Japan's workforce of about 56 million has only 1.13 per cent unemployed, or two per cent of the total population, a bit higher by unofficial rates.

The irony of Japanese success is particularly striking compared to the U.S. The watchword of American economic policy is revitalization, a rebuilding of geriatric sectors with aged plant and equipment.[1] The difficulty and challenge are doubly compounded by declining productivity and the need to adjust to high priced energy. By contrast, almost a decade after the first oil shock, Japan has modernized and re-equipped the industrial structure to world energy prices, at once shedding energy-intensive sectors and reallocating resources to reduce oil requirements. In 1973, compared to the U.S., Japan used only 57 percent as much energy for every unit of GNP; by 1980, this percent dropped to only 43 percent (Yergin, 1982). Notwithstanding the election of a pro-business Presi-

---

[1] For representative approaches, see Thurow (1982), Dewar (1982), Magaziner and Reich (1981), and Rohatyn (1982).

dent in 1980 an atmosphere of despondency, pessimism and defeat characterize many centers of U.S. society. "From the boardroom to the research laboratory," writes Yale business school Dean and Director of Amdahl computers, Burton Maltciel, "The consensus seems to be that U.S. enterprise has lost its innovative touch." The American correspondent for Britain's *Management Today* adds the view that "there is an unbridgeable gulf between business and truly advanced science. Business is still animated by the works, if not the spirit, of the 'gifted tinkerers', by the pragmatic outlook, by the urge to maximize the returns on what is, rather than speculate on what might be" (Thackery, 1980).

The introspective analyses of American writers have prompted a fresh look at everything from the efficiency of government programmes and the need for coherent industrial policy, to the way corporations are managed, the way workers are treated, the way technology is introduced. Thus, for example, foreign models from West Germany, Sweden and Japan are the order of the day, particularly in the area of business/government relations. The relative decline of the American economy is almost taken for granted. Do the facts and figures bear out this pessimistic analysis? For one thing, it is easy to go to one of two extremes – to take, for instance, detailed comparisons of particular industries such as cars or textiles, which have taken a severe battering in recent years. Similarly, one can place unwarranted emphasis on macro aggregate statistics which gloss over major differences by industry groupings or variations in the industrial structure of different countries. Another difficulty is to make claims about differential growth rates and productivity based on single hypotheses or single variable explanations (Dennison, 1979).

Exhibit 1/1: Real GDP Per Employed Person Own Country Price Weights, Selected Years, 1950–1980 (United States = 100)

Country	1950	1970	1980
Canada	84.5	91.9	91.4
Japan	13.5	42.1	58.4
Belgium	45.6	59.8	69.3
France	38.6	64.3	80.0
Germany	32.6	61.9	74.4
Italy	23.1	48.1	54.2
Netherlands	46.5	63.4	72.8
United Kingdom	47.2	50.3	54.5
Unweighted average, eight countries	41.4	60.2	69.4

Source: Daly (1980)

The overwhelming evidence is that on a per capita basis, the United States has the highest gross domestic product, not only in 1950 or 1970 but in 1980 and

Exhibit 1/2: Comparative Indices of Macro Economic Goals

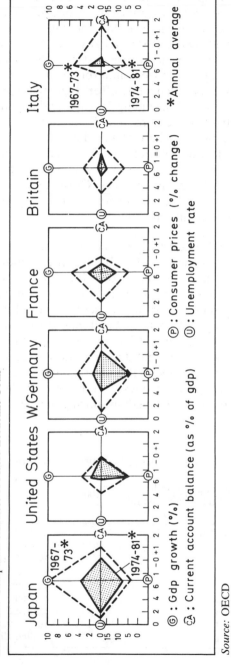

Source: OECD

beyond. Moreover, despite perceptions to the contrary, U.S. growth has never exceeded two per cent over any significant period, yet the growth between 1950 and 1980, despite the slowdown since 1973, actually exceeded the growth rates between 1890 to 1950 (Daly, 1981). To say that U.S. wealth and economic growth have declined relative to historical standards does not mean that other countries have not gained. Indeed, inherent in U.S. economic and foreign policy since 1945 has been a deliberate effort to increase productivity and trade in other areas of the world, including Europe and Japan. Their relative improvements are actually a measure of U.S. economic policy success (Calleo, 1981.) For instance, the U.S. share of world exports in 1955 amounted to 16.6 per cent; a quarter of a century later, that figure had declined to 11 per cent, or only a sixth of all developed countries' world exports. Japan, by contrast, went from 2.2 per cent to 6.3 per cent and West Germany went from 6.6 per cent to 10.5 per cent. Yet the level of U.S. exports both as a percentage of GNP and dollar amounts are at an all time high.

Economic growth and productivity indices are not the only standard of macroeconomic policy. As shown in Exhibit 1/2, the diamond shaped charts reflect the balance of macroeconomic goals for any one country, namely economic growth, inflation, unemployment, and external balance of payments. The larger the diamond, the better the score on the four economic targets. Although Japan clearly had a better record than any other major country prior to the 1973 oil shock, Japan still led the world in the post OPEC period. However, what is striking is that Japan is now experiencing much slower growth. Indeed in one analysis, that undertaken by The New York Stock Exchange, Japan actually performed less well between 1974–1980 than the worst economic laggard, the United Kingdom, during the 1960–1973 period (Exhibit 1/3a, b).

Exhibit 1/3 a: Economic Performance Index: 1960–1973, 1974–1980

$$\text{EPI} = \frac{\text{real rate of gdp growth}}{\text{unemployment rate + inflation rate}} \times 100$$

	1960–1973		1974–1980
Japan	145.9	Japan	37.8
West Germany	123.9	West Germany	29.0
France	85.5	France	18.0
Italy	67.7	Canada	16.5
Canada	64.2	Sweden	15.3
Sweden	55.6	United States	15.2
United States	50.4	Italy	13.4
United Kingdom	43.1	United Kingdom	2.2

Source: NYSE

Exhibit 1/3b: Comparative Productivity Growth by Sector, 1963–1973, 1973–1980

| | Agriculture | | Manufacturing | | Services | | Total | |
| | 1963 | 1973 | 1963 | 1973 | 1963 | 1973 | 1963 | 1973 |
	1973	1980	1973	1980	1973	1980	1973	1980
Britain	5.6	3.2	4.3	0.2	1.8	0.1	3.4	0.6
France	6.8	4.0	5.4	3.8	1.8	1.7	4.6	2.6
W. Germany	7.1	4.1	6.0	2.5	2.6	2.7	4.7	2.9
Japan	8.3	1.6*	10.4	6.4*	6.1	1.8*	8.1	3.0*
U.S.A.	4.0	2.1*	2.8	1.2*	1.8	—0.1*	1.8	0.2*

* output per employee 1973–1979   * 1973–1979

Source: Economist (February 27, 1982).

What these two sets of figures show is that simplistic explanations of the Japanese economic miracle are grossly misleading. Not only has Japan had notable years of very fast growth, but also years of production slowdown and declining productivity. Overall value added labour productivity in manufacturing is still only four-fifths of the U.S., although it is notably high in such sectors as steel, electrical machinery, and precision machinery. Foreign explanations of Japanese economic success have cited a number of diverse factors – permanent employment, close business/government interaction, quality circles, Sogoshosha trading firms, long range investment horizons, Theory Z, superior industrial engineering, and the like. Ironically, most Japanese do not believe many of the superlatives written about their economy or their management capabilities, and indeed, see their few strengths as the product more of hard work and careful planning than any brilliant technique worthy of foreign emulation. What's more, just as Europe and the U.S. have discovered the merits of Japanese management, most of the countries of South East Asia have already learned them.

1.3 Paradoxes of Asian Growth

The East Asian countries of the Pacific Rim – the two Koreas, Taiwan, Singapore and Malaysia, the Phillipines and Hong Kong, stand in the economic pecking order as Japan stands to the West – today's rivals, tomorrow's leaders. By all the standards of economic growth – the levels of investment, productivity, technology diffusion, rate of exports – the countries of South East Asia, often called the other Japans, or the newly industrialized countries, stand in the vanguard of the world's most dynamic economic area. Together with Japan, they represent what Norman Macrae (1975) calls the dawn of the Pacific Century, the era to replace the earlier periods of the American Century 1875–1975, or the British Century 1775–1875. In this perspective, the center of gravity in business terms dominates trends for politics, culture, technology, and lifestyles as much as it does economy and commerce. Moreover, as Hofheinz and Calder (1982) properly note, "The countries of the region have longer recorded histories, larger and denser populations, and more collective experience in commerce and statecraft than the rest of the world combined."

For Americans and Europeans, the enviable growth patterns in South East Asia are no more understandable simply because they rest on Japanese emulation. After all, the U.S. and Europe have a long history of association with this region, both by politics and war, as well as commerce. Most of the region has been a European colony of one sort or another, and many countries like Hong Kong, Singapore and South Korea have special relations with Britain and the United States. Three of the last military conflicts experienced by the United States have been fought in the region, at a cost of a quarter of a million lives. One of the major American foreign policy changes of this century touches on the region, namely the U.S. recognition of The Chinese People's Republic. Trade between the United States and Asia has, since 1975, surpassed trade with Europe.

Indeed, the dynamism of the Pacific Rim countries, as shown in Exhibit 1/4, stands as a major challenge more serious for Europe than for the United States. The paradox is that as Japan increases its rivalry in high technology products with the United States – in computers, microchips, biotechnology, electronics of all forms – the likelihood is that the countries of Europe, lacking coherent industrial policies in continental unison, will be caught in an industrial squeeze between the low wage standardized technologies of Asia and the high technology products of Japan and the U.S.[2] (In 1981 and 1982, the U.S. trade surplus with Europe actually was larger than Japan's surplus with the U.S.) The particular advantage of the South East Asian countries is their highly complementary economic structures with Japan. As Japan discards industries no longer

[2] Christien Stoffaes, in *La Grande Menace Industrielle* (1978), establishes this argument specifically for France, and includes German high technology with that of the U.S. and Japan. Important studies carried out by CEPII, Le Centre d'Etudes Prospectives et d'Informations Internationales, provides detailed comparisons of the world's economic zones and the threatened position of Europe vis a vis Japan and the U.S. See Fouquin (1981), Lefay and Fouquin (1980), and Soutter (1980). As a specific example, Europe's production of integrated circuits in 1980 was about five percent of world production, as against twenty-five percent for Japan and seventy percent for the U.S. By 1990, Europe will still have less than fifteen percent of world production share, as against 85 percent shared between Japan and the U.S. The U.S. and Japan will be net exporters of chips, Europe a net importer, even with the presence in Europe of major U.S. and Japanese chip manufacturers. Expressed differently, American and Japanese chipmakers had sales worldwide of $5.6 billion in 1980, of which $1.28 billion, or more than twenty percent, was to Europe. European chipmakers, whose worldwide sales were only $693 million, had sales at home of $552 million, or less than half that of the Japanese and American exports to their own market.

suitable for its evolving economic structure, these sunset sectors become relocated in Korea, Taiwan, or Singapore. Already Korean shipbuilding rivals Japanese yards, electronics of all sorts compete against Japanese exports, and South East Asia is actually supplanting market share in Japan once supplied by the U.S. (Abegglen and Hout, 1979).

Exhibit 1/4: Selected Economic Indicators for Developing Asia

	Annual Average GDP Groth		Inflation rate		Saving as % GDP		Investment as % GDP		Annual Average Growth in Exports		Imports	
	1960–70	70–81	1960–70	70–81	1960	1980	1960	1980	1960–70	70–80	60–70	70–80
Japan	10.9	4.7	4.9	8.6	34	31	34	32	17.2	8.9	13.7	4.4
Hongkong	10.0	9.4	2.4	12.9	6	24	18	29	12.7	9.4	9.2	11.7
S. Korea	8.6	9.3	17.4	16.9	1	23	11	31	34.1	23.0	20.5	11.8
Taiwan	9.6	9.2	3.4	10.4	13	33	20	36	20.0	17.7	22.0	12.1
Singapore	8.8	8.6	1.1	7.1	−3	30	11	43	4.2	12.0	5.9	9.9
Malaysia	6.5	7.7	−0.3	6.2	27	32	14	29	5.8	7.4	2.3	7.0
Indonesia	3.9	7.6	184†	17.1	8	30	8	22	4.0	8.7	2.0	11.9
Thailand	8.4	7.3	1.8	10.0	14	22	16	27	5.2	11.8	11.2	5.4
Philippines	5.1	6.1	5.8	13.5	16	25	16	30	2.2	7.0	7.1	3.4
Middle-income countries	5.9	5.6*	2.7	13.2	19	25	20	27	5.4	3.9	6.4	4.2

Sources: World Bank. IMF * 1970–80, † 1962–70.
Average figures for countries with gnp per head of $ 420–4500 in 1980.

Asia's competitive advantages go well beyond its considerable resources such as raw materials, large internal markets and highly literate workforce. As Confucian cultures, they reflect what Kahn (1979) has called the New Protestant Ethic:

Most are familiar with the argument of Max Weber that the Protestant Ethic was extremely useful in promoting the rise and spread of modernization. Most will be much less familiar with the notion that societies based upon the Confucian ethnic ways may be superior to the West in the pursuit of industrialization, affluence and modernization.

All of the countries of South East Asia are tied into a regional (and increasingly global) logistical system based on water transport, modern communications, and informational intelligence gathering by large trading firms. Seen globally, the rise of southeast Asia on water transport links illustrates how the Mediterranean has been the sea of the past, the Atlantic is the sea of the present and the Pacific is the sea of the future. The countries are all Friedmanite economies, with governments accounting for a fraction of the GNP of Western countries. Despite these characteristics as free enterprise economies, they combine complex industrial planning mechanisms to allocate resources and promote technology development. They are all countries where the combination of restrictive union work rules and luddite attitudes to technology are least developed. This advantage means that with a highly literate and numerate citizenry they will be able to adopt, quickly and cheaply, technology developed elsewhere. In this respect the technological changes ushered in by the new micro electronics revolution will be least disruptive to traditional social values and work habits, and to modern forms of job design. These countries have the added advantage of learning from Japan, a notion far less removed culturally and socially than Japan's former teachers, the U.S. and Europe.

1.4 Japan as Learner and Teacher

Since Japan opened its ports and its eyes to Western commerce and trade in the period known as Meiji (1868), Japanese leaders have guided their economic visions with the slogan *Wakon Yohsai* (Japanese Spirit, Western Technology). Since that period, Japan has consistently devoted enormous resources to education of all kinds, not just to young people in the form of schooling, or in factory careers in the form of on-the-job training, but in a systematic approach to learning techniques and processes from abroad. Whether the examples were naval and shipbuilding techniques from Britain, law and chemistry from Germany, or management, engineering and baseball from the United States, Japanese leaders and citizens have adopted foreign ideas, skills and technologies from the West so completely and so intensively that foreign learning is almost second nature.

From a managerial perspective, the question of learning has far less importance in the general scheme of things when the key role is that of teacher. For most of the post war period, there was no question which role the U.S. played and there was little question which institution was the key teaching vehicle, namely the U.S. management education and its leading star, The Harvard Business School. All over the Western world, the technological and economic performance gaps between the U.S. and elsewhere were explained as a management talent gap. U.S. style business schools sprung up all over Europe as well as in Canada. Whether the teaching methodology was case oriented or theory oriented, the pitch was largely the same: MBA education. The correlates of American style MBA executives were everywhere: superior performance of U.S. multinationals, more aggressive marketing strategies in products as diverse as Pampers and Kleenex to banking and blue jeans. The ultimate praise was voiced by Jean Jacques Servan-Schreiber, who praised the glories of American management and organization, and by John Kenneth Galbraith, who coined the phrase "technostructure" to describe the managerial wizards behind the new industrial state.

The apex of MBA ascendancy came in the 1960's and 1970's both in the U.S. government and many of the key corporations. The crowning example was Robert MacNamara, first at Ford and then at the U.S. State Department, who brought in his "whiz kids" with PERT, PPBS, flow charts, critical path, and rational management techniques and the new world of cybernetics, systems, and policy analysis. At Defense, the new techniques were such ideas as zero-based budgeting and, during the Viet Nam War, precision bombing for maximum effect. At Ford, the example was the Mustang. The long term results were not dissimilar to the Asian adventure. Not just Ford but all of Detroit was drowning in a sea of red ink, faulty products, and the worst employee relations in a generation.

The one industrialized country not to go the MBA management education route was Japan. The recent productivity problems in the U.S. have recently been defined as a management gap problem – a problem of style, substance, vision and technique. American economist Lester Thurow put the matter squarely on the shoulders of U.S. top managers. In a brutal article entitled "Where Management Fails," Thurow laments:

As the list of industries – textiles, consumer electronics, steel, autos – that have been conquered or need government protection to survive, has grown, it has become increasingly obvious that something is systematically wrong with American management. Not long ago General Motors was commonly referred to as the "best-managed firm in America." Why couldn't the best-managed firm in America see the Japanese challenge coming and defeat it? *Fortune Magazine's* current candidate for the best-managed firm in America, General Electric, has essentially become a marketer of foreign products in its consumer electronics division. Why can't the best-managed firm in America compete with American made products?

In a controversial analysis of American competitive decline, Harvard professors Abernathy and Hayes (1980) identify the key problem in what they call the new American management orthodoxy – short-run financial criteria, corporate diversification and risk minimization, and over-reliance on marketing rather than production and technology. They also cite the career patterns of top managers, particularly those with backgrounds in finance and law. The result is an emphasis on what *Business Week* calls "paper management" – the shuffling of assets rather than knowing "the speed and feed of machines." In a related vein, the familiar comment in Osaka or Tokyo makes the same point: when the Clean Air Act was introduced in the U.S., senior management at Ford and GM called in their lawyers; at Toyota and Nissan, senior managers called in their engineers. Indeed, the question of a management gap may well be in reality a matter of an engineering gap, where Japan now has substantially more engineers in senior management positions than the U.S., and graduates more engineers than any other Western country (Exhibit 1/5).

Despite these anecdotes about the merits and demerits of U.S. management, there can be little doubt about the relative knowledge Japanese managers possess about Western concepts of organization, compared to Western managers' knowledge of Japanese management and the workings of the total econ-

Exhibit 1/5: Comparative Output of Engineering Graduates: 1965–1977

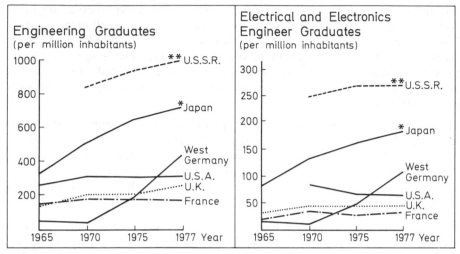

* 1979   ** 1978

Sources: "International Financial Statistics Yearbook", 1980; "Economic Statistics Yearbook", 1980 (Japan); "Statistic Abstract of U.S.A."; "Statistisches Jahrbuch", "Annuaire Statistique de la France"; "APN" (U.S.S.R.); British Embassy in Tokyo.

omy. Moreover, much of the recent interest in Japanese management – such as human resource strategies and production techniques – tends to stress the positive and beneficial aspects, without seeing either the cost side or the functional limits of one approach compared to another.

This more balanced view of Japanese management, while relatively underdeveloped in Europe or North America, forms part of a debate almost three decades old in Japan. In government circles, in business groups, and in journalistic outlets, the advantages and disadvantages of American concepts have been debated, particularly in the context of Japanese cultural values and environment.

The evident success of the Japanese economy, and the persistence of certain institutional practices such as permanent employment, high debt financing, and the trading firm marketing philosophy, have raised anew the benefits of *Nihonteki Keiei,* or Japanese style of management. The shift of Japan then from learner to teacher is of more than academic interest, since economic studies of organizational productivity have recently elevated management to a key role (Caves, 1981).[3] At an even more general level, the success of Japan's economy

---

[3] The economic literature on productivity, particularly the field of growth accounting, has emphasized traditional factor inputs (labour and capital) in the framework of neoclassical produc-

has prompted a fresh thinking about the general direction of industrial nations towards societal convergence, i.e., a growing similarity in social values and organization. The standard interpretation clearly pointed the direction of change towards Western practice and behaviour. Japan's success has now re-kindled that debate and, to some scholars, turns the argument on its head. Is Western management, in short, becoming more like the Japanese model, especially in high technology?

1.5 From Late Development to Leader

Organizations and management techniques are forms of social technology which are products of a particular age and state of knowledge. As Stinchcombe (1965) argues, the design and functioning of organizations reflect the level and patterns of industrialization. On the other hand, not all societies industrialize at the same time, or in the same way – indeed there may well be a 'penalty of taking the lead' in the path to industrialization, to use Veblen's classic phrase. In this sense, Britain was the first industrialized nation and has perhaps incurred the penalty in obsolescence of many kinds; the path then followed by France and Germany, or the United States was also different. Japan, as a nation with industrialization dating only since 1868, has been on a growth path different again since it has had the advantage of learning from the greatest number of previously industrialized nations (Kassem, 1974). New starters can emulate the latest organization and management practices without having to slowly reform already existing norms and behaviours.

Dore (1973) has taken up this point as a late development hypothesis, namely that late starter countries will show in their organizations advantages which allow them to get ahead – processes which "in the countries which industrialized earlier are still emerging, still struggling to get out from the chrysalis of nineteenth century institutions." Dore's (1973) study relates primarily to British-Japanese comparisons of social organization. Moreover, the historical basis of many specific aspects of Dore's interpretations have been questioned (Cole, 1979). What is different about the late development perspective is that in Dore's view, there is a tendancy towards social convergence but the direction

tion functions. Empirical studies have widened the framework to incorporate technological advance, energy, and natural resources. Labour input and capital input have been disaggregated: for example, age, sex, and education for labour, and age and stock of machinery for capital. More recent analysis, relaxing neoclassical assumptions, draws on the organizational analysis literature wherein such variables as mangement style, leadership patterns, union-management relations, and organizational culture are recognized. For a review, see Nelson (1981).

Exhibit 1/6: Conjectional Trends in Labour Management Relations

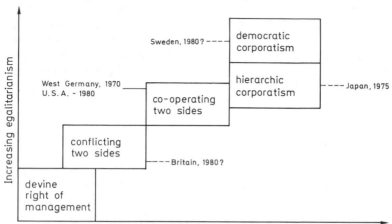

Source: Adapted from Dore (1973).

is towards Japanese practice, rather than the other way around, i.e. towards the West (Exhibit 1/6).

This redirection of thinking of Japan not as follower but as leader coincides with predictions about Japan overtaking the United States in per capita GNP within a decade (Kahn, 1979), becoming a pioneer in many leading areas of microelectronics technology (Casement, 1982) and taking the same path to multinational corporate expansion as the United States, to a projected fifty billion dollars by 1985. The issue therefore of Japanese forms of management and social organization merit serious analysis both for their appropriateness as models for foreign learning, and for what they explain about Japanese managerial strategies in the 1980's.

1.6 Strategies for the 1980's

This book focuses on Japanese management strategies for the 1980's. The word strategy is perhaps a source of ambiguity, because the concept of strategy in the Western sense has no meaning in the Japanese culture. It does not denote, for instance, a carefully thought out, completely logical, highly related set of policies and procedures to get from A to B to C. In Japan, strategy really implies a state of preparedness for events which unfold largely outside management's control. True, Japanese plan, but the aim is largely informational. Few countries come close to the enormous statistical bureaus in the government, the data intelligence gathering in the trading firms, and the mammoth environmental scanning and information search of the industrial corporations.

Japan is undergoing a massive shift in its industrial structure, i.e. in the weighting of key industry sectors and all that that implies for various import requirements (such as energy, minterals, commodities, and technologies) and obviously for exports. The catalyst for many changes in Japan's industry structure has been the new environment of expensive energy, but the real engine behind the country's dramatic evolution is technology – especially microelectronics but also new forms of materials (e.g. cyramics for car engines) and new forms of production, such as automated offices and plants.

Much of the foreign writing on Japan has stressed various aspects of the culture and the human side of organization – the software systems. Much less recognized is the tremendous importance of technology issues – of hardware and its use and applications in promoting productivity and social innovation. Because of Japan's overwhelming committment to hardware development, particularly in what the Japanese truly believe is a new industrial revolution in the form of microelectronics, the general direction of the country's evolution thus takes on the form of strategies emerging piecemeal, haphazardly, sometimes with luck, guile, and even questionable legalities. Nevertheless, what does unfold is a rather clear and economically logical path of development.

To understand Japan's evolution to a high technology manufacturing and service society, one must understand the general international context of trade relations with developed areas such as North America and Europe as well as the dynamic areas of the Pacific Basin. As Drucker (1968) noted years ago, Japan is one of the few countries totally oriented in its industrial and corporate strategies to the global economy. Even though Japan is only half the size of the United States in population (117 million versus 240 million), and external trade for both countries is a fraction of Canada and Northern Europe (12 and 10 per cent versus 25 for West Germany and Britain, 33 for Canada), the actual structure of economic decision-making at the government and corporate levels in Japan is vastly more international in outlook and analysis than the U.S. or Europe. This general orientation to the global economy means that management of industries and corporations has for decades detailed experience in competitive analysis not only within Japan, where competition in most sectors is fierce, but in international comparisons. Ironically competitive analysis at the firm level – i.e., the study of the basic determinants of industry competition and selection of a defensible corporate strategy – is a relatively new approach in the U.S. (Porter, 1980) although business schools are incorporating this concept into MBA courses. Japan's approaches are not necessarily novel, but the extent of the understanding of its importance is probably greater, as judged by the pervasive shift of Japanese forms from being oriented primarily for the domestic market to global markets and the speed and extent of achieving international market share.

In this respect, attention must be given to the clear linkages between industrial policy at the societal level and that at the firm level. Japan is a country which does a great deal of planning, but there is much confusion over its advantages and disadvantages. Industrial planning at the national level typically means setting general directions over very long time horizons – it is up to the private sector to flesh out the broad visions in terms of specific products and services. The importance of planning as a particular tool of economic development, and thus one to be emulated by other countries, misses the underlying advantage for Japan. In the first instance, planning is a powerful educational tool for managers and the population at large – it serves to elevate economic debate to a fairly high level. The second point is that Japan's general planning makes the consistency between public policy goals and private corporate objectives relatively strong – they are not working at cross purposes. The third advantage is that planning is seen less as a guide to the future but as an interpretation of the past. In an age of profound discontinuities – in technologies, politics, trade flows, energy and social values – planning is seen as a tool to shape current thinking based on interpretations of past assumptions and behaviours. As noted already, Japanese thinking patterns do not easily lend themselves to detailed, highly rational strategic norms favoured in the west, so this point must be kept in mind when Japanese management "strategies" are discussed in the chapters which follow.

1.7 Summary and Conclusion

The emergence of Japan as the second largest capitalist economy coincides with fundamentally new directions in the global economy. As a major economic player on the world stage, attention has started to focus on Japan's new directions in response to high priced energy, new technologies, and new competitors from southeast Asia. Parallel to this development is a growing interest in Japanese management and social organization – in short, management as a social technology. The importance of management – both in quantitative and qualitative terms – is now increasingly recognized by economists, although precise estimates are somewhat primitive. More to the point, while Japanese management techniques appear to be somewhat different in many respects from European or American practice, the approach to management training and education is very different – the MBA business school in North America, for instance, or in house training of university educated graduates in science and engineering.

Much of the foreign interpretation of Japanese management is either one sided – with more recent emphasis on success factors – or one dimensional. The soft areas such as decision making, training and employment practices are treated in isolation from the hardware or technology issues, such as equipment, production processes, and industrial engineering. Another deficiency is that specific firm level types of factors – human resource strategies or marketing issues – are isolated from broader industrial goals and public policies. To fully comprehend Japan's industrial evolution and direction in the decades ahead, these linkages must be recognized and set in a general context of economic goals and policies. The next chapter establishes a framework for linking these software/hardware and macro/micro dimensions into an integrated map.

Chapter 2
Samurai Management: A Framework for Analysis

"The Japanese should have no concern with business. The Jap has no
business savvy."

Rudyard Kipling

2.1 Introduction

This chapter outlines a framework for studying the Japanese system of management and social organization. As noted previously, there has been ample
oversimplification of Japan's industrial system based on one dimensional and
single variable interpretations – an approach which does considerable injustice
to what is an extremely old and rich cultural heritage and which is downright
misleading for any outsider trying to interpret the competitive dynamics of the
world's second largest capitalist economy. The framework is an attempt to
overcome the simplistic perspectives of many writings on Japan.

Another compelling reason to focus on the complex relationships in Japan's
industrial system comes from what writers such as Bruce Scott (1982) and
William Abernathy et al (1982) call the new industrial competition. By this they
mean the radical new forms of market forces brought about not only by higher
energy prices, but internationalization of entire industry segments, novel production systems, and new technologies. "Managers must recognize that they
have entered a period of competition that requires of them a technology –
driven strategy, a mastery of efficient production, and an unprecedent capacity
for workforce management." Detailed studies of particular industries – from
automobiles and steel to televisions, motorcycles, and computers – demonstrate a recurring theme – the strategic impact to how these competitive forces
alter global markets.[1] Japanese managers have had amazing success in this new
industrial competition, partly to be sure, because European or U.S. managers
have been blind to opportunities in their own markets, partly because they
have simply surrendered many niches to the Japanese once they gained market
entry. More detailed analysis tends to show, however, a rather basic emphasis

---

[1] At the more general level, changes in technology, communications, and transportation can turn
industries which were once regional or national in scope (e.g. cars, television, banking) into
global markets. The key is to understand how strategies at the national level and the corporate
level can influence these broader forces. For one perspective, see Hout et al, (1982). The point
is taken up again in Chapter 11.

on underlying productivity dynamics – the relationships, for instance, between people and technology on the one hand, or between government policies and corporate strategies, and changing locational advantages of particular industries and infrastructure arrangements. Single variable models fail to understand, or illuminate these relationships. This chapter addresses these productivity issues in a general conceptual framework of hardware and software management technologies.

2.2 Japanese Society: Adversity Management

Studies of "national character" explain the distinctive features of a given country in terms of particular geographical, physical or environmental conditions. Many writers comment on Britain's lagging economic growth, for instance, on the persistance of hierarchical class structures and limited educational opportunities (Jamieson, 1980; Caves et al, 1981). Writers on the American national character, such as Frederick Jackson Turner, explain distinctive U.S. qualities in terms of a frontier thesis: the historical expanson westward, the taming of geographical adversity and individual optimism. David Potter (1954) has defined the American character in terms of the economy of abundance, where U.S. attitudes and values stem from the immense physical and natural resources of an entire continent.

S. M. Lipset's (1962) four country analysis of national character builds on the dissimilarities of the educational systems, labour organizations, religious tendancies and political values. Not only do environmental differences impact on social character – the vigilantism, limited law and order, and lynching in the U.S. compared to the law and order, peaceful settlement and few massacres of the Indian population in Canada – but the historical experience of each country has led to different institutional outcomes and norms of accepted behaviour. Where the U.S. Constitution, for instance, speaks of "life, liberty, and the pursuit of happiness," the Canadian speaks of "peace, order, and good government."

Studies of Japan's national character are few. Ruth Benedict, whose book *Patterns of Culture* forms the genesis of the scientific study of national character, wrote the highly influential work on Japan's culture, *The Chrysanthemum and the Sword*. More recently, the very well known work, Chie Nakane's (1973) *Japanese Society,* dwells primarily on sociological models of behaviour and social organization. Her approach leaves out questions of the physical and geographical features of Japan. Yet if there is one quality which stands out in Japan, certainly compared to North America, but also to an extent Europe, is the recurrent theme in Japanese history of geographical and physical adversity. Not only have the forces of resource scarcity (food, energy, and raw materials) coincided with extreme land density to accompany very rapid economic growth, but so has the persistence of basic social values and leadership norms which appear on the surface to be antithetical to Western industrial logic.

Consider the case of resource scarcity and physical density. Japan's extreme dependence on virtually all major types of raw materials, energy and food stuffs have been extensively documented. Not only does Japan differ from almost all the major industrial countries in this respect, but also the physical environment of scarcity raises a social awareness of the fact which is truly surprising to a visitor from, for example, resource abundant Canada, the United States or France. Given the geographical pressures on the Japanese people during the last century of industrialization, it is not surprising that various institutions and social behaviours have evolved to counterbalance the extreme costs of this economic weakness. Externally, Japan's outward investment policies, government foreign policy, and scientific thrust have all been aimed at the goal of reducing external dependence on any one source country (including the United States), and of maximizing flexibility on payment terms and securing long term contracts. Internally, the Japanese government and political leaders have been particularly adept at using this pressure of dependency and scarcity for maximum effect for social ideology. The average high school graduate is probably more aware of Japan's relative standing in the international pecking order than any other country. The two most important economic events of the past decade – Nixon shock and oil schock – have reinforced the well inculcated values of living with scarcity and the need for constant social innovation in their aim of catching up with the West.

From a purely managerial perspective, such values have enormous significance. Japanese managers have developed policies on such issues as material handling, transportation, quality control, cutting out waste, energy conservation, and energy convertibility which go far beyond programs elsewhere, even in the United States. In part, of course, luck has been on the side of the Japanese. Faced with geographical isolation from major Western markets just at a time when the energy balance between oil and coal were changing and when major new technologies were being introduced (oxygen blast furnaces in steel, micro circuitry in electronics and telecommunications, and machinery in agriculture), Japan could make startling social innovations in several industries which improved her competitive position. By way of example, not only did the steel plants built in the fifties have more than double the economies of sale which American engineers thought feasible,[2] they were located on deep water seaports adjacent to steel customers, just when Britain and the United States found themselves with land-locked steel facilities of smaller scale located near

---

[2] For analysis, see Gold (1974).

low grade raw materials rather than near customers. In addition, Japan then turned its military technology in shipbuilding, mostly acquired from Britain (which had fifty percent of the world market in 1950 and most of the best welding technology) to revolutionize global transport systems and long-range bulk carriers. In other words, a physically-imposed problem of scarcity has been seen as a major policy threat and a whole series of managerial actions have been a direct consequence – ranging from Japan's record as the most energy efficient industrial structure and highest expenditure on energy R&D to its energy efficient products in radial tires, small cars, and commercial motors.

Consider briefly the second issue, physical density. Turner's theme of conquering geography and expanding frontiers in American history has a modern counterpart in President Kennedy's New Frontier slogan and conquering space with a moon landing. The geographical theme of Japan's physical structure has received much less attention among writers who dwell on its managerial practices. Yet Japan is one of the most densely populated countries of the industrialized world and certain areas, the Tokyo-Yokohama conurbation, for example, puts it in a league with New York City. Japan's density is not only the pressure of so many people among its four main islands, but the problem that so much of its land area is mountainous, volcanic, or otherwise unusable.[3]

The impact of Japan's population density shows in several ways, many of which have pervasive managerial implications. Severe land density makes housing extremely expensive and, aside from any tax law absurdities, commuter time for workers is considerable (often up to two hours). Expensive housing reduces the per capita/square meter housing ratio and encourages multiple use of rooms and combined inter-generational families. The high cost of housing – opinion polls consistently show that owning a house is the main goal of young people – affects the pattern of savings, and the percentage of income spent on

---

[3] By way of comparison, certain density figures for selected areas are as follows (population per sq. kilometer) – from Kahn and Pepper (1980:92):

Japan	299	Tokyo	9,499
Holland	374	New York City	10,162
Taiwan	472	Paris	8,455

Since much of Japan is mountainous and forested, a more relevant measure is habitable land. The following table, adopted from the Japanese Economic Research Center data, gives Japan-Europe comparisons:

	People/Km	GNP/Km	Energy Consumption*
Japan	928	787m.	299
Britain	248	213m.	134
W. Germany	351	502m.	190
Italy	227	139m.	63
France	127	164m.	63

* tonnes of coal equivalent of energy consumed/area of habitable land.

housing (Japan's is twice, for example, that of Britain's) with a consequent lessoning of income spent for other products. It is little wonder that the average Japanese citizen is very conscious of price/quality features of consumer products.[4]

In this respect, Japan's physical and geographical characteristics give social reinforcement to its social history of groupism, interdependence, and sense of ON and GIRI – debt and obligation. The fact is, Japanese citizens have been forced to cope with social interdependence and close living for centuries. As a result, there has been great capacity to transfer rural values to urban living. By contrast, what has existed in some societies as agrarian or community values – the sense of belonging, social togetherness, and mutual interdependence – gets transformed in urban industrialization as individual anomie or a sense of personal alienation. According to Phillip Hauser (1969), and more recently Ezra Vogel (1979), this is precisely the problem of American forms of industrialization and transformation to urban values in a post-industrial, high technology age. Again, however, Japan has turned a necessity into a virtue. Since the Meiji era, the notion of IE (household) has been the predominant form of small firm and farm, and this is extended to the DOZOKU (confederation of households by kin, or "tribe") with the consequent notion of exclusion/inclusion, with resulting loyalties and supportive belief systems. Today this basic value system remains intact, with Japanese management placing great emphasis on human resource management and software systems.

In this respect, there can be some appreciation for Dore's (1973) view that Japan may indeed be a model for Western countries. Not only has there been a clear attempt, especially in big firms, to reconcile the economic advantages of scientific management with the human conditions requisite in the social side of work behaviour, the movement for such conditions has been led by prominent Japanese industrial leaders and business groups.

Japan's physical and geographical characteristics have nurtured a consciousness into the national character through literature, theatre, myths and traditions. (Western children learn about the man on the moon, which is made of

---

[4] Consider the following comment: "Japanese consumers are choosier than their foreign counterpart. When purchasing a bucket, for instance, a Japanese will examine it from every angle, even scrutinizing the underside of the bottom plate, and will not buy it if there is the slightest dent in any part of it . . .

There is an experimental device that consists of a steel cylinder about 50 cm in length, inside which is a steel ball of such an exact fit that when water is poured in the top of the cylinder not a drop will leak through to the bottom. Moreover, the ball is made to move slowly downward in the cylinder at such a speed that it reaches the bottom in 24 hours. A study has shown that only Japan and West Germany have technicians capable of producing this precisions cylinder and ball" (Takeuchi, 1978).

cheese. Japanese children learn of the moon where two rabbits make rice cakes.) The staples of the traditional Japanese diet – tea, rice, and fish – are products of small scale peasant farming and fishing traditions which illustrate the close proximity of rural and urban values throughout Japan, even in big cities.[5] Some of Japan's worst disasters – fires in the last century, flooding of rural areas on a regular basis, and recurrent earthquakes, including the memory of the 1923 earthquake when 100,000 people died – are constant reminders of the link with geography and nature's perils.

Even the esthetic arts of Japan, imported a thousand years ago from China, have a link with nature and the land. Flower arrangement, landscape gardening, monochrome landscape painting, and the graceful tea ceremony – these are the cultivated expressions of simplicity, natural beauty, and discipline to which the Japanese of every age can relate and identify. Japanese cultural sensibilities reflect the human interpretation of the world of nature. There is almost a religious reverence for natural beauty (e.g. Mount Fuji) and the Japanese people, as expressed in art, sculpture, and architecture, attempt to assimilate themselves in nature and even interpret it in human emotions. The traditional Japanese house, for example, is constructed according to nature's dictates (facing south) to reflect the four seasons. The classical Japanese garden also reflects this symbiosis with nature, with trees, stones, and water serving as symbols of the natural environment. Water, of course, is a central feature of the natural order, and because rice grown in wet paddies has been the staple diet, great attention has been placed on its management. Even from ancient times, irrigation, drainage, land filling, water control and water use have given the Japanese strong traditions in resource management – influences which persist in many functions of management practice in modern industrial organizations.

An interpretation then of the Japanese character stems from the powerful impact of the country's isolation and separateness from the industrial West and from the imperatives of living in a challenging and often inhospitable geogra-

---

[5] E. J. Mishan makes the same point as follows: "In the older forms of social organization which began to disappear in the early nineteenth century it was just (the) inescapable fact of close interdependence that held the family and the community together. In the historical circumstances the interdependence was inevitable, yet there was unabashed satisfaction in affirming it . . . Narrow though their lives might appear by our megalopolitan standards they had, rich and poor, young and old, their place in the natural order of things, a settled relationship to one another guided by a network of custom and mutual obligation. Inevitably, then they were, all of them, at the center of the gossip and the interest, all of them part of the prior and absorbing concern of the community they dwelt in . . .

Thus in the unending pursuit of progress men are driven even farther apart and come to depend instead, for all their services and experiences, directly upon the creations of technology (Mishan, 1969:154–155).

phical environment. As Krause and Sekiguchi (1976:450) note, "part of the Japanese economic miracle, however, may be the results of inherent weakness – the Japanese learned to make the best of adversity . . . The lesson the world might learn from the Japanese example is not, of course, to seek adversity, but to recognize that most difficulties can be transformed in such a way as to advance societies."

2.3 Hardware and Software as Core Concepts

The conceptual framework presented in this chapter employs two key dimensions – the notion of hardware and software management systems, and macro and micro levels of analysis.[6] The software/hardware analogy with computers is intentional because the key relationship is their interdependence, not their separate impact. It encompasses a range of strategic issues involving the stock of technology embodied in physical plant and equipment, and the major determinants of changes in that stock. The intended meaning is to combine both the knowledge aspects of technology, as treated by conventional economics, and capital as a factor of production. In received economic wisdom, capital goods, as distinct from consumption goods, yield their use only over time, i.e. they depreciate in value and productivity. The difficulty is that productivity of capital goods forms a complex and little understood relationship not only with labour but the state of technology. Optimum factor allocation provides efficiency, but this in turn, depends on the nature of technology, which happens to be a social as well as an engineering activity.

The meaning of the hardware metaphor is to separate, for analytical purposes, the other end of the dimension, management software. Management software may be defined as the system of rules, regulations and standard operating procedures governing work, tasks and human behaviour.[7] Software in management systems consists of the type of management styles and institutional arrangements to organize production. At the societal level, software management systems include industry associations, worker-management groupings, and business-government organization. Software management systems at the micro level include decision-making modes, employment practices, orientations to time and learning and organization design. Management theory suggests that these types of software can vary considerably even within a single firm (e.g. differences in production, research, and marketing) as well as across

---

[6] Earlier versions of the framework were developed in previously published materials: McMillan (1978, 1980).

[7] For a detailed analysis relating to human abilities, see Blackmore (1981). A perspective at the organizational level is given in Cyert and March (1963).

a single industry. The real essence of software management technology is the system of personal relationships, values, and social interactions in an organization. Societal values and culture in an advanced industrialized society may well influence and condition such processes, but the variation within any one country are likely to be considerable (Azumi and McMillan, 1980).

Social scientists have coined the term "socio-technical" system to describe the linkages between software and hardware aspects of management and worker relationships in social organization (Emery and Trist, 1975). Many writers stress one aspect over the other as the primary influence on the shape and structure of organization. For example, Marxian analysis emphasizes technology and the mode of production, i.e. hardware, as the primary determinant of social and class relations. More recently, writers as diverse as Galbraith (1967) ("the technostructure") in economics, and Joan Woodward (1965) ("production technologies") in management, and Robert Blauner (1964) in psychology, stress technology while some put the emphasis on social values and socio-psychological systems, e.g. McClelland's (1961) analysis of achievement norms.

This distinction between macro and micro levels of analysis pervades all of the social sciences (e.g. macro economics/micro economics) although the exact boundary between the two is rarely made clear. The essential idea is that macro factors provide the large setting, the big picture or context within which micro forces operate. In terms of hardware issues, these forces include tax and investment policies, and science and energy policy, which in turn impact on the types and patterns of plant, equipment and production processes at the level of the firm and industry.

The macro/micro distinction is consistent with the notion of systems and subsystems. "From a societal point of view the organization is a subsystem of one or more larger systems, and its linkage or integration with these systems affects its mode of operation and its level of activity" (Katz and Kahn, 1978:63). For a particular country, this approach means that culture patterns in any society extend across micro organizational features in complex ways. As Lammers and Hickson (1979:403) point out, "the culture and sub-cultures in a society have a potential impact on organizational forms and processes; because outside agencies set cultural constraints for an organization; because dominant elites in an organization design and redesign organizational life in terms of culturally given models of organizing; because members themselves unofficially tend to organize and to 'counter-organize' in ways derived from sub-cultures."

In the Japanese case, there is often an explicit view that culture is a prime influence on organizational processes and practices, although the linkage between the macro and micro levels of analysis are expressed only in terms of values and norms. In fact, the emphasis is typically on software features of social behaviour, in isolation from hardware technologies.[8]

Moreover, the software features go beyond merely cultural values and norms; they include and express the social and intellectual capital arising from the educational and institutional processes of society at large. The intensive consultative mechanisms, to cite a specific case, between businesss and government develop a stock of knowledge and information about trends, competitive forces, and intentions which are at least as important as the raw statistics and impersonal data gathered by various bureaus.

The framework presented here, as shown in Exhibit 2/1, is that both hardware and software are critical. The common denominator is the influence of technology. As Furkiss (1969:37) has noted, "technology is more than tool-making . . . (It is) a self conscious organized means of affecting the physical or social environment, capable of being objectified and transmitted to others, and effective largely independently of the subjective disposition or personal talent of those involved." The next two sections elaborate this theme in the context of hardware and software systems at the macro and micro levels.

Exhibit 2/1: A Framework for Comparative Analysis

	Macro	Micro
H A R D W A R E	Tax Policy Investment Policy Science Policy Energy Policy	Automation Plant and Equipment Computerization Energy Utilization
S O F T W A R E	Business-Government Industry Association Management-Labour Ideologies and Values	Employment Practices Decision-making Information Diffusion Social Innovation

---

[8] This marriage of software and hardware goes to the heart of Britain's productivity problem. In many sectors (cars and steel), detailed statistical analysis has shown no superior labour productivity as a result of more capital per employee. But as Prais (1976:195) points out, "A possible explanation is that capital intensive-industries tend to have large plants. In Britain, however, the greater contribution of capital in these industries is partly or wholly offset by the greater labour-relations problems that arise in larger plants."

2.4 Japanese Hardware: A Comparative Perspective

The total amount of goods and services in an economy is defined as gross
national product. However useful this concept is for aggregate comparisons of
economic performance, it glosses over major differences in the composition of
GNP – such as government expenditure, consumption, investment, and exports. The long term path to economic growth lies in the flexible and productive approach to changes in the composition of aggregate demand. What is
striking about Japan's approach to hardware development is the special emphasis placed on investment and technology.

Japanese investment in new plant and equipment, i.e. gross fixed capital formation, is the highest in the western world, and double that of the U.S. Not
only is the stock of plant and equipment in Japan on average far newer as a
result, but in most instances, they embody new production ideas and processes
over a protracted period. For many years, Japan's rate of new investment was
not notably higher than Canada, France or West Germany, but what is striking
(Exhibit 2/2) is the continued low investment levels of the U.K. and the U.S.

Exhibit 2/2: The Relation of Growth in Output to Investment in Eight Countries, 1970–77

Country	Percentage change in per capita GDP from 1970 to 1977 (1)	Average percentage of GDP devoted to capital formation 1970–77 (2)	Ratio of column 1 to column 2
United Kingdom	10.0	19.4	0.52
United States	15.6	17.6	0.89
Japan	17.3	33.5	0.52
Belgium	24.6	21.6	1.14
France	25.0	23.5	1.06
West Germany	18.8	23.4	0.80
Italy	21.3	20.6	1.03
Netherlands	22.4	22.7	0.99

Source: Blume (1980)

(Blume, 1980). Estimates vary, but studies show that at least in the past, for
each incremental percentage of GNP invested in new capital, economic growth
increased by .2 percent, employment grew by .3 percent, and inflation decreased by about one percent. Japan's investment advantages are clearly consistent with these variations, independent of many other factors such as energy,
defense spending, or tax rates. Just how significant the growth of capital stock
is in the short and medium term as measured by macro economic statistics is
debatable (Dennison, 1979) but there can be little doubt that when viewed in

the context of particular industry sectors, the differences can be startling. In many sectors – steel, shipbuilding, and petrochemicals, for instance – productivity is inherent in the actual hardware in place, with only minor productivity differences resulting from software management systems. However, in many others – consumer electronics, computers, autos and telecommunications – the key to productivity is the successful marriage of software and hardware – precisely the area of Japanese emphasis. As detailed in subsequent chapters on industrial planning and technology strategies, Japanese managers and MITI bureaucrats have consistently aimed to establish particular sectors around the most advanced hardware available and to exit from sunset or low growth sectors made obsolete by new technology or cheaper imports. Labour market and human resource strategies are consistent with this approach.

The other side of high investment rates is high personal savings which, in Japan, have been among the highest in the world and over the past decade and a half, double that of American and British rates (Blume, 1980:299). Various explanations have been advanced for Japan's high savings rates – low levels of social welfare, the twice yearly bonus system, limited development of consumer credit, the legacy of a low income rural society, social values oriented to frugality, and so on. From an economic perspective, the high savings rates are consistent with rapid economic growth and rising disposable income. In addition, very high rates of productivity in the most modern sectors have meant that it has been consumers in Japan (and elsewhere) which were (and are) the main beneficiaries, rather than workers alone through high wages. In general, retail prices of many consumer products have remained static or have fallen, while compensation for employees in these sectors have increased no faster than productivity or international competition. (The most notable example of this pattern is the car industry: in the U.S., and to a lesser extent in Europe, the exact opposite has occurred in the past decade: high wage rates and increasing consumer sales prices in the face of international competition.)

Japan's macro policies for investment, taxation, technology, and competition – while not particularly unique as separate instruments – have been orchestrated into a highly successful industrial policy oriented to a progressive increase in the level of capital stock and entry into high value – added sectors. The efficacy of Japan's industrial policy can be analyzed in relation to the prognosis made by an American expert during the post war occupation. According to one view put forward in 1949:

In the light of an analysis of its resources, the Japan of the next three decades appears likely to have one of two aspects, if its population continues to grow to 100 million or more. (1) It may have a standard of living equivalent to that of 1930–34, if foreign financial assistance is continued indefinitely. (2) It may be 'self-supporting' but with internal political, economic, and social distress and a standard of living gradually approaching the bare subsistence level. Either of these alternatives seems more likely than that of a Japan which will have made itself self-supporting at a 1930–34 standard through foreign trade and improved resources utilization (Ackerman, 1949:528).

As an indication of just how the Japanese economy fared, in 1948, if the prewar index (1934–36) was 100, industrial production was 58.5, agricultural production 91.1, that of quantity exported 7 and of urban per family consumption level as 63.8 (Tsuru, 1977:17). What specific elements account for such changes?

There is plainly no single factor which accounts for Japan's post-war productivity, but a common starting point is the very high level of fixed non residential investment to gross national productivity (Kendrick, 1982). High savings, high levels of investment, high productivity, and low inflation are, of course, reinforcing mechanisms for economic growth, much in the same way as low rates of savings, low levels of investment and low productivity produce a downward growth spiral. In the absence of other influences (e.g. government policies or foreign investment), old plant and equipment are a symptom of geriatric decline and lack of competitiveness which is virtually impossible to arrest once set in motion. Macro fiscal and monetary policies extended over long time periods translate into growth rates of capital stock per employee at the firm and plant level, which in turn impact on labour productivity. Japan's fifty per cent or more increase in the rate of plant and equipment growth, and the resulting capital stock per employee, now provide a major cost advantage in key sectors. For example, one study conducted in 1977 showed that in the car industry, the capital intensity of Toyota and Nissan were 29.2 and 22.4 thousand dollars per

Exhibit 2/3: Government in G.N.P. Comparative Indicators of Government Spending

Ratio to GNP (%)

		Public consumption expenditure	Public general capital formation	Transfer expenditure	Other expenditure	Total (differential)	
U.S.	1970	19.0	2.6	7.9	3.4	32.9	(0.6)
	1978	18.0	1.6	10.4	3.5	33.5	
U.K.	1970	17.6	4.8	8.6	6.6	37.7	(5.2)
	1979	20.2	2.7	11.6	8.5	42.9	
West Germany	1970	15.9	4.3	12.2	3.7	36.1	(8.2)
	1979	19.8	3.5	15.3	5.6	44.3	
France	1970	13.4	3.8	17.0	˙4.3	38.4	(6.5)
	1979	14.7	2.9	22.4	4.8	44.9	
Japan	1970	7.5	4.6	4.7	2.6	19.5	(13.5)
	1980	10.1	6.3	10.4	6.3	33.0	

Source: Keidanren

worker, compared to 15.5 at Volkswagen, 15.1 at Ford, 11.4 at GM, and only 4.1 at British Leyland (MITI, 1977).

Japan's investment record cannot be isolated from the role of government in the economy and the overall tax system. Contrary to accepted opinion, Japan's level of government expenditure, while historically very low (because of limited welfare programs and low defense expenditures), is not notably less compared to the U.S. or other western countries (Exhibit 2/3). For example, Japan's ratio of total government expenditure to GNP was 33 percent in 1980, as against the same ratio of the U.S. in 1970 and only .5 percent more in 1980. With Japan's defense expenditure being only 1 percent of GNP compared to seven or more in the U.S., the Japanese government role in civilian aspects of expenditure is actually higher than the U.S., despite the smaller size of the government bureaucracy (see Chapter 3).

The major difference between the U.S. and Japan does not lie in the level of government expenditure as such. The more relevant issue is the impact of the tax structure and its impact on personal savings and corporate investment. Japan's savings rates are very high; the U.S. is very low. Marginal tax rates on personal salaries vary by country – Sweden has one of the highest schedules, France one of the lowest. The U.S. is among the western countries with the most onerous tax burdens on the individual – like Sweden. The U.S. taxes corporate dividends as interest income (most countries allow a tax credit for taxes paid by the corporation). In the area of taxes on investment income, the U.S. rates are second to Sweden, and marginally ahead of Britain but double the rate charged in Japan, West Germany, and France.

Exhibit 2/4 shows an international comparison of statutory tax rates for five western countries, as well as special measures (e.g. excise taxes on particular industrial products) which change the real rate of tax burden. Japan and West

Exhibit 2/4: Comparative Tax Rates in Five Countries

	Statutory Rate (according to tax law provisions)	Rate of real tax burden (taking into account the special measures for tax expenditure)
Japan[1] (1982)	53.24%	52.50%
U.S. (1983)[2]	51.18%	37.95%
U.K. (1980)	52 %	18.41%
West Germany[12] (1978)	56.52%	46.65%
France (1980)	50 %	43.35%

[1] Assuming that 30% of corporate income is directed to dividend.
[2] Including local taxes charged against corporate income.

Source: MITI

Exhibit 2/5: Aggregate Capital Cost Allowances on New Machinery
in a Number of Industrialized Countries

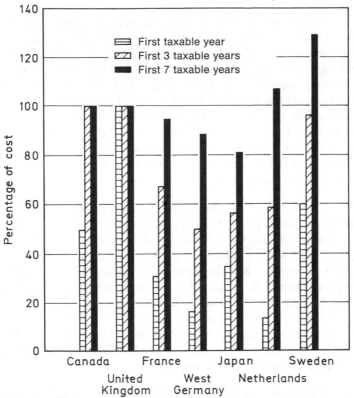

Source: Canadian Tax Foundation

Germany have the highest real rates, well above U.S. rates or British rates.
Comparisons internationally of tax rates are extremely difficult, because national policy typically offers incentives for particular types of investment (pollution control equipment, export activities, regional development, etc.). In
1975, the Organization for Economic Cooperation and Development (OECD)
conducted a study to compare tax depreciation policies for twenty-two countries. The aim was to measure the comparative tax cost of investing in selected
assets. As shown in Exhibit 2/5, Japan had the lowest index of the countries
studied. Economic studies have questioned the real impact of tax incentives on
growth, especially in the absence of other policy instruments (e.g. access to
capital and loan assistance). Pechman and Kaizuka (1976:367–368) make the
point that the real message from Japanese investment is the great success in

coordination of separate policy instruments, not the importance of any one instrument like taxation as such:

Two econometric studies argue that the special tax measures have been fairly effective in raising the level of investment. Both studies, however, use an investment function that tends to make tax incentives appear to be much more effective than do other investment functions. In our view, the access of growing firms to abundant amounts of borrowed capital through the banking system is at least as important as the special tax measures. This is particularly true in Japan because the various policy instruments are coordinated to an unusual degree in the interest of promoting private investment.

Japan's hardware strategies in support of high investment rates in new plant and equipment, coupled with favourable tax laws and sector specific depreciation policies, reinforce the impact of carefully nurtured science policies.

Japanese hardware management has received growing recognition in the area of science policy or, as elaborated in Chapter 4 and Chapter 5, knowledge intensification, training and education, and research and development. Computers represent the most dramatic area where Japanese companies have developed expertise, mainly because as an industry, computers represent the apex of the micro electronics industrial revolution and the key to automated office and manufacturing systems. Already Japanese companies account for 60 percent of video display screens and printers worldwide, 35 percent of disk drives and 25 percent of semiconductors used in computers.

There are three policy approaches which have formed the basis of Japan's science policy: reliance on the private sector, rapid technology diffusion, and corporate competition, "The United States," reports an advertisement by Motorola Inc. in the series 'Meeting Japan's Challenge', "spends three times more than Japan on research and development." The Japanese government's technology planning for the 1980's spells out a goal of spending up to four percent of GNP by 1990, more than double the present level. However, these aggregate figures do not reveal that about two thirds of the investment in technology in Japan is carried out by private sector firms, and a much higher level of investment is in the form of applications and product development than in fundamental science or mission research. The government has carefully monitored foreign licensing agreements in order to assure that no domestic firm can thereby gain a monopoly or a competitive advantage in a particular sector. Where one Japanese firm links up with a foreign company through a technology agreement, the government exerts pressure to have a second or third Japanese firm develop equivalent links with other overseas corporations. This approach has meant greater technology diffusion throughout each industry sector. In addition, the subcontracting system promotes technological diffusion between big firms and small and medium-sized firms, where technological barriers often exist in other countries. Japanese hardware policies must be examined for their interdependencies and coordinated effects, rather than in their separate impact per se.[9] Moreover, their overall development must be seen in context, namely how they impact at the micro level of the corporation and how they relate to software policies.

2.5 Organizational Software Systems

The strong economic and technological explanations for Japanese productivity gains form only one side of a complex equation where organizational and behavioural norms and structures influence managerial activities and systems. In North America, especially, the academic separation of economic and social models of organizational reality and the search for productivity clues in Japan practice naturally leads to simplistic models of explanation. Economists typically play down the role of attitudes, norms and management style, while behaviouralists typically ignore the impact of technology, the constraints of market structures and competition, and competitive pressures.[10]

Of all the approaches to the analysis of Japan, the cultural thesis has been the most enduring. Evident differences in language, history, race, religion, and social ettiquette have often provided the starting point for culturalist explanation. The usual litany of basic contrasts in Japanese and Western culture has become widely accepted. Westerners are individualists, highly mobile, heterogeneous, and boast short term horizons. By contrast, the stereotype of the

---

[9] According to Wassily Leontief, the father of input-output analysis, or the branch of economics called econometrics, there is in the U.S. an ideological aversion to input-output analysis and, in the 1950's, it was actually prohibited. Although routine computations are now made, their use is ineffective. As Leontief (1982) notes:
  What remains particularly self-defeating in the United States is the inability – or occasionally the reluctance – of official statistical organizations to collect the readily available specialized information that is needed not only for input-output analysis but for other projects as well. The U.S. is the only advanced industrialized country that still does not possess an effective central statistical office responsible for systematically obtaining information about population, natural resource, technology and other aspects of the national economy and society. The Census Bureau hardly qualifies as a central statistical office . . .
  What a contrast with the statistical organization of Japan or even that of a small country like Norway . . . In the U.S. the task of compiling a dicentennial U.S. input-output table is assigned to a small team tucked away in one of the many bureaus of the Department of Commerce. The most recent Japanese input-output table is produced by the combined efforts of thirteen ministries under the general supervision of a committee of the Council of Ministers. The five hardcover folio volumes containing the Japanese table are several times as large as their U.S. counterparts. The table was compiled much faster, and is indispensable to the Japanese government and businesses in deciding, among other things, which industries have good prospects for growth and which do not (Leontief, 1982:32–33).

[10] An important intellecutal bridge has been made between those academic fields by Liebenstein (1966, 1975, and 1976).

Japanese is one of collective consensus, high stability, homogeneous race and discipline, and long term horizons.

The difficulty with this broad reliance on cultural stereotypes, aside from the clear racial overtones implicit in the approach, is the rather basic point that increasingly, all high technology industrialzied societies require basic organizational systems to achieve efficiency. This is not to deny the impact of national culture specific to any one country. The more fundamental point is the consistency between corporate culture at the micro level and national culture and tradition at the societal level.

Corporate culture is a system of beliefs and expectations which is "reflected in the attitudes and values, the management style, and the problem-solving behaviour of its people" (Schwarz and Davis, 1980:477). Corporate culture goes beyond the narrow meaning of attitudes and expectations which define organizational climate. Culture defines the deeper meaning and symbolism of behavioural norms. Hall (1970), for instance, sees culture as a form of communication, often highly implicit and subtle. Communication can take the form of gift giving, touch, non-verbal symbols (eye contact, use of hands) and orientations to time.

In a more extended analysis, Hall (1977) speaks of societies being either low context of high context cultures. Context refers to the underlying structure of culture, where "meaning and context are inextricably bound up." To communicate properly and meaningfully, it is necessary to understand the context of communications, to pay attention to the right things. According to Hall, Japan, unlike the U.S., is a high context culture (Hall, 1977:45). In this sense, Japanese socialize meaning and experience into a deep value structure which can form the context of particular events or situations. Social relationships and communications in Japan reflect the way Japanese use uncertainty and interdependence in subtle ways and in what appear to be ambiguous communication signals. What this reflects in reality however, is the high context culture wherein contextual factors provide meaning and value to social relations.

As shown in Exhibit 2/6, there are basic differences between high context and low context cultures. In a high context culture, organizational meaning is transmitted not just through direct verbal forms of communications, but also through a plethora of symbols, ideologies, historical events serving as decision-premises, rituals and ideologies.

The essential point of this kind of distinction between high and low context culture is to indicate that Japanese management practices are a function more of the high context culture than Japanese social culture per se. There are diverse examples of organizations in numerous fields which clearly illustrate the basic characteristics of high context cultures: The Jesuit order in the Ca-

Exhibit 2/6: Characteristics of High and Low Context Cultures

High context	Low context
* Business . . .	* Business . . .
– low pressure sales	– high pressure sales
– long sale cycle	– short sale cycle
– high customer and employee involvement	– low customer and employee involvement
– eshews protagonist–antagonist	– 'us' vs. 'them'
– gray issues	– black and white
– circumscribed committments	– specifically defined committments
* Communication	* Communication
– indirect	– to the point
– economical	– explanative
– expects much from listener	– expects little from listener
– form important	– content important
– difficult to change	– no unification
	– easily changed
* Rules	* Rules
– wholistic	– must stand on own
– cannot be manipulated	– consciously manipulated
* Generally	* Generally
– covert knowledge required	– legal
– ethical	– not responsible for others
– responsible for subordinates	– exclusive
– situational inclusiveness	
– distinction between outsiders and insiders	

Source: Hall (1977)

tholic Church, Michelin Tire in France, the Royal Canadian Mounted Police in Canada, IBM or the U.S. Marines in the U.S..

Numerous studies have been made on the so-called particularistic traits of Japanese culture. These software aspects of the larger (or societal) culture do provide some basis for accepting the importance of their influence on social behaviour. It is a complex empirical question as to the relative importance of software management influences such as societal values as compared to hardware technology issues. It is a management imperative to take both factors into account – not to give undue primacy to one at the expense of the other. As Crozier (1964:210) notes, "Intuitively, however, people have always assumed that bureaucratic structures and patterns of action differ in the different countries of the world and even more markedly between East and West. Men of action know it and never fail to take it into account. But contemporary social scientists . . . have not been concerned with such comparisons."

What then are the main cultural traits of Japanese society? Volumes have been written on this subject; it should not go unmentioned that many Japanese

Exhibit 2/7: Cultural Traits of Japanese Society

	IE	DOZOKU	IEMOTO	ON	OYABUN-KOBUN
Japanese Expression Cultural Trait	Household	Set of Households	Voluntary Association	debt/obligation	parent–child patron–client relation
Traditional Role	defines social boundaries inclusion/exclusion	defines economic relationships among groups	defines primacy social unit	defines social obligations	defines norms for social exchange
Example	father/eldest son	rice paddy community	samurai/ronin bonds	individual joining an alien group	parent/child relations
Modern Role	voluntary economic association	allegiance to organizational system	human relations in factory setting	mentoring system	social norms of reciprocity
Value meaning	instill sense of ordered hierarchy and boundaries	collective norms of obligations and status in vertical hierarchy	defines code of behaviour to meet joint objectives	transmits loyalty and attachment through obligations and responsibilities	identifies rules for social obligations hierarchical relationship

scholars place great weight on the measure of Japanese value differences and even cultural uniqueness. As Azumi (1974:516) suggests, "the idea that Japan is unique is perhaps responsible for the large number of studies of that country which has taken a particularistic in contrast to a universalistic approach." Exhibit 2/7 provides a simplified, but illustrative, indication of what such cultural traits mean for Japanese social behaviour. What are the main themes?

A good starting point is the concept IE, which indicates the idea of household or basic social unit. In Japan IE implies a name group, not a blood relationship. Permanent relationship in the family unit starts from the head of the household as an organizing principle. Traditionally the head of the household was a man (but might have been a woman); strength and leadership ability often superceded strict blood lines. As a result, there were strict norms of behaviour over all aspects of household activities, including, for instance, the inheritance passing to the oldest son with other sons moving elsewhere. In general the social roles of the head of the household involve the management of outside relations; the actual responsibilities of the household itself were left to his wife or mother (Hosegawa, 1965).

The contemporary importance of the IE concept reflects many aspects of Japanese corporate life. The modern corporation is a social institution where bonds of loyalty and internal/external ties are part of the corporate culture. This is the meaning of Nakane's (1973) interpretation of the Japanese emphasis on "frame" or social context, as distinct from the Western emphasis on "attribute" or personal criteria or job characteristic (job, achievement, status, etc). The typical Japanese firm thus has more social integration around the IE concept of membership, regardless of attribute differences by hierarchical level or job classification.

The extension of the IE concept is the DOZOKU which refers to the set of households forming an economic relationship, much like a clan or community. The DOZOKU had its origins in the agricultural rice communites, where shared roles were important for rice growing and harvesting. These activities reinforced the norms of obligations, social relations and rituals and symbols of the vertical supervisor/subordinate relations. The modern counterpart of the DO-ZOKU is seen at the corporate level by the group structure of major Japanese firms linked to key suppliers and subcontractors, and the total responsibility of top executives, who, like the DOZOKU head, assume the obligations of authority for the whole organization.

Even surpassing these forms of social influences is what some writers (Hsu, 1975) consider to be the primary social unit of organizational life in twentieth century Japan, the IEMOTO. In Western terms, the IEMOTO is much like a club of voluntary membership. The IEMOTO is an integral value system reflecting bonds between master and disciple, expressed in terms of authority, discipline and loyalty. The modern counterpart to the historical meaning of IEMOTO is the factory life of modern industrial Japan.

Such a dependence/authority concept is not unknown in the West, but there the meaning is usually derogatory or has negative connotations. The sense of ON in Japan is an expression of obligation or indebtedness which arises from voluntary social exchange. Japanese culture defines this meaning in a more thorough way than in most Western nations. In a spiritual sense, the ON obligation reflects GIMU – a payment is never complete in the fullest sense. A more materialistic sense of ON is Giri, which is somewhat like moral bonds between friends or colleagues. Workers, for instance, give gifts at New Years to the boss. For the boss to reciprocate with gifts, rather than tea or a drink, would mean increasing the sense of ON.

The OYABUN-KOBUN relationship reinforces this bonding in hierarchical relationships and obligations. The OYABUN-KOBUN is like a parent-child or patron-client relationship, and indicates a dynamic social responsibilities and obligations within an ordered structure of authority and decision-making. The Japanese practice of mentoring, of linking senior managers as patrons or godfathers to young workers, is an illustrative case in point, much like the wandering individual becoming accepted in a community in historic times under the shogun or household elder.

For the foreigner trying to penetrate the subtleties and complexities of Japanese culture, such traits and values easily lead to beliefs about clear and major differences between Japan and other societies. In this sense, the shared norms and mores of Japanese social life do indeed amount to a high context culture in Hall's (1977) useful terminology. From a management and organizational perspective, however, it is clearly an overstatement to argue that Japanese culture is in and by itself the critical point, because many of the sociological ideas expressed in Japanese cultural traits are universal – they apply equally to many other organizational and societal settings. Different societies are high context cultures and many countries reflect differences within them (e.g. Francophone and Anglophone Canadians).

What must be recognized is the way Japanese manage their social affairs as expressions of their high context culture. Employees have a strong work ethic but managers equally demonstrate, at least in the larger firms, a very strong employee welfare ethic. One supports the other: they can't be seen in isolation. The family unit still remains the basic unit of Japanese society. Children are the central focus of the core family and in a country where education is worshipped, the family unit has remained consistently stable. In 1962, there were 0.75 divorces per 1000 persons; in more recent years, the trend has been slowly upward, 0.79 in 1965, 0.99 in 1971, 1.14 in 1977. Yet this is only a fraction of the rate in the U.S. for instance (5.02 in 1976), where the divorce rate is one in three in the population at large, and one in two among professional occupations (partly as a result of students moving from rural areas to urban universities).

The family and school socialization have done much to maintain the high context culture of Japanese society. Modernization trends of industrialization have not blurred out traditional mores and cultural patterns. What appear to many as rural folkways continue to exist even in large urban centres. An obvious implication of this transformation has been the remarkably low crime rate – a measure of societal integration and consensus. Exhibit 2/8 shows the low crime rates in Japan (or more accurately, the extremely high crime rates of the U.S. compared to Japan, European countries, and its neighbour to the north, Canada: in the U.S., one American in 600 is in prison).

The low crime rates in Japan may have a deep cultural meaning, but Japanese military history and the samurai tradition weaken that argument. More tellingly is Japan's police system, which neatly illustrates the connection between hardware and software management systems. Japan's police system is at once highly centralized and highly decentralized. Centralized are the main information systems, the senior police and security services, and the overall administration. Within a city like Tokyo, the operating system is highly decentralized – 94 main police stations and 1236 Koban or neighbourhood police box – i.e. one for every 8800 citizens or 2500 nuclear families. Each of these neighbourhood policemen is equipped with radios, information on local crime conditions, plus bicycle or skooter. Most police recruits are from rural areas and have training

Exhibit 2/8: Comparative Indicators of Violent Crime*

Country	Homicide	Rape	Robbery
Britain	2.5	10.1	25.4
Canada	2.4	9.6	102.7
France	3.6	3.6	60.0
Germany	4.3	10.7	35.8
Japan	1.6	2.4	1.8
U.S.	9.7	34.5	212.1

* Crime rate per 100,000 people 1979/80

Source: Japanese National Police Agency

in judo, karate and unarmed combat, even though they wear guns. Their mandate is to visit each household at least twice a year to become informed of the neighbourhoods, new families, special problems and the like. When crime does occur, these Kobun police are the first to inspect a suspect area supported by backup units from central dispatch and high technology crime equipment, such as mechanical and electronic drawing machines for crime witnesses.

The result of this system is the most productive arrest rate in the world. In Japan, 96.9 percent of murderers are arrested, compared to 92.2 percent in Britain, 94.2 in Germany, 78.9 percent in Canada, and 75.5 percent in the U.S. For rape, only 51.2 percent are arrested in the U.S., 72.7 in Germany, 88.6 percent in Britain, and 90 percent in Japan. For robbery, Britain and the U.S. have the lowest arrest rate (27.7 vs. 26.9) compared to 52.3 in Germany and 78 percent in Japan.

Japan's software mangement systems in short are a mirror reflection of a deep historical tradition of personal relationships at every level and these personal bonds are woven into the modern institutional fabric of the society through extended families, schooling, and intricate corporate networks (school/university, university/corporation, company/supplier, business-government, business firm/trading firm, corporation/bank, trade association/government department etc.). These networks are a pervasive and all encompassing mosaic of personal relationships, shared experiences, common schooling, and identical social origins. In Japan's high context culture, information, values, traditions, and skills become the instruments for shared goals and common objectives. Elites in the society at large, whether in the bureaucracy, in politics, or in the private sector, have managed economic and social affairs around the elements of traditional Japanese culture, not in opposition to it. It is because the key traits of Japanese culture are generally based around social relationships (e.g. work groups), interdependence (rice culture, assembly lines, business and labour) and the high context society. Even where labour unions are largely excluded from central economic decision-making bodies, enterprise unions and leaders are fully accepted in the context of the corporate household.

2.6 Summary and Conclusions

This chapter has outlined a framework for analyzing Japan's industrial system and managerial strategies in the 1980's. The main point of the framework is to show the broader relationships behind Japan's industrial competitiveness and the complexity of the factors accounting for the country's success. Numerous studies of Japanese management have gone to one of two extremes. Studies by Brzezinski (1973) and Kahn (1970), for instance, cite as many as sixteen or seventeen variables which point to Japanese growth. Some of these variables are highly interdependent, others actually work inconsistently with one another. At the other extreme, and notably by academics, there is the propensity to reduce Japan's success to single variable explanations. At the societal level, there is the question of good business-government relations or a low level of welfare or defense spending. At the corporate level, there is the role of the Sogoshosha or the permenant employment system (Theory Z) or the style of management and the soft s. Most recently, there is critical role of marketing (Kotler and Fahey, 1982).

The fact is, there is no simple explanation for Japan's staggering economic success. At the government level, the very structure of departments and bureaus is designed to orient the total economy to international trends – a telling point is that the much touted MITI – to many, the heart of Japan Inc. – is called the Ministry of International Trade and Industry. Though exports account for only ten per cent of GNP, scarcely more than the relatively closed economy of the U.S., the total thrust of government economic decision making has a decidedly international character, which is similarly reflected at the corporate level in such matters as international market research, technological scanning, and the like.

The macro/micro linkages are clearly important, but as the next three chapters will show, the patterns are neither rigidly fixed nor totally coherent. Japan is a much more pluralistic society than foreigners often perceive and behind the overall facade of cooperation and consensus is a fierce competitiveness which carries the samurai tradition to a modern day, economic and industrial counterpart. If Japan does have an advantage, the hardware/software issues are an important point to consider internationally. No country has been so successful at applying technology – indiginously developed or internationally imported – as the Japanese. Whether it was numerically controlled machine tools, the transistor, or the computer a generation ago, or the automated factory, robotics, and micro electronics of every form in today's society, the Japanese have developed work systems which combine human intellectual effort with machine precision and computational facility in a way unrivalled by Western societies. It is not hardware alone, nor software alone – it is both.

Studies in Britain (Caves, 1981) show that managers are reluctant to operate large plants because of industrial relations posing unbearably high risks of work stoppages. Others show that Britain's productivity deficiencies owing to labour relations is one-fourth compared to the U.S. and Canada, one-third relative to France, and one half relative to West Germany. Another study pointing to the direct hardware-software relationship is in the automobile industry. Citing seven specific factors affecting productivity, Abernathy et al (1982) found such hardware issues as process automation accounted for only ten percent of U.S.-Japan differences – the key factor was process yield (40%) relating to engineering layout and supply and work cycles, followed by job structure (18%), absenteeism (12%) and quality systems (9%).

The framework presented in this chapter ist to underscore the dynamic relationships which provide the basis for Japan's managerial strategies in the 1980's. The pieces fit together in a holistic fashion – they have evolved and are evolving from a constant interplay of all major economic decision-makers. Even the concept of strategy may be misleading in a Western sense. Japan's enormous information output relating every facet of the economy to past and future, and to other industrial countries, provides an unparallel level of economic literacy. In many ways, strategy is a form of rationalization of past achievements rather than a blueprint for future action. Government white papers are the major examples of this kind of exercise – individual decision-makers think more in terms of reacting to and anticipating uncontrollable events and activities rather than designing a strategy to control or manage events in the face of uncertainty. The information base for Japan's decision-makers is the key to understanding this point – it is best evidenced in the business-government relationship. That issue is taken up in the next chapter.

Chapter 3
The Visible Hand: Business-Government Relations

> "I would suggest that there could be
> no more devastating weakness for
> any major nation in the 1980's than
> the inability to define the role of gov-
> ernment in the economy."
> *Louis Mulkern*

3.1 Introduction

Like all Western capitalist nations, Japan has a mixed economy. The government's role in Japanese economic development has received a great deal of academic and managerial attention, although there is considerable controversy on the matter of just how important the state has been. Kaplan (1972:10), for example, argues that "it is the special and unique way in which that Japanese government has guided the economy's development and the interaction of government and enterprise which is the peculiar hall-mark of the Japanese economy. Japan's economic destiny has not been left to the free play of market forces." At the other extreme lies this assessment: "Careful examination of Japan's postwar trade and industrial development in comparison with general world performance indicates that the Japanese pattern was not unique at all; thus, while government policy may have been important, its impact on economic performance was not 'uniquely Japanese'" (Patrick and Rosovsky, 1976:47–48).

Part of the reason for the difference of opinion concerning the role of the Japanese government in the economy is the absence of clear benchmarks. Curiously there is no accepted theoretical answer in classical economics on this important question, except of course at the two extremes, i.e., a hundred percent, total market economy (which doesn't exist in any advanced country) or a hundred percent total 'command' economy, which only exists in fully totalitarian states. Thus on any basic quantitative index, such as the percentage of government activity in the total GNP, or the level of tax spending, there is no simple correlation with economic performance. High spending Sweden is not appreciably different from low spending Switzerland; the bigger government activity in West Germany scores higher on productivity than the USA (Samuelson, 1980).

Traditionally, the major government levers used in the capitalist economies have been in three categories: broad stabilization policies within a Keynesian framework; monetary policy affecting interest rates, inflation, and the value of the currency; and defense policy. To a more or less extent among all Western countries, but starting in Britain with the Beveridge report, which outlined the basis of the welfare state, governments have added to their portfolio of programs and thereby greatly increased the role of government in the economy at large. Among these activities are extensive programs in education, health, pensions and welfare, which encompass at the extreme an entire range of programs covering economic security from birth to the grave. In recent years, the trends towards international competition and competitive threat have added a new dimension to the government's role, namely industrial strategy-making or planned industrial development.[1]

In the United States, where the ideological committments to laissez-faire and the separation of business and government are relatively strong, there is a tendency often to compare foreign practices and institutions in relation to US experience. Abegglen (1970:71) once described the business-government relationship in Japan as a tightly coordinated, centrally directed mechanism to achieve specific policies, much like a large multidivisional corporation:

The Japanese government corresponds to corporate headquaters, responsible for planning and coordination, formation of long-term policies and major investment decisions. The large corporations of Japan are akin to corporate divisions, with a good deal of operating autonomy within the overall policy framework laid down by coorporate headquarters, free to compete with each other within broad limits, and charged with direct operating responsibility.

This version of Japan Incorporated, or Japan Inc., has many adherents among foreigners, both in the public at large and in key institutions, not simply because prominent writers have simplified a complex institutional arrangement in Japan, but because there is a certain measure of truth in the idea. Certainly by comparison with the United States, the Japanese government through key ministries like the Ministry of International Trade and Industry in industrial matters and the Ministry of Finance in banking and finance matters, has a far larger role to play than equivalent or near equivalent ministries in Washington. Moreover, there is an enormous difference in the approach to business-government relations which in Japan involves constant and quite detailed levels of interaction between executives in the corporate sector and the government ministries, even among low level officials, in an attempt to reach overall consensus on a coherent and long range vision of the forward direction of the economy. By contrast, the US case typically involves almost no coherence

---

[1] The literature on industrial strategy is small, although separate studies by the Boston Consulting Group in Sweden, Franch, and Germany, plus works like Magaziner and Hout (1982) on Japan, have prompted a new look at the role of planning and competitiveness. See Reich (1982), Steiner (1979) and Dewar (1982).

across government departments, constant turnover of key officials, treatment of major domestic economic issues in isolation from foreign policy issues, and virtually no high level bureaucratic apparatus to link trade and investment policies to domestic programs and policies. In this respect, there can be some appreciation to Patrick and Rosovsky's (1976) observation that for Japan," the nature and extent of the government-business relationship is in many respects similar to that in France, West Germany, and other continental European nations; the United States is perhaps the atypical case."[2]

This chapter examines the business-government relationship in Japan with specific reference to industrial policy and economic development. Japan's macro hardware and software policies have been called "the most intelligently dirigiste system in the world today" (*The Economist,* May 27, 1967). The first section examines the historical context of Japan's business-government relationship, particularly the absense of a strong anti-business ideology on the part of government officials or anti-government on the part of business. The following section examines the structure of modern government decision-making, including the mechanisms for consultation and communication. The last two sections focus on this macro structure for big business and for small business. The next two chapters analyze the actual strategy outcomes and examine industrial policy making and science and technology policy.

3.2 The Social Origins of Business-Government

While the history of the contempory business government relationship[3] can be traced to the Meiji Restoration, and the almost single minded devotion to economic affairs relates to the desire to catch up with the West, the preconditions for the modern era were established in the centuries before 1868. For one thing, Japan's feudal era developed a strong social legitimacy for the key in-

---

[2] Senator Daniel Patrick Moynihan (1983) has written an argument for centralizing trade policy in the U.S., as follows:

"Eight Cabinet departments now have statutory roles in international trade policy: State, Treasury, Agriculture, Defense, Commerce, Labor, Transportation, and Energy. There are five important independent agencies involved as well. And there is a sign of sure chaos: Within the Executive Office of the President is the Office of the U.S. Trade Representative, where a succession of brave men have tried to impose some order.

It is time to get it all together. The Commerce Department is a perfectly good organization but one with practically no role in policy making. Hasn't had since Herbert Hoover was Secretary and the department helped create a system of nationwide markets for American industries."

[3] The volume of essays edited by Nakagawa (1980) traces Japan's business-government relationship, as compared to Britain, Germany, and the U.S.

stitutions, while at the same time accepting a high level of competition and pluralism within a centrally controlled polity. Of the four traditional social classes, or SHI NO KO SHO – the samurai, the peasants, the artisans and the merchants – it was the samurai who dropped their military roles and accepted administrative tasks with high levels of status. By developing a strong bureaucratic power base in the Meiji period prior to the development of strong political parties, the samurai bureaucrats achieved a level of influence totally out of significance to their numbers. Another factor was that for all the defects and negatives relating to Japan's long period of isolation between the Tokugawa period in the sixteenth century and the Meiji restoration in the nineteenth, Japan escaped from the centuries of European (and later, American) debate concerning the merits and demerits of conservative and liberal rule, capitalist or socialist political economy, or an Adam Smith or Karl Marx interpretation of the role of the state. As a result, Japanese policy-makers and institutions reflect a remarkable degree of non-ideological or pragmatic adjustment to circumstances.

Some writers depict the social origins of the business-government relationship in terms of the familiar metaphor of the family:

The state bureaucrats exercise authority not in the name of the people, but in the name of the House of Japan. To the Japanese way of thinking, then, the state does not 'interfere' with the affairs of private business. It merely manages itself, exercising authority and control of its constituencies. The productive activities of private businesses is very much a part of the business of the whole nation state (Haitani, 1975).

The difficulty with the family metaphor is that it does not go far enough: it is unsatisfactory in the instances when the government undertook projects not entirely to big business' liking; and it fails to explain the strong nation building role that governments have taken in all capitalist countries, including in the United States. Most Americans would be embarassed at the notion of the House of the United States, yet the American government has always provided a strong and direct promotional role – in canals, in railways, in credit, and in federal aid to business (Cochran, 1974). Chatov (1982:490) makes the point as follows:

From the outset of their nationhood, Americans tried to reconcile laissez-faire ideology with governmental promotion of business. It was apparent that a healthy economy depended on government promotion. Secretary Treasury Alexander Hamilton proposed a series of programs designed to provide for the national credit, a safe and uniform currency via the offices of a national bank, communications and transportation networks, and planned development of manufacturing. Hamilton's programs were, by and large, adopted; they fostered commercial expansion, although full-scale industrialization did not take place until after the Civil War ended in 1865.

However, the parallels between Japan and Western countries in terms of the state's role in economic development are actually much closer to Europe's aristocratic traditions than the US model. Unlike the US legacy of a Madison-style division of powers and factions of minorities, Japan's post Meiji government was headed by an Emperor who "was simultaneously head of state, head of government, highest lawgiver, supreme judge, and commander in chief of all armed forces" (Sumiya and Taira, 1979:191). Absolutism was the form of government during the formative years of Japan's market economy; the absolutism turned to militarism, which in defeat changed to an imposed democracy.

When the major choices for economic development were made in the last century, the national slogan, *Fukoku Kyohei* – rich country and strong army – was reflected in the major institutional arrangements for the society at large. Because the actual choices for emulating foreign countries were not great – capitalist in North America or Europe, where the image of national richness originated – the role of the merchant class and the new bureaucracy quickly became apparent. The state machinery of samurai administrators built a web of enterprises and institutions tied to the "political merchants" who joined forces with the government while letting the state take many of the social risks. Social ideologies based around nationalism and a type of manifest destiny provided a form of social glue with the masses, even though the bureaucracy operated on the feudal principle of *Kanson Minpi* – revere the official, despise the common man.

The internal struggles within the bureaucracy were essentially between the younger and low level administrators from humble social origins, who desired modernization and development, and higher level bureaucrats who promoted the role of the bureaucracy through the cult of the emperor. While the industrial emphasis was in large scale mines and factories, as well as in military arsenals, the financing came mostly from land taxes imposed on the peasantry and labour conditions remained feudal and authoritarian. By the time the Meiji period ended in 1912, the state had developed modernized institutions in banking, trade, and transportation, mainly in coalition with the so-called political merchants, while the government legitimized the role of private enterprise and private property. However, the servile peasant class was still subject to high tax payments, agriculture remained feudal, and the government links to the military establishment grew stronger as a result of vistory in the Russo-Japanese war (1904–1905) and the Korean annexation in 1910.

In other words, the basis of the institutional character of Japan up to the end of 1945 was firmly in place two generations before. The large and efficient industrial sector, supported by government and exploited by the political merchants, contrasted with the position of the agricultural and light industry sectors. While the economy itself was developing a modern merchant and entrepreneurial class, the government was dominated by a traditional and self-serving bureaucracy which increasingly merged its own interests with imperialistic militaristic adventures. As Boulding and Gleason (1972:247) have pointed out, there was a basic continuity between the Pacific War aims in the 1940's and the movements in Asia from the Meiji period: "But the Meiji government, once isolationism had been abandoned, resumed the imperialistic practices of an earlier era. The policy of expansion was supported by a powerful traditional nationalistic sentiment or pride which rested on the belief that the Japanese were a nation divinely established and favoured, a kind of chosen people of the Orient, destined to rule the less favored".

The high level of centralization in the economy, and the general attempt to mobilize resources for government-imposed goals, such as imperialism in the decades up to the Pacific War and then war itself, shaped not only the institutional character of the government but left a legacy of values, attitudes, and even language among the bureaucrats and their subordinates. The result was a surprising level of continuity between the prewar years and the post war years when, for example, during the occupation years, the level of government control reached unparalleled. Johnson (1982:308) goes so far as to argue that the prewar experience was not entirely negative for postwar economic development:

The experience of the 1930's and the 1940's was not by any means totally negative for postwar Japan; these were the years in which the managerial tools of the developmental state were first tested, some being rejected and others proving useful. Overcoming the depression required economic development, war preparation and war fighting required economic development, postwar reconstruction required economic development, and independence from US aid required economic development. The means to achieve development from one cause ultimately proved to be equally good for the other causes.

The emergence of a new order after 1945 broke down a stable pattern of coalitions whose power, privileges, and positions owed much to a delicate balance of mutual protection from outside interests. While the basic coalition was a blend of the industrial elites, the political establishment, and the government administrators, the internal factions of each group were never monolithic: in big business there was the tension between the old *Zaibatsus* and the emerging enterprises; in the government, there were the clashes between the militarists and the bureaucratic conservatives; among the political elites, there was the tension between the old nobility and the new privileged class. By breaking up this historical interplay of protected elites, the post-war Occupation Forces unleashed a new set of coalitions, whose aim was to survive the Occupation and rebuild the economy. The very fact of Occupation control left little room for mutual antagonism among the elites; the result was a rebuilt elite structure formed from a new generation of managers whose number one priority was on industrial rebuilding.

3.3 The Structure of Modern Government

A good starting point for understanding the modern form of Japanese government is the nation's twelve government ministries and eight cabinet level agencies. Housed in the Kasumigaseki district of Tokyo,[4] Japan's bueaucracy consists of some of the country's best educated and most gifted personnel. Despite
the considerable power exercised by this public elite, the bureaucracy is not
large, at only a million employees, plus another three million at the prefectural
level. Using a ratio of the number of national government officials per thousand of the working population, Dahlby (1981) calculates that Japan has 17.1
bureaucrats, compared to 20.2 in Britain, 22.5 in the USA, and 84.5 per cent in
France.

Exhibit 3/1 shows an outline of the government structure in Japan. Despite the
importance of the local administrations in the forty-seven Prefectural governments, the strong ministries at the national level not only have vastly more
power but also they are staffed by Japan's best and the brightest, such that
Craig (1975:5–6) characterizes the bureaucracy as one of bimodality,

of exceedingly able men directing the work of the central ministries, but much less able
men in the offices of local government; of graduates from the two or three best universities versus those from lesser schools and, at a lower level yet, high school graduates; of
generalists versus specialists, technicians and clerks; of relative freedom in creative
work versus mechanical rote tasks; of the satisfaction of power versus the frustration of
narrow routine. Of course, the bimodality is not simply between the central ministries
and local government. Those who will reach the highest appointive positions in the
central government will spend some time in prefectural-level officies. There are planning and executive posts at the prefectural level that are highly demanding, and many of
the sections of the central ministries are filled with clerks, assistants, researchers, and
temporary employees performing the most routine kind of work.

The elite bureaucrats move frequently from post to post and often occupy certain
positions which are, as it were, on a special track, reserved for the most promising
careerists . . .

In one sense, this description of the bimodality with the Japanese bureaucracy
fits well with the notions of Max Weber (1947), who first explored the idea of
bureaucracy as an "ideal type" of organization, emphasizing the norms of
impersonality, rationality, specialization, and control. In another sense, the
power and influence of the central bureaucracy in Japan rests also on the
recruiting and training of the most intelligent graduates into elite positions, its
strategic control over the drafting of legislation, its nonpolitical character during a very long period of essentially one party rule.

---

[4] KASUMIGASEKI translates freely as "misty gates"; the pecking order among the Ministries is
evident from the addresses: The Ministry of Finance and Economic Planning Board at No. 1
Chome, MITI at No. 2 Chome, and The Foreign Office at No. 3 Chome.

Exhibit 3/1: Government of Japan

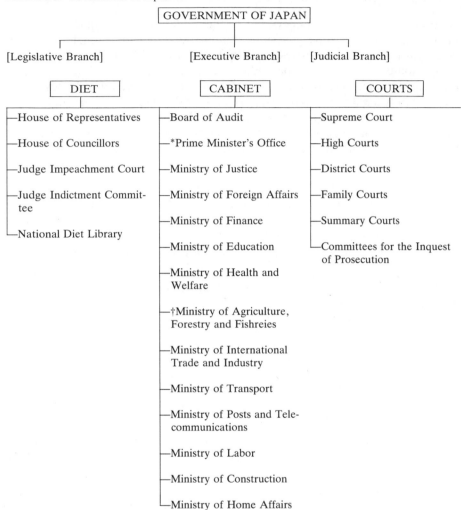

* The Prime Minister's Office consists of the Defense Agency, Economic Planning Agency, Science and Technology Agency, Environment Agency, Fair Trade Commission, and other offices.
† Formerly, Ministry of Agriculture and Forestry.

Adapted from: *Politics and Economics in Contemporary Japan*, Tokyo: Japan Culture Institute, 1979.

Indeed, it is the sense of constant forward direction within a coherent framework of planning, together with a low rate of turnover among high level elites, that contrasts with most other Western countries. Not only is the bureaucracy apolitical, with very few changes of high level personnel with each change of political administrations, the internal dynamics within the economic ministries and agencies stress strict adherence to the basic tenants of Japan's forward progress in economic and technological development. This is not to say that the system is monolithic: ministries have constant battles over resources and main policies, but the level of interaction, discussion, circulation of planning documents, and consultation does much to reduce the level of open conflict and to reach consensus on the broad outlines of economic policies. As will be discussed below, the interactions of the bureaucrats within the government and between the bureaucrats and the company executives in the private sector appear to be incredibly complex; in fact the modus operandi of business government consultation goes to the heart of Japan's success in industrial policy-making.

Of all the ministries touching on economic and management issues, the two most important are the Ministry of Finance and the Ministry of International Trade and Industry. These two ministries share a very high reputation for the quality of their personnel and the sophistication of their policies during Japan's postwar success, but there are important if subtle broad differences. As a general rule, the Ministry of Finance is more internationalist and nonprotectionist than MITI, where the international reputation of MITI is almost synonymous with protection and quotas. MITI, for instance, is much more interventionist in the economy, and because of its particular role in shaping industrial policy, it has a more focused strategic framework for particular sectors. The Ministry of Finance, because it is in charge of the total budget, has a more balanced view of the societal requirements than MITI: the rise since 1974 in the budget deficit has exacerbated, for instance, the budgetary needs of MOF on the one hand, and the desires of MITI for subsidies and tax relief for industry on the other. Despite these differences, the Ministries are not without certain similarities in their aims to build a strong economy. MOF, after all, controls the bureau of Customs and Tariffs, and the Ministry's control over central banking policies and credit allocation to the large commercial banks, exercises extraordinary power with MITI over the basic direction of the economy.

The Ministry of Finance drafts and implements the national budget: as such it has the pivotal role in the entire government bureaucracy and also controls the entire financial system, external financing and banking, social security and tax collection. Obviously, with so many large companies operating with debt to equity ratios of 80:20 or more, the Ministry is also the pivotal government institution behind the banking system, thus placing it at the center of international controversies surrounding such questions as the role of the yen in inter-

Exhibit 3/2: Stucture of The Ministry of Finance

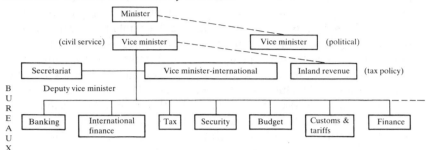

national finance and the use of the exchange rate as an instrument of industrial policy (see Chapter 12).

Structurally, the Ministry of Finance has seven specialized bureaux, which handle day to day operating decisions with a considerable degree of autonomy (Exhibit 3/2). Informally there is a status ranking, with the Budget bureau highest, followed by Tax, Finance, Banking, and International Banking. However, domestic crises and international events can change this ranking to some extent; moreover, because of the highly specialized nature of each of the bureaux, business groups must know intimately the key officials, internal politics, and principal policies of each.

The Minister of Finance and the Vice-Minister are appointees of the Prime Minister; the other high level officials are career bureaucrats within the Ministry. The prestige of the Ministry comes not just from the overall control of the national budget and the quality of the Ministry Staff; the Minister of Finance has been an important route to the Prime Minister's job – a parallel in countries like Britain, France, and West Germany, but not the United States.

The Ministry of International Trade and Industry, whose name clearly spells out the central thrust of Japan's industrial policies, dates back to the Ministry of Agriculture and Commerce founded in 1881 and which became the separated Ministry of Commerce and the Ministry of Agriculture and Forestry in 1925. During World War II, these same ministries became the Ministry of Munitions and the Ministry of Agriculture and Commerce, which in turn became MITI in 1949. As shown in Exhibit 3/3, the Ministry is organized along both horizontal and vertical lines.

There is a close parallel with the Ministry of Finance in the MITI structure. At the highest level is the Cabinet Minister, followed by two parliamentary vice-ministers and an administrative vice-minister *(Jimu Jikan)*. Real power resides at the bureaux level, followed by the section chiefs and assistants. The various industrial bureaux, or *Genkyoku,* focus on quite detailed plans and strategies for various sectors. As discussed in Chapter 4, this approach goes to the heart of Japan's industrial planning, with incredibly detailed information and statistics pertaining to each sector's output, competitiveness, and potential relative to international competitors. For example, these industrial bureaux monitor Japan's performance sector by sector along such dimensions as demand growth, capacity utilization, factor input cost, productivity performance, market share, technology, import competition and the like with international comparisons monitored to a degree likely unmatched by any Western country. So high is the quality of this statistical base, carefully nurtured and developed over the years, that in a fundamental sense, MITI actually externalizes the costs of environmental scanning for corporate strategy making. In short, MITI turns the information gathering and environmental scanning function into a public good, freely available to all companies, big or small, Japanese or foreign.

The work at the level of the sector bureaux is complemented by the Industrial Policy Bureau which carries out the planning of aggregate or horizontal policies common to all industrial sectors. Examples of this form of industrial planning include industrial reorganization, industrial land allocation, raw materials sourcing and distribution, and the like. Within this bureau, the details are worked out for implementing particular policies and programs. The Industrial Structure Division copes with the projected structure of industrial demand and output with policies aimed towards a specific targeted year, with provision for a "rolling plan" continuously revised and updated.

At a more specific level, the Business Behaviour Division works on areas like tax measures and labour questions to study the impact of changes in the industrial structure, while the Price Policy Division examines the growth prospects in terms of financing implications. Overall there is on overlapping set of consultative committees, which provide input to the work of the various divisions. The output is an integrated plan which pulls the separate aspects together. The continuing nature of this approach means that MITI is primarily interested in constant, incremental adjustments within an overall framework or "vision".

The report *Japan's Industrial Structure – A Long Range Vision*, which was first published in 1975, and then updated in 1980, exemplifies this approach. In it the powerful and pervasive influence of the international environment are clearly spelled out, as are the changing energy situation and the competitive impact of technology. In practice, the horizontal and vertical sections of MITI's organization operate as a matrix with a great deal of cross fertilization of ideas, data, and strategies, including liason and coordination with other government ministries. It is because there is a broad consensus of the basic vision or direction of the economy, such as the vision of shifting towards a technology-intensive[5] knowledge economy (see Chapter 5) that the various departments,

---

[5] The intellectual case for developing "Knowledge-intensive" industries was set out by Naohiro

Exhibit 3/3: Structure MITI

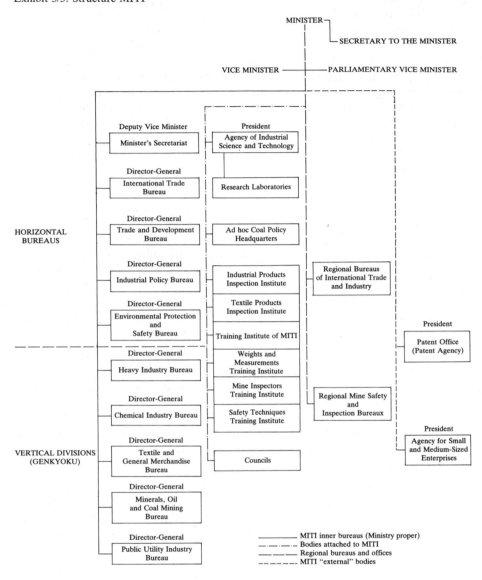

Source: O.E.C.D., Paris 1972

bureaux and commissions can work together. Moreover, there is an enormous amount of continuous consultation with the private sector companies and economic organizations. These in turn also conduct a great deal of parallel forward planning. Some leading executives share work with academics and bureaucrats on certain MITI committees, such as the important Industrial Structure Council. Japanese consensus building and harmony may be the typical Western characterization of this broad approach, but that simply does not adequately describe both the level of effort or the depth of sophistication which the planning approach covers. Chapters 4 and 5 go into the details of the intended output of the planning approach; the next section examines the nature of consultative mechanisms between business and government.

3.4 Government and Big Business

Conventional economic theory places great emphasis on the notion of atomistic competition, where the role of size and power are of peripheral concern and where control of the market are seen as the exception. Galbraith's (1967) tract, *The New Industrial State,* attempted to right the balance for the US, but ironically, his description in many ways applies more to Japan, where the concept of forward planning has much greater acceptance both in government and in business. The idea of the "Military Industrial Complex" is an inferior description[6] of the business-government interface, while Marxian views[6] of a dominant interlocking power elite do not do justice to the fierce competition across industrial sectors and to disagreements between business and government. Notwithstanding these conventional academic perspectives of business as atomistic market competition, or as part of an elite structure, some scholars have attempted to see the business-government role in different and, at times, controversial ways.

In one of the earliest works of its kind, Dahl and Lindblom (1952) presented a societal model of three distinct social systems operating in any advanced society: the price system or market, the bureaucratic system, or government, and the bargaining system, covering individual micro decisions. In a similar vein, Boulding (1968) established a framework for understanding the social decision processes of any advanced society: the price system for the production of goods and services; the government system or hierarchy for producing public goods and services; and the grants economy, governing voluntary exchange and gift relations. What is critical in assessing business-government relations in a complex economy is how well both business and government understand the

---

Amaya, a leading thinker in MITI, and Motoyuki Miyano, who presented their vision in a paper "70 Nendai No Tsusho Sangyo Sisaku" (Trade and Industrial Policies For The 1979's).

[6] The best Marxian analysis of the Japanese system is provided by Halliday (1975).

strengths and limitations of these different social systems or mechanisms for action. The argument presented here is that the strength of the business-government relationship in Japan stems from the fundamental legitimacy held for both business and government by each of the principal economic actors, a legitimacy which exists to a far lesser extent in Western countries. Further, the strength of that fundamental understanding is developed and nurtured by the quality and the pragmatism of the consultative mechanisms between business and government.

Lindblom (1977:174–175) is unambiguous in describing the true nature of business and government in a modern market economy:

One of the great misconceptions of conventional economic theory is that businessmen are induced to perform their functions by purchases of their goods and services, as though the vast productive tasks performed in market-oriented systems could be motivated solely by exchange relations between buyers and sellers. On so slender a foundation no great production system can be established. What is required in addition is a set of governmentally provided inducements in the form of market and political benefits. And because market demands themselves do not spontaneously spring up, they too have to be nurtured by government . . .

To understand the peculiar character of politics in market-oriented systems requires, however, no conspiracy theory of politics, no theory of common social origins uniting government and business officials, no crude allegation of a power elite established by clandestine forces. Business simply needs inducements, hence a privileged position in government and politics, if it is to do its job.

The literature on business government-relations in Japan, whether of the left or the right, conveniently strips away pluralist theory and focuses overwelmingly on a ruling elite model, or the more crudely put Japan Inc. stereotype. Recent studies of particular decisions and the growing complexity of the Japanese economy, including the important international dimension, shows that a more sophisticated pluralist approach is required (Curtis, 1975; Johnson, 1982).

The pluralist perspective of business-government relations in Japan is reflected in the set of business associations, the basis of transmitting the business view to the government. As in most areas of social affairs, the Japanese business world has a set of organizations which on paper represent particular groupings and espouse different points of view, and they bring to the business-government relationship a rather comprehensive and generally consistent form of interaction and political lobbying.

At the top is the *Zaikai,* which translates as "business world" or financial circles; to many people in Japan, the *Zaikai* represents the apex of business power and is the main focus for top executive influence on the government. Historically the *Zaikai* was seen to be synonymous with the two major political merchants, Mitsui and Mitsubishi, the two dominant *Zaibatsu* groups which funded the two main political parties. Mitsui supported the Seiyukai (Political Friends' Society) while Mitsubishi supported Minseito (Democratic Party). In the 1930's the Zaibatsu groups joined forces with the military and the bureaucracy to build a coalition for militarism.

In the postwar breakup of the Zaibatsu, and the reorganization of government, the seeds of the new business government relationship were established. While related to the *Zaikai,* four distinct business organizations are involved: the Keidanren, Japan Chamber of Commerce and Industry, Nikkeiren, and Keizai Doyukai.

Keidanren is the leading economic organization. It is a federation of more than 110 leading industrial associations, such as the Japanese Automobile Manufacturers Association, the Japan Iron and Steel Federation, the Japan Chemical Industry Association and the like. The membership is so extensive, encompassing banks, insurance, trading firms, wholesale and retail, as well as the full range of manufacturing associations, that it is generally recognized that the President of Keidanren is effectively the Prime Minister of Zaikai.

There is no real equivalent to the Keidanren, although France's "patronat" – (La Confédération Générale du Patronat Français) and Britain's Confederation of British Industry, founded in 1965, come closest in terms of power and prestige. However, the Keidanren operates with a panel of 39 standing committees involving the most senior executives of major corporations–committees which do detailed research on issues ranging from small business and taxation to technology and industrial policy. This work involves an extensive and constant process of consultation across companies, academe, other economic groups and, of course, government. While the basic ideology of the Keidanren is essentially conservative and free enterprise, it derives much of its strength from its understanding not just of the private sector but the government[7] decision-making apparatus and Japan's relative economic and technological standing as compared to competitors.

The Keidanren dates from 1946. A leading force at the time was what became known as the "Miyajima group" led by Miyajima Seijiro, who was President of Nisshin Spinning Co.. The Miyajima group were instrumental in establishing in 1948 a second employers association, Nikkeiran, or Japan Federation of Employers' Association. When Nikkeiran was first established, its primary aim was to serve as the employers' power base in labour-management relations. Although the Occupation forces had legalized union formation and collective

---

[7] This stereotype is not simply a post-war phenomena. Consider the following comments: "Allied propaganda had pictured Japan as a typically 'absolutist' country, belonging to the same category as Nazi Germany. It was only natural therefore that the Americans and others should have been astonished to discover how great was the split among the leading groups in Japan and how unstable its political situation, especially when compared to Nazi Germany . . ." (Maruyama, 1969:86).

bargaining as part of the post-war reforms, there was widespread fear that the labour movement would become communist controlled. Starting with a strike at the Toho Movie Company, and in quick succession in conflicts at Toshiba, Hitachi, and Nissan Motors, the Nikkeiran took up support for management and quickly gained the reputation as the Zaikai's anti-labour center.

Throughout the 1950's and 1960's, the Nikkeiran attempted to confront the General Council of Trade Unions of Japan, the SOHYO, which pressed their labour wage demands in the nationwide "spring offensive" or SHUNTO. In the early years management generally adopted the wage guidelines advanced by Neikkeiran, which typically meant that the monies not paid out to workers in the form of wages went to capital investment and modernization. In addition to the wage guideline function, Nikkeiran conducted a public relations campaign against the left leaning press but it is not clear that this function had much success when compared to the impact of rising prosperity and better wages on the public's attitude towards socialism or free enterprise. A more successful role for Nikkeiran has been an educational one: training young executives through its own offices and offering on the job training for foremen for the 29,000 member companies and 54 industry associations.

A third organization is the Japan Committee for Economic Development which, while it has lost considerable influence in recent years, has played a very important role as the voice of "amended capitalism" or social responsibility. Founded in 1946 as *Keizai Doyukai,* the organization was seen as a progressive side of management, devoted to the study of economic reconstruction and production issues, involving middle-rank businessmen. Its most famous declaration was a principle that the business organization consisted of three equal stakeholders – management, labour, and shareholders – and that the supreme decision-making body should consist of a council representing these three groups. While this declaration was widely denounced and later shelved,[8] it gave the organization a reputation for conciliation in management-labour matters, a reputation in contrast to the anti-labour, fighting Nikkeiran. Another important function of the group was the ten member "Sanken" (*Sangyo Mondai Kenkyukai*), or Industrial Issues Study Council. This Council, which at first did not include Mitsui and Mitsubishi among the major corporate group members, became the leading private sector organization for studying Japan's industrial structure, including the impact of internationalization, technological change, and capital liberalization – issues which the major economic ministries were also studying.

The fourth organization is the Japan Chamber of Commerce and Industry (JCCI) which evolved from the Tokyo Chamber of Commerce founded in 1878 by one of the Meiji era's most prominent entrepreneurs, Shibusawa Eiichi. The

[8] For a more elaborate analysis of this declaration, see Yoshino (1968).

JCCI has traditionally represented small business, but the organization fell on hard times after the War when the President, Fujiyama Aiichiro, became a victim of the Occupation's executive purge. While reinstated in 1950, Fujiyama was unable to bring about a reorganization of the JCCI, and it was not until a successor, Nagano Shigeo, took over as successor in 1970 that the small business organization began to gather strength and gain influence in both business and government circles.

Nagano, ironically, joined the JCCI after a successful career at Nippon Steel, the largest Western steel manufacturer, where he served as Chairman. His task was to organize Japan's eleven million small business enterprises into the JCCI by allowing a stronger regional voice to the membership. Instead of having the Presidency come from the Tokyo Chamber of Commerce, with vice-presidents representing the big cities of Osaka, Yokohama, Nagoya, Kyoto, and Kobe, Nagano introduced a structure with an executive council representing nine regional blocks – Tokyo, Osaka, and Nagoya, plus Sapporo, Fukuoka, Hiroshima, Sendai, Niigata, and Takamatsu. Today there are about 475 urban-based Chambers and Commerce and Industry, financed from the public sector for about a fifth of its revenue and representing a million firms; the rural based Societies of Commerce and Industry receive about 62 per cent of their revenues from the public sector and represent another million firms in the 2,852 chambers.

Nagano's essential contribution was to raise the profile of Japan's small business sector, and to give it clout in the bureaucratic corridors of MITI and the Ministry of Finance. At first, he started to invite Cabinet Ministers and key bureaucrats to the monthly meetings. Their presence increased the profile and prestige of the JCCI and, in turn, added to the cohesion of the once weakened organization. By 1972, the JCCI proposed that a special fund of one trillion yen be created to help small business financing, where the local chamber approved the project. This approach was accepted, and MITI created such specialized financial institutions as the Small Business Finance Corporation, the Central Bank for Commercial Industrial Cooperatives, and the Peoples Finance Corporation.

Since then, MITI has developed a number of programs to assist the small business sector, including the establishment of the Small Business Promotion Corporation, provision of technical guidance and subsidies for R&D, policies for accelerated depreciation for certain machinery and facilities, programs for management consulting and management education, encouragement of cooperatives formed through prefectural federations of small business associations, regulation of sub-contracting relations, and funding of the Small Business Investment Company. In all there are sixteen major laws on small business in Japan (ten passed since 1961) which both individually and in combination with Japan's Fundamental Law of Small-Medium Enterprises, passed in 1963, form an integrated framework for small business development. Not only is the tenor of this legislation interventionist in flavour and biased towards "eliminating the barriers associated with smallness", it is aimed at making the small sector modern and efficient within the context of the total economy.[9]

To realize what this means, Japan's small business sector must be put in an international context. Small business in Japan is not only larger than in most other Western economies, as shown in Exhibit 3/4, much of it is also integrated with large businesses through the sub-contracting system. This dual structure of big firms and small firms is usually analyzed in terms of the two-tiered wage and employment practices, but the implications go much deeper. Big companies have the resources and staff to deal directly with the main agencies of government, but because of the sub-contracting relations with small enterprises, they serve as linking pins in the tos and fros of government policy and international trade debates.

The sub-contracting system is not necessarily unique to Japan – indeed subcontracting is but one form of interorganizational relations, as compared to arms' length exchange on the one side and vertical integration on the other (McMillan, 1983; Williamson, 1975) – what is different is the extent of the

Exhibit 3/4: Comparative Ratios of Small Firm Manufacturing

Country	Year	Manufacturing establishments		Manufacturing employment		
		Total ('000s)	Small firm share (%)	Total (m)	No. of establishments per 100,000 employed	Average no. of employees per establishment
Austria	1980	6.5	88	0.61	1 070	94
South Africa	1976	15.5	91	1.36	1 140	88
Germany, Fed. Rep.	1975	93.1	93	7.48	1 240	80
UK	1978	108.0	94	7.11	1 520	66
United States	1977	350.8	94	18.52	1 890	53
Canada	1978	32.0	95	1.70	1 880	53
Australia	1978	21.5	95	1.15	1 870	53
Norway	1979	13.2	98	0.37	3 570	28
Switzerland	1975	62.7	99	0.95	6 600	15
Japan	1978	744.3	99	10.89	6 830	15
Spain	1978	164.8	97	2.30	7 170	14
Italy	1971	628.5	99	5.30	11 850	8

Notes: Reduced small firms coverage in Federal Republic of Germany after 1975. Australian figures relate to enterprises.

Source: British Business, Vol. 9 (November 1982).

[9] The following works survey small business in Japan: Haselitz (1980), Tamotsu (1980), Yamanaka (1971).

[10] The subcontracting system is described in general by Ikeda (1983) and with respect to the auto industry in McMillan (1982).

approach across many sectors and the degree to which the small firms acting as suppliers and subcontractors are integrated into the long range planning of the big firms, which themselves are heavily influenced by government industrial policy. Small business represents the source of flexibility and entrepreneurial creativity for big firms: by one estimate, Japan's small business sector of fewer than 100 workers per firm employs 58 per cent of total manufacturing, as against only 16–18 per cent in Britain, Germany, or the US (Twaalhoven and Hattori, 1982)[10].

As subsequent chapters will demonstrate, the difference between Japan and other Western countries lies not so much in the basic distinction between small business on the one side and big business on the other, as many analysts have put it (Peterson, 1979). In Japan, the key is the pivotal role that an intermediary sector plays between the small stand alone owner-managed firms and the very large, internationally competitive firms. This intermediary sector is the long list of companies such as those in automobiles, consumer electronics, computers, and telecommunication who act in concert with their family of suppliers and sub-contractors, together with the banking and trading firm arms, as shown schematically in Exhibit 3/5.

Unlike in Europe or the US, such sectors involve extensive forward planning, some ownership links, technology transfer, intra-corporate banking and financing, and interchange of personnel. The bigger firms are well connected

Exhibit 3/5: The Small Business-Big Business Link: Japan and the U.S.

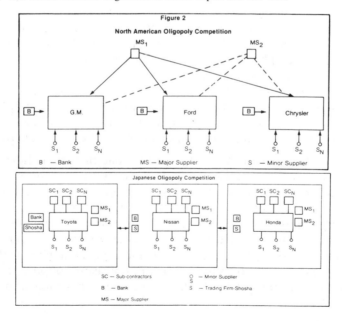

through the economic organizations to the corridors of bureaucratic power, and through interpersonal connections and contacts *(Kone)* to political channels of influence. Because the small business sector is mostly non-unionized, big business must be extremely conscious how its preferred policies impact on small business: in the same way, the acquiescence by the government to big business at the expense of small firms, or *Chusho Kigyo,* can mean a severe loss of political support over the election cycle.

The business-government relationship, in short, is built on a mutually reinforcing structure of building and improving the entire economy on internationally competitive lines. Ideology in the conventional sense has very little impact on the fundamental issues. To outsiders, this close business-government dialogue has overtones of a conspiracy – a pyramid of bureaucratic officials keeping foreigners at bay. In reality, there is a remarkable pluralism of interests within the private sector and fierce competition among the major firms in each industry. Indeed the nature of the exclusive subcontracting system, while reducing the level of uncertainly for the major firms in their supplier relationships, are actually in a stronger position to compete more aggressively against other similarly structured companies in the sector. Public policy is oriented to promote this kind of direct competition, especially where price, technology, and quality are the critical competitive weapons.

3.5 Summary and Conclusions

This chapter has analysed the business government relationship in Japan. Two broad themes have characterized this literature. The first, found in older academic studies but frequently highlighted in Western periodicals and the business press, places great emphasis on the monolithic nature of Japanese society and the close nexus of interests between big business and the Liberal Democratic Party, which has ruled Japan for most of the post-war era. Tariff and non-tariff protection, closed markets, targeting of industries, selective import controls, low defense spending – such is the type of issue usually subscribed to the Japan Inc. interpretation of Japanese industrial success and export penetration.

Since the end of the Pacific War and the Occupation period, Japan has had invoked a whole series of legislative and administrative measures to help rebuild the war torn economy and to rejuvenate the corporate sector to international standards of competitiveness. Restrictive tactics of all descriptions, plus focused legislation on foreign investment, plus weak antimonopoly laws and legalized cartels, have provided the broad framework for this industrial rejuvenation. Some thirty years after the Occupation, Japan now rivals the US on per capita income and outstrips the US on most measures of productivity. It is little wonder that proponents of the Japan Inc. model have much to complain about.

The truth is, the past is a better guide to the future than many writers fully appreciate. To explain Japan's industrial success in terms of the narrow vision of Japan Inc. is simply to miss the real message. All countries have their basket of protectionist inward policies – one estimate suggests that from 35–40 per cent of manufactured trade is "managed" i.e. not determined by market forces (Page, 1982). Japan is hardly alone in this approach, but it is the trends which are critical. By 1973, Japan has been shifting out of the post-war construction and rebuilding effort, and the degree of internationalization of the economy has started first in the trading firm sector, has extended into manufacturing, especially in cars and electronics, and has begun in banking and finance. Unless the backdrop of the wartime experience is fully appreciated, it is easy to ignore how Japan's business-government relationship fits into the wider context of shaping the Japanese economy into the global system. Japan's industrial policy is one of orchestrating national levers – taxation, banking, monetary and fiscal measures, administrative guidance, science policy, and the like into a coherent framework of investment decisions, for both big and small firms, public and private enterprises.[11]

Japan is one of the few countries to have managers in the public and private sector with a vision of where the country fits in the global system, and what this means for developing strategies at the societal, industry, and corporate level. Contrary to what anti-planners think, Japanese planners put far less emphasis on a plan but on a process. The vision is forward-directed, but the impact is one of using the plan to interpret the past. The planning process obviously brings an enormous statistical and information gathering apparatus into play, but this process of constant dialogue serves an educational purpose of widening choices and increasing analytical depth.

Japan's personnel practices known as *Amakudari* (literally meaning "descending from heaven") involves the transfer of young officials from the central government to rural posts, government agencies or, in some cases, to private sector companies. Usually the elite of the bureaucratic corps, qualified through the demanding Higher Civil Servants Examinations, these officials learn the network of contacts relevant to their government role and build information bridges both within the bureaucracy and to the industrial world. At the other end of the career spectrum, retiring bureaucrats who have been responsible for an industrial section often transfer to companies as advisers or consultants,

---

[11] Nobuyoshi Nimiki, a leading thinker in MITI, has explained MITI's future role as follows: "This formula is meant to revolutionize the attitude of MITI bureaucrats and ultimately bring about a cultural revolution. Put differently, I want them to work hard so that they can supply industry with top quality information relevant to actual conditions. MITI must transform itself into a research and coordinating mechanism specializing in interindustrial relationships, a source of advice respected by private industry." Quoted in Saito (1978), who analyzes the recent changes in MITI.

bringing their information contacts and years of experience into the decision-making process at the corporate level.

The strong acceptance of both big government and big business underlines the argument made earlier by Lindblom (1977). There is a cyclical bout of anti-big business feeling in the population at large, especially when incidents like the Lockheed bribery scandal of 1974 and the Hitachi-Mitsubishi "computer sting" scandal of 1983 serve to highlight the underside of corruption, racketeering, and questionable judgement in some circles. However, there is a pervasive awareness throughout Japan that any modern economy needs a careful balance among the sectors, between the big scale sectors of banking, trading, and manufacturing, and the small and medium size sectors of entrepreneurial creativity. The business-government relationship reflects this balance, with the tensions and visions of each side providing a force for destabilizing the inertia and rigidities common in European forms of industrial policy.

In many respects, Japan has had the best of both worlds – a global economy geared to fast post-war growth, and a competitive environment where the fundamentals of productivity improvement at the corporate level were finely turned, just when Europe and the US let those fundamentals fall by the way side. The Japanese have taken the lessons of the post-industrial and information revolution and turned them to competitive advantage. It is not just the software and hardware management techniques per so which are key, but the collection and utilization of information in all areas – economic, political, technological and competitive – which rejuvenates and challenges the thinking processes of today's industries and managers. As the next two chapters argue, Japanese business and bureaucratic planners have made the goal of international competiveness the central dictum of industrial policy. There are numerous secondary issues – social and regional policy, stretching the life cycle of sunset industries, protecting various political interest groups, not to mention political power, bureaucratic in-fighting, and the like. However, these secondary issues are usually kept off center to the main goal of improving Japan's competitive edge in the global economy.

The central point remains: business and government share the goal of making Japan internationally competitive. This goal is at once a strength and a weakness. As a strength it highlights the country's unparalleled capacity to mobilize human skills towards economic and social endeavours. While MITI is usually the main catalyst in creating the vision, whether in cars, electronics or computers, the private sector is the locomotive which drives the long range vision into commercial success. Because each sector is not dominated by any one firm, domestic competition forces cost efficiencies and market applications far faster than any government plan could. The next two chapters examine the detailed processes of industrial and technology strategy in contemporary Japan.

Chapter 4
The Visible Hand: Industrial Planning

"If government economic interventions are inherently inefficient, then American firms should rejoice to see other countries 'helping' their industries, because regardless of how well intentioned it might be, such 'help' will hurt foreign firms more than it helps them."

Lester Thurow, Newsweek

4.1 Introduction

Industrial planning in Japan is a judicious mixture of government intervention often associated with a socialist economy, of jawboning and cajoling usually seen in the American economy, and long range vision normally recognized as characteristic of good management. At the heart of the country's industrial planning is the view of the total economy as a portfolio of sectors, many inter-related and interdependent, each having specific features such as energy intensity, technological sophistication, export orientation, and the like. The term "industrial structure" is the general phrase used to capture this concept, and various government white papers provide detailed statistical analysis of its evaluation and direction.

During the 1980 American presidential campaign, there was considerable discussion about the need for revitalization and "reindustrialization" of the U.S. economy. Except for such specific factors as continuing low productivity, high energy costs, and aged plant and equipment, most if not all of the description of the problems were surprisingly short of much serious analysis and prescriptive solutions. Indeed, the few positive statements made tended to argue on the one hand for less government involvement in the economy (lower spending, reduced regulation, lower taxes) and on the other, for greater government intervention, even for a Japanese-style system of industrial planning (Fallows, 1980).

In this respect, the understanding held abroad of Japan's system is rather low and superficial. The popular image of Japan Inc. is well ingrained abroad, and the element of truth in it is reinforced in the popular press by such well publicized issues as Nippon Telephone and Telegraph's intransigence on foreign sourcing, or the government's well known efforts at protecting domestic agriculture.[1]

Analytically, however, Japan's industrial planning is considerably more complex than the popular images portray it. For one thing, the planning exercise is not one of creating fixed blueprints of a static industrial structure, as planning critics often argue (Sharpe, 1975). The major body responsible for developing and deliberating on industrial structure, The Industrial Structure Council (*Sangyo Kozo Shingrikai,* or *Sankashin* in brief), is actually an advisory body of a cross-section of well informed industrial, academic, financial, bureaucratic and trade union leaders. The chairman of the council is the head of the Keidanren and 130 authorized members serve renewable two year terms.

A second consideration in Japan's industrial planning is that there is virtually no ideological component to the process, at least in the sense of being "capitalist" or "socialist."[2] Planning, of course, is a highly loaded term in this context, and in recent years, elections have been fought on the role of government in Canada, Britain, Sweden, France, and the United States, to name some notable examples. In Japan, business-government relations are not governed by such ideological overtones and it is for this reason that a general consensus is probably easier on the broad thrust of the evolving industrial structure.

The conceptual basis of its evaluation from one largely based on unskilled, low cost labour-intensive industries to one based on high wage cost, knowledge-intensive industry is shown in Exhibit 4/1. Planning in the past two decades has focused the industrial structure around heavy industrial goods, or *jukagaku kogyoko*. The main beneficiaries of these policies were in the heavy machinery, chemical, and machine tool sectors where high income elasticity of demand prevailed. In this situation, as world income levels increased with more global trade, demand for such Japanese goods via exports would be even higher.

The present direction of the industrial structure is towards a service-oriented, knowledge-based economy based on micro electronics, biotechnology and new materials technology. This approach, called *chishiki sangyo,* is a response to the upward revaluation of the yen, rising energy prices, the terms of trade for raw materials, land shortages and rising costs, and pollution abatement. The aim is to move away from sectors which are land-intensive, pollution-intensive,

---

[1] For an excellent treatment of the agricultural issues and their relationship to domestic political problems, see Donnelly and Hay (1980).

[2] Chie Nakane, in an interview in *Newsweek* (October 15, 1973; 60) makes the point as follows: "The Japanese way of thinking depends on the situation rather than principle – while with the Chinese it is the other way around. The Chinese are the people who developed the classics and so can't do anything without principle. But we Japanese have no principles. Some people think we hide our intentions, but we have no intentions to hide. Except for some few leftists or rightists, we have no dogma and don't ourselves know where we are going."

Exhibit 4/1: Comparative Characteristics of Export Structure

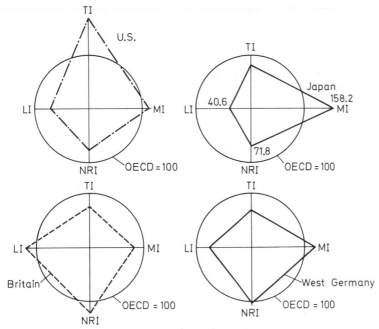

LI   = Labour Intensive Industries (textiles, rubber, sundries, etc.)
NRI = Natural Resource Utilization Industries (pulp and paper, steel, chemicals, nonferrous metals, etc.)
MI   = Machinery and Tools Industries (electrical machinery, transport, general machinery)
TI   = Technology Intensive Industries (Medicine, medical instruments, electronic parts, communication instruments, precision machines)

Source: Adapted from MITI, Japanese Statistics Bureau, 1982.

and energy-intensive (the so-called *Keiretsu* sectors such as steel, shipbuilding, and chemicals) into high value added knowledge sectors (computers, electronics, fashions, pharmaceuticals, fine chemicals, and the like).

4.2 Origins of Industrial Planning

For much of the post-war period when Japan was rebuilding its shattered economy, the foreign image of this far off Asian country was a mixture of disdain for its cheap trinkets, memory of Pearl Harbour and its foreign occupations, and admiration for human resilience. By the time Japan had become the second largest GNP economy in 1968, just when the U.S. was in the quagmire of Vietnam and Britain was spurned by De Gaulle as he was faced with student rebellion at home, revisionist thougth on Japanese economic performance rekindled foreign views of comparative performance. In the first place, there was the wartime bombing and destruction view which, by requiring totally new buildings and equipment, gave Japan (like West Germany) a fresh start. Britain, by contrast, was left with its old plants and equipment largely intact, and thus had an uncompetitive edge to enter the post-war era. A related view was that without handsome payouts of American dollars via aid plans and foreign investment, Japan would never have recovered in so short a time frame. Britain by contrast, had a major disadvantage in its way. So goes one refrain on Japan's post-war comparative success.

The second major interpretation of Japan's performance was best set out by Herman Kahn (1970) in his popular book, *The Emerging Japanese Superstate.* In his view, economic, social, and psychological factors combine to give Japan unique performance growth rates and only time awaits the point when the economy overtakes the USSR, and later the U.S., to be what Vogel (1979) calls, *Japan As No. 1.* Surprisingly, however much the Japanese enjoy and read the foreign comments on Japan's success and future status, as witnessed by the best selling books on the subject, few Japanese really believe that the country is anywhere near the apex of the economic pecking order.

In point of fact, Japan's progress in reconstruction and development of a modern, competitive industrial structure has no real parallel in world history. In many crucial areas, Japan has actually defied the historical trends of other Western countries, such as achieving industrialization and urbanization while actually lowering crime rates, and doubling and tripling the demand for automobiles and reducing the number of accidents. Yet the origins of such successes go back to the war period of 1945 and the occupation period led by MacArthur. Ironically the efforts and activities of both occupier and the occupied reinforced the basic tendency in Japanese industrial planning to focus on specific sectors in the economy and to weigh up strengths and weaknesses of each, precisely the kind of activity common in military strategy and in the textbooks on corporate planning.

On the Japanese side, a group of gifted bureaucrats in The Research Bureau of The Foreign Ministry began intensive (and secret) discussions of how Japan should rebuild the economy after the war's end in total defeat. This group wrote a book-length report of 200 pages called *Basic Tasks for Japan's Economic Reconstruction.* It is a remarkably prescient document and also surprisingly open-minded, especially considering that its origins date just when American bombing raids were freely smashing Tokyo and other industrial centers into ruins. One of the major authors was Saburo Okita, a brilliant planner in the Japanese bureaucracy, who later directed the 1960 Income Doubling

Plan, held the post as Japan's Foreign Minister in 1979, and published his economic philosophy in book form in 1980.

The document started from the premise that all countries, even Britain and the U.S., would have some measure of economic planning. Improving living standards and opening the world to international trade would be major national objectives. Despite Japan's loss of territories, lack of raw materials, heavy reliance on foreign trade, and feudal work conditions, there were strengths to build on. The first was human resources.[3]

Through the experience of a wartime economy Japan has acquired the technology to be self-sufficient in a wide variety of machinery . . . Furthermore large numbers of technicians, trainees, and other categories of heavy industrial workers have been fostered to meet the needs of the time. Today one can find young people in any village, no matter how remote, capable of running a lathe.

Reallocation of resources from wartime to peacetime activities, and the productive capacity unleashed by an imposed democratic structure, would build on the wartime developments in agriculture, particularly the "introduction of farm machines and communal labour patterns." The final condition favourable to economic reconstruction was the experience in planning, namely a capacity to learn from the mistakes of the past.

As it turned out, this committee favoured a form of industrial strategy which fused central planning and ownership of key sections with democratic control. The apporach, the report argued,

must be determined from the standpoint of the kind of economic system that is best able to guarantee the people's livelihood and, as the prerequisite for this, to improve productive capacity . . .

Perfectly fair and free competition is not the only alternative, no matter from what angle one views the issue. For Japan's economy to be made democratic we need public control over financial institutions and key industries, a planned economy, and a strong measure of state controls. But the government, as the body exercising this control, must be a government *for the people* (emphasis in original) and not a reincarnation of past bureaucratic institutions.

In the event, the actual choice of structure was not left in Japanese hands, although this document had a powerful influence on the occupation forces' thinking. Within only three weeks of Japan's official surrender, President Truman instructed General MacArthur "to favour a program for the dissolution of the large industrial and banking combinations which have exercised control of a great part of Japan's trade and industry" and "the elimination in Japan of

---

[3] The following paragraphs and quotes are based on Hideichino Nakamura, "Plotting a New Economic Course," *Japan Echo* Vol. VI (Special Issue, 1979), 11–20.

those selected industries or branches of production whose chief value to Japan is in preparing for war . . . and the limitation of the size and character of Japan's heavy industries to its future peaceful requirements."

The details of the occupation's plans were known by December 1945, with the preparation by the American reparations committee of specific targets to remove Japan's surplus excess capacity: all tools and equipment in army and navy arsenals, in aircraft, light metals, and ball and roller bearings, in process sulfuric acid and in a quarter of all shipyards. Half the machine tool industry's capacity, half the termal power generation, and twenty new plants in caustic soda were to go, and steel capacity was limited to 1.5 million tons.

The thoroughness of this purge on Japanese industry surprised even the leading businessmen and industrialists, and led to such views that Japan should turn away from industry and become a nation of agriculture. Despite Japan's large urban population among the 80 million people, and the three generations of industrialization since Meiji, the notion that Japan's future could be in agriculture was hardly novel. In fact, a major component of Japanese fascist thought in the prewar period was a belief in the need for strengthening rural villages as a counter to the growing centralization and power of the urban centers. A major faction in this development was The Village Government League, which argued that Japanese nationalist spirit should be an extention and enlargement of the family-system principle, namely service to the society at large, not to individual rights (Maruyama, 1979:39). Closely related to these pro-agrarian sentiments were an almost utopian sentiment for village life and suspicion and mistrust of large scale commerce and the zaibatsu industrial structure.[4]

Yet while these undercurrents of Japanese ideology were recognized by various groups within the country, the deteriorating war effort and the need to develop some vision of post-war reconstruction before the occupation prompted bureaucrats like Yonosuke Goto and Saburo Okita to seize the initiative. Within weeks after the war ended, a brilliant critic of prewar and wartime policies (and future prime minister, if only for two weeks), Tonson Ishibashi, wrote a survey of Japanese reconstruction and conversion to peacetime industry. Two quotes from Ishibashi's report give not only a flavour of the thinking process central to Japan's post-war rebuilding and industrial planning, but also the statistical and conceptual work on which the planning was based. The plan itself was called Essentials of Industrial Reconstruction Policy (Sangyo Saiken-Saku No Yoryo). According to the document:

---

[4] A major spokesman for this view was Gondo Seikyo, who spoke for the rural population as follows: "In the present state of fear and apprehension the villages suffer most. Our villages are the foundation of the country and source of our habits and customs. At present the farmers form one half of our total population; they utilize the greater portion of the land; and they produce a large proportion not only of stable foodstuffs of the nation but also of its industrial raw materials and commercial goods." This perspective still has strong roots in rural Japan.

The prompt execution of a statistical investigation by us Japanese ourselves to determine exactly what industries with how much capacity are required for Japan to support a peacekeeping economy. It will be important, based on the study, to draft and decisively implement a plan for the rapid conversion of war industries to peaceful industries and for the rehabilitation of other industries.

Conversion of industry, according to Ishibashi, would challenge the agricultural society thesis. A well presented plan would convince the Allies (i.e., the Americans) of its merits. Further the effort had to be of long term consequence, not just peace time conversion of existing industry:

Tremendous industrial capacity will be a prerequisite for producing the materials, tools, and machines needed just to rebuild our war-ravaged cities and repair our roads, railways, and communications networks. In urban rehabilitation, it will not be adequate simply to set up paper and wood barracks as we have in the past. And in railway construction, such as on the Tokyo-Osaka line, where work was under way before, we need to switch to broad-gauge tracks as well as to lay double tracks at all places where one set of tracks exist . . . Unfortunately, the surplus industrial capacity we are accused of enjoying beyond the requirements for a peace-seeking economy simply do not exist in Japan . . . I do not think that anyone will argue with us on this point if we explain it in a well-documented report.

The major policies undertaken by the American occupation forces under General MacArthur are generally well known. The Zaibatsu enterprises were disbanded; some 200,000 major bureaucratic and industrial executives were purged. Major land reform was implemented, a total revolution in access to education was introduced, and a vast array of civil and judicial rights were guaranteed. By the time Japan regained its independence after the occupation, per capita income was approaching the levels of the prewar (1934–1936 period) and major reforms had been implemented in big business, education, the bureaucracy and local government. By this time, Japan was firmly entrenched with other countries, notably Europe, Britain, Canada, and Australia, in adopting broadly Keynesian stabilization policies and preventing serious unemployment and distruptive business fluctuations (ironically the major exception during the period, the Korean war excepted, was the United States). The relationship between SCAP and official Japanese government policy was often tense: the Americans seeking to obliterate "old" Japanese ways in favour of American ideals of democracy, the Japanese totally subservient to occupational aims but subtlely testing post-occupation independence. The point of departure in this period was the 1954 transfer of power from the strongly pro-American prime minister, Shigeru Yoshida, who held office for over seven years, to Ichiro Hatoyama, who had criticized his predecessor as "undeviatingly pro-American" and as excessively laissez-faire. Hatoyama and his cabinet adopted an official five year plan – the first of its kind since the war and the model for all succeeding governments.

4.3 Japan's Five Year Plan

In the lexicon of liberal economic thinkers, industrial planning is a twin of public ownership and thus of socialist progeny. The Chinese, Russian, and East European all have their five year plans and that fact in itself is usually sufficient evidence for avoiding a similar fate by Western governments, at least by the accepted wisdom of anti-planners in Europe and the United States. The enormous literature on this subject in recent years has predictably taken on a deep ideological flavour, and this has obscured the rationale and motives for industrial planning at the national level, even if it is conventional wisdom to conduct five or ten year planning at the corporate level. What makes good corporate sense at one remove is satanic blasphemy at the national level. In Japan, no such ideological fears arise. If anything the debate on industrial planning has a strikingly discordant note. The search for long run goals, the basic rationale for industrial planning, is necessarily a process of reaching consensus, over however long a period, an then developing targets to accomplish them. Yet according to some Japanese, this is precisely what Japan is good at, without any barometer to withstrain performance. As Chie Nakane (1973:56) has remarked

I think it is better not to do anything. If we establish any goal we will proceed to attain it without considering any other factors. It is better for us to remain just as we are. For if we are set in motion toward any direction, we have just too much energy and no mechanisms to check its direction. So it is better to remain as we are – without doing anything.

Despite this warning, Japan adopted a series of regular plans in the post-war period to guide and direct its industrial activities, as shown in Exhibit 4/2. The first plan, adopted in December 1955, was called the "Five Year Plan For Self-Support" with an aim of five per cent annual growth during the life of the plan. Part of the thinking behind the plan's title was a basic belief that the two billion dollars in aid received from the United States after the war, and perhaps another billion a year during the Korean conflict, were not appropriate ways to support the economy's recovery and autonomous, self-supporting policies were superior (Okita, 1980).

At the government level, there are public sector groups which parallel the structuring of private sector organizations, and trade associations which take these five years plans as a starting point. In addition to the five year plans are a variety of publications and white papers which focus on particular issues and departments, or very broad conceptual issues such as knowledge intensification, import liberalization, and the like. Such documents provide both a framework for the corporate sector, including the pervasive industry associations, and a barometer to compare past performance with future direction. Even

Exhibit 4/2: Economic Plans

Plan name	Five-year plan for economic autonomy	New long-term economic plan	National income-doubling plan	Medium-term economic plan
Date established	Dec. 1955 (July 1955, Dec. 1955)*	Dec. 1957 (Aug. 1957, Nov. 1957)	Dec. 1960 (Nov. 1959, Nov. 1960)	Jan. 1965 (Jan. 1964, Nov. 1965)
Drafting Cabinet	Hatoyama	Kishi	Ikeda	Satō
Duration	1956–60 (5 yrs.)	1958–62 (5 yrs.)	1961–70 (10 yrs.)	1964–68 (5 yrs.)
Method	Colm system	Estimated growth rate	Estimated growth rate	Economic model
Goals	Economic autonomy, full employment	Maximum growth, improved living standards, full employment	Maximum growth, improved living standards, full employment	Correction of distortions
Economic growth rate				
Planned	5.0%	6.5%	7.2%	8.1%
Actual	8.7%	9.9%	10.7%	10.6%
Production growth rate of mining and manufacturing industries				
Planned	7.4% (1955–60)	8.2% (1957–62)	10.5%	9.9%
Actual	15.6% (1955–60)	13.5% (1957–62)	13.8%	13.6%
Consumer price increase				
Planned	none	none	none	2.5%
Actual	2.0%	3.5%	5.7%	5.0%
Current balance of payment in target year				
Planned	0	—$ 0.15 bil.	$ 0.18 bil.	0
Actual	—$ 0.01 bil.	—$ 0.02 bil.	$ 2.36 bil.	$ 1.47 bil.
Objectives	Attainment of economic autonomy and full employment based on stable economy	Attainment of sustained growth at highest possible rate while maintaining stable economy, thereby converging on full employment and achieving real improvement of living standards	Advancement toward marked improvement of living standards and achievment of full employment; stable growth at maximum speed for this purpose	Development of harmonious economy and society by rectification of distorsions to bring backward sectors into line with tempo of socioeconomic progress
Tasks	1. Strengthening the industrial base 2. Promoting trade 3. Improving domestic self-sufficiency and reducing foreign-currency spending 4. Expediting land development 5. Promoting science and technology 6. Fostering small and medium enterprises 7. Increasing employment and enriching social services 8. Maintaining sound financing and normalizing money markets 9. Stabilizing prices 10. Stabilizing national livelihood and economizing consumption	1. Expanding exports 2. Building up capital accumulation 3. Developing basic industrial sectors 4. Improving industrial structure 5. Modernizing agricultural production structure 6. Improving employment and national livelihood	1. Replenishing social capital 2. Improving industrial stucture 3. Promoting trade and international economic cooperation 4. Fostering human capabilities and promoting science and technology 5. Adjusting dual economic structure and ensuring social stability	"Accelerating Social Development" 1. Promoting trade and improving industrial structure 2. Fostering human capabilities and promoting science and technology 3. Modernizing low-productivity sectors 4. Increasing mobility and effective use of labor 5. Improving the quality of life, adjusting the living environment, enriching social services, and eliminating pollution

* The first date in parentheses is the date when the government instructed the competent advisory organ to prepare a recommendation, the second is the date when the recommendation was submitted.

Exhibit 4/2 continued

Plan name	Economic and social development plan	New economic and social development plan	Basic economic and social plan	National economic plan
Date established	Mar. 1967 (May 1966, Feb. 1967)	May 1970 (Sept. 1969, Apr. 1970)	Feb. 1973 (Aug. 1972, Feb. 1973)	May 1976 (July 1975, May 1976)
Drafting Cabinet	Satō	Satō	Tanaka	Miki
Duration	1967–71 (5yrs.)	1970–75 (6 yrs.)	1973–77 (5 yrs.)	1976–80 (5 yrs.)
Method	Econometric model	Econometric model	Econometric model	Econometric model
Goals	Development of balanced, affluent economy and society	Creation of a comfortable environment by balanced growth	Simultaneous attainment of national welfare and international harmony	Simultaneous attainment of national welfare and international harmony
Economic growth rate				
Planned	8.2%	10.6%	9.4%	6.25%
Actual	10.9%	6.1%	4.1%	5.5% (1976–77)
Production growth rate of mining and manufacturing industries	(A) 10.2% (1966–71)†			
Planned	(B) 10.4%	12.4%	10.0%	9.5%
Actual	13.2% (1966–71)	3.6%	2.1%	6.9% (1976–77)
Consumer price increase		4.4% (annual average), about		6.75% (annual average), under
Planned	about 3% by end of plan	3% by end of plan	about 4% (annual average)	6.0% by end of plan
Actual	5.7%	10.9%		
Current balance of payments in target year			12.8%	8.0% (1977)
Planned	$ 1.45 bil.	$ 3.5 bil.	$ 5.9 bil.	about $ 4.0 bil.
Actual	$ 6.32 bil.	$ 0.13 bil.	$ 14.03 bil.	$ 14.03 bil. (1977)
Objectives	Consolidation of Japan's economic position in changing world society; corresponding creation of basic conditions for popular enjoyment of affluent livelihood; development of balanced and rich economy and society	Construction of economically adjusted, comfortable nation through balanced developement while also encouraging internationalization ("Toward a Humanistic Economy and Society")	Presentation of basic line for policy management during the first five years (1973–77) in the long-range process to replenish national welfare and promote international cooperation simultaneously, thus realizing a vigorous welfare society ("For a Healthy Welfare Society")	Realization of stable domestic development and affluent national livelihood while maintaining harmony in the international economic and social community during a time of fluctuating internal and external conditions
Tasks	1. Stabilizing prices 2. Realizing efficient economy 3. Expediting social development (These are the three major tasks.) 4. Adjusting conditions for long-term economic growth 5. Replenishing social capital	1. Realizing efficient economy from global viewpoint 2. Stabilizing prices 3. Expediting social development 4. Maintaining proper economic growth level and laying groundwork for future development	1. Creating an affluent environment 2. Ensuring comfortable and stable life 3. Stabilizing prices 4. Promoting international cooperation	1. Stabilizing prices and achieving full employment 2. Ensuring stable life and creating a comfortable environment 3. Cooperating with and contributing to world economic development 4. Attaining economic security and building a foundation for long-term growth

† (A) Based on medium-term macro-model.
(B) Based on accumulation of item-by-item supply and demand prospects.

other levels of government use this information, such as the prefectural governments issuing annual prefects throughout Japan. All of this planning really involves data analysis and communications across government departments and between public and private sectors. The interaction among public and private sector officials is much more intense than in most Western countries; conversely, the level of awareness of even quite low level public officials towards the problems of private sector issues is probably the highest in the world.

4.4 Industrial Structure Goals

Japan undertakes two basic types of economic planning. The first type is typical of most Western market societies and is based on the Keynesian framework of stabilization policy, using fiscal, monetary, and commercial instruments to guide and direct the level of economic activity. However, the Japanese go beyond this first approach and develop detailed long term industrial structure goals for the entire economy. These structural goals are decided within a general framework of market forces operating in the international economy (Koyima, 1975).

Broadly speaking, there have been three transformations of the industrial structure (actually the third is now underway). The first took place at the turn of this century and centered on the textile trade to sustain export earnings for development. The second period, extending from about 1920 to the next forty years (but heavily interrupted by the war), consisted of the construction and development of heavy industry such as steel, shipbuilding, and chemicals to support mass production consumer goods as well as industrial production. This period is characterized by a massive shift away from agriculture and a support for small and medium size manufacturing. For example, as recently as 1960, the proportion of the labour force engaged in agriculture, forestry and fishing was over 30 percent; it has declined now to 14.5 and will fall to about 9 percent in 1985, more than double the figure for the U.S. in 1970.

The third transformation, namely the move out of heavy industry (e.g., steel and shipbuilding) into knowledge intensive, high technology industries is accelerating. The oil crisis and the resulting high energy costs, as well as changing social values on such issues as pollution and environmental protection, have served to accelerate this broad shift in industrial structure during the 1980's (Exhibit 4/3).

The extent of Japan's progression to this third transformation can be indicated in two ways. First, there is the shift in employment among various sectors; second, there is the changing pattern of R and D expenditures. Employment in

Exhibit 4/3: Changes in the Value of Output by Industry (Billion yen at 1970 market prices)

	1970**		1980		1985		Average Annual Growth Rate 1965-1970	Average Annual Annual Growth Rate 1970-1980	Average Annual Growth Rate 1980-1985	Average Annual Growth Rate 1970-1985
	Output	Compo- nent Ratio	Output	Compo- nent Ratio	Output	Compo- nent Ratio				
Agriculture, forestry, and fisheries	7.113	4.4	8.510	2.8	9.470	2.3	1.5	1.8	2.2	1.9
Mining	959	0.6	1.330	0.4	1.590	0.4	5.3	3.3	3.6	3.4
Foodstuffs	9.620	6.0	16.240	5.3	22.150	5.3	5.7	5.4	6.4	5.7
Textiles	5.349	3.3	7.240	2.4	8.310	2.0	5.7	3.1	2.8	3.0
Paper and pulp	2.621	1.6	4.850	1.6	6.250	1.5	12.1	6.3	5.2	6.0
Chemicals	5.191	3.2	10.750	3.5	14.870	3.6	15.1	7.6	6.7	7.3
Petroleum and coal products	3.019	1.9	5.820	1.9	7.720	1.9	17.1	6.8	5.8	6.5
Stone and clay and glass pro- ducts	2.670	1.7	5.150	1.7	7.190	1.7	12.0	6.8	6.9	6.8
Iron and steel	11.286	7.0	21.140	6.9	24.470	5.9	18.0	6.5	3.0	5.3
Nonferrous metals	1.857	1.2	4.350	1.4	5.320	1.3	15.2	8.9	4.1	7.3
Fabricated metal products	3.777	2.3	8.870	2.9	12.480	3.0	19.1	8.9	7.1	8.3
General machinery	8.324	5.2	17.900	5.8	26.140	6.3	21.7	8.0	7.9	7.9
Electrical machinery	7.632	4.7	19.220	6.3	28.500	6.8	26.1	9.7	8.2	9.2
Transport machinery	7.624	4.7	14.090	4.6	17.920	4.3	27.4	6.3	4.9	5.9
Precision machinery	1.103	0.7	2.190	0.7	3.190	0.8	14.3	7.1	7.8	7.3
Miscellaneous industrial pro- ducts	10.106	6.3	19.610	6.4	28.590	6.8	13.0	6.9	7.8	7.2
Construction	16.259	10.1	31.120	10.2	45.380	10.9	13.6	6.7	7.6	7.1
Electricity and gas utilities	2.100	1.3	3.980	1.3	5.550	1.3	12.6	6.5	6.9	6.7
Transportation and commu- nications	7.444	4.6	14.510	4.7	20.060	4.8	13.4	6.9	6.7	6.8
Commerce	14.290	8.8	26.580	8.6	35.560	8.5	12.4	6.4	6.0	6.3
Banking, insurance, and real estate dealing	4.907	3.0	8.080	2.6	10.300	2.5	10.2	5.1	5.0	5.1
Services	28.267	17.5	56.140	18.3	77.290	18.5	8.8	7.1	6.6	6.9
Total	161.518	100.0	307.670	100.0	418.300	100.0	12.8	6.7	6.4	6.6
Primary industry	7.113	4.4	8.150	2.8	9.470	2.3	1.5	1.8	6.2	1.9
Secondary industry*	97.397	60.3	189.870	61.7	260.070	62.1	14.8	6.9	6.5	6.8
(Manufacturing)	80.179	49.6	157.420	51.2	213.100	50.9	15.1	7.0	6.3	6.7
Tertiary industry	57.008	35.3	109.290	35.5	148.760	35.6	11.0	6.7	6.4	6.6

* Secondary industry covers mining, manufacturing, and construction industries.
** 1970 performance is domestic output value based on the Input-Output Tables.

service occupations passed the 50% mark of the total labour force in 1975 and is expected to reach U.S. levels by the mid 1980's. Within manufacturing there is an emphasis on knowledge industries not only for R and D intensive products (computers, industrial robots, integrated circuit electronics, and electric cars) but also in the development of highly sophisticated production processes (digital process control devices, on-line communications equipment). Policies are developed to facilitate the adjustments these changes imply, including the employment and occupational structure, capital formation, energy consumption, and government expenditure.

Exhibit 4/4 outlines the general framework for the execution of industrial structure programs and policy tools. These tools consist of a general macro frame-

Exhibit 4/4: Japan's General Framework for Industrial Structural Planning

Policy Directions and Tools	Institutional Framework (controls, standards)	Loans	Inducements		Implementation by Government	Administrative Guidance
			Tax Measures	Subsidies		
Response to National Needs		·	·	·	·	· Investment Adjustment
Countermeasures against Constraints:		·	·		·	· Lower Discharge Volume
Resources and Energy Conversation	· Targets for Lowering Energy Units	·	·		Technology Development	
Environmental Standards	· Environmental Controls	·				
Nurturing Leading Industries		·	·	·	· Aircraft Computers	
Promotion of Care Technology		·	·	·	· R & D Programs	
Industry Relocation		·	·	·		
Internationalization	· Ensuring Propriety in Business Behavior	·	·			· Overseas-Investment
Structural Improvements of Specific Sectors		·	·	·		
Sophistication of Small Business		·	·			

Policy Directions and Tools	Institutional Factors	Inducements Subsidies	External Measures	Legal Codes
Response to National Needs		· Tax Measures · Loans · Subsidies		
Countermeasures against Constraints (Energy conservation & environmental standards)	Lowering Energy Base Units	·	· International Co-operation in Technology	· Antipollution Laws
Nurturing Leading Industries		·	· Adjustment of Imports	Aircraft Industry Promotion Law
Promotion of Care Technology		·		Machinery and Electronic Industry Promotion Law
Industry Relocation		·		Factor Location Law Industrial Relocation Promotion Law
Internationalization	Code of Business Behavior		· Adjustment of Relations with Host Countries	
Structural Improvements of Specific Industry Sectors				Small and Medium Enterprise Bank Law
Small Business Programs				Modernization Promotions Law

work, based on a consensus reached by business and government, and shaped by international economic and political forces. Positive inducements or incentives are those used by most countries, namely industry loans, subsidies, and direct government action such as R and D support. What distinguished the Japanese use of these tools is their coordination for maximum impact and their clearly understood use for given ends, namely an internationally competitive industrial structure. The overall vision of the industrial structure is based on a realistic perspective of market forces, not bureaucratic planning mechanisms. As a recent government publication noted, "The accumulation of policy information within the government and its presentation are probably the most fundamental tools to compensate for the limitations of the market mechanism and to guide industry in the right direction from a dynamic viewpoint in the present, fast changing and complicated times. An old saying claims, 'To have foresight, one has to see' but perhaps that ought now to be rendered, 'To be prepared one has to foresee' (Jetro, 1975).

4.5 Resource Dependence Planning

Japan is essentially a through-put economy, importing raw materials from sources around the world and processing them for end markets. Resource dependence is highest among all the world's major industrialized countries (see Exhibit 4/5) so that it is no accident that Japanese logistical and transportation technology to serve global water routes is unrivaled. Such high rates of dependence often raises the spectre of supply cutoffs and Brzezinski (1973), for example, cites this issue as an inherent weakness in any economic power. In point of fact, however, Japan has not been notably affected by this dependence.[5] Indeed, the country has many inherent advantages by strategically managing this import problem so shrewdly. Why is this the case?

For one thing, Japan benefitted like all Western countries by the availability of cheap energy after the Second World War. While domestic prices were high relative to North America, for example, Japan from the 1950's began to substitute domestic coal supplies and hydro electricity with imported oil. Japan contracted for long periods (e.g., ten years) and thereby achieved stable supply sources at predictable prices. By 1970, imported crude oil accounted for almost 75 percent of energy consumption.

In the case of raw materials such as coal, minerals, and food, Japan has diversified its source markets and, in some cases, plays one country off against

[5] Brzezinski (1972) has written as follows: "Japan may also encounter increasing difficulties in her access to raw materials . . . Yet it is far from certain that access to these supplies will be readily available or that their costs will not rise perceptibly, given social and political instability in some areas of supply, mounting international competition, and rising resentment in some areas (e.g., Indonesia or Australia) over Japanese investment efforts designed to assure Japan firm control of the needed supplies." In the decade since those words were written, despite revolution, political instability and war in the Middle East, South Africa, and South East Asia, the real costs of raw materials are no higher than 1972, the availability of supply is greater, and the desire for Japanese investment is intense.

Exhibit 4/5: Overseas Dependency on Key Resources (1978) (Unit: %)

	Japan	U.S.	West Germany	U.K.	France
Energy	92.4	21.9	56.9	21.2	81.4
Coal	75.2	7.9	9.8	0.1	51.3
Crude Oil	99.8	37.7	95.0	45.6	97.7
Natural Gas	82.6	4.5	62.3	7.8	70.6
Iron Ore	98.4	30.4	96.4	78.7	39.6
Copper	94.1	38.0	99.9	99.9	99.8
Lead	78.6	61.3	89.4	99.5	84.6
Zinc	62.4	67.0	69.1	99.4	85.8
Tin	98.0	100.0	100.0	79.9	100.0
Aluminium	100.0	66.5	100.0	100.0	271.3
Nickel	100.0	92.9	100.0	100.0	100.0

Source: White Paper on International Trade, MITI, Tokyo, 1980.

another. The phase ABC policy (Australia, Brazil, and Canada) is a term applied to describe this approach, and to recognize the need for vigilant management of security of supply, quality, and delivery. Government policy has consistently reinforced this general framework, but has sometimes added such tactics as stockpiling, developing new sources, and overseas joint ventures. For example, energy-related projects received up to 80 percent of exploration costs and 70 percent of development costs.

What is less well appreciated or understood outside Japan has been the question of how successful the government has used brilliant sourcing strategies to aid the underlying cost structure of the manufacturing sector. Ministries like MITI and Finance regularly publish reports on the relative standing of Japan's industrial sector in such areas as elasticity of energy consumption to GNP, energy productivity by sector and rates of primary energy consumption.

It is for these reasons that while Japan suffered severe shocks after the 1973 oil crisis, including major declines in investment, reduced profit-sales ratio of firms, and very high inflation, the government was able to weather the second oil shock in 1979 better than any Western country. Both of these energy crises have helped to reinforce Japan's desire for the lowest priced imports consistent with supply security. There have also been some unrecognized impacts on Japan's competitive position.

As illustrated in Exhibit 4/6, there are really two stages of production prior to full manufacturing. Japanese government policy has consistently used an ABC style approach to maximize supply security and favourable cost purchases for raw materials. Throughout the 1950's and 1960's, MITI attempted to keep the level of fragmentation of the resource-based industries high by discouraging vertical integration. The trading firms were major importers of raw materials.

Exhibit 4/6: Japanese Planning: Primary, Intermediate and Secondary Sectors

	PRIMARY	INTERMEDIATE	SECONDARY
Sectors	Minerals Fuels Food Commodities	Iron and steel Petrochemicals (Micro circuits)	Cars Consumer goods Appliances Plastics Cameras Industrial equipment Etc.
Policy Issues	Transportation Logistics Infrastructure	Technology Global economics Cost elements	Marketing info R & D support Tariffs

While acting in an intermediary role in crude oil supplies, they were prohibited by law from importing crude themselves. Since the 1979 Iranian crisis, the trading firms have been active in the spot market and in deals with state-owned oil companies. By 1980–81, about a third of all crude oil imports entered Japan through the large trading houses (*Petroleum Economist,* August 1981).

The impact of this sourcing approach has been to increase price competition for resource needs, and to provide a measure of monopsonist powers to end users in the intermediate stage sectors. It is no accident therefore that the Japanese steel industry, or until recently, the petrochemical industry, has been world scale competitive, combining the latest technology, optimal scale economies, and location advantages near end users. The strategy has been clear: supply basic intermediate feedstock materials to downstream assembling and processing manufacturing industries at the lowest possible cost.

4.6 Portfolio Approach to Sectors

In Japan the broad framework of the manufacturing sectors gets translated into analyses of specific industry sectors. Conceptually, industry sectors can be viewed somewhat akin to an investment portfolio. The portfolio consists of a series of investments, each giving a different return depending on its age, risk, size, sophistication and the like. Like any other portfolio there is a combination which represents the values of the investor – short term versus long term gain, security versus risk, future winners versus today's breadwinners. What is critical to this conception of industrial structure as a portfolio of investments is the perspective that there are industries to enter but also industries to exist. Divesture in Japan is seen as a critical function and unlike many market countries of the West, is ruthlessly followed, as shown by the level of bankruptcies in small, medium and large companies and by the patterns of industrial incentives. As one U.S. study reported in this regard, "It remains a pleasant surprise in Japan to have quite minor functionaires address public meetings and discuss programs to divest the economy of inappropriate industries. We have already looked at the consequences, and some of the quandaries, of this basic strategy, like the question of what proportion of production of an essential product should be kept on shore. But the entire thrust of Japan's tax laws, depreciation schedules, trade policies and government programs is directed along the lines of this agreed strategy" (Abegglen and Hout, 1978:165).

The basis of the sectoral analysis of Japan's industrial structural planning is shown in Exhibit 4/7. This figure and Exhibit 4/8, which shows the empirical results for the period 1965–1970, is based on two fundamental dimensions for Japanese economic analysis. These two dimensions are first, estimates of production growth and second, Relative Productivity of Labour. Production growth in industries is considered as a function of a number of factors, both domestic and international. For examples, because careful calculation is made of each sector with international considerations, there is the possibility to consider Japanese potential for production in terms of domestic demand, import substitution, export demand, and export substitution of current foreign producers (e.g. automobiles). In industries where Japan is a technological/product pioneer, production growth can be considered as a function of domestic demand potential, and foreign export market potential, divided among developed countries and less developed countries (the latter probably timed at a later date).

Relative productivity of labour relates each industrial sector's productivity of labour to the Japanese average productivity in manufacturing. The peculiar features of the Japanese economy are an important consideration here, given

Exhibit 4/7: Dynamic Comparative Advantage Model

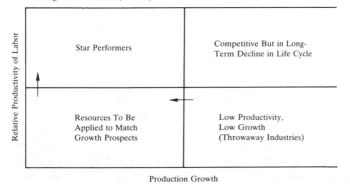

- Most Productive Use of Resources
- Strong Future Demand (Growth)

| | Star Performers | Competitive But in Long-Term Decline in Life Cycle |

Relative Productivity of Labor

Resources To Be Applied to Match Growth Prospects — Low Productivity, Low Growth (Throwaway Industries)

Production Growth

Exhibit 4/8: Productivity/Growth Matrix Japan's Productivity/Growth Matrix Manufacturing Industry Ratio: 1.0

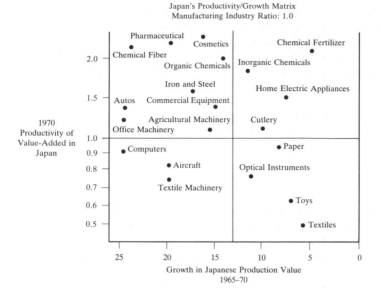

the presence of the dual economy – i.e. small and medium sized firms, with lower economies of scale, productivity and wage rates, persisting with the presence of large, technology and capital intensive firms often with unmatched economies of scale. By international and especially North American standards, the smaller and medium sized firms are considerably lower in productivity, yet the large firms are considerably above the Japanese average.

Small firms are about 20 percent below average productivity, and account for a higher percentage of total manufacturing output. The difference is that Japanese labour productivity among large corporations (with plants employing above 1,000 employees) is about 50 percent above average for all manufacturing due to such firm specific factors as economics of scale, labour relations, worker-capital ratios, organizational structure, and technology absorbtion (Caves and Uekusa, 1976; Daly, 1980).

Together these two dimensions can be cross-classified to represent a model of dynamic comparative advantage for the total industrial structure. Firms in low growth, low value added sectors (e.g. textiles) are considered as expendable industries – the actual term applied is "throw-away" industries. In the opposite quadrant are the Star Performers, i.e. sectors which feature at once both high production growth and high value added. For Japan, these star sectors have been such sectors as chemical fibers, automobiles, iron and steel, and agriculturel equipment and implements. They have experienced in the 1965–1970 period above average growth in demand and above average increases in value added.

Sectors in the lower left quadrant represent potential future stars, if the appropriate resources are applied to match growth prospects. The resources necessary to develop these potential winners can vary according to the sector, but such factors as financing, capital equipment, research and development, scale economies, and appropriate manpower are central considerations. Two examples illustrate these developments. In the computer industry, MITI has engineered mergers among the smaller firms to promote world scale production and research and development and there are now three main Japanese producers (Yasaki, 1976). In aerospace, the government has been very active in promoting technology licensing agreements with foreign producers to develop manpower and production capabilities within Japan: the results have been spectacularly successful (Hall and Johnson, 1970).

The fourth quadrant represents the sectors where technological and marketing considerations restrict growth prospects – these areas are at the end of the product life cycle and face decline. In many cases, these are sectors which were yesterday's star performers: today they face competition from off-shore production sights since labour is cheaper, the technology is standardized, and energy sources may be more abundant. There may be short term prospects to prolong the life cycle by improvements in production processes (e.g. replacing expensive labour with industrial robots) but these are interim adjustments before the inevitable shift into the "throw away" industry category.

4.7 Japan's Export Strategy

No country in the world, at least during the past twenty-five years, has so correctly perceived the dynamics of the international economy, including the emergence of labour-intensive third world economies, as has Japan. As a consequence of this realistic assessment of world trading patterns, Japan has oriented its domestic manufacturing mix with a specific orientation to the global patterns of trade and foreign investment. Even though exports comprise one of the lowest percentages of GNP of any major Western nation (10–11% of GNP, compared to 8–9% in the U.S., 25% in Canada and Britain, 40% in West Germany), in manufacturing alone, the Japanese rate is about 50 percent.

The planning of industrial structure outlined above relates directly to the country's export strategy. The composition of exports is not entirely identical to the domestic mix of the manufacturing sector, for two reasons. First, for many products (e.g. color televisions), exports from Japan actually preceded the growth in production for the domestic market, a fact which reflected the dif-

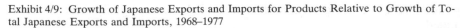

Exhibit 4/9: Growth of Japanese Exports and Imports for Products Relative to Growth of Total Japanese Exports and Imports, 1968–1977

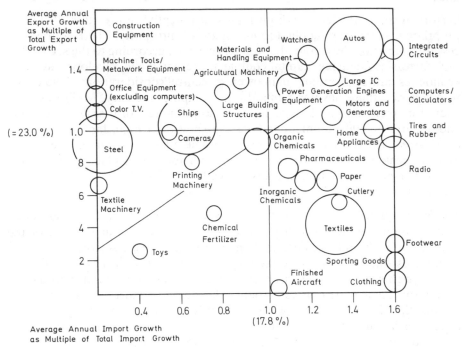

Average Annual Import Growth
as Multiple of Total Import Growth

Note: Circle size proportional to total trade.

Source: Summary Reports Trade of Japan (Ministry of Finance) and BCG.

ferences in incomes and consumer tastes between foreign markets and Japan. Second, Japan is capable of relating the level of exports to domestic demand such that by long production runs of fairly specific products (e.g. watches), huge productivity gains are possible which allow entry and penetration of foreign markets even as domestic demand is growing. By contrast, in many Western countries, export growth occurs after domestic market saturation has been reached.[6]

The dynamics of Japan's export strategy is outlined in Exhibit 4/9. It represents a realistic national economic strategy of continually shifting into higher value added, high productivity sectors and, of course, exiting from industries which

---

[6] In many sectors, the Japanese producers have focused on particular niches abandoned (small black and white televisions) or poorly developed (sporty motorcycles). By aggressive marketing and in too many cases by passive foreign rivalry, Japanese firms have quickly gained market share to reinforce their long production runs and resulting lower unit costs. The pattern becomes a reinforcing vicious circle in favour of Japanese productivity.

do not meet these criteria. Exhibit 4/9, pieced together by the Boston Consulting Group using government data, outlines the industrial sector strategy relating exports to domestic production.

The top half of the figure represents the fastest growing and higher value added sectors. The top left quadrant consists of industries with growth in exports higher than average; for the most part, technology and capital intensive sectors where Japan has been consistently competitive. The right quadrant is also the competitive sector, but here growth in exports and imports has been above average. This quadrant represents the most competitive sectors, since neither Japan or any other exporter clearly dominates trade patterns at present. They have even higher levels of technological sophistication and R and D backing, which are as necessary as pricing and marketing strategies. Japan's recent efforts to move away from strictly small cars, with standardized technology and mass production assembly, into medium priced, high value added, technically sophisticated components, is the latest reflection of this general strategic development.

The bottom quadrants represent a mixture of Japan's declining industries, or those whose days are numbered because high domestic wages, or raw material and energy costs create comparative disadvantage. There may be potentials to prolong the adjustment, for example, by exporting technology and turnkey projects in these sectors (as in the Middle East or South East Asia) but the capacity for Japan to remain competitive is severely constrained (the one exception in this chart may be pharmaceuticals, where improvements in production value-added and R and D investments may push the sector into the upper right quadrant).

The planning behind these structural adjustments are typically related to two additional considerations at the firm level in Japan. First, by adding export potential to domestic production growth concurrently, rather than in a step wise fashion of many Western competitors, Japanese firms gain enormous productivity advantages from scale economies. In many sectors, Japanese firms are unrivaled for building optimal scale plants.[7] Second, by recognizing the managerial and labour advantages from fast growth, Japanese firms accumulate the economics of the learning curve, or experience curves. Very fast

---

[7] In this connection Bela Gold, an expert on the economics of scale and specialization, writes as follows: "An interesting and important example of this was the confidence of American engineers in the mid-1950's that the optimal size of blast furnaces had already been reached, only to have the Japanese subsequently demonstrate the superiority of furnaces with several times greater capacity – although no major advances in technology were involved. Japanese engineers have also assured me that no major advances in technology were involved in the designing and construction of the giant ships built by them after the war, which dwarfed those previously regarded as most economical." Bela Gold (1981:14).

growth can mean spectacular improvements in per unit costs as output increases. This cost volume relationship, often depicted as progress cost curves, means that savings can be as much as 20 percent with a doubling of output, e.g., 20 percent in steel, 15 percent in televisions, 10 percent in automobiles (Rose, 1978).

Indeed, it is these kinds of plant level skills and managerial capabilities which make the model of dynamic comparative advantage so successful for the Japanese. Moreover, it shows that the macro vision or framework of the Japanese economy is not etched in some static government blueprint, which invites inflexibility, protectionism, and organizational inertia. The emphasis is on the dynamics and this approach means there are winners and losers, sunrise as well as sunset sectors.

4.8 Japan's Sunset Industries

Japan's penchant for gathering and reporting economic statistics is well known. One very important role such statistics can serve is to distinguish between sectors with falling demand or temporary dislocation problems (e.g., the need to invest in new machinery) and sectors with fundamental structural problems of obsolete technology, declining productivity, or uncompetitive cost position. More than in most countries, Japan has been able to identify these sectors, to recognize the difference between short run and long run difficulties, and to reallocate resources away from sunset sectors to sunrise sectors.

A report prepared on United States – Japan trade by The Comptroller General put the difference starkly:

In comparing U.S. and Japanese trade policies, GAO finds the sharpest contrast in the different approaches toward export industries. Japan's commercial policy rests on identifying industries with strong export potential and providing them with support. In the United States there is no analysis of export potential among industries. Shoes and computers are regarded equally. Before targeting an "export industry," Japan asks "Do the products of this industry have a high value-added content? Will the demand for this product rise with rising income?" These questions are not asked in the United States. Japan encourages its strong industries; the United States protects its weak ones.

Declining industries are sectors where there is a sustained absolute decrease in unit sales and where lower cost imports threaten a permanent challenge for cost competitiveness.[8] Individual firms have a mixture of strategic options in the

---

[8] Porter (1980:255) writes: "Industries differ markedly in the way competition responds to decline; some industries age gracefully; whereas others are characterized by bitter warfare, prolonged excess capacity, and heavy operating losses. Successful strategies vary just as widely. Some firms have reaped high returns from strategies actually involving heavy reinvestment in a

face of a declining industry environment, such as the selection of market niches, controlled disinvestment, or quick liquidation. The significance of the Japanese approach to sunset sectors is, however, a pervasive willingness to face up to the dislocation costs of uncompetitive industrial sectors and to develop a planning approach to long term decline. How is this planning function carried out?

The two major bureaucratic players in this exercise is The Industrial Structure Council and MITI. (Japan's Fair trade Commission is rather weak and doesn't have the communication links of other government units.) MITI bureaucrats work from comparative growth statistics and import data to analyze the underlying cost structure of raw material, production, technology and the like to ascertain the degree of severity of a sunset sector's competitive disadvantage. Once a sector is targeted as a lame duck, the signals in the business community are quickly picked up and a rather typical pattern develops.

The first move is to reduce industry capacity, often in staged cuts. In the aftermath of the second energy crisis in 1979, this pattern has been in force in aluminum smelting, synthetic fibres, oil refinery, steel, and petrochemicals, and shipbuilding, chemical fertilizers and paper, to cite examples. Cuts in capacity are closely linked to market share and production rates – between 1976 and 1981, as one prominent instance, the top five steel producers maintained output of crude steel at exactly the same share of total output. The costs of these cuts in capacity are borne first by the companies involved and by tariff revenues. For example, the cost of shifting capacity out of coal mining was covered in part by a ten percent duty on petroleum imports. More recently, where MITI forced a reduction in aluminum smelter capacity, tariffs on imported ingots were used to pay for the structural adjustments.

The second move in declining sectors is to establish new ground rules for the adjustment period. Outright cartels,[9] i.e., industry cooperation on such fundamental issues as production volume, pricing, inventories and sales agreements is permissible under the law; for example, this approach has been widely used in shipbuilding and in steel. In some cases, import controls may be permitted, especially when modernization of equipment with new technology or energy

---

declining industry that make their businesses better cash cows later. Others have avoided losses subsequently borne by their competitors by exiting before the decline was generally recognized, and not harvesting at all." For an examination of corporate strategies for declining industries, see Harrigan (1980).

[9] According to a French government study, "The formation of cartels, authorized by MITI, in accord with the antimonopoly law, for treating particular industrial problems constitutes a very powerful tool of industrial policy. It is one of the keys of capacity adjustment of Japanese enterprises and what presents a common front in matters of industrial questions (exports and divisions of markets, investment, transfer of technology)." Jean-Pierre Souviron, *Stratégie de Réponse au Défi Japonais* (Paris, 1981), p. 22.

savings may signal a return to profitability. However, such instances have been quite rare in the post-war period; import controls really signal a prelude to long term decline. A related response is to specialize in high value added areas, even if the market niche is limited or involves export development.

The third move involves a reallocation of workers. Policies which are key to this approach involve subsidized retraining programs, early retirement of older workers, movement of labour into other sectors or to other business units of the bigger corporations. In the post-war period generally strong economic growth has allowed this reallocation approach to work well, and there has been limited union resistance to shifting employment because layoffs have usually been seen as a last managerial response to competitive decline.

The underlying processes of decision-making for declining sectors are identical to sunrise sectors. At the most general level, there is an enormous statistical basis for major decisions; there is also a constant interplay of communications, lobbying, cajoling, and industrial gamesmenship. On the government side, there is not only the pressure of individual politicians, representing declining industry prefectures, but the *gen Kyoku* or "original bureau" responsible for each industry sector. Their institutional counterpart in the private sector are the hundreds of trade associations representing specific industrial interests. Both sides hold constant and elaborate meetings and consider a wide range of such issues as technology, tariff policy, tax law, imports, foreign investment and the like.[10] There may well be sharp disagreement between both sides on some issues, such as, for example, the timing of import liberalization.[11] However, judged by the reduction in relative importance of major sectors of the Japanese economy over the past two decades, and the emerging prominence of new sectors such as electronics, life sciences, and new materials, Japan's approach to sunset industries can be seen as a costly but ruthless recognition of

[10] In the steel industry, for example, top executives meet each Monday, sometimes with MITI officials in attendance. MITI itself publishes quarterly guidelines for production based on forecasted output requirements. As one former viceminister of MITI stated (Ojimi, 1975:107), "MITI may have been used as a tool by industry and yet there are still problems which cannot be settled without strong leadership from the bureaucracy."

[11] There has been a clear trend away from MITI's activist interventionist approach towards the arms length, market philosophy of the Ministry of Finance. As far back as the mid-1960's, there were two well publicized incidents which illustrate not only this contrasting government philosophy at the ministerial level but the conflict between MITI and private sector firms. In 1962, in the Takushinho incident, MITI attempted to have legislation passed to promote mergers via tax measures in key sectors facing tariff liberalization. The Ministry of Finance and private lending institutions fought this approach and won. Three years later, MITI attempted steel production cuts, only to be faced with strong opposition from Sumitomo Metals. A compromise was reached. In the current automobile crisis, there is the paradox of MITI favouring export quotas – the private sector is not in agreement with them.

comparative disadvantage in the industrial structure. As subsequent chapters will elaborate, the route for declining industries may not be a closing down of a business unit but one of shifting production via foreign investment to offshore markets where comparative advantage is higher. The idea is to shift the production site from Japan where unit costs are too high to a foreign site where input costs are lower than the domestic industry structure.

This pattern is not only eminently rational from the point of view of Japan's industrial evolution, it usually means as well that Japanese foreign investment complements the trade characteristics of the host country. Much of Japan's first foreign investment took place in South East Asia, usually in the form of joint ventures, in sectors where low cost production was greater than onshore (e.g., textiles and cutlery). This process is now being extended to include high wage countries like the United States and Western Europe, because of their domestic comparative advantage in labour and raw materials supplies. For the domestic economy, this approach has two major consequences. First, by the process of "throw away" industries, the economy can allocate its main resources to sectors where Japan has comparative advantage, now or in the future. There is considerably less pressure to prop up lame duck industries where there is no hope of salvage. Second, the diversion of the domestic industrial structure into high value added, high growth sectors means that each sector can feed on the improvements and developments in other sectors. For example, large scale firms promote the sophisticated products or processes into small firms; consumer industries are spurred by the new equipment processes developed by the industrial goods sectors. The overall impact is for the major sectors of the economy to develop a momentum by the major actors – managers, workers, and government officials to understand the basic direction and ruthlessly assess performance on relative growth and productivity.

4.9 Summary and Conclusions

The planning process for developing Japan's industrial structure has no parallel either in the mixed market economies of the West or the planned economies of the communist regimes. Ironically, while many Western observers would suggest that Japan is indeed a unique case, the fact is that Japan is the model of most of the countries of South East Asia. Both these countries and Japan share an economic feature not readily perceived in the West, namely that while a planning process is in force, buttressed by strong business-government relations, they are all Friedmanite economies where governments account for less than 30 percent GNP, or in some cases no more than half that of the capitalistic U.S..

The main point of Japan's economic planning is not to produce a blueprint but to give direction, and that direction is clearly market- and trade-oriented. For the Western countries, there is a major lag in perceptions of what Japan is doing. There can be no question that in years past, Japan has used all kinds of trade and non-trade barriers to keep exports at bay and foreign investment to a minimum. Moreover, there are still some sectors which remain protectionist and inward looking (agriculture being the primary example). Yet it is another matter to generalize the workings of the entire economy on the basis of these worst examples. It is equally wrong to ignore the basic path of Japan's industrial structure based on the pattern of exports in the sixties and early seventies. Japan is well past the stage of post-war reconstruction and needs no government props to remain technologically and industrially competitive.

Further, contrary to evidence from planning skeptics, the Japanese model serves a very useful purpose, namely the educational function of clarifying past mistakes and future direction. In this respect, Japan's approach is ruthlessly performance oriented, and acts as a barometer against international standards. Countries in South East Asia have started to emulate Japan's analytical techniques to design their evolving industrial structures and indeed, in a number of instances, they are now severely threatening many once highly competitive sectors such as traditional consumer electronics (e.g., radios and television), steel and shipbuilding.

However, the particular features of the new industrializing countries of South East Asia – their geographical proximity to Japan, their capacity to buy catch up technology, their transportation advantages – are quite different from the major economies of North America and Western Europe. In those countries, there has been much debate on the relative merits of industrial planning, even in the United States. Most of this discussion has taken on the flavour of highly charged ideological overtones. France has become the one Western country most obsessed with Japanese style industrial planning, and since 1980 has studied the approach in some detail.

Despite the attention given to the Japanese model, most foreign observers fail to recognize why, at bottom, the system has been successful. For one thing, there is limited recognition of the incredibly thorough discussions and information exchange between industry and government. A typical description of this dialogue is explained in cultural terms of conformity and consensus, but too little appreciation is given to the efforts on both sides to achieve a competitive industrial structure.

A related point is that while the Japanese plan, they are fiercely market oriented. There is little sympathy for the view usually found in Europe of picking a single industrial champion for each sector: the Japanese approach is like the stable of race horses with many champions competing in each sector.

The elaborate set of government levels for industry – tariffs, foreign investment controls, government purchasing, tax policies, and financial loans – are all geared to an optimal industrial structure which is globally competitive. The competitive difficulties of many European industries in their own markets is a measure of the ineffectiveness of excessive reliance on planning and protection.

A third issue is the Japanese obsession with technology as a key to industrial productivity. Value added has been a recurrent theme of the planning approach and the underlying rationale for growth in some sectors and not others. Japanese dependence on foreign resources and foreign technology have reinforced the desire for an effective national response. The model of industrial structure planning has several decades of practice and the decision-making processes between business and the government and internal to the corporation or the bureaucracy reinforce it.

So the question remains: Would the Japanese planning approach work in North America or Western Europe? This question is hardly academic: As far back as 1975, a bill was introduced to the U.S. Congress calling for the development of a balanced economic growth plan in the United States. The preamble to the bill argued that basic economic problems were largely the consequence of a previous "failure to develop a long-term national economic policy."

Proponents of national planning often draw a parallel between corporate planning and government planning. "If corporations are to take a look at where their companies are heading," states Senator Jacob K. Javits of New York, "it seems appropriate for the government to do the same." A basic distinction, however, is that a corporation acts on its own purposes and its own resources; a government acts on the society as a whole. As Weidenbaum and Rockwood (1977) caution, "Unlike a private organization, government may not only plan, it can also command. While a business firm can set goals only for itself, government can establish goals for society as a whole."

Much of the foreign analogies with industrial planning in Japan are either mistaken or misplaced. In terms of the overall economy, the role of the government – or specific departments like MITI – is vastly overrated, especially in recent years. Where the government does have a role, the clear lesson for Western countries is one of maximum coordination of effort – for example, tax policies, manpower programs, R and D support, regional policy. Japan's resource dependence and export trade consciousness heavily reinforce this coordinated effort.

A second point is that Japanese industrial planning is most influential at the two extremes of the industrial structure – in emerging sunrise sectors or the declining sunset sectors. While the government's role is clearly powerful, it is by no means blindly supportive to corporate interests when competitiveness is low. Unlike most European countries,[12] the Japanese government rigorously promotes strong, indeed ferocious, competition in each sector by assuring several entrants in each sector. Even in the area of sunset sectors, the government's success has largely been due to careful coordination of the various levers in the policy arsenal. Because the planning approach is fundamentally microeconomic in nature, the basic differences across sectors can be learned, assessed, studied and acted on. In the United States, for instance, most government programs for ailing industries are not coordinated and many policies are macroeconomic in nature. As a *Business Week* report on the U.S. economy noted,

Relying solely on macroeconomic policies is not likely to solve the problem of sectoral fragmentation now confronting the U.S. Instead government policies will have to be carefully targeted to meet special needs. The requirements of ailing basic industries are obviously different than those of the energy and high-technology industries.

Another basic distinction with the Japanese approach is continual commitment to analyzing significant global economic and technological trends and their likely impact on the domestic economy. Corporations and trading firms do this in Japan, of course, but certain national objectives – energy, transportation, housing, food, education – can only be met by government input. Some work undertaken by MITI has American counterparts in the Defense and Space Programs in the U.S., but the U.S. approach is piecemeal and fragmented, partly because this need is not publicly admitted. This constant monitoring of Japan's relative position, publicized in an endless array of statistical sources, greatly increases the public awareness of economic and trade issues and makes for informed public policy. The next chapter takes up this theme in the context of the second side of Japan's industrial planning, namely technology and knowledge-intensification strategies for the 1980's.

---

[12] Despite dramatic mergers or takeovers in certain sectors – Dai-Ichi and Kango in banks on Yawata-Fuji in steel, or mergers in the computer sector – Japan has not had the forced restructuring found in Britain and France, for example. In Britain, planning efforts have created mergers and takeovers such that there are only one or two major firms in key sectors – British Steel in steel, Hawker-Siddley and British Aircraft in aerospace; ICL in computers, British Leyland in cars. France has followed a similar effort. Ironically much of this effort took place just when many energy-intensive and capital-intensive industries were becoming obsolete, and where new industries based on new technologies and processes were favouring small scale, low entry barrier industries largely based on individual entrepreneurship. For detailed country analyses and industry case studies, see Vernon (1974).

Chapter 5
Technology and Knowledge Intensification

"Science Finds – Industry Applies –
Man Conforms"
Theme of Chicago World's Fair 1933

5.1 Introduction

Probably no single factor explains the continuing success of Japan's industrial system as the management of knowledge and technology. Economists such as Edward Dennison (1976) have indicated that about a fifth of Japan's 1953–1971 growth in income can be accounted for by technological change. Vogel (1979) argues that "in virtually every important organization and community where people share a common interest, from the national government to individual private firms, from cities to villages, devoted leaders worry about the future of their organizations, and to these leaders, nothing is more important than the information and knowledge that the organizations might one day need". French journalist Jean Jacques Servan-Schreiber (1979) notes that throughout the 1930's, 1940's, 1950's and 1960's, from Roosevelt to Kennedy, nothing could compare with the great universities of Harvard, MIT, or Princeton, all on the east coast. It should be recognized, he argues, that it is now West coast universities – Stanford, California Tech, Berkeley and U.C.L.A. – which are at the cutting edge of U.S. technology. They are all on the Pacific, facing Japan and not Western Europe.

Yet for all the success of Japan's technological achievements, there is no doubting the myopia of the United States in the area of technological trade. Almost two decades ago, Peter Drucker (1968) called attention to the view that "the international balance of technology is as important as the old standbys, 'the balance of trade' or the 'balance of payments' – and maybe more so." As in many areas of management, this was a theory that took better root in Japan than in the U.S. Today, industrialized and newly developing countries alike are worried about this balance of technology and technological sovereignty[1].

---

[1] An excerpt from Canada's Science Council's annual report exemplifies this perspective: "For Canada, a technological sovereignty consistent with international interdependence must replace technological imbalance. We must develop an appropriate amount of original technology, 'high' as well as 'low' (i.e. complex and simple), and apply it vigourously. We need to stimulate innovation" (Science Council of Canada, 1977:26).

Exhibit 5/1: Comparative Patent Registration (1980)

Country	Total Patent Applications	Resident	Non Resident	Patents Per 100,000 Capita
Japan	191,020	165,730	25,290	147
Australia	15,936	6,582	9,354	48
Canada	24,974	1,785	23,189	7.7
Sweden	9,192	4,106	5,086	50
U.S.	104,329	62,098	42,231	28.8
U.K.	41,640	9,612	22,028	35

In the immediate post-war period, Japanese productivity in comparison to the U.S.A. was incredibly low: five percent, for example in coal mining and chemicals, ten percent in rubber and twenty percent in rayon. Within decades, this position has been totally reversed. Japan rivals the U.S. in integrated circuits, main frame computers, and leads both Europe and the United States in high technology trade. How has Japan been able to make these phenomenal leaps in technology, especially in contrast to a country like Britain? Have Japan's government and corporate strategies been the key? Are there other factors at play, such as the unwitting role of American corporations?

Consider the case of U.S. sales of technology to Japan in the 1950's and 1960's. Japan imported an enormous amount of U.S. technology, which is often credited with the "catch up" hypothesis of Japanese economic growth. The use of foreign technology to close the gap with the West has certainly been a major policy of the Japanese government ever since Meiji. In point of fact, however, the central role placed on technology by Japanese managers and policy makers persists even today, when Japanese technology is on a par with Western countries. Japan is innovating technology in many new sectors. Despite the persistence of factors favouring imitative strategies, there remains an insatiable thirst for technology contracts with Western countries, and technology trade deficits are sizeable with, for example, the U.S. and France. Why? According to Abegglen and Hout (1978), "the cumulative cost to Japan of technology purchases from abroad – more than 25,000 contracts covering essentially all the technology the West had to offer, most of it from the United States – has been about six billion dollars. This is a little more than ten percent of the annual R & D expenditure of the United States. More to the point, that technology has nurtured competitors who now enter or threaten U.S. markets. And as a final irony, technology which might have been a lever to enter the Japanese market has been surrendered and with it the advantage that might have made entry successful."

This picture of trade in technology is important because it illustrates so well some basic themes of Japan's industrial system. The emphasis is on the long term, not the short term. The emphasis is on learning and knowhow, or process, rather than end product. The rationale is to develop sunrise sectors. The emphasis is on knowledge intensive sectors with high value added and export potential. Too often Western analysts emphasize Japan's technology strategy in terms of imports (particularly from the U.S.) and the imitation tactics of applying foreign technology. Yet technological policies and practices go hand in hand with many micro and macro strategies at the level of the firm, industry and society. For example, Japan's R & D policies help explain the strong emphasis and skills at process development and enviable record in productivity and quality control. In addition, technology policies can be seen as pivotal to the understanding of Japan's export development and evolving industrial structure around knowledge intensive industries. Whereas in the 1960's, Japan's exports were heavily concentrated in industries with low R and D (e.g., textiles, iron and steel, cars), the exports in this decade and in the 1990's are in high R & D sectors, with electronics, production processes, and biotechnology at the forefront. Nor is this technology plan one of imitating or buying foreign technology. Japan now registers more than two and a half times the number of patents as the U.S., eight times the rate of Britain and, at 147 per capita for resident patents, compares with 28.8 in the U.S., 35 in Britain, and 64 in Switzerland. The seeds of Japan's technology future lie in these investments. Technology is a central element of Japan's general approach to industrial planning and highlights the priorities for new products, materials, and production systems. In Japan this approach is called knowledge intensification of the industrial structure and forms the basis of management strategies in the 1980's.

5.2 Technology and Economy

The importance of technology in societal modernization and economic development has long been recognized, and today the role of technology and the "knowledge factor" in international trade has taken a central place in the theory of the multinational firm and foreign investment (Vernon, 1970). In the broadest sense, Japanese policy makers have carefully studied the implications of such issues and adopted a policy geared towards "making" technology via licensing and development rather than "buying" technology directly via foreign investment by multinational subsidiaries (e.g., as Canada does).

The recognition given to technology and science as an instrument of economic and industrial policy is indicated by the emphasis placed on science in government departments such as the Science and Technology Agency, and publication of its annual report. The government collects and analyzes more statistics on technology trade than most countries, and regularly outlines broad goals for technological research. For example, research on energy savings and resources conservation has taken almost twenty percent of total technology research in the 1980's, compared to less than five percent in the 1960's. By contrast, research in the areas of quality control and mass production has been greatly reduced in the scale of priorities. Increasingly, Japan's export performance in global markets is directly linked to its technology strategy. As outlined in the last chapter, planning for the next decade is geared towards another radical movement away from land-intensive, pollution-intensive and energy-intensive sectors (the so-called Keiretsu sectors such as steel, shipbuilding, and chemicals) into high value added, knowledge sectors (computers, machinery, electronics, fine chemicals).

Japan's technological emphasis has been a central factor in catching up to the West. While the government has played a leading role, the success of individual entrepreneurs, various research institutes, and the universities should not be underestimated. For example, businessmen such as S. Ishibashi, founder of Bridgestone Tire, was innovating in "jika-tabi" or rubber sole socks in the tire industry independently of Michelin in France. Sakichi Toyoda, founder of Toyota, pioneered many innovations in automatic weaving machines and even sold his equipment abroad. As far back as 1918, The Nitrogen Research Institute carried out basic research based on German patents in such areas as ammonia synthesis, production of nitric acid and hydrogen, and methanol. In the development of the imperial universities, the government created chairs for research in applied chemistry – these have become the forerunners of chairs in industrial chemistry and several new fields today. For example, Tokyo Imperial University had chairs in such areas as acid, alkali and fertilizer, dyestuff and coal chemistry, fiber and cellulose chemistry, plastic and petroleum chemistry, and electric and photochemistry.[2]

A theme of Japan's post Meiji technological development, when compared to other industrial countries such as Britain, the U.S. and Germany, was the remarkable "information awareness," partly as a result of inviting foreign engineers and technicians to Japan, and sending elites abroad to learn foreign technology (Uchida, 1980). As indicated in Exhibit 5/2, Japan's institutional conditions and managerial attitudes were positive influences for technological diffusion and development and indicate a pattern which exists even today. In other words, the government's lead role has been important, but the understanding of technology in economic development has been pervasive, and no where so important as in management.

---

[2] For excellent case studies on Japan's early technological development, see Okochi and Uchida (1980).

Exhibit 5/2: International Comparison of Technological Development and Diffusion in Electrical and Chemical Industries (1870–1920)

	Britain		United States		Germany		Japan	
	Electrical	Chemical	Electrical	Chemical	Electrical	Chemical	Electrical	Chemical
Information Awareness	Very good Foreign experts (USA) Physical Society Royal Society I.E.E. (1890–)	Good Foreign experts (GERMAN, SWISS) Chemical Society Soc. of Chemical Industry	Limited in science Good in engineering A.C.A. Journals Urbanization	Much borrowed from U.K. etc.	Dingler (since 1821) VDI-Journal (1857–) ETV-Journal (1880–)	Chemical Journal (1867–) Excellent	Booklearning Studying abroad (incl. army & navy officers) Foreign employees Translation of technical terms	Foreign engineering firms
Profitability	Not very good until W.W.I.	Very good until 1880 Very bad afterwards	Long term capital Agricultural rate-of-return vs. industrial rate-of-return	Unprofitable until W.W.I.	Medium Siemens: private Co. AEG founded in 1883	Very good Four big companies founded in 1863 as Ltd. company	Non profitable	Profitable in the long run, uncertain in short term
Institutional Conditions	Poor except pure science	Very poor	Military academy Engineering science Late	Training in chemical technology improving from mid-19c.; very good by 1914	Technical high school Patent office very favorable ETV, VDE	D. Ch. G.: KWG (1910–)	Higher technical education Trading companies Government and bank	
Managerial Attitude	Negative	Poor management	Poor management Risk-bearing vs. risk-avoiding		Till 1897, Siemens was more profitable than Ltd. companies	Scientifically & commercially very good	Active Copy-oriented	
Others	Could not compete with gas until 1900	Very cheap raw materials; coal, salt, lime, sulfur	Hydraulic power	Very cheap raw materials No dyestuffs	Scientific publications of industrial research also in other ways	Dependent on some imports until 1880	Hydraulic power	Competition with imported goods

Source: Uchida (1980: 226–227)

Japan's current policy of knowledge-intensification goes hand in hand with science policy oriented specifically to increase international competitiveness.[3] Spending on research and development now amounts to about 2.01 percent of GNP, compared to 2.47 in the United States and 2.42 in West Germany (see Exhibit 5/3). However, there are significant variations in the allocation of R & D effort. In Japan the private sector contributes more than two thirds R & D spending, as against 28% for the public sector (in the U.K., the percentages are 52–48 respectively). France, whose industry sector now provides 58 per cent of R & D funds, is closest to Japanese funding patterns but has much fewer researchers per capita. Preferential tax measures are an important factor. Moreover, unlike the United States, very little of Japan's research effort is financed via defense contracts, where economic spinoffs have shown to be less valuable than mission-oriented, commercial R & D. In Japan, the vast proportion of R & D expenditure is on product development (75% compared to only 5% in basic research and 20% in applied research). Even though Japan has historically spent less on R & D, in overall terms, research in specific sectors such as electronic and mechanical engineering, chemicals, and automobiles, to cite specific examples, has been notably greater and more successful. In terms of the number of researchers per 100,000 population, Japan is second to the U.S. with 240 versus 280, compared to 150 in Sweden and West Germany, 140 in Britain, 130 in France, and 90 in Canada (*Focus Japan,* 1981).

The emphasis on developmental work relates to Japan's historical dependence on foreign technology, and the willingness of foreigners to sell Japan their latest products and processes. Japanese companies have excelled in process innovations arising from the application of reverse engineering techniques to foreign designed goods. The priority given to process innovations has been assisted and even accelerated by the predominance of Japanese managers with science and engineering backgrounds. In their review of Japanese undergrad-

Exhibit 5/3: Comparative Indicators of Science Policy

	Japan	U.S.	W. G.	France	U.K.
R & D Spending Index (1979)	100	281	87	52	35
R & D Spending as % GNP (1979)	2.0	2.4	2.3	2.0	2.2
Researchers Per 10,000 population	24	28	15	13	14
Private Sector Research Funding	72	49.6	48.3	58.7	47.3

Source: Agency of Science and Technology

---

[3] Japan's technological policies are set out in MITI's *The Industrial Structure of Japan in the* 1980's (Tokyo 1981). For related analyses, see Abegglen and Etari (1980), Gregori and Etari (1981), and *Business Week,* "Japan's Strategies For the 1980's" (December 14, 1981).

uate training, Peck and Tamura (1976) argue that the traditional emphasis is more suitable to catch up technological development than pioneering innovation. However, other factors are involved, including managerial career patterns, incentive schemes for productivity improvements, and the very high percentage of engineers employed in production (McMillan, 1982).

Japan's dependence on imported technology in general, and imports from the United States in particular (64.6% of the total), have often been cited as a major bottleneck for future growth along the path of recent years. A decade ago Ohkawa and Rosovsky (1973) argued "there is . . . a fundamental difference between closing a gap (or eliminating a lag) and depending on the extension of a domestic or foreign technological frontier. In the former case, if other conditions are right, one can proceed at great speed. Gains can accrue in a relatively short time. In the latter case, one may face lengthy bottlenecks. The technological frontier is inevitably surrounded by uncertainties, hesitations, and false starts."

Overall Japan, like West Germany, is a major importer of foreign technology. The largest deficits are in the electrical machinery and transportation equipment sectors; steel and construction are the largest technology earners. As shown in Exhibit 5/4, Japan has run a substantial trade deficit in technology, although there are large variations by sector. The reason for this pattern is the growing export of technology from Japan to Asian and other markets. In 1980 Japan earned 2.7 times the payments for technology acquisitions, mainly because it sells not only high technology to Europe and North America but also

Exhibit 5/4: Technology trade balance in selected countries (in millions of dollars)

	Japan			U.S.A.			France			W. Germany			U.K.		
	R	P	R/P	R	P	R/P	R	P	R/P	R	P	R/P	R	P	R/P
1965	17	166	0.10	1534	135	11.4	169	215	0.79	75	166	0.45	138	131	1.06
1966	19	192	0.10	1515	140	10.8	181	244	0.74	73	175	0.42	168	143	1.18
1967	27	239	0.11	1747	166	10.5	195	231	0.85	90	193	0.47	183	174	1.05
1968	34	314	0.11	1867	186	10.0	270	282	0.96	99	219	0.45	211	195	1.08
1969	46	368	0.13	2019	221	9.1	336	332	1.01	98	256	0.38	218	223	0.98
1970	59	433	0.14	2331	225	10.4	344	357	0.96	119	306	0.39	273	255	1.07
1971	60	488	0.12	2545	241	10.6	398	467	0.85	149	377	0.39	288	270	1.07
1972	74	572	0.13	2770	294	9.4	585	587	1.00	201	433	0.46	339	307	1.10
1973	88	715	0.12	3225	385	8.4	844	741	1.14	216	539	0.40	410	350	1.17
1974	113	718	0.16	3821	346	11.0	989	823	1.20	262	582	0.45	465	413	1.12
1975	161	712	0.23	4300	473	9.1	1332	1035	1.29	308	729	0.42	493	484	1.02
1976	173	846	0.20	4353	482	9.0	1461	1180	1.24	289	692	0.42	–	–	–
1977	233	1027	0.23	4725	447	10.6	–	–	–	335	816	0.41	–	–	–

Note: R = receipts, P = payments.

Source: Peck (1981)

Exhibit 5/5: Percent of Total U.S. Patents Issued by Country

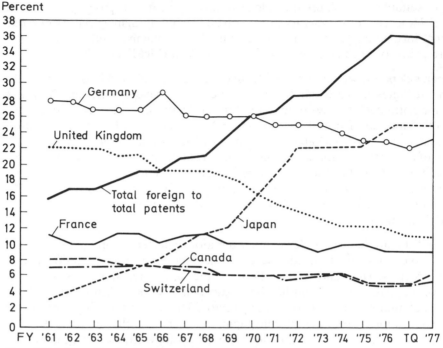

Note: TQ is Transition Quarter
Source: Annual Report of Commissioner of Patents 1971, 1974 and 1977

acts as a relay station to countries in Asia. Asia accounts for 48.7 of Japan's technology exports, compared to 17.3 per cent in North America and 16.7 per cent in Europe. Imports from North America, by contrast, are 64.8 per cent in 1979, mostly from the U.S. and 33.6 per cent in Europe. In this approach, as in many products Japan is a clearing house for European and American technology to Asia. For example, Japan supplied two-thirds of the 737 know-how agreements with Korea between 1962–1976, compared to only 158 from the U.S. (21%). Yet the U.S. is the overwhelming source of technology exports and U.S. patents to Japan (Exhibit 5/5). Japan has thus become the center of high technology/low technology societies, where the key trade is licenses, patents, and technology agreements. Japanese industry is still in a technology deficit position with U.S. industry but even here the gap is narrowing with more licencing by U.S. firms in such areas as robotics where Japan has a technological edge.[4] Comparative data on the ratio of R and D expenditures to

---

[4] Japan has a positive export-import technology surplus with the U.S. in iron and steel, construction and textiles. While the overall technology surplus on new contracts has existed for a decade,

total sales for many sectors show that the U.S. is still ahead in most areas (Exhibit 5/6) although the gap has narrowed considerably.

Exhibit 5/6: Ratio of R & D Expenditure to Total Sales

	Japan (1977)	U.S. (1975)	W. Germany (1975)
Electrical Machinery	3.6	7.1	6.7
Precision Machinery	2.9	5.3	4.5
Chemicals	2.6	3.6	3.2
Transport Machinery	2.3	3.5	2.9
General Machinery	2.0	4.1	3.1
Rubber Products	2.0	1.7	2.1
Clay, Glass, and Stone Products	1.2	1.5	1.3
Iron and Steel	1.1	0.5	0.4
Textiles	0.6	0.4	1.0
Lumber, Paper and Pulp	0.5	0.7	0.7
Foods and Beverages	0.5	0.4	0.5
Aircraft	13.8		44.0

Yet there are even now major changes taking place in Japan's approach to imported technology. In the past decade, the government has promoted multiple purchases of foreign technology, that is, imports of the same technology by more than one firm. Statistics are unclear for this trend – The E.I.U. (1981) states that as far back as 1971, 74 per cent of technology were for duplicates, Peck and Goto (1981) claim that in 1977 the figure was 15 per cent. There can be little question, however, that the government has played a central role in technology trade both as an instrument to improve Japanese productivity and to increase competition by technology diffusion. Another trend is that a small amount, perhaps ten per cent, consists of technology imports in unmodified form. The Japanese now combine indigenous technology with imports for product improvements. However, the major bottleneck for Japan, aside from the fact that Japan is now on a technological par with the West (and thus less likely to make major advances on proven technology), is the new pattern of restrictions being placed on imported technology. Just as imported technology is competing with Japanese technology in Japan, foreign technology in Japan is competing with Japanese technology in offshore markets, hence the rise to about 80 per cent the number of licenses placing export restrictions on Japanese manufacturers (Tsurumi, 1976).

Japan still pays out over a billion a year in net royalty payments on contracts signed many years ago.

5.3 Technological Diffusion

A common theme expressed in the popular literature on Japan is that country's capacity to copy or imitate foreign technology rather than to invent or pioneer technology (Abegglen, 1970; Peck and Tamura, 1976). This "follower" instead of "leader" takes various forms. For example, it is felt that Japan does very little basic research compared to Western countries but has taken advantage of Western sales of technology to promote growth. Another variation is that Japan concentrates only on imitation technology rather than innovation. Still another theme is that Japan promotes extensive diffusion of foreign technology to all industry, so that most firms adopt best practice usage more quickly than Western companies, even though the technology has been produced in the West, not Japan.

In many respects, there is an element of truth in these assertions. As already noted, Japan has persistently run a trade deficit in technology with the West, and there is a greater emphasis on the development side of research compared to the mission approach. Yet there are certain elements in Japan's approach to technological diffusion which aren't often recognized and appreciated.

For one thing, unlike the United States or Britain, Japan's primary research emphasis is not in government or the universities, so the pattern of rewards and psychic incomes are quite different. In the U. S., for example, it is common practice for scientists working in the commercial sector to publish, to participate in academic gatherings, and to aspire to scientific reputation. In Japan, where there is an equivalent number of researchers per capita as the U.S. (about double the number in France and Germany), the thrust of rewards and career incentives is for economic and corporate success, as well as for short run commercial payoff. This pattern is fostered by close consultation and research support for university faculty. In the field of robotics, it is not unusual to have university faculty provided "on permanent loan" experimental equipment for testing and trials. Some companies in chemicals and pharmaceuticals publish research undertaken by faculty members.[5]

A second consideration in Japan's diffusion of technology is the country's very high level of literacy, and knowledge of mathematics, economics, and basic engineering. On balance, Japanese managers and workers are among the most educated in the world,[6] and this formal training combines with a strong moti-

---

[5] This difference is one of degree. In the United States, even in consumer and industrial sectors, it is not unusual for company personnel to work closely and publish articles with academics. The student riots at universities during Viet Nam protests perhaps accelerated the shift of some research based in universities to industry research centers. The most obvious discipline where this has occurred is in economics. For a perceptive analysis, see Hoffman (1970).

[6] According to findings by Professor Richard Lynn of The New University of Ulster, results of the Wechsler Intelligence Scale for Children, a standardized test to avoid cultural bias, only about

vation to succeed and a value system emphasizing learning and curiosity. In a sample of almost 1,000 managers, Mannari (1974) found that 100 per cent of managers under 40 and eighty-one percent between 40–50 had university degrees. In an international perspective, he notes: "It may however be of some surprise to find Japan still more committed to advanced education than the United States, which itself emphasizes a university degree for elite careers to a greater degree than does Western Europe. The rapid progress of Japanese business and industry in the recent period may be due to the fact that business executives who are university graduates are by training receptive to new ideas, new technology and new management practices." Historically, of course, scholars have now recognized that Japanese success at absorption of foreign technology since Meiji (1868) has been built on a very high level of indigenous technology and very high rates of literacy. A policy of technology imitation, in short, can't be built in a vacuum.

Another factor often overlooked in Japan's technology policy is the collective capacity to carry out what might be called "environmental scanning" or surveillance of market and technological trends globally. Various studies have documented the systematic approach to learn from Western companies – e.g. in textiles, in steel, in shipbuilding – and this learning desire is often expressed in the Meiji slogan *Wakon Yohsai* ("Japanese essence, Western technology"). One approach adopted involves programs such as hiring foreign specialists, sending students and workers to offshore countries, and establishing middle management tours to the West. Then there is the vastly more complicated system of translating foreign technical journals, monitoring and screening foreign trade flows with Japan, and surveying firms and their "scanning activities". In this regard two methods stand out.

By far the most sophisticated and advanced, relatively speaking, is the *Sogo Shosha* – the trading firms, of which there are over 8,000, specialized by size, by product, or by geography, and of which ten account for about 60% of total trade. The large *Soga Shoshas* do regular monitoring of the technological environment of all the major Western nations and much of this data is linked on line to corporate headquarters in Tokyo and Osaka. Major foreign cities like London, New York, and Frankfurt are the base of a beehive of intelligence sourcing from technical magazines, trade journals, company reports, and government studies. However, even small firms are active in industrial scanning: Bylinsky (1980), for example, discusses the approach of Japanese firms to gain information in the semiconductor sector by hiring American employees and consultants familiar with their previous employers.

two percent of North American and European populations score above 130, but about 10 percent score above 130 in Japan. Among the youth generation, Japanese scored an average of 111, compared with 100 for youth in Canada and the United States (*Globe and Mail,* June 11, 1982).

Other sources of technological scanning include surveys by such government agencies as Science and Technology, the Japanese External Trade Organization (Jetro), and industry associations. Jetro, an affiliate of Miti, operates with more than 100 offices in major trade centers and acts as a listening post for economic and technology trends. It publishes numerous brochures on the Japanese economy, conducts seminars for Western businessmen, and more recently, promotes foreign imports to Japan.[7]

All these activities serve to build a large data profile of all foreign markets and technological trends which are then supplemented by detailed company studies. Tsurumi (1968), for example, has shown the kind of scanning pursued by almost 1000 Japanese firms in search of technology: 97.9% used systemic use of data available from patent offices, trade conventions and academic journals; 53.2% stationed or sent research staff offshore; 36.4% employed private information and universities; 19.9% employed overseas information services, licensees and contacts in business; 17.1% used trading firm data; 16.1% used the industry associations and the facilities of the Japan Scientific and Technical Information Center.

A more recent survey carried out by MITI of 200 firms reveals that the largest sources of information for technology were business associates (54.6%), patent office reports (52.1%), companies in related businesses (45.4%), trade and professional journals (38.8%) and trading companies (37.9%). A reexamination by Robert Cole of the original data of this MITI survey shows that overall differences by industry and size of firms are rather small, thus indicating a well operating infrastructure for information diffusion of technology. By size of firms some differences exist. According to Cole (1981) "The smaller the firm (as measured by the amount of capitalization), the more they tend to rely on industrial, trade and professional journals, industrial fairs, and merchandise catalogues".

Behind these scanning activities are, of course, the administrative guidance procedures and processes of the Japanese government. Especially in the postwar period but even during the Zaibatsu-dominated era prior and during World War II, there have been formal and informal pressures to diffuse technological know-how from large to small enterprises, and from "core" firms to subcontractors. The government itself has been an important vehicle for monitoring and screening foreign technology (especially before technology liberalization in 1968). MITI has also played both a direct role (via case to case screening) and an indirect role (by Japanese firms threatening government

---

[7] JETRO has served as the model for Korea's KOTRA (Korean Organization for Trade Advancement), Taiwan's CETDC (China Exports Trade Development Council, and Hong Kong's Trade Development Council.

intervention if concessions weren't granted by foreigners) in technological negotiations (Blumenthal, 1976).

The government's role in technology planning should not obscure the basic
market orientation and competitive focus of Japanese industry. In this respect,
many foreign perceptions of Japanese technology policy, especially in such
areas as licensing restrictions and foreign investment regulations, are a basic
legacy of programs in existence before trade liberalization under the GATT
tariff reductions. The government has consistently favoured the presence of
many firms in all leading sectors – indeed, promotion by the government of
technology diffusion is partly explained by this desire for market-based competition. As Peck and Goto (1982:238) note: "We also regard the competitive
character of Japanese industry as a factor that promoted technical change.
While there is a stereotype of Japan as the home of cartels and government
limitations on competition, the extent of competition appears significantly high
for the industrialized oligopolistic economy that is found in all major market
economies."

In short the Japanese program of adopting and developing Western technology
has neither been a simple process of "borrowing" or imitating, as if anyone else
could adopt the same approach, as the simplistic notions of Japan Inc. theorists
have suggested. The simple catch up hypothesis of Japanese economic and
technological development is not supportable. By contrast, a realistic appraisal
of Japan's technological diffusion strategy must point to the large, sustained
and sophisticated efforts to monitor and understand global trends in technology and the dynamics of trade flows. It is this global orientation to technology
trade, Japanese mangers' shrewd assessment of the country's competitive
strengths and weaknesses, and their negotiating strategies which have raised
the competence of so many domestic firms to that of foreign competition.
Increasingly they are now forming the basis for medium-size and small firms.
Both new product development and process technology are critical to competitive survival. Industrial planning and technological policy go hand in hand
with proactive corporate strategies for the firm.

5.4 Creative Technology Policies

As part of the catching up with the West in economic development and technological sophistication, Japan's main emphasis has been in the core industries
consuming natural resources (e.g., iron and steel and petro chemicals), their
engineering off-shoots (e.g., cars, shipbuilding and fibres, plastics), and in
pollution industries allied to chemical processes. Aside from the social costs of
this rapid development, there has been a fairly clear recognition that other
basic technologies had to be mastered, such as the electronic and computer
revolution with its implications for work, production processes, and spinoff

industries. Research by MITI officials has argued for new technologies for the 1980's. The emphasis is on three areas – overcoming energy constraints, improved quality of life, and new knowledge intensive industries. The key to these developments are new materials technology, biotechnology, and new functional technology. As Japan reorders its industrial priorities and undertakes a major restructuring, this program amounts to the most significant change in direction certainly since the Second World War, possibly since Meiji. The basic thrust of the shift in industrial structure is depicted in Exhibit 5/7. Up to 20 per cent of Japan's GNP will be directed towards new high technology industries. The aim is to spend up to four per cent of GNP on research and development by 1990, 3.5 by 1985.

Exhibit 5/7: Forecast Shift in Japan's Industrial Structure

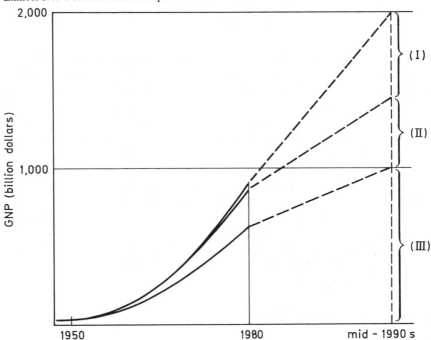

(I) High-Tech industries (15–20% of GNP):
     Aircraft/Space, Data Processing, Electronics, New Energy, Life Sciences, New Basic Materials, etc.
(II) Key industries (15–20% of GNP):
     Steel, Automotive, Electric Machinery, Chemical, etc.
(III) Other industries:
     Agriculture and Fishery, Construction, Electric Power and Gas, Wholesale and Retail, Finance and Insurance, Services, etc.

Source: MITI

The changes signalled by this shift in direction are profound, not simply for Japan but for the competitive position of Japanese industry. This new direction signals a shift in exports, the role of government in financing research and the impact of Japan's production technologies on existing imports. For example, while spending in the private sector will remain high and have a strong applications bias, government outlays for R & D will reach the levels of the US and Europe, or about 50 per cent of total R & D spending. The impact on corporate strategies of particular companies will be equally profound, since the style of management and organizational practices will undergo major changes. Already the top firms on the Tokyo Stock Exchange are committing almost eight per cent of sales on R & D spending, and this pattern will increasingly prevail for all major Japanese corporations and will be reflected in the composition of future Japanese exports. As stated in *The Vision of Miti Policies In The 1980's,* "Japan needs to behave itself in the international community in a manner different from the past". Technology planning in Japan is increasingly being directed at two levels: innovation directed towards daily life and specific industries. In each case, technology is considered in terms of three basic areas, namely new product development, production process development, and application of existing products and technologies to related areas.

Less reliance on foreign technology, less dependence on foreign energy and raw materials and greater reliance on technology related exports form only half the basic change in technology planning. Japanese corporations expect to pioneer new products based around biotechnology, micro-electronics and microcircuitry as well as highly advanced production systems, including automated factories and flexible manufacturing systems linked to robotics, computer aided design and manufacturing, and a new generation of numerically controlled machine tools. The elements in these strategies are still being worked out, but they point to what the Industrial Structure Council calls "a higher level of creative knowledge – intensiveness in the 1980's": In the present decade, Japan aspires to build a technology-based nation through self-inspired and imaginative technological innovations.

More specifically, consider the case of social innovation directed towards human needs. Seven areas have been identified: diet, clothing, dwelling, health, locomotion, intellect (education) and leisure. For each area, it is possible to identify general tasks for technological innovation, which then involves resource allocation for product development. In the case of food, for example, where Japan has only 55% self sufficiency on a calory basis (and 77% on a value basis), the following tasks have been identified:

a) development of foods and fertilizers
   – to develop safe and non-polluting agrichemicals
   – to develop effective fertilizers

   - to develop untapped biological resources
   - to develop new foods and feeds

b) development of food systems
   - to transform farm management to factory management
   - to develop new fishing methods (e.g. submarine fishing ships)
   - to develop resources nurturing fish systems
   - to establish methods to foresee blight and insect attacks
   - to systemize data on weather and ocean resources
   - to develop sophisticated food processing technologies

c) development of machines and materials
   - farm machinery and implements (e.g. automatic harvesters)
   - fishing machinery (large scale aerators, automatic feeders)
   - food processing machines (automatic cookers, food freshness gauging
     machines)
   - development of effective environment adjusted materials (artificial soil,
     high performance plants for cultivation).

In some cases – housing is perhaps the most obvious – technological innovation
implies a historic change for Japan, although some aspects of it (e.g., artifically
created land space, centralized garbage disposal, and electronic locks) would
have applications in countries with more advanced housing technology. (During the seventies, almost a quarter of Japan's fixed capital investment went into
housing.) The three areas considered to have the biggest social significance are
in education, housing, and health and welfare, as outlined in more detail in
Exhibit 5/8.

The conceptual basis of planning for these "city-related" living needs can be
equally applied to private sector business opportunities, both in terms of product development and production processes. From a competitive perspective,
the Japanese have gone a long way in formalizing the trends in technology such
that both government ministries and private sector groups (e.g., industry associations and firms) have a framework to understand, plan, process, control
data, and register patents for technological applications. Information is at the
core of these trends, and Japan has made computers and information processing a major national goal of its technological thrust. Technical journals of all
major countries are regularly scanned and studied, and translation into Japanese is quick and efficient. By way of example, Exhibit 5/9 outlines the direction of technology planning for the industrial mechanical equipment sector and
for automobiles. The primary emphasis is on new product development, but
closely related is the improvement of production processes. In many cases,
firms which pioneer in new product development innovate in new process work
as well – Japanese car makers, for example, have become major producers of
robot equipment. Equally important is the stress on developing more syste-

Exhibit 5/8: Needs of Daily Life and Tasks for Development of Technology

Needs Involving Conditions of the Environment of Life	Tasks for Development of Technology
Dwelling Life Enrichment of the Dwelling Life – Mass supply of housing – Improvement of the quality of housing – Full development of room furniture and furnishings and their trend toward fashion articles Enrichment of the Community Life and Its Conveniences – Securing good regional environment – Amenity of the environment of the dwelling life	– Industrially manufactured housing – Standardization and objectivization of housing quality and performance – Unit-prefabricated housing – High-rise prefabricated housing – Transforming housing functions into units and parts – Industrialization of *wachsende haus* ("waxing house") which is adaptable to expansion or replacement construction – Artificially created land space – Inorganic materials for construction purposes – Technology for performing adhesive building construction – Non-combustible interior decoration materials – Magnetic heating plates – Surface illuminants – Electronic locks – Mobile homes – Wired city – CATV (Cable Associated Television) – Home facsimile – Centralized heating and air-conditioning – Centralized garbage disposal technology – High-rise structure demolition technology – Calamity prevention system – Regional environment protection system
Health A Healthy and Civilized Life and the Full Development of Medical Care – Prevention and cure of illness – Expansion and improvement of medical facilities Expansion and Improvement of Welfare Facilities	– Automatic medical examination system – Automatic brain-wave analyzing system – Nursing and rehabilitation facilities – Welfare facilities for the physically handicapped – Artificial organs, artificial skin – Health foods
Intellect (Education) Enrichment and Sophistication of Education – Increase in education opportunities – Expansion and improvement of educational institutions Expansion and Improvement of Educational Equipment of the Welfare Type	– Man-machine responsive educational system using the computer – Simulators for training and education using the computer – Educational system utilizing the cassette video – Training equipment for the physically handicapped – Learn-in sleep technology – Educational system through international correspondence – Pattern-data processing system

Source: Japan External Trade Organization (JETRO)

matic applications for existing technologies and products. This approach means that small and medium sized firms are able to gain access to new technology trends much faster than in most countries. It means that novel uses of existing technology prolong the underlying technology life cycle, thereby reducing the unit cost of technology development. (Studies have found that while the level of spending of many Japanese firms is lower than their counterparts in Europe or the U.S., Japanese efficiency in using the R & D is higher.) An added but unquantified factor which promotes this research intensification is the high

Exhibit 5/9: Direction of Technology Development in Major Industries

Industry Group	Development of New Products	Improvement of Production Processes	Application and Systemization of Existing Technologies and Products
Industrial mechanical equipment	• Development of automation machinery for manufacturing processes to increase labor-saving and safety • Development of unmanned factories • Application of man-machine systems, promotion of safety-improvement by attaching failsafe mechanisms and other measures • Development of unmanned factories by integrating automation machinery • Development of bio-mechanic technology substituting for human functions, such as sensors, artificial organs, molluscan machines, etc. • Development of new material technology such as functional materials, function-assisting materials and structural materials in order to expand functions and to improve reliability	• Development of automation machinery for manufacturing processes such as casting, forging, thermal treating, working, assembling, conveying, wrapping, and packing (for example, robots, transfer machines, numerical controllization, group technology) • Development of new handling technologies and conveying technologies such as robots which have visual functions • Improvement of reliability by making design more precise, homogenizing materials, improving inspecting technologies, etc. • Development of automatic processing technologies such as learning control technology • Optimization of processing conditions by such measures as full development of processing data banks, etc.	• Improving labor-saving and work precision by introduction of the computer for individual machines, such as metal working machinery, plastic forming machinery and casting and forging devices (NC-ization, accommodation control, learning control, group technology) • Automation of manufacturing processes such as materials-supply, product-conveying, inspecting, working and assembling • Development of unmanned factories • Development of machinery and apparatus deemed necessary for community-systems such as calamity-prevention, water supply and sewerage, solid waste disposal, new traffic systems, etc., and their systemization

Industry Group	Development of New Products	Improvement of Production Processes	Application and Systemization of Existing Technologies and Products
	• Development of nuclear energy related equipment, cryogenic machinery, etc. by applying technologies adapted to extreme conditions • Development of resource and energy recycling systems to conserve resources and energy and eliminate pollution	• Development of ultra-deep drilling systems • Underwater stockpiling systems • Underwater oil production systems	• Development of pollution preventing machinery systems, safety-plant systems for solving the problems of pollution and safety • Application of industrial mechanical systems such as rehabilitation systems and artificial organ systems to life sciences • Automation and systemization of food production, such as indoor agricultural production systems and cultivated fishing systems
Automobiles	• Development of vehicles with engines which apply new theories, such as gas-turbine vehicles, rankine cycle engine vehicles, stirling engine vehicles, electrical automobiles, etc. • Development of antipollution equipment (such as engine enclosures) and low-pollution vehicles • Development of safety in automobiles by adopting, among other measures, air bag systems, anti-skid systems, and safety tires	• Automation and labor conservation in the assembly process by utilizing the computer, for example • Improvement of heat efficiency of boilers and other equipment and adoption of cold-working for conserving energy • Development of pollution countermeasure technology in such sectors as casting and forging • Standardization of parts and improvement of painting methods in order to raise productivity	• Development of new traffic systems by combining automobile technology with the computer, such as demand-bus systems, and city-car dual mode systems • Development of the automobile comprehensive control system by unifying the automobile and wireless communications

Source: Japan External Trade Organization (JETRO)

level of vertical integration of firms in each major sector arising from the large number of firms attempting to gain competitive advantages (e.g., Exhibit 5/10).[8] While government policy has attempted to prevent individual firms gaining a temporary monopoly from foreign technology licenses (and at times actively interceding to make sure a competing Japanese firm will have equal access to one already getting foreign licenses), the shift to superior domestic technology makes this role less important. This point is still not a view widely appreciated in North America and Europe. Fierce domestic competition provides the impetus to greater technology diffusion and productivity far better than government edict or bureaucratic mandates.

This strategy for knowledge intensiveness and creative technology raises two fundamental questions for Japan. First, what is the actual state of Japanese technology relative to other countries? Second, now that Japan is entering a

Exhibit 5/10: Office Automation Equipment Manufacturers

Company	PPCs	Facsimiles	Office computers	Word processors
Konishiroku Photo Industry	•			
Hitachi Ltd		•	•	
Toshiba Corp	•	•	•	•
Mitsubishi Electric		•	•	
Nippon Electric		•	•	•
Fujitsu Ltd		•	•	•
Oki Electric Industry		•	•	•
Matsushita Electric Industrial	•	•	•	
Sharp	•	•	•	•
Matsushita Communication Industrial				•
NCR Japan			•	
Casio Computer		•	•	
Sanyo Electric			•	
Olympus Optical	•			
Canon	•	•	•	•
Ricoh	•	•	•	•
Minolta Camera	•			
Uchida Yoko			•	
Nippon Univac			•	
Copyer	•			

Source: Yamaichi Securities

---

[8] Gregori and Etari (1981) note the point as follows: "Leading Japanese electronics manufacturers are, therefore, characteristically large-scale enterprises. Although there is a vast number of smaller electronics firms in Japan, most of these are subcontracting production which is inherently small scale and has been less conducive to mechanization in the past. Others fill special niches, some in global markets which require custom or batch labour intensive production technologies. In the main, however, major electronics firms in Japan are now more diversified and highly integrated than their competitors abroad."

new era of development, can the past emphasis on innovation – productive commercial exploitation of ideas developed by foreign invention – be successfully shifted to fundamental creative technology, whether by individuals or by organization-based research?

As part of its technology strategies for the 1980's, MITI's Industry Structure Council undertook two studies to assess Japanese technological performance. The first involved a technology performance index, based on patents registered, the technology trade balance, value added in manufacturing, and proportion of exports being knowledge intensive. With the United States as the barometer, the study (Exhibit 5/11) indicates that in the late 1960's, Japan still trailed behind West Germany, and was only one fourth that of the United States. Other factors enter into this kind of comparison, such as the high level of defense and space related research effort in the United States, so Japan's actual technological level may even be understated.

Support for this view comes from the second study by the Industry Structure Council, namely a survey of businessmen. This study asked a group of business

Exhibit 5/11: Japanese Technology Levels

General Index of Technological Level

	Late 1960s	Late 1970s
United States	100	200
West Germany	40	56
France	24	38
United Kingdom	25	26
Japan	22	50

Index: Using U.S. as 100 the average of index positions in patents registered, technological trade balance, value added in manufacturing, and proportion of exports which are technology intensive

Source: Vision of Industrial Policy in the 1980's, p. 277

Businessmen's Evaluation of Japan's Technology (71 industrial sectors)		
	Technological Level (number of sectors)	
	U.S.	Western Europe
Japan superior to	2	2
Japan equal to	41	55
Japan inferior to	26	8
No rated	2	6

Source: Vision of Industrial Policy in the 1980's, pp. 279–80

men in 71 industry sectors how Japan's technology ranked in comparison to the United States and Europe. In almost two thirds of the sectors, the business men rated Japan's technology as either equal to or superior to US technology; in sectors rated, the business men felt Japan's technology was equal to or superior to eighty per cent of West European technology. Japanese technology was seen to be inferior to the US in one-third the sectors, in the case of West Europe, only eight sectors.

Despite these kinds of statistics, there are many Western commentators and even many Japanese, who doubt that Japan has the necessary individualism to overcome the country's lack of original research. For example, of the major scientific discoveries of the past fifty years, Japan has made fewer than a half dozen. There have been only four Japanese awarded the Nobel prize in science. According to Dr. Leo Esaki, one of Japan's two surviving Nobel prize winner in science, too many Japanese scientists favour the worn treads of scientific research: "The Japanese never challenge the unknown. There is a lack of the sprit of exploration . . . Eventually you really come down to the lack of individualism." A related cultural argument is made by Professor Tadatsugar Taniguchi: "excellent scientists are generally pushy and a little bit arrogant, but these attitudes are never, or hardly ever, accepted here, even if you are very good."[9]

Beneath these cultural arguments, however, are two additional considerations, one historical, one linguistic. The different emphasis in Japan on applied research, especially during the post-war period, has been heavily influenced by the country's relative economic backwardness, the shortage of money for funding independent research institutions, and the absence of immigrant scientists who could train and inspire young researchers. Professor Samuelson (1976) notes the contrast with American academe: "By American economics one cannot mean economics as taught and discussed by persons *born* in this country. Scarcely one professor in twenty was born outside of France. But of twenty outstanding American economists at the time of World War II, perhaps two came here from England, six to eight from Europe . . . An American University that tried to recruit its economics department from Mayflower descendents would, I fear, have a tough time of it. These and other characteristics of the American economics profession would also be quite typical of other disciplines: mathematics, physics, chemistry, classics, sociology, medicine – and in some degree law and history."

The economic/financial gap hypothesis contrasts with another view, namely the role of the Japanese language and its impact on thinking patterns. The ideographic patterns of the Japanese and other Asian countries promotes the re-

---

[9] See "Original Thinkers," *The Economist* (September 26, 1981).

cognition of complex patterns and interrelationships – the kind of synthesis needed for creative work in the medical sciences where the Japanese have excelled. By contrast, there is the view that English and other alphabetic languages "foster individualism, generalization and abstraction, which find easy expression in higher mathematics (the crest of Western thought)" (Uenishi, 1982:4).

As noted, many Japanese believe their country excels much more at innovation than invention, on developing and improving ideas rather than original work. Certainly many of the institutional barriers inhibiting Japanese inventive work – poor facilities, lack of funding, few research centers, low levels of education, limited public support, ease of access to existing technology – have greatly changed in Japan's favour. Moreover, the Thomas Edison stereotype of the creative individualist has long since become obsolete in high value-added industries of the future where Japan wishes to excell – aerospace, bio-technology, pharmaceuticals and information. Even in the US, most industrial research in these fields is team oriented and organizationally based, precisely the areas where Japanese have major strengths.[10]

5.5 Technology Policy in Comparative Perspective

Beginning with the impact on public policy in the U.S. of the Russian Sputnik success, and extending to the debate over the perceived technology gap between Europe (or Canada) with the United States, and more recently, the productivity gap between Japan and other industrialized countries, technology and science planning are increasingly viewed as central to industrial strategy and economic development. In virtually every European country, this issue has taken on a level of importance which has elevated technological development to the level of national prestige and sovereignty. One author has raised the fear that European countries will get caught in the competitive squeeze between the high technology products of the U.S. and Japan and the low wage products of the Third World (Soffaes, 1979).[11] Even in the United States, where a coordinated approach to technology and industrial development is the least devel-

---

[10] In these fields, there may also be a parallel with many of Japan's traditional arts and crafts, where intricacy, manual dexterity and discipline go with precision, quality, and perfection in production.

[11] Seven of the eleven new antibiotics introduced worldwide in 1979 originated in Japanese laboratories. In August 1981, a new technical research association consisting of 14 leading chemical, pharmaceutical and food corporations was organized with plans to spend upwards of 26 billion yen on biotechnology in the decade ahead. See *Far Eastern Economic Review* (December 4, 1981).

oped, there has been a major concentration of government R & D expenditure in three areas – space, defense and atomic energy (Mansfield, 1968). France, West Germany and Britain have likewise concentrated government resources on high technology sectors such as computers, nuclear power, and aerospace. Even small countries like Holland, Belgium and Sweden have attempted to specialize in particular technologies to win export markets and gain national prestige.

There are some major parallels across European and North American approaches, but also some important differences. In both cases, the government has increasingly played the lead role, although in the United States, there is more reliance on the private sector, even when the government may foot the bill. Another issue is that national objectives, rather than international cooperation or even global market opportunities, are the overriding concerns. Nuclear power, defense products, and solar energy are notable examples. A third aspect, and one which has led to the term coined by *Time* magazine – "innovation recession" – is the increasing divorce of technological goals and objectives from market potential and commercial applications. The Concorde in aerospace is the notable if overworked example.

There are a variety of institutional reasons for these developments and they tend to reinforce one another. Government spending, for example, involves complicated budgetary pressures which reinforce incremental growth of existing programs rather than radical shifts to new ones (of Britain's research budget of about $ 5 billion, only about five per cent is allocated to industrial innovation). A related issue is government procurement practices, which often favour inefficient local companies to competitive foreign suppliers. Another side of government procurement is the myopic desire of bureaucrats to favour technological designs for products and services which are custom tailored rather than designed to sell in global markets as well as for domestic use.

Political concerns with industrial development have prompted a variety of initiatives to promote domestic technological capacity. Here the basic conflicts over appropriate resource allocation become more evident. The United States has favoured a more pluralist, decentralized approach, relying, for example, on such tools as grants and research contracts, government procurement, defense contracts, and experimental programs such as Research Applied to National Needs (RANN) administered by the National Science Foundation. The more centralized approach favoured in Europe includes funding for major government research units and, in France, particular institutions for new fields, such as 'Centres Nationaux' for areas like ocean exploration, bio-technology, informatique, and nuclear energy.

The contrasts with government policies in most Western countries with Japan rest in two basic areas – commercial applications for global markets and what might be termed technology pull government programs. The contrasts are really matters of degree but they reflect a basic understanding on the part of Japanese corporations, academics, and science bureaucrats of international market and technology trends of knowledge intensification.

As noted, Japan's R & D thrust is primarily in the private sector, and where the role of government is strong, it typically is on the side of equalizing competitive forces for particular technologies or encouraging technology diffusion throughout a sector or region. By contrast, for R & D in most European countries and in the defense and space establishments of the U.S., the emphasis has been on government laboratories which often produce spectacular scientific knowledge of questionable commercial usage. Organizational inertia and individual's scientific reputation are often two reasons promoting this result. In West Germany, during the last decade, government support concentrated on only ten key companies; in France, almost three quarters of government effort went into defense and nuclear programs.

The second issue – technology pull – refers to the range of incentives and inducements which promote technological innovation. These processes contrast with technology push, the processes of direct support for new technology development or modification of existing technology. Research in this area is spotty, but some studies of U.S. examples suggest that the technology push orientation are likely to fail unless, as Abernathy and Chakravarthy (1979) argue, "the technology creation action of the government is intensified by giving it more of a mission orientation, and complemented by appropriate technology pull actions."

Despite the efforts of the European governments to "plan" technology on a national basis, success has been minimal. In areas where European technology has been as good as or superior to the U.S. – defense and aerospace, to cite two major examples – Japanese technology and competition have been weak or non-existent. In the basic technologies likely to have the most significance in the next decades – information technology, bio-technology, and energy – European technology trails both the U.S. and Japan.

The most fundamental area is in information technology, which covers the full range of basic technology (micro circuits, microprocessors and semi-conductors) through to computers, office technology, telecommunications, and data transmission devices.[12] So significant is this development that it has been li-

---

[12] The heart of Japan's new direction in computer technology is the G5 project, or Fifth Generation Computer System, involving a long term research program involving 26 major themes. MITI has funded the project with $430 million, which will be matched by private sector funds in the order of $1.5 billion. The aim is to develop intelligent interface hardware which offers natural language access, the ability to learn and infer, and understanding data base content. The

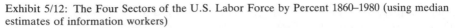

Exhibit 5/12: The Four Sectors of the U.S. Labor Force by Percent 1860–1980 (using median estimates of information workers)

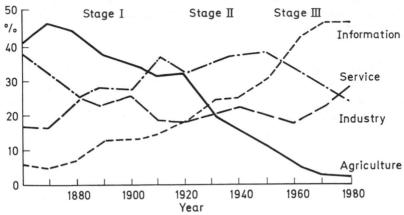

Source: Marc Porat, The Information Economy: Definition and Measurement, Office of Tele-communications Special Publication 77–12(1), May 1977

kened to a second industrial revolution: in the 1980's, the United States has more employment in the information sector than in agriculture, manufacturing, and services combined (Exhibit 5/12). Japan and the U.S. have great strengths in these production areas but the long term impact of their competition may well be to leave their European counterparts behind. As a European union Institute noted: "In the United States and Japan, the governments have controlled and aided the development of the electronics industry. The governments of Western Europe must do likewise in the action plans coordinated and encouraged at the European level."

In the area of biotechnology, there is some question whether Europe can keep up to Japan and the United States. In certain areas, such as in the production of amino acids from fermentation, Japan has gained a leading edge; biotechnology as a field already accounts for about five per cent of GNP, about the same level of electronic equipment.[13] One estimate of patents in various biotechnology fields shows Europe training both the U.S. and Japan by a significant margin (Exhibit 5/13).

Energy represents the most obvious area where Europe has considerable advantages over Japan. North Sea oil and gas, coal and nuclear reactors are the

President of The British Computer Society was quoted as saying, "If this project had been prepared by anyone else except the Japanese, it would be declared science fiction".

[13] MITI has established a program called "The Sunshine Project". It covers areas such as solar energy, coal, subterranean, ocean and wind energy, and hydrogen energy. The project examines not only core technologies but spin-off areas such as housing and office construction technology, and machinery and robotics.

Exhibit 5/13: Percentage of Patents Taken out by Europe, Japan, and U.S.A.

Field	Europe	Japan	U.S.A.
Enzyme Technologies (1969–1975)	20	50	30
Enzyme Immobilization (1977–1979)	10	21	69
Chemical Products from Fermentation	15	18	67

Source: Godet and Ruyssen (1980)

most obvious strengths for domestic industries. Even here, however, neither Europe nor the U.S. has developed or exploited any significant competitive advantages in such energy related fields as energy conservation technology, renewable energies and coal liquification. Moreover, while the abundance of energy resources in Europe and the United Stated provide an overall balance in total production/consumption, the actual imbalances in particular energy sources, the political problems of securing world prices, and difficulties in developing spin-off technologies on balance provide no great or insurmountable competitive edge against Japanese industry dependent on foreign supply sourcing.

5.6 Summary and Conclusions

As in most areas, foreign stereotypes of Japanese technology abound. The most common of these nations have depicted the country as a nation of industrial copiers only too willing to apply whatever ideas were developed in the West for Japan's vast production machine. The fact is, Japan has learned a great deal from the West, both as a licensor of foreign technology and as a skillful adapter of particular ideas pioneered in the West but improved in Japan and developed for global markets.

As in most fields where Japanese and Western standards are compared, the Japanese view of themselves is not totally unreceptive to the foreign stereotype. Japan's century old desire to catch up to the West has made the country a giant industrial mirror, where copious statistics reflect the comparison of Western and domestic products and processes and success makes front page news. The historic development of Japanese heavy industry – steel, chemicals, shipbuilding, machinery – has required close contact first with European technological developments, more recently with American. The simplistic notion that Japan has merely copied foreign technology clearly overlooks certain fundamental issues which, if ignored, may possibly lead to basic misunderstanding of Japanese management strategies in the future.

The first point is that while Japan has been an importer of foreign technology, as if this implies a weakening of her technological sovereignty, so have most other Western countries at one point or another. Indeed, the cost of developing new technologies in many fields may well be beyond the resources of even the richest countries, including the United States. More than any other country, Japan has recognized the economic calculus of buying technology in global markets rather than making it because of a desire for technological sovereignty. At the other extreme, France and Britain have gone the other route and have devoted enormous sums to basic research in a wide spectrum of fields. The underlying cost advantage to Japan of this technology division of labour has been to provide Japanese industry with opportunities for more widespread and faster diffusion of existing technology than any Western country.

The second issue is related to the first and involves the organizational skills not only to absorb new technology via "gatekeepers" and scanning techniques. It also involves the organizational decision-making and coordination across production, marketing, and research and development departments to mobilize technology for commercial applications. In this respect, technology is market driven, but the key is a management system which can transform complex ideas and techniques into a simplified stream of processes, components, and end products for volume production with perfect quality and high price elasticities.

The third issue is that at a time when Japan has caught up to the West in many areas and, indeed, is selling technology in fields as diverse as subway cars and robotics, the country is still aggressively searching for foreign technology. In part, this can be explained by the historical search for foreign ideas and a perception that foreign technology was superior to domestic industry. The other side is that Japan is situated in a part of the world where the entire country can act as a technological gatekeeper to the aggressive countries of South East Asia and even to the Third World. Where countries are not active in promoting their own technology abroad, Japanese firms are willing to buy even standardized technology and resell it as part of a commercial package in Third World countries.

In this chapter, the outlines of Japanese technology trends have been examined, particularly the designs of new technologies for the decades ahead. This change in technology "vision" signals a fundamental shift not only in sectoral priorities and in the role of government, but introduces a new era of Japan as a fundamental pioneer in new and creative technologies. As it happens, the emphasis analyzed and reported abroad has concentrated on such high glamour items as computers and memory chips and the competition with the best and brightest of U.S. industry. In the long run, some of Japan's major technological creativity may come in other fields, in such areas as food technology, housing, lift style and the environment. In a world where a million people a year die of malnutrition, substandard living and sanitary conditions, and poor medicine, Japan's role in world welfare development could be more profound than even MITI planners have thought so far.

Chapter 6
Samurai Education and Management Recruitment

"One of the solutions to the Japanese threat is to export a number of our MBA programs to Japan."

William F. Hamilton, University of Pennsylvania

6.1 Introduction

It is a generally accepted tenet of economic development that investment in human capital is as important as investment in physical resources. Beyond this generalization, arguments abound concerning the nature of education and training, the balance between general versus specialized (e.g. professional schools) education, and the economic and social consequences of accessibility to higher education.

Japan's educational system is of interest for several reasons. In sheer numbers, it is very large, with one of the highest percentage of the relevant age cohort receiving postsecondary degree. It is fiercely competitive, since access to the top universities greatly influences career ladders in government and the largest corporations. It is relatively new, in terms of the level of expansion and of the curriculum content, both shaped by post-war American influences. It is highly controversial, because of the close university-business career and job hierarchy relationship, and the alleged rigidities.[1]

Although the precise causal linkages between economic growth and education remain subject to debate, there can be little doubt that Japan's interest in human capital is both widespread and dates back more than a century. Japan's education system merits attention for the links between education and technology, especially as a model for other countries. Moreover, Japan's investment in education also supports the development of human and intellectual capital to promote new industries and technologies to compete globally in the 1980's and beyond. This chapter outlines the basic features of Japan's education system, the vocational linkages with industry, and the impact of universities as an instrument of elite formation and corporate linkages. The chapter concludes with a discussion of women in the education system and workforce.

---

[1] For an excellent overview, see Cummings (1980).

6.2 Education and the Meiji Legacy

Although the contemporary education system of Japan demonstrates the legacies of the American post-war reforms, the broader role of education in society among the Japanese elites reflects basic continuities with policy initiatives instituted after the Meiji restoration. Prior to the Meiji reforms, particularly the fundamental code of education patterned on the French school system in 1872, the main feature of Japanese education was the samurai "han" schools distributed among about 300 large and small feudal domains. The emphasis was primarily on the teaching of Confucian classics, but as late as the eighteenth century, courses included practical subjects like applied mathematics, military science, medicine and astronomy.[2]

For commoners, the most important educational institution was the *terakoya*. The *terakoya* were essentially voluntary schools, ranging in size from about twenty to fifty, open to boys and girls. Between 1789 and 1867, 104 such schools were established. In the large cities of Edo (Tokyo) and Osaka, some had as many as a hundred pupils. The curriculum was based on individual tutoring, usually by a single teacher, supported by small fees; the teaching emphasis was the three basics (reading, writing, calculations) and, for girls, sewing. A lower strata of one room schools was the *gogaku* or village school, which emphasized moral indoctrination for the individual working class in the feudal order (Aso and Iku, 1972).

The system produced a very high level of literacy through-out the country with perhaps 40 percent of the population literate prior to 1868 (Passin,

Exhibit 6/1: Estimated Literacy in Japan before 1868

Social Group		Estimated Literacy	Proportion of Total
Samurai	men	Almost 100%	7%
	women	50%	
Merchants	in large towns	70–80%	3%
	in smaller towns	50–60%	
Artisans	in large cities	50–60%	2%
	in smaller towns	40–50%	
Farmers	village notables	Almost 100%	87%
	village middle	50–60%	
	lower peasant levels	30–40%	
	peasants in more isolated areas	20%	

Source: Fuse (1973)

---

[2] Historical works on Japanese education and Meiji reforms include Nagai (1971), Passin (1965), Roden (1980) and Shimahara (1979).

1965:58–59), a high figure even by European standards, outstanding by Asian levels.

The 1872 Educational Code was a new master plan to reorganize the school system under a central Ministry of Education. Japan was divided into eight academic districts, each with a university, and these were further divided into thirty-two school districts based on a secondary school and 210 elementary schools. Throughout the period of the Meiji changes ranging from industrial policies to educational reform, the theme of strengthening Japan against foreign power domination is constant. Despite severe criticisms by Confucian scholars like Motuda Eifu, who wished to strengthen Samurai traditions and the existing social order, reformists such as Mori Arinarni instituted reforms for imitating elements of Western education and technology. There was also a strong element of nationalistic indoctrination, especially for the compulsory sector and an acceptance that education was to serve the needs of the state – a relationship reflected in the phrase *Seikyo-itchi* or unity of education and politics. Although the reforms were widely criticized at the time, these policies helped to shape the subsequent development of Japanese education and their impact remains even today. Three factors stand out.

First, the educational reforms after Meiji served to abolish the feudal status system and effectively stripped the samurai class of its official privileges (Azumi, 1969). Second, the reforms established scholastic achievements as the channel to elite recruitment. With the formation of the University of Tokyo in 1897 (founded from Tokyo Imperial University in 1886), university education became the substitute for feudal class status as the primary avenue to elite status. Third, even with the formation of other universities – 47 were developed by 1947 – an effective ranking of universities as centers for elite formation was well established and entrenched. This elite pecking order promoted the use of severe, competitive exams as the critical screening for university enrolment. Together, these changes virtually abolished at a stroke the feudal social order perpetuated on Confucian theories of rule, and the four classes ranked from Samurai-administrator, the peasant, and the artisan to the lowly merchant *(shi-no-ko-sho)*. The educational reforms instituted a new class structure based around the elite occupations of merchants, industrialists, and bureaucrats, and these, despite the upheavals after the Second World War, survive to this day. Paradoxically, the development of these elites and the mass education system instituted after the war have fostered a new social phenomenon, namely Japan as a nation of predominantly middle class citizens.

6.3 The Post War Reforms

As already noted in many areas of Japanese life, the post-war reforms were based on American ideals, in this case mass education and rapid expansion of the school system. Elementary and junior high school (nine years) were made compulsory; twenty five years after the occupation, about 95 percent of all students of junior high complete senior high school, and over forty percent of these graduates entered university. The number of two year colleges, professional schools and universities has increased to over 1,000; the number of students enrolled exceeds two million. In other words, expressed in sheer numbers, the educational reforms have moved Japan much closer to the United States than Europe in terms of universal access to higher learning; indeed, as Kahn and Pepper (1980) note, "Japan may very well have overtaken the United States in high school education; the drop out rate is much lower, making the rate of those who finish high school in Japan higher than that in the United States."

The social consequence of Japan's contemporary approach to education system has been to establish a new social ranking which transforms the traditional Marxian perspective on its ear. As a post-industrial society, Japan now has a clearly multi layer educational class which provides career ladders marked by entry points determined by educational credentials.[3] Unlike the Marxian view, wherein social class is largely a function of inherited wealth and a perpetuation of elite power, Japan is a stratified society where social class is a function of university education, which in turn is a function of egalitarian meritocratic performance.[4]

In the past twenty-five to thirty years, Japan's education system has become a gruelling rat race for the best university positions. As in any competitive market, the educational rat race is now highly differentiated by product, quality, and price. This gradation applies at every level, from kindergartens and junior schools, to high schools, colleges and universities. Japan's reputation abroad as a tightly knit, orderly and consensual society is a thin veneer which hides a

---

[3] The emphasis on educational credentials in business recruiting is hardly unique to Japan, although the intensity of rivalry for top positions is probably more extreme. In his analysis of education credentials as a passport to elite positions, Collins (1979:73) writes as follows: "Education prepares students in the skills necessary for work, and skills are the main determinant of occupational success. That is, the hierarchy of educational attainment is assumed to be another such skill hierarchy. Hence education determines success, and all the more so as the modern economy allegedly shifts towards an increasing predominance of highly skilled positions."

[4] To be sure, a Marxian perspective would argue that it is not market forces which shape the supply and demand of labour and education but instead, the economic and financial interests of capitalist forces which in turn control the processes of educational and training needs. See Bowles and Gintis (1975).

ruthlessly competitive social order wherein the educational system is but one layer.

The rat race starts at the level of kindergarten, which are for three to five year olds. Under the "Kindergarten Educational Promotion Plan" (for fiscal 1972–1981), the aim was to provide openings for all 4 and 5 year old applicants by 1981. Since 1960, the percentage of young people enrolled in kindergartens and day nurseries has gone from 26.9 percent of the age group to over 90 percent in two decades. Only France, with its extensive development of *écoles maternelles* for three to six year olds, comes close to Japan's schooling for very young children. However, where the French system is largely state supported, the vast majority of kindergartens in Japan are private – over 95 percent for three year olds, over eighty percent for four year olds, and over 67 percent for five year olds.[5]

The widespread growth of kindergarten education reflects the general increase of almost universal education at the high school level, and more recently, even post secondary education. Kitamura (1979) notes the rising percentage of parents wishing to send their children to university: 22 percent in 1951, 50 percent in 1964, 70 percent in 1977. As recently as a decade ago, over forty percent of students entered the labour market. Today this percentage has greatly fallen and has compressed the supply of labour for blue collar jobs. An indicator of the competition for university places is the new breed of students in the educational rat race – the *Ronin. Ronin* refers to the class of high school graduates who spend one or two extra years of preparatory studies after high school graduation for the university entrance examinations. (The term literally means *samurai* with a lord or feudal attachments.) An extension of the *Ronin* system is the *Yobiko* – the cram schools which service the Ronin and which themselves are ranked by a system of examinations. Azumi (1969) reports that at the University of Tokyo, three quarters of the successful first year entrants were Ronin, forty-two percent of whom were Ronin, 32 percent were two or more years as Ronin. The competitiveness of the educational rat race is thus totally pervasive – from kindergarten through to university.

Curiously the examination aspect of Japanese education may be more important than the nature of the curriculum, teaching methods, and low quality of much university research.[6] Critics point to the high suicide rate among even young students, the lack of individuality promoted by the curriculum, and the gloss of equality on top of a highly regimented, business oriented system. Defenders of the rat race system point to the success of Japanese education. In

---

[5] For statistics on Japanese education and sources, see *Facts and Figures of Japan 1980*.
[6] On the Japanese examination hell, see Dore (1976).

comparative studies of such areas as music, mathematics and natural science, Japanese students rank at the top in terms of common exams.[7] (More tellingly perhaps is that in one test among students in nineteen countries, the U.S. ranked fifteenth.) What is more important, however, is the success of the Japanese educational system in producing minimal standards of performance for all students at each level. Unlike in the U.S., for example, where less than half the number of senior high school students take at least one science or math course, the Japanese aim for a balance of all basic courses. Here there is a clear parallel with the Japanese government's approach to industrial policy and technological planning. The aim is to produce improvements in quality of standards to a high minimum degree. In the same way that all firms in an industry are encouraged to adopt technological process which meets a certain standard of productivity, the Japanese government encourages and promotes equal facilities among all regions and school districts, such that the spread between the best and the worst is substantially reduced. The best may not be equal to the best in England or the U.S., but the average is substantially above the average in those countries.

There are other aspects of the education system which defenders of the system emphasize, namely the role of socialization.[8] The competitiveness of the educational rat race is a prelude to the kind of rivalry which exists among industries and corporate groupings. The close ties between *oyabun-kobun* (parent child) change to *sensei-deshi* (teacher disciple) as a prelude to the horizontal relationships emphasized by Nakane (1973) in the Japanese company. The strong emphasis on educational performance socializes students to accept status differences based largely on merit rather than social class. The system also promotes a much greater egalitarianism and this is reinforced by the school uniforms which are common of all students, rich or poor. It is no accident that workers and managers in Japanese factories also wear identical uniforms. Finally, even the distinction between physical labour and intellectual labour is minimized, because both students and teachers share in janitorial and cleaning duties. Vogel (1977:177) makes the point as follows:

The uniformly high quality of training provides Japan with an unexcelled supply of generally competent labour power prepared for company life and receptive to learning more specialized skills at the workplace. If anything, the high level of education has overtrained students for their jobs and has created shortages of blue-collar workers. However, the Japanese do not share the disdain for physical labour found in some countries. Japanese schools, for example, use fewer cleaning personnel than America, and because teachers and all students share the "dirty" cleaning work in the schools, students learn to take physical labour for granted, not as something to be done only by those at the bottom of the social scale.

[7] See Glaser (1976) for details.
[8] This theme is developed by Kiefer (1970).

6.4 Social Origins of the Managerial Elite

The stereotype of Japan Inc. is based on the intimate set of personal relationships between business and government. The key link is organizational, namely informational and executive circulation between the private sector firms, particularly the large corporations, and the government bureaucracy, especially The Ministry of Finance and International Trade and Industry. There is a well known Japanese expression to describe this process – *amakudara*. As suggested in Chapter 3, *amakudara* is the practice of transferring officials in the civil service to the private sector on retirement, often from ministries dealing with business directly. As one study notes, "Former officials of economy-related agencies, in particular, are much sought after by corporations which hope to benefit from the personal bonds these people have built up with the 'family' of colleagues in their former ministry. A vice minister or bureau chief is virtually guaranteed such a post retirement job and even high officials outside the economy-related ministries can count on leadership positions in semi-governmental organizations" (Japan Culture Institute, 1979:89).

Such a system is hardly unique, of course, among most Western countries and often gives rise to criticisms of the workings of the corporate elite and the role of elite education in capitalist society. The theme of this line of corporate research is that social factors relating to age, schooling, and interlocking boards and private clubs create a cohesive and self serving capitalist class. The description of the U.S. corporate elite would apply internationally:

Although divided by sector, size, and other schisms, the corporate elite is united by its primary commitment to capital accumulation; it possesses a degree of internal integration, particularly within the dominant stratum, unmatched by other social class. Class exclusiveness enhances its cohesion by seeking to keep membership hereditary. Cohesion and intergenerational continuity endow the corporate elite with autonomy and power that can reactively shape the very corporate foundation from which it was formed (Useem, 1980:68).

Most studies with this theme focus on particular countries; comparative data across countries are rare, except perhaps for broad statements or generalizations such as "England expected its 'old Boys' to lead; America to succeed." Fortunately, there is some limited research in this area, which this section draws on. The data are drawn from questionnaire information from the top 500 Japanese corporations; the respondents were the top five executive positions in each firm: the chairman of the board of directors, the president, the vice president, and two senior managing directors (Mannari, 1974: Appendix I). In all there were 1080 respondents, or about a third of the total population, and they were broken down in the following percentages – 6, 13, 15, 26, and 40. Before looking at the comparisons of these executives with U.S. and European elites, it is instructive to examine certain patterns of the Japanese business hierarchy.

In terms of age, there seems little doubt that the practice of recruiting on the basis of a long career in the firm has persisted. The median age of presidents in 1979 was 58.9 – only 1 per cent was under 40 years of age and only seven per cent were under 50 years. In fact, viewing the age issue on a comparative basis (Exhibit 6/2), Japanese executives are not only older than their European and American counterparts, they become chief executives when their counterparts are ready to retire. If anything, this age gap has probably widened in recent years.

Exhibit 6/2: Comparative Age Distributing of Presidents

Age	Japan 1970	U.S. 1966	All Europe 1968	France 1968	U.K. 1968	Germany 1968
Under 50	6	23	26	15	25	30
50–59	30	51	34	36	46	25
over 60	64	26	40	49	29	45
%	100	100	100	100	100	100
N	140	492	576			

Source: Mannari (1976: 211)

In terms of social origins, the study found that the majority of business leaders in 1970 came from the occupational groups with the highest social ranking. Executives who came from families of government officials, professors, lawyers and businessmen were over represented; the least represented were sons of farmers and manual workers of all kinds. "For sons of men of upper status, chances of assuming leadership are markedly high. In spite of the great increase in top executive positions that has accompanied rapid industrialization, big business firms in Japan have tended to recruit their top executive cadre principally from the urban upper class."

The openness of executive recruitment by social class is relative, of course, and in this respect, Japan is more socially mobile than Europe, with France being the least mobile. As indicated in Exhibit 6/3, the upper class is heavily represented; only five per cent come from the working class, less than twenty-per cent from the middle class. (Lower class refers to farmers and skilled or unskilled workers; middle class refers to occupations like salesmen, school teachers, junior civil servants, and office workers.)

Equivalent U.S. data is not available, but Thanheiser (1976), in a comparison of U.S. and German chief executives, argues that "top positions in Germany seem to be more accessible to a wider cross section of the population than in the U.S." In Germany, seventeen per cent of the chief executives come from upper

Exhibit 6/3: Social Origins of Japanese and European Presidents

Social Class	Japan 1970	All Europe 1968	France 1968	U.K. 1968	Germany 1968
Lower	9	5	2	8	11
Middle	30	16	12	23	16
Upper	61	79	86	69	73
(Father-son same firm)	(14)	(26)	(34)		
Percent Total	100	100	100	100	100
N	138	576			

Source: Mannari (1974: 220)

Exhibit 6/4: Type of President and Firm Performance

	Year	Founder Score	%	Successor Score	%	Company-Bred Score	%	Amakudari Score	%
	1975	5.59	(10.7)	5.12	(20.7)	5.00	(36.2)	4.69	(32.4)
Manufacturing	1976	5.06	(9.8)	5.03	(21.0)	5.08	(34.7)	4.87	(34.5)
	1977	5.08	(10.9)	4.91	(21.5)	4.99	(35.7)	4.90	(31.9)
	1975	5.84	(7.6)	5.15	(17.5)	5.01	(46.9)	4.88	(28.1)
Large Firms	1976	5.17	(7.4)	5.10	(15.9)	5.17	(45.2)	4.81	(31.4)
	1977	5.22	(8.2)	4.98	(18.7)	5.05	(47.1)	4.90	(26.0)
	1975	5.38	(16.0)	5.08	(26.3)	4.94	(17.7)	4.47	(40.0)
Medium Firms	1976	4.95	(14.2)	4.95	(30.3)	4.60	(15.5)	4.94	(40.0)
	1977	4.96	(15.3)	4.83	(25.8)	4.72	(17.7)	4.90	(41.1)

Source: Adapted from Shimizu (1980), Table 3–3

class backgrounds, compared to 45 per cent of U.S. chief executives who were sons of presidents, chairmen or company founders."

Just how much the past represents future practice in Japan is open to debate. The purge of a sizeable percentage of executives among the *Zaibatsu* companies after the war opened up career ladders for many younger executives from a wide range of social and educational backgrounds. The intensification of university education as a basic credential to corporate careers favours the urban, upper class elites to the detriment of labourers and lower white collar.[9] The transformation of many companies from owner-managed to professionally managed firms may well continue, although Shimizu (1980) found that among manufacturers generally, or large firms and medium-sized firms, entrepreneurial founder companies consistently out performed firms led by other kinds of presidents. Using a composite index of business results which includes sales

[9] Kitamura (1979:58) argues that an increasing number of students in private colleges and schools come from "high income" families, more than three times the number for low income families. See also Collins (1979).

growth and profit rates, his study compares four kinds of presidents and firm performance; founder, successor, company-bred, and *amakudari*. The firms with founder presidents had higher performance scores in almost all cases – a finding which is consistent with Channon's (1979) research on service firms in Britain. Three year results are shown in Exhibit 6/4, showing the scores and percentages for the four types.

6.5 Japanese Management Education

There is a paradox concerning American influence on Japanese education since the post-war reforms. The trends towards mass education and greater social mobility among the elite, and to the emphasis on meritocratic performance standards, have done much to remove the particularistic criteria in use before the Pacific War. In one major respect, the Japanese have not copied the American model, and that area is management education. To be sure, the emphasis on education for management is real and pervasive. Comparative data show, for example, that formal university education among chief executives is highest among U.S. businessmen, followed by those from France and Japan. Britain scores the lowest. Although the data are now a decade old, the likelihood is that the gap between Japan and the U.S. has closed (because of the high participation rates for university education since 1950). If anything, the gap between Britain and other countries has widened, since so few of the 18–24 age cohort in Britain (about 13 per cent) attend university.

Exhibit 6/5: Chief Executives and University Attendance

Education	Japan 1970	U.S. 1979	France 1968	U.K. 1968	Germany 1968
Attended University	89%	94%	89%	40%	78%
Did Not Attend	11%	6%	11%	60%	22%

Source: Mannari (1974), Table 10

The major difference across industrialized countries is less in the level of university education among Western countries (Britain begin the exception), as in the type of education. Among French and German executives, the main emphasis is on science or engineering (see Exhibit 6/6). In Germany, the larger the company, the more likely the chief executive has a Ph.D. Post-graduate education among U.S. executives is also high.

The pattern of education among Japanese executives indicates certain fundamental characteristics of the education system at large, namely that the level of university education in Japan is very high. There are, however, three features

Exhibit 6/6: Educational Background of Chief Executives

	Japan 1970	U.S. 1979	France 1968	U.K. 1968	Germany 1968
Science/Engineering	23	53	59	43	54
Business/Economics	44	32	34	47	29
Law/Government/Social Sciences	24	9	7	10	17
Other	9	6	–	–	–
	100	100	100	100	100

Source: Mannari (1980), Table 11

Exhibit 6/7: Business Leaders and Universities Attended

University	1960	1970
Tokyo	36	32
Kyoto	11	12
Hitotsubashi	10	5
Keio	7	6
Kobe	6	2
Waseda	5	4
Kyushu	3	3
Tokyo Institute of Technology	2	2
Osaka	2	2
Tohoku	1	2
Other	17	30
	100	100
	N = 902	N = 1026

Source: Mannari (1974)

about management education which differ and which will very likely continue in the future. First, Japanese executives, like most of the population at large who attend university, do not continue to graduate school. By contrast, about 44 percent of U.S. chief executives have university post graduate education; in Germany, more than half have doctoral education. Among the population at large, only three percent of university graduates go to graduate school, compared to fifteen percent in France and twenty percent in the U.K. and the U.S. (MESC, 1975:56).

A second contrast between Japanese executives and those from other countries is the role of the elite schools. Tokyo University is at the apex of a clear university hierarchy (See Exhibit 6.7), but departments and faculties within particular schools play a role in streaming graduates towards specific careers. For example, while Todai is a main supplier of bureaucrats to the government, the Tokyo University Law School is particularly well connected through alumni to the Ministry of Finance. Keio University is a major supplier of graduates to business, while Waseda has many alumni in journalism. This elite streaming contrasts with the U.S., but has parallels with Britain and France.

A third major difference, and a paradox given the role of U.S. education reforms and the influence of American business techniques during the post-war period, is the absence of any significant development towards formal management education. In the U.S., of course, the key educational credential for management is the Master of Business Administration. From the mid-1960's to 1980's, the output of MBA's increased from about 7,000 per year to over 60,000, an eight fold increase. Although university schools of business in the U.S. go back at least a century – Wharton was founded in 1881, Harvard in 1911 – the technology of training managers via business school methods has been uniquely American until the last two decades.

Unlike Japan, other countries have now embraced this American technology. The fear of *Le Défi Americain* in the late 1960's, and the view that the productivity gap between Europe and the U.S. was in fact a management gap, largely explain the growth of management schools both in Britain and on the Continent. As it turns out, France has pushed this development the most, first by sending a large cadre of university personnel to U.S. business schools, then by establishing a large network of the *École Superieure de Commerce* in major business centers. Unlike their North American counterparts, these French schools are rather loosely connected to the university. They are often allied to the Chamber of Commerce, they are relatively elitist in student enrollment, and they have a strong international business curriculum (including language training). Similar developments have occurred in Britain, Sweden, and Switzerland; in Germany, most business education is primarily in traditional business economics.

The absence of the U.S.-style MBA professional management school in Japan's universities – Keio University perhaps comes closest to a U.S. model – has meant that Japanese companies prefer to "make" business education via company training programs rather than "buy" through university education. In fact this model is not accidental; it stems quite clearly from Japanese educational traditions and basic cultural values.

Japanese executives and university professors typically make a major distinction between education and professional training. Kobayashi (1969) makes the point as follows:

The purpose of a university is to develop a rounded personality while providing the student with a general academic background. They believe that it is not their responsibility but rather that of the employer to offer graduates specialized professional training . . .

Japanese business, with its strong desire for harmony, has generally preferred the so-called amateur managers to aggressive professionals. Further it must be borne in mind that in the long run in Japan it is what you know rather than whom you know that will determine how fast and how far your ride up the escalator will be; and at the top, relations between businessmen and bureaucrats help to vitalize a status-oriented system that might otherwise grow dangerously static. These two factors are, in a sense, "built-in mechanisms" to keep Japan's tradition-ridden and paternalistic system from stulification.

Ironically, the contrast in the Japanese and U.S. approach to management training exists just at a time when U.S. management techniques and the MBA are increasingly under attack. Major articles along this theme have appeared in *Time, Business Week* and *The New York Times. Business Week,* for instance, cites the complaint about "The inability of newly minted MBA's to communicate, their over reliance on mathematical techniques of management and . . . expectations of becoming chairman in four weeks." Business school students from Japan are typically unimpressed with the U.S. focus on abstract quantitative models, and the emphasis on human relations and organization behaviour seems redundant to Japanese students experienced in consensus oriented, cooperative environments.[10]

If there is one contrast which stands out in regard to management education, it is the surprising strength of spiritualism among the bureaucratic and business elite.[11] Religion has always been strong in Japan, but in recent years, the development of new sects and groups now compliments the broad interest in spiritual themes in society at large. Indications of this interest include the formation of voluntary religious clubs, weekend Zen training, and widespread interest in books and television programs on traditional Japanese values, legends, and spiritual discipline. The popularity of such writers on the Samuri ethic as Yukio Mishima has taught young people in Japan about these themes and has rekindled the old Meiji slogan of *wakon yohsai* (Japanese spirit and

---

[10] "Japan Gives The B-Schools an A- for Contacts," *Business Week* (October 19, 1981). Asked why they studied in the U.S., Japanese students indicated "They wished to develop a theoretical underpinning for some of their existing knowledge, to establish a network of American contacts, to learn how management thinks and acts in the U.S., and to polish their English. Conspiciously absent from the list was a desire to learn U.S. management skills." *Business Week* (April 25, 1983) also reports U.S. business schools may have to shift their curriculum towards operational issues rather than mere number crunching, partly to compete against competition from in-house schools for managers.

[11] In his treatise on education, Max Weber (1946, 426–427) called attention to the contrasts in educational traditions in Europe and Asia, particularly Japan and China. On the latter, he noted the emphasis on exams, career patterns and asceticism. The Western model of rational and bureaucratic domination emphasizes special training. "Specialized and expert schooling attempts to *train* the pupil for practical usefulness for administrative workshops, scientific or industrial laboratories, disciplined armies." By contrast, "The charismatic procedure of ancient magical asceticism and the hero trials, which sorcerers and warrior heroes have applied to boys, tried to aid the novice to acquire a 'new soul', in the animish sense, and hence, to be reborn."

Western technology). A related theme in Japanese religious mentality is that of joint suffering and individual weakness, and these ideas are exemplified in such novelists as Endo Shusaku. Studies analyzing the Japanese character , such as Isaiah Ben-Dasan's *The Japanese and The Jews* or Tokeo Dai's *The Anatomy of Dependence,* have become best sellers.

While the interest in spiritualism and aesthetic traditions is hardly unique to Japan – consider the interest in Zen, martial arts, Yoga and spiritual fulfillment in industrialized areas as diverse as France, California, Quebec and West Germany – the spread of spiritual values among the bureaucratic and business elite, and the role of *Seishen* or spirit in management education, is uniquely Japanese. The Seishen spirit, recording to one analysis, aims at the "containment of tendencies towards selfishness and egotism." The expression *messhi hoko* – "destroy ego and serve others" describes the relationship between seishen training and social involvement. According to Frager and Rohlen (1976:26), "In a position of subordination to authority, the individual may not be required to give up his life, as in the time-honored example of samuri and modern soldiers, but he is often required to give up personal opinions, pleasures, or privileges if they interfere with the achievement of greater goals or duties."

Many company education programs involve Seishen training not only for new recruits but for older workers. Spiritual training such as Zen, or physical endurance training[12] such as hikes or camping reinforce the desire for a proper mental outlook and career orientation. Individual ambition, selfishness, or impatience are personal attributes which Seishen training attempts to avoid:

Of note here is the fact that the difficulties accompanying work tend to be regarded as tests of strong character. The strains of working in a hierarchical system, the tedious repetition of daily tasks, and the anxieties that accompany new work situations are all regarded as problems that try a person's spirit. Those who prove most capable of perserverance in the face of such difficulties and who show themselves dedicated over the long haul to their work are the ones judged (according to the Seishen perspective) to be most suited for future leadership. In other words, the very nature of the promotions system serves to preserve a concern with Seishen as a crucial framework of evaluation.

In this approach, the rationalist, quantitative orientation of U.S. style management training stands in contrast to the on the job, training philosophy of the Japanese corporate and government bureaucracy. Many of the concepts and

---

[12] The emphasis on physical endurance and development has been a constant theme in Japanese education since the Meiji reforms. Mari Arinori, the controversial Minister of Education from 1886 to 1889 when he was assassinated, travelled widely in the West, including to utopian Christian colonies in New York. The importance of physical development was to be able to put into practice sound knowledge. See Passin (1965).

techniques taught in the business school cirriculum are also included in Japanese company training courses, but these are considered quite secondary to a broad organizational philosophy and spirit. In all of this educational emphasis, there is an implicit meaning that one sector of the population is not included, namely women.

6.6 Elite Exclusion: Women in Japan

No where does the contrast between traditional and modern Japan focus so clearly as the role of women in a business-dominated country. Geishas, arranged marriages, dress-making, flower arranging, and tea ceremonies – such are the evocative words to illustrate the kinds of women's roles in traditional Japanese society. In contemporary Japan, there are few signs of basic shifts in regard to management. Although there are more women in the work force, pay is only marginally above fifty percent of males. There is the expression "education mama" (*Kyoiku* Mama) to refer to the powerful and dominant role of mothers in the family, and their doting ambition for young children and their studies. Many mothers even accompany their children to get their final high schools grades – the key to placement in the top ranked university. Despite changes, there is the male bias in the Japanese constitution which favours husbands rights over those of wives in the case of divorce. There are "love hotels" for couples even though oral contraceptive devices are illegal. Sex tours to Taiwan, Manila and Bangkok are openly advertised – for men. What does all this say about the role of Japanese women in business and the corporation? What are the patterns over the next decade?

Japan seems the ideal description of Douglas MacGregor's observations on management as a male preserve: "The model of the successful manager in our culture is a masculine one. The good manager is aggressive, competitive, firm and just. He is not feminine, he is not soft and yielding, or dependent or intuitive in the womanly sense."

As in most industrialized countries, recent trends have seen advances for Japanese women, and education has been the primary vehicle. A growing proportion of women, for instance, continue from lower secondary school to upper secondary school – over fifty percent compared to more than 80 percent for males. In 1976, thirteen percent of the female population attended university (41 percent for males) and another twenty percent attended Junior College (only 2.4 percent for males). In terms of the labour force, there are more than twenty million women in Japan working outside the home (about 46 percent of the total female population and thirty-seven percent of the total Japanese labour force). However, jobs for women are heavily weighted towards small and medium sized firms (70 percent) compared to large firms. In 1978 salaries were 57.4 percent of male wages, and the majority of women are employed in production and clerical jobs where mobility is limited, permanent employment benefits are minimal, and retirement is about ten years earlier than men. In other words, despite the strides made in education levels and labour force participation rates, women are in a much more inferior position relative to men in almost all job categories. Indeed, national surveys conducted since 1953 indicate that while the lot of females is improving, a surprising percentage of female respondents reveals that, if given the chance, they would prefer to be born a male: 64 percent in 1953, 43 percent in 1973. Data for the same question in the U.S. show that female preferences are only 17 percent in 1959, and 16 percent in 1970 (Exhibit 6/8).

Exhibit 6/8: Relative Preferences to be Born Male or Female

		Men		Women	
		Born Male	Born Female	Born Male	Born Female
Japan	1953	94	2	64	27
	1973	89	6	43	50
U.S.A.	1959	96	4	17	83
	1970	96	4	16	84

Source: Iwao (1976)

While these figures would tend to show Japanese women in a less than perfect position, surveys reveal a paradox in that women are generally more content than men with all aspects of life (both male and female respondents report being more satisfied than dissatisfied). In such specific areas as personal physical comfort, personal sense of well being, and interpersonal relations, for instance, women consistently report being more satisfied than men. How can this paradox be explained?

A common expression reflecting the status of women goes to the effect that the "two things in Japan which have become strong since the war are nylon stockings and women." There is also the expression *maihomushugi* (love of family life; literally "my-home-ism") to refer in the modern sense to a devotion to the nuclear family and an accepted division of labour between husband and wife.

If these sayings imply that Japanese women are now liberated, it was not always so. The roles of women as mother, wife, and citizen stem from a long history of codified norms covering the entire life cycle.[13] The traditional legal

---

[13] The feudalistic emphasis on the Japanese "house" in the continuation of family lineage means that "the whole family is placed under the control of the head of the house of paternal rights. It

code adopted by the Meiji government was unambiguous in many areas. Family status and lineage took precedence over affection and love. Marriages were arranged "by the family and for the family." The wife entered the husband's "family" and accordingly assumed the husband's family name. In the event of the husband's death, the inheritance went to direct lineal descendants, not to the wife. The strict code was equally reflected in the conformity to the three obediences, and seven grounds for divorce. The family obediences were clear: the unmarried girl must obey her father; the married woman must obey her husband, and the widow must obey her children. The grounds for divorce were similarly codified: disobedience to parents-in-law, failure to conceive, sexual indulgence, jealousy, serious disease, talkativeness, and diverting household money for personal use.

Such was the status of women in a patriarchial family structure in which the father was the revered head of the household and only male children could inherit land and pecuniary holdings. The mother was responsible for upbringing of the children, controlling household finances, and distributing food and clothing. Daughters were a welcome asset around the house but they were distinctly secondary to sons on the land. With the rise in industrialization and the growth of the textile industry in the late nineteenth century, there was a job outlet for young women who became of age at fifteen and in some areas, as young as thirteen. Almost two-thirds of the factory labourers were female and by 1930, this decreased to fifty-two-percent.

During the war children were moved to the countryside to avoid the heavy bombings in urban centers and girls and wives were recruited to munitions factories and thus broke the traditional view that women should remain at home. After 1945, the Occupation Forces introduced reforms to grant women suffrage, provide equal legal status to men in marriage, and to liberalize educational opportunities. The 1947 reforms allowed females to inherit family wealth, equalized the grounds for divorce for men and women, permitted women to marry without third party consent, and provided for the mother, in the event of the husband's death, to be head of the household. Other reforms included amendments to the labour laws reducing clear discrimination and exploitation of women in the workplace.

Workplace reforms involved health and safety protection on such issues as guidelines on harmful or unsafe jobs, compulsory work past midnight, restric-

is no wonder that in such a 'house' the freedom and development of its individual members, especially of the female sex, should be regarded as of only secondary importance, rarely being considered a matter of any account . . . Submission being considered the foremost feminine virtue, women in this country have long been deprived of the freedom of criticism in the name of obedience, gracefulness, or the women gentleness to hush up a matter . . . Resignation has offered a place of refuge to Japanese women, and in resignation have they found their only life – philosophy" (Hatusiko, 1948:9–13).

tions on underground mine work, provisions for maternity leave, and wage discrimination solely on the basis of sex. In addition, the government has introduced measures to assist women, such as a law specifying that a woman may not be dismissed during maternity leave or for thirty days after her return to work. A twice per day, half hour nursing allowance is also provided but few women take advantage of it since only a minority of companies provide good nursing facilities. Women in Japan are also allowed a monthly menstrual leave of two days, but in 1978, only 16 percent of the female labour force requested it (Cook and Hayashi, 1980).

Education rather than social class has had the biggest impact on changing women's values in the modern era. Because the majority of Japanese citizens were born after the war and the occupation inspired changes, many young people of both sexes have altered the traditional feudalistic sex stereotypes. More young women finish high school than men, and the rising percentage of female university graduates is approaching the level of men. Starting pay differentials between male and female workers favour men at all educational levels, although the gap has been narrowing. Two thirds of all women employed are married. Potentially these trends will be reflected in positions in industry and eventually the overall occupational structure. Yet any prediction of the future role of women in Japanese society, and more specifically, in senior management, must take account of various conflicting trends.[14]

The general demographics are quite clear. The female participation rate is below males at all age levels except 15–19. The age group 25–34 has the smallest proportion of women employed (Exhibit 6/9) except for the over 65 age group. Although many women return to work after 35, it is unlikely they would

Exhibit 6/9: Age and Labour Force Participation Rates (1976)

	Total Labour Force	Male Labour Force	Participation Rate (%)	(000's) Female Labour Force	Participation Rate (%)
15–19	1,510	770	19.2	740	19.2
20–24	6,160	3,290	74.9	2,870	66.4
25–34	14,320	9,870	97.2	4,450	44.2
35–44	13,080	8,250	97.6	4,830	57.4
45–54	10,550	6,340	96.8	4,210	60.0
55–59	3,220	1,900	91.8	1,320	50.0
60–64	2,450	1,560	80.3	890	37.4
Over 65	2,490	1,700	43.2	790	15.2
Total	53,780	33,680	81.1	20,100	45.8

Source: Labour Force Survey, Japan 1979

[14] For a related analysis, and an attempt to predict trends, see Kiefer (1976) and Pharr (1976).

Exhibit 6/10: Female Employees (Married or Single) by Occupation, Japan 1976

Occupation	No. of Workers	% of Female Workers	(000's) % of Total Labour Force
Professional & Technical	1,620	8.2	42.6
Managerial	120	0.6	5.6
Clerical	4,270	21.6	51.6
Sales	2,820	14.3	37.4
Farmers	3,140	15.9	49.5
Transportation & Communications	170	0.9	7.0
Crafts & Production	4,520	22.8	28.3
Labourers	580	2.9	38.4
Service Workers	2,520	12.8	55.1
Total	19,760	100.0	

Sources: Labour Force Survey, Prime Minister's Office, Japan 1976

return to the same job or even the same employer. Indeed a large percentage of such people get classified as part-time staff, and receive lower benefits. Production remains the major area of female employment, followed by clerical work (51.6%) and professional and technical (42.6%). The high percentage of women engaged in agriculture reflects the exodus of young men to the factories in cities and the consequent aging of the diminishing farm labour force (Exhibit 6/10).

In terms of current employment and education statistics, the data point to a moderate advance in salary and job content but within the confines of a partiarchial, male career hierarchy. Women are rarely in top positions, although the shift to a service economy has opened some doors for female entrepreneurship. Music, fashion and television are examples. Yet many remained closed, as female journalists discovered at the daily newspaper, *The Asahi Shibun,* where women numbered only one percent of the three thousand journalists. The same trend applies in government.

The basic patterns analyzed here suggest that women have roles in organizations consistent with traditional cultural and social norms of Japanese society. In fact, the evidence tends to be quite consistent with research data in other countries of Europe and North America. As Acker and Van Houten (1974) argue, sex differences in organizational participation are related to (1) differential recruitment of women into jobs requiring dependence and passivity, (2) selective recruitment of particularly compliant women into these jobs, and (3) control mechanisms used in organizations for women, which reinforce control mechanisms to which they are subjected in other areas of society.

The permanent employment system among the major corporations and public bureaucracies reinforces the male career hierarchy and the likelihood of male

Exhibit 6/11: Women in National Legislatures of Western Countries*

	House	No. of Legislators	No. of Women	Female Share (%)
Australia	Upper	64	6	9.4
	Lower	124	0	0
Britain	Upper	unfixed	55	1
	Lower	635	19	3.0
Canada	Upper	102	14	13.7
	Lower	282	12	4.3
France	Upper	295	4	1.4
	Lower	491	19	3.9
W. Germany	Upper	45	0	0
	Lower	496	36	7.3
Italy	Upper	315	11	3.5
	Lower	630	52	8.3
Sweden		349	80	22.9
US	Upper	100	1	1.0
	Lower	435	16	3.7
Japan	National Diet	743	22	3.0
	Judges	2731	72	2.6
	Public Prosecutors	2125	24	1.1

Source: Prime Ministers Office, Special Unit on Women's Affairs, August, 1979

leadership roles for years to come. Female participation in influential political positions has not yet occurred, so there is no obvious impetus for major structural change. Nor is there much opportunity for female monopoly of particular professional occupations which offer an outlet for widespread participation on an equal level. Even in government, where there might be some voting pressure for change, women have very low participation rates in Japan, although the same situation seems to apply to most western countries (Exhibit 6/11).

"In the beginning," says a Japanese expression in the women's movement, "There was the sun, and the sun was a woman." What does this say about the future, and the impact on corporate management? The women's movement is not strong in Japan, less so than in the U.S. or Europe, as comparative wage levels tend to confirm (Exhibit 6/12). Curiously, in some aspects multilateral codes such as those developed in International Women's Year, may have more influence on government than domestic political pressure – for example, in citizenship rights of female Japanese married to foreigners. In many respects, the centuries of codified norms and the traditional roles of men and women make serious change unlikely, even with advances in education and kinship

Exhibit 6/12: Comparative Hourly Wage Differentials by Sex (Males = 100)

	Japan	US	France	W. Germany	Britain	Australia	Denmark	Switzerland
		(1974)						
1975	55.8	60.8	86.3	72.2	67.9	91.9	83.0	66.7
1976	56.1	–	86.4	72.4	71.4	93.4	83.7	66.3
1977	55.8	–	86.4	72.9	–	94.1	84.4	66.2

Source: Ministry of Labour (1979)

households. The well developed channels of in-company training reinforce the male preserve for elite positions.

6.7 Summary and Conclusions

The rapid and extensive growth of mass education in education has major technological and social implications for the economy. Seen primarily from the perspective of the corporate sector, the rapid increase in the supply of a well educated, highly literate and well disciplined workforce puts the incoming Japanese labour force in a highly advantageous position vis-a-vis foreign competitors. The high priority put on general education for the population, high levels of on-the-job training for workers, and in-house executive training for managers are a natural development of linking software organizational systems to hardware technology and innovation.

Better educated workers easily fit into the Japanese corporation where the relationship between individual and job is not clearly defined as in the West. New recruits can be easily shifted from one task to the next on a regular basis, a process called *teiki ido* (regular shifting). Familiarity with many different tasks and responsibilities increases the flexibility of work allocation when technology is changing, and serves to enhance individual socialization into the firm's corporate philosophy. This emphasis on continuous training enhances the Japanese strategy of knowledge intensification of the key industrial sectors, especially in electronics, pharmaceuticals, computers, and biotechnology. Already the number of researchers in Japan has reached equivalent levels with the U.S.

The benefits to the corporate sector are not all positive, however. Increased enrollments in universities, plus declining numbers of young people, have reduced the supply of high school graduates and greatly exacerbated the shortage of skilled blue collar workers. Locked into a relatively static permanent employment system, large corporations have less room for university graduates at lower career ladders – as recently as 1977, only one in six graduates went to the biggest companies. These demographic trends have led to significant problems and challenges. In the big companies, university graduates are being pushed into new jobs such as sales hitherto reserved for less educated personnel. Smaller firms are hiring more university graduates from the better schools, thus reducing the pay differentials between big and smaller firms for some types of jobs.

The trend to mass university education and a transformation of the age structure have a massive impact on many aspects of Japanese management, as subsequent chapters will analyze. The shortage of high school graduates, for instance, at a time when the overwhelming percentage of Japanese who reach retirement age are manual workers, implies that the corporation is caught in a form of demographic sandwich. At the recruitment end and the retirement end, the labour supply is drying up. In the middle is a growing pool of young educated workers with higher expectations and salaries facing lower promotion prospects for supervisory and managerial positions.

The problems of the education market and their impact on internal human resource management should, however, be kept in perspective. Japan is far ahead of many industrial competitors in the level of educational quality and quantity of human skills, and the economy is rapidly moving out of many industrial sectors dominated by blue collar workers. As Japanese industry intensifies its growth in high technology areas, and shifts production to offshore markets, the need for highly educated Japanese expatriates will greatly increase. Moreover, better housing and social conditions will be a positive incentive for many young Japanese to take up this challenge, particularly when so many middle-aged Japanese have very weak foreign language skills. An additional consideration is that, for all the increases in productivity and success in export performance, there are many areas where Japanese still trail foreign competitors: numbers of young people becoming entrepreneurs, application of microelectronics to the office and white collar work, number of holidays and reduction of the work week, and modernization of the service and distribution sector.

The changes in the education system thus bring mixed blessings. In one area, the role of women, the trends point to more of the same in the key areas. As in other countries, Japanese women will be concentrated in the low paying job sectors, with a major pay differential between men and women. The rising percentage of university-educated females entering the labour force, together with the generally higher rates of female participation rates, will tend to push up the percentage of dual career, two income families in Japan and further reduce the traditional three generation core family. These trends have major consumer marketing implications but, for management recruitment, the traditional male preserve will likely stay intact.

The difference in Japan is twofold, despite the broad economic and demographic parallels with Europe and North America. Aside from the strong impact of Confucian values among males in regard to the role of women, Japanese females face two particular barriers to top management roles. First, Japanese women can't use graduate school and professional training as an easy credential for career advancement as in the U.S., for instance (where about one in four M.B.A.'s, or C.A.'s or M.D.'s are women). Second, there are almost no important allies in senior echelons of the business world or the government to instigate major reforms which will change the traditional recruitment patterns in the corporation. Indeed, the pressures on the corporations owing from the changing age structure could even reduce opportunities for women in most sectors. Japanese traditions continue to exist in a path of modernization.

Chapter 7
Management Strategy and Organization

"The dominant culture in most big companies demands punishment for a mistake, no matter how useful, small, invisible."

Thomas J. Peters and Robert H. Waterman, Jr., In Search of Excellence

7.1 Introduction

It is a popular cliche in texts on organizations to speak of modern society as the "organizational society". As Presthus (1978) notes, "contemporary organizations have a pervasive influence upon individual and group behaviors, expressed through a web of rewards, sanctions, and other inducements that range from patent coercion to the subtle of group appeals to conformity. Indeed, bureaucratic organizations often seem less concerned with the self-realization of their members than with the relevance of such individuals for organizational goals of size, power, and survival."

No where is the foreign perception of the organizational power of big business stronger than in Japan. Whether the perception derives from the pre-war Zaibatsu families, or journalistic cover stories on Mitsui, Sumitomo and Mitsubishi, there is a pervasive view that Japanese industry is one large extended corporate bureaucracy. It is thus an extreme irony that much recent research on Japanese mangement strategy and organization singles out the paradoxes of Western and oriental differences. Japanese management downplays merit as a basis for promotion and wages as a basis of incentives. Western managers emphasize both, and resort to individual mobility, legal contracts, and detailed directives. The administrative structure of Western industrial corporation is derived from the military (including such terminology as strategy and tactics, divisions and business units, logistics and compaigns). The corporate model in Japan is the village, the dominant values are consensus and harmony and the practices are permanent employment, consultative decision-making, and parental guidance *(Sempai/Kohai)* of newly recruited employees.

The permanent employment feature of large corporations is generally viewed as the predominant characteristic of Japanese organizational form. Analysis of this form of organization, viewed from Western perspectives, often leads to a unique cultural interpretation, based on Japanese values such as groupism, harmony, consensus and the like. Unfortunately, this kind of approach views the Japanese form of organization from the vantage of a narrow paradigm or theory. This traditional view is one based on a centralized technocratic bureaucracy. This form of organization has a particular internal logic, regardless of variations by size, industry, or machine technology. Authors vary in their choice of terminology – mechanistic structure, closed system, theory X, rational organization, single loop models of decision-making.

Trist (1980) describes the traditional organization in these terms:

Traditional organizations follow the technological imperative which regards man simply as an extension of the machine and therefore as an expendable spare part . . . Traditional organizations are also characterized by maximum work breakdown, which leads to circumscribed job descriptions and single skills – the narrower the better. Workers in such roles are often unable to manage the uncertainty, or variance, that characterizes their immediate environment. They therefore require strict external controls. Layer upon layer of supervision comes into existence supported by a wise variety of specialist staffs and formal procedures. A tall pyramidic organization results, which is autocratically managed throughout, even if the paternalism is benign . . .

In the traditional organization each member has first of all to compete with and defend himself against everyone else, whether as an individual or as a member of a functional group – maintenance versus production, staff versus line. Rewards such as promotion and privilege go to those who, in the metaphor introduced by Michael Maccoby (1976), are "gamesmen" – those who excel in playing the political game of organization. Cooperation, though formally required wherever tasks are interdependent, take second place as a value.

As shown in Exhibit 7/1, the traditional paradigm and the new form or organization represents different structures to meet the demands of technology and

Exhibit 7/1: Features of Old and New Paradigms

Old Paradigm	New Paradigm
The technological imperative	Joint optimization
People as extensions of machines	People as complementary to machines
People as expendable spare parts	People as a resource to be developed
Maximum task breakdown, simple narrow skills	Optimum task grouping, multiple broad skills
External controls (supervisors, specialist staffs, procedures)	Internal controls (self-regulating subsystems)
Tall organization chart, autocratic style	Flat organization chart, participative style
Competition, gamesmanship	Collaboration, collegiality
Organization's purposes only	Members' and society's purposes also
Alienation	Commitment
Low risk-taking	Innovation

Source: E. Trist (1981)

industrialization. The traditional form exhibits a response to standardized technology and stable environments, where work is guided by the machine as the major resource, not people. The new paradigm is a response to rapid change, highly skilled workers, new technology and environmental turbulence, such as global competition.

The modern approach to organization represents an ideal blending of human values, organizational learning, and continuous adaptation. Software management systems are critical both for senior echelon personnel and for workers. Software technologies consists of the types of managerial styles and institutional arrangements to organize work. Familiar examples of important software technologies include decision-making modes, employment practices, orientations to time and learning, and organization design. Western interest in Japanese style decision-making – *Ringi* – and in shopfloor use of quality control circles – must be seen as a rational response to the newer paradigm of work and organization. In other countries, the labels differ – industrial democracy, quality of work life, socio-technical system, worker councils – but they all form a broad pattern of new work values and software systems heralding post industrial society.[1] The real essence of software management technology is the system of personal relationships, values and social interactions in the organization. As it turns out, Japanese societal values of consensus and cooperation, discipline and learning, equality and curiosity reinforce and encourage the adoption of the new paradigm. Further, as outlined in other chapters, Japan's historic emphasis on production technology and the principles of scientific management have resulted in an ideal integration of rational work methods humanized and blended with software employment practices.

The Japanese approach to organization, typically studied in the context of unique cultural values, should be viewed in this broader picture of post-industrial society. Industrial and technological planning at the society level have placed enormous demands for high value added, high growth products and services. These demands have been met by strategically adaptive organizational structures, and by mobilizing the skills of the most educated and continuously trained workers in the industrial world. The irony thus is well stated in the U.S. Senate study on U.S. – Japan trade relations (p. 168):

In its ideology the United States, with much higher levels of capital accumulation than Japan, has placed and continues to place primary emphasis on capital. In Japan, there is the saying "The company is the worker"; in the United States, one could paraphrase and say, "The company is the shareholder". And to carry the anomaly one step further, it is in hierarchical Japan that there is greater egalitarianism in the work place than in egalitarian United States.

---

[1] For a comprehensive review, see Adams (1982) and Dunlop and Galanson (1982).

This chapter focuses on management strategy and organization in three areas: the evolving strategy and structure of corporate organization, the impact of structure on organizational processes, and contrasts and similarities with Western style organization.

The framework for analyzing the model of Japanese management and organization is given in Exhibit 7/2. There are two broad features of this model, namely the emphasis on an articulated management philosophy, and corporate culture and an internal labour market. Management philosophy, the focus of this chapter, refers to the articulated goals and objectives of the organization within a framework of societal and employee needs. Organizational culture is "a pattern of beliefs and expectations shared by members of an organization. These beliefs and expectations produce rules for behaviour – norms – that powerfully shape the behaviour of individuals and groups in the organization" (Schwartz and Davis, 1981).[2] In the Japanese company, management philosophy and corporate culture typically translate into an emphasis on team work and clan socialization, where the norms of harmony *(Wa)* and community

Exhibit 7/2: A Model Japanese Management and Organization

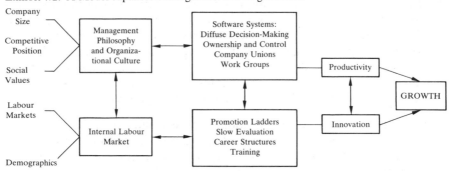

(Kaisha) proedominate. As Nakane (1973) notes, "in most cases the company provides the whole social existence of a person, and has authority over all aspects of his life; he is deeply emotionally involved in the association." The internal labour market characteristic of larger Japanese organizations is treated in the next chapter.

---

[2] The concept of corporate culture is hardly novel, but its impact on strategy, productivity and organizational change has only recently been recognized. See Baker (1980), Swartz and Davis (1981), Pettigrew (1981).

7.2 Strategy and Structure in Context

Modern industrial societies exhibit many common features everywhere, and no where is this more apparent than in the case of corporate organization. What is striking is how so many people accept that all organizations everywhere are basically identical. Preston (1975:437) makes the point as follows: "The general point that managerial organizations of all types are fundamentally similar with respect both to internal features and to environmental relationships is now commonplace in management literature." Another perspective is to see national culture as a major influence on organizational form.

In his analysis of U.S. investment in Europe, Servan-Schreiber (1967) singled out American management's strength as one of "organization."

This is the problem, and it cannot be phrased only in economic terms. It involves our capacity for organization: The ability to work under different conditions to take advantage of an enormous market, to know how to make a profit from it and adopt to its needs. Europe's lag seems to concern *Methods of Organization* above all.

Despite this view, U.S. industry has consistently lost ground to foreign competition not only in Europe and in Japan but in the home U.S. market. The rhetorical question posed by Lester Thurow (1981) is relevant:

Not so long ago General Motors was commonly referred to as the "best-managed firm in America." Why couldn't the best managed firm in America see the Japanese challenge coming and defeat it? *Fortune* Magazine's current candidate for the best managed firm in America, General Electric, has essentially become a marketer of foreign products in its consumer electronics division. Why can't the best managed firm in America compete with American-made products?

Are Japanese organizations that different in the basic structural features from their North American or European counterparts? Are the basic influences shaping structure, such as technology, economies of scale, and markets any different in Japan than elsewhere?

In recent years, these questions have been high on the business school research agenda. The basic pattern seems clear: there are few major differences in the design features of organizations, that is, in the way organizations are structured along product or market lines, or the broad separation of strategic and operating decisions and the like. But that is not the whole story, for societal values have an influence on individual behaviour.

But first, what of the similarities? Alfred Chandler (1962), the American business historian has outlined the growth strategies of U.S. industrial firms:

Growth came either from an expansion of the firm's existing lines to much the same type of customers, or it resulted from a quest for new markets and sources of supplies in distant lands, or finally it came from the opening of new markets by developing a wide range of new products for different types of customers.

Historically, business firms displayed a clear, top down structure organized around functions – e.g., finance, personnel, production, sales, etc. However, as firms changed their product market strategies from single products serving single markets to more complex strategies, i.e. geographic expansion and product diversification, new administrative problems arose. Many firms tried to maintain their existing structures, i.e., the functional form, others compromised the central control inherent in that form for the looser holding company structure of semi-autonomous divisions. Yet the more complex strategies placed great pressure on top management for coordination among products and markets, and for budget allocation across the organization. The pressure resulted in the adoption of a new form, the divisional structure.

Thus the new structure left the broad strategic decisions as to allocation of existing resources to different divisions and the acquisition of new ones in the hands of a top team of generalists. Relieved of operating duties and tactical decisions, a general executive was less likely to reflect the position of just one part of the whole – functional area – even though old ties and attitudes were often hard to break . . . At the same time, the new structure eased the problems of coordination and appraisal. Coordinating product flow and determining costs in relation to volume as well as adapting design or make up to changing demands were all left to the multifunction divisions . . . In this way, the new structure left the divisional executives to run the business, while the general office set the goals and policies and provided overall approval . . . Besides allocating decision-making more efficiently and assuring more precise communication and control, the new structure proved to have another advantage over the functionally departmentalized organization. It provided a place to train and test general executives.

The essence of Chandler's (1962) analysis, and numerous theoretical and empirical studies (Thompson, 1967; Williamson, 1976; Scott, 1973) point to the basic managerial strategies required to operate with functional, divisional, and multidivisional systems. The functional structure is most suited to stable unchanging environments and, like bureaucracy, is guided by norms of efficiency. In more unstable environments, with changing technologies and growing markets, the divisional structure is more adaptive, since decisions can be taken at a more decentralized level. The most flexible organization is the multidivisional or matrix structure, which has features of both horizontal and vertical communications to aid managerial decision making.

For the U.S., the first organizational changes took place at the turn of the twentieth century – in the railroads, the telegraph, and mass merchandising. By the time of the Second World War, the multidivisional form had become the dominant kind of economic organization, spreading from such firms as General Motors, Standard Oil and Sears Roebuck to most American corporations at home and abroad.[3]

---

[3] The classical study was Alfred Chandler's (1966) *Strategy and Structure*.

Exhibit 7/3: Structural Change in Japanese and British Companies

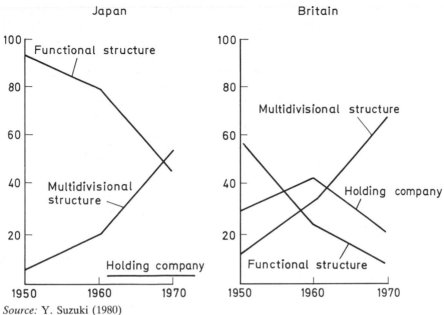

Source: Y. Suzuki (1980)

Indeed, it was the presence of successful U.S. multinationals, largely organized around the multidivisional structure, that helped spread this form in Britain, France, Sweden, and West Germany.[4] There was also the influence of U.S. consulting firms such as McKinsey. Not only were the basic managerial techniques associated with the multidivisional structure increasingly common – especially the emphasis on financial budgeting and computer controls – the source of recruitment for many European subsidiaries and domestic firms were U.S. business school graduates. While this latter trend had less influence in Japan, the broad trend was to multidivisional organizational structures.[5]

As shown in Exhibit 7/3, 56 of the top 100 Japanese firms had adopted the divisional structure, compared to 78 per cent in the U.S., 72 per cent in Britain, 50 in Germany, and 54 per cent in France. Various theories have been advanced as to the differences in time spans between the early adoption of the multidivisional form in the U.S. and the rather late diffusion of this form to Europe and Japan. Franko (1974), for example, argues that it was the capacity of European firms to negotiate cartels, receive government support, and main-

---

[4] For a theoretical analysis and review, see Horvath and McMillan (1978).
[5] For important historical accounts, see Nakagawa (1976).

tain tariffs and other forms of anti-competitive behaviour which allowed them to survive with more traditional organizational forms. Unlike the large, relatively open U.S. market, with a history of anti-trust and free trade, continental Europe (and Canada) had a developed set of trade barriers, at least until the formation of the European Economic Community through the Treaty of Rome. Similarly, in Japan, until the dismemberment of the large Zaibatsu and fostering of competition among the business groups during the post-war American occupation, the competitive environment did not require the more developed multidivisional structures. Like their European counterparts, the Japanese firms were introduced to U.S. organizational principles by the many technical agreements with American firms and a minority of firms adopted a divisional form of structure. For example, in electronics, Toshiba was related to General Electric, Mitsubishi to Westinghouse, Nippon Electric to Western Electric, and Fuji Electric to Siemens. In terms of dates, Toshiba, employed the word division as early as 1931, and Matsushita introduced a multidivisional structure as early as 1933 (Suzuki, 1981).

However, the pioneer for developing an indigenous multidivisional form in Japan was Mitsubishi, long before it became a *Konzern* or *Zaibatsu*. In 1895, the Mitsubishi enterprises were reorganized with the addition of banking to its other business lines of shipbuilding, trading, mining and real estate. Under the leadership of Heigoro Shoda, who acted as *Kanji* or general manager, Mitsubishi evolved by 1908 to organize the mining, banking, and shipbuilding divisions as independent profit centers. Each was allowed independent investment autonomy to the limit of allocated capital, and lines of communications between each operating unit and central office was prohibited. In this way, the basic elements of the federated, divisional structure pioneered in the U.S. by Alfred Sloan at General Motors were taking shape in parallel lines in Japan at Mitsubishi (Marikawa, 1975).

Did the development of similar architectural features of the largest industrial firms in Europe, the U.S., and Japan imply similar management strategies and decision styles? On the surface, the answer is yes, since there were many common procedures common across cultures. In practice, however, the organizational processes within the multidivisional structures operate quite differently.

Organizational Processes

The common strategic requirements of the multidivisionalized structure among all Western countries tend to downplay the role of culture in the design of organizations. In Japan as in Europe, certain U.S. principles have had a major impact, yet differences remain. Obviously, language, tradition, and interpersonal relationships have a bearing, but one should be cautious about over generalizations. There are as many variations within most countries as there are among them (Hickson and McMillan, 1980).

Academic research on these issues show that it is not the macro organizational features, that is the general administrative structure for managing the planning and operating functions, where national culture will predominate. It is at the micro level, the type of individual attitudes, norms, and interpersonal relationships, where cultural variables impact on behaviour. For individuals and groups, this means that societal values and norms, and the patterns of socialization from parents, the family, schooling, and friends are most pronounced and reflect cultural traditions. Language, food and eating, even religion and rural/urban experiences, reinforce these norms for the individual.

In Europe, studies of the adoption of multidivisional structures in France and Germany show pronounced differences in the style of organizational behaviour when compared to American practice.[6] In Germany, for example, two factors stood out in major firms, collegial vs. individual management responsibility and the type of reward systems. More specifically, the use in Germany of an executive board or *Vorstand,* consisting of between three and fifteen members, meant that divisional managers would not report to a single general manager, as in U.S. firms, but to the Vorstand. It operated effectively because different functional managers were represented on the same board, even if there was a dominance of production and R & D, compared to finance or marketing. These collegial management practices meant different reporting relationships and control features (Dyas and Thanheiser, 1976).

Another difference in Germany, and one found also in France, was the type of reward systems. In the American firm, it is common practice to link divisional performance to divisional management's compensation.[7] Culturally, this style is a reflection of American cultural values with the emphasis on the individual and focused responsibility. In management terms, this value is indicated in the system of management by objectives, providing a basis to integrate goal setting, motivation, and individual performance. Yet Europeans dislike the system. As one study found,

In Germany, monetary incentives to division managements on this basis were extremely rare, and were even considered undesirable by the managers interviewed. They generally felt that such direct incentives were not only unnecessary, but might actually do harm. If a significant portion of a division manager's income depended on his division's profit, it was argued, his anxiety would interfere with the objectivity of his business judgement, plan discussions between divisions and headquarters would become negotiations, and corporate interests might come into sharp conflict with divisional interests (Dyas and Thanheiser 1976).

---

[6] Dyas and Thanheiser (1976).
[7] A typical approach is given in Salter (1973).

In France, similar features exist, namely, the absence of variable financial rewards for executives based on divisional results, the fear of the negative effects on perceived inequity on organizational climate, and the view that variable rewards encourage shorter horizons for managerial decision-making.

The foregoing emphasis on European practice with the multi-divisional structure, which is largely a U.S. organizational innovation, serves to underscore that Japanese organizational behaviour, while different from U.S. practice in many respects, is not necessarily unique. Indeed, in many aspects, it may be the case that U.S. managerial practice as presently performed is the odd man out among Western countries, with the possible exception of Britain. Certainly in terms of performance of many key industries – steel, automobiles, consumer electronics, watches, and shipbuilding – there is nothing inherently successful in U.S. management style.

What then can be said of Japanese practice? First, there are obvious parallels with European practice in the rejection of U.S. style executive compensation. Although the bonus system to employees is widespread, being paid twice annually, it does not exist for management. In fact, the structure of rewards is clearly biased in favour of the long term. Because managers are tied to a long term, lifetime career structure, with a fairly clear wage level based on seniority and experience, middle managers can focus on sales growth, market shares, and productivity. In Japan, of course, there is not the pressure of the stock exchange to maximize earnings per share, as in the U.S. The result is that Japanese managers can afford to emphasize long range planning. Internally, their wages aren't linked to short term divisional performance, where sales objectives, for example, might otherwise take precedence over quality or technical proficiency.

However, the long term horizon of Japanese managers stems more concretely from the Japanese view of organizations as situational entities of shared values. Principles in the Western sense have much less emphasis or value than shared emotional bonds usually associated with the family. In the U.S., the principles of market exchange and impersonal, financial values are widely accepted. Organizational commitment of workers is primarily an economic contract between the individual and the organization, although elements of a social contract exist (Schein, 1970).

Theoretically, the emotional bonds of Japanese organizations, commonly linked to Japanese village life or family structures, are not limited to industrial firms or even government bureaucracies. Sport teams, religious orders, tribes, political groups, professions, interest groups, clans and voluntary organizations are cases in point. However, as Ouchi (1979:136) has argued, such organizational forms typically display high levels of cohesion, a high degree of discipline, and social mechanisms to assure the reduction of differences between individual and collective goals. For business firms, these organizations are typically in technologically advanced or closely integrated industries, where teamwork is common, technologies change often, and therefore individual performance is highly ambiguous.

These issues notwithstanding, there are important structural factors which reinforce the sense of community and shared values favouring long term strategies. It is not simply a matter of management philosophy, or a Theory Z model (Ouchi, 1980) which produces this result. The structures and constraints faced by Japanese management must be recognized in context. The two main issues are the role of stockholders and the enterprise union.

Ownership and Management Control

The high debt equity ratios characteristic of Japanese corporations is one of the most common indicators of the special role of Japanese banks in the industrial system. Whereas the debt-equity ratio in Japan is in the order of 80–20, in the U.S. the ratio is more like 40–60 or 50–50. Of the total financing of Japanese corporations, the overwhelming proportion is of bank borrowing rather than bonds.

As a result of the post war dissolution of the *Zaibatsu* family holding companies, the identification between stockholders and the corporation has been lessened. As a result, "stockholders essentially are subordinated creditors from whom the enterprise, an entity responsible only to itself, in effect borrows equity capital" (Wallich and Wallich, 1976). Unlike the U.S., where the U.S. Securities and Exchange Commission requires quarterly reporting of corporate earnings, there are substantially less pressures for short term results. As a consequence, real authority rests with the board of directors, which effectively replaces stockholder meetings as the vehicle to replace old and to nominate new directors and auditors.

Unlike in Britain and the U.S. for instance, outside directors in Japanese companies are rare. The system of appointing directors who hold executive positions in the company has parallels with the German system (Japan's Commercial Law, passed originally in 1896 and revised during the U.S. occupation, was based on German practice).

Directors in Japanese companies do not form a single decision making body based on one man, one vote. The most senior positions in the company hold directors positions, such as vice-presidents *(Fuku Shocho)*, executive managing directors *(Sennu)* and managing directors *(Joma)*. However, lower level directors, such as heads of divisions and heads of functional departments like accounting, marketing, or manufacturing, extend the link between senior and middle management in a more direct way, despite the differential status among them. Notwithstanding the importance of the company president who appoints and removes these directors, the system of directors adds greatly to the sense of collective responsibility for executive decision-making. The *Jomukai,* or managing directors board, is the real locus of power in the organization. The composition of this group greatly influences the overall decision-making system in ways not usually understood in Western countries.

The *Jomukai* cabinet style board of directors has various implications. For one thing, the decision emphasis is heavily operational, that is on current problems rather than long term strategic planning. This does not mean that Japanese corporations don't do strategic planning. In fact, partly as a result of copying planning techniques from Western companies, Japanese managers have introduced more complex planning technologies, including computer forecasts, long range (5–10 years) strategic plans, and planning departments. However, the emphasis is clearly on the short term – six months to a year. Middle management and divisional heads have the responsibility for outlining planning projections, and the typical short term plan covers all aspects of organizational performance. While the two year or five year plans provide an overall framework for strategy, they receive far less emphasis from top management. As Hayashi (1978:222) notes, "the primary purpose of corporate planning as viewed by some firms was not to formulate strategic programs and to implement them, but a) to set up targets of endeavour and to draw the future portrait of the company, b) to unify managerial thoughts within the organization, and c) to create an achievement orientation and motivational effect in the organization." On the surface, this points to a paradox. Where U.S. director positions are usually filled by outsiders often experienced in long range planning, American corporation are criticized for short term horizons. Where Japanese directors have little training in strategic management and hold executive positions on internal boards, the efficiency emphasis is short term but performance goals long term. A major reason for this situation is the fact that directors in Japanese corporations typically hold line responsibilities. Given the collective norms and pressures in the Japanese economy generally, the dominant group on most company boards are production oriented. By way of example, Dore (1973) found that in his comparative study of Hitachi and Britain's English Electric, fourteen of Hitachi's twenty directors were engineers. The others were educated in law and commerce. At English Electric, ten of the sixteen held internal executive positions and six were external – a scientist, an ex diplomat, bankers and chairmen of other companies. In all only six were chartered engineers and one a scientist. Unlike Hitachi, the personnel director was not a member of the board.

The strong production emphasis in Japanese companies influences decision-making in other ways. The vertical structure of directors means that staff roles are not separated as in the West, but operate either as fairly low level administrative personnel, or as appendages to committee structures crossing departmental lines. This, for example, is one of the reasons why engineers in Japan are better integrated into manufacturing operations than in many Western countries (Cole, 1979; McMillan 1982). By integrating staff and advisory personnel into line departments, Japanese management unwittingly emphasizes a more comprehensive and thorough analysis of operational decisions. In this way Japanese companies rarely focus on a large strategic decision as a separate agenda item. Strategic decision-making in the Japanese firm is very much a continuous stream of operational decisions.

7.3 The Enterprise Union

The diffuse character of decision-making and communications in Japanese organizations stems from the managerial structure which emphasizes persuasion more than direction, implementation more than strategy formulation. Another factor which reinforces this pattern in Japan is the enterprise union. Like many institutions, the enterprise union owes its current form to the American occupation. As a result there are some parallels with the U.S. trade union philosophy, as compared to the European.

In the U.S., the major building block of the trade union movement is the plant local of an industrial union. It follows that there may be several locals, depending on the size of the company. The same unions organize workers across the industry to assure minimal wage standards and work conditions by all plants in the same competitive sector. The steel workers' union thus represents employees in the iron and steel sector (even for Canadian plants which compete against U.S. firms), the auto workers in cars, meatpackers in meat plants, and so on. The focus is on the industry as a whole; the issues are traditionally bread and butter ones of pay, work conditions, safety and security.

Japan's enterprise unions have certain parallels. The building block is the enterprise local or branch union. In small firms with one plant, there will be one local; in large firms, the locals combine to form a company-wide body. Compared to European labour philosophy, with the emphasis on government initiatives for workers, Japanese unions are primarily concerned with lifetime employment security. Wage increases are determined much more as a function of enterprise productivity and national wage norms.

The enterprise union influences management and decisionmaking within the company in several ways. Because the unions are company wide, rather than industry wide as in the U.S. or occupation wide as in British craft unions, management's approach to unions is more cooperative than adverserial. When unionization grew very rapidly after the war, management-union relations were marked by strife and conflict. However, unlike management in many

Western companies, management in many Japanese companies came from union ranks. Membership in the union local is open to all permanent employees, white collar and blue collar employees alike. Since management positions above the rank of section chief and higher are exluded, it follows that most managers in the hierarchy rising above section chief at about age forty and reaching the position of director, moved through union ranks, and possibly participated as an official in the union. In such circumstances, the bitterness and anti-unionism found in Western countries is substantially lower. The more prevalent Japanese norm is 'wa' or harmony.

Another implication of the enterprise union is the dynamic convergence of management-worker interests as a result of interfirm wage differentials. The lack of common occupational wage rates across the whole economy means that wages for different job groupings depend on each firm. The more successful the firm, the higher the wages of employees at all levels. Since mobility across firms is minimal as a result of permanent employment, enterprise unionism increases the conformity of employees both to the union and to the company. Among larger firms, this process is especially strong, because larger firms are not only more productive and pay higher wages, they tend to recruit the best students from the universities and thereby raise the stock of human capital and talents of the work force. The result is better personnel policies. As stated by Sakurabashi (1969).

". . . The effect of enterprise unions upon their firms, as compared to conditions in a non-union situation, is not so much that of the so-called 'economy of high wages' or the 'shock effect of high wages' as it is of improvements in personnel administration, such as more careful policies of recruitment and transfer, more thoughtful systemization of personnel administration itself and a concomitant increase in professionalization of the personnel department, and more explicit attention being given by top management to personnel policies in general."

Sakurabashi's (1969) comments are born out by some empirical research on the personnel function. Azumi and McMillan (1975) compared specialist functions and their importance in British and Japanese companies. In Japanese firms, of all the major specialist functions, production and personnel ranked highest,[8] as compared to accounting and finance in British firms. The same result on British firms were found in Jamieson's (1980) comparison of U.S. – Britain organizational differences: "American firms are likely to regard personnel as a more important function than the British firms. Their personnel departments were bigger, they spent more money and effort upon recruitment, and they organized the careers of the managerial recruits in a broader and more systematic way than the British companies."

---

[8] Cole's (1979) research showed that firms like Toyota had personnel policies for production workers that U.S. companies hadn't developed even for managers.

7.4 Software Management Systems

The firm as village or family metaphor is now widespread in Western literature on Japan. Theories and concepts have sprung up to elaborate this community relationship in Japanese organizations. *Theory Z* and *The Art of Japanese Management* are two popular tracts to underscore a comment too infrequently recognized, namely the importance of software systems of management, such as staffing, management style, and competitive skills. In this view, Japanese management comes much closer to organizational systems based on behavioural science principles than Western firms.

To understand the application of Japanese practices, one must recognize the nature of the internalized labour market. Because workers are hired for a career and not for a job, the employment relationship involves many dimensions, social as well as economic. Both managers and workers recognize this, and both groups fully recognize the consequences of the relationship, especially the issue of job security. For managers, this point means that in return for considerable flexibility on job allocation, manning by subcontractors, and technological change, managers commit themselves to worker security and life time organizational careers. Despite resentment from time to time over specific issues – holiday pay, excessive work or bonuses, there is more legitimacy of workers in a Weberian sense held by managers than in most countries, even in organizations which are professionally managed. For one thing the symbols of management status common in Britain and North America which indicate status differences – private toilets, separate parking, three piece suits, and private dining – are downplayed in Japan except for very senior management. Further the pay differentials between white collar and blue collar workers are probably the lowest of all industrialized countries. Equally important, organizational status differences are generally acknowledged, but they are perceived as stemming from educational levels and qualifications, which themselves are recognized as acquired in a fair and meritocratic way.

What these factors add up to is that the typical Japanese industrial organization is administered much less on the basis of formal authority rankings, as defined by role and position, and more by consensus and expertise. Despite the status differences between the lordly samurai and lowly peasant were ot that great, as ethos among organizational members. During the last war, this egalitarianism was said to be nurtured by the "equality of suffering" experienced during the period of bombing, food shortages, and fires. Historically, however, the status differences between the lordly samuri and lowly peasant were not that great, as Chie Nakane (1973) points out: "A man living in a society with this organizational basis and cultural background believes in basic equality and communal rights; while he is conscious of delicately graded rankings among his fellows, he will not recognize over stratification in his world."

During the post war period, most Japanese companies pursued manpower policies and administrative practices largely consistent with the precepts of scientific management. More specifically, Japanese factories combined an element of piece rate incentives to the overall compensation scheme which was heavily weighted by seniority and job classification. In most factories, however, the piece rate system was based on group output, not the individual rate, and thereby mobilized the norms and expectations of the group. Since a vast preponderance of workers hired in the post war period were recruited directly from rural areas in the regions where the factories were located, the scientific management theories of time and motion studies, group incentives and annual bonuses were extensively applied.

In this context, why does the modern Japanese factory seem to be the prototype of modern human relations practice when historically, scientific management took such a strong root. Cole (1979) notes the paradox that Japanese management followed through on some of the logical implications of Western theories of human relations and worker motivation in advance of Western firms: "One way to understand this puzzle is that the American engineering and managerial professions became locked into the earlier "solution" for raising worker productivity associated with scientific management, while the Japanese version of scientific management always allowed for more behaviouralistic approaches involving attempts to increase worker motivation" (p. 132).

One of the most highlighted aspects of Japanese software management is the decision-making process. The broad approach is referred to as *Nemawashi, or opinion seeking* at all levels.

Nemawashi literally means "root trimming." When a tree is transplanted, there must be preparations in the form of trimming the roots, wrapping the soil, and binding the branches. These steps improve the transition to new soil and provide the basis for future growth. In the same way, when new policies on strategies are introduced, the proper groundwork must be carried out. Surprise, poor spade work, or open conflict have to be avoided. *Nemawashi* is the practice of testing the climate of opinion, checking the broader implications, learning the potential grounds for conflict. Loss of face, hostility, or suspicion of distrust are the diplomatic shoals to get over.

The actual decision process is *Ringi Seido*. This process involves an elaborate circulation of ideas and tactical plans initiated at lower levels to reach a consensus. The procedure can be extraordinarily slow and cumbersome and requires long lead times to be effective. The involvement of several departments and organizational levels, plus interminable meetings, fits well with the diffuse authority patterns of Japanese organizations and the capacity of managers to cope with ambiguity and political in-fighting.

Viewed from the traditional paradigm of top down decision-making, *Ringi* does not make sense to most Western managers. However, as Drucker (1971) argues, the distinction is really on what is meant by making a decision and in this regard, he argues, the West is moving in the Japanese direction.

In the West, all the emphasis is on the *answer* to the question. Our books on decision-making try to develop systematic approaches to giving an answer. To the Japanese, however, the important element in decision-making is *defining the question.* The important and crucial steps are to decide whether there is a need for a decision and what the decision is about. And it is at this step that the Japanese aim at attaining consensus. Indeed it is this step that, to the Japanese, is the essence of the decision. The answer to the question (what the West considers *the* decision) follows from its definition.

The Japanese approach to decision-making is not in principle unique, although as a process it reflects cultural norms and values of implicit communication. For example, as a response to overly structured decision models, authors such as George (1972) and Argyris (1976) have developed approaches not dissimilar to the Japanese, such as multiple advocacy. The attempt in multiple advocacy is to open up the decision-process to harness diversity of views and to avoid the bureaucratic politics which tend to narrow the range of options too easily.

Nemawashi and *Ringi,* despite their cultural origins and long history, are evolving methods and in many organizations are often ignored or downplayed for particular issues. The long lead times make the ringi system cumbersome and unsuited for crisis, or when conditions force quick action by top management. Moreover, the consensus approach reinforces and is reinforced by other software management systems, such as the diffuse responsibility in the hierarchy and the emphasis on managers as generalists, not specialists, in the Western sense. As indicated in the next section, even though the formal architecture of Japanese corporation has similar features to North American and European firms, the decision-making processes also reflect social values and adoptive requirements of learning and information. Ezra Vogel (1979) has stated, "Japanese loyalty and patriotism are not inherited but are constantly recreated by organizational practice, and perhaps no practice is more important than the shared search for more information and the optimal solutions to which it leads." In other words, the loyalty and consensus displayed in a Japanese company owes as much to managerial strategy and leadership style, as to any treatise on cultural values and feudal traditions. The best example of such a strategy has been institutionalized, in the form of quality control circles.

7.5 Quality Control Circles

Origins of QC Circles

Although QC circles now have three decades of practice, and are being widely copied in the West, and especially in the United States, their origins stem from the Japanese desire to improve production techniques and productivity, by integrating worker values into the organization.

In reality, the QC movement actually originates with the desire of Japanese management to improve the knowledge level of individual operatives and most importantly, the foremen. There were a variety of reasons for this development. In the factory itself, the foremen had special responsibilities in the operation of the incentive and piece rate system. Further, the rapidly advancing level of education of newly recruited workers, largely due to the educational reforms during the American occupation, meant that the vast proportion had received senior high school. At the same time, Japanese industry itself was rapidly being transformed into higher technology areas requiring more sophisticated work skills, at a time when it was increasingly difficult to recruit and keep employees in traditional job categories.

Within the Japanese industrial firm, managers had adopted, or had at least learned about, new applications in scientific management in the form of statistical quality control. The inspiration for this movement came from two prominant American experts in applied statistics, W. Edwards Deming and J. M. Juran. These two American lectured extensively in Japan about the development of wartime industrial standards in the U.S. At the same time, Japanese industrialists travelled extensively in the United States in an attempt to update their knowledge about quality control and U.S. production techniques. A new organization, the Japanese Union of Scientists and Engineers, was established as a forum for diffusion of production and quality techniques.

Historically, American management has put about 85 per cent of the responsibility for quality control on line managers and engineering staff – only about fifteen per cent could be attributed to plant workers. The essence of the Deming/Juran philosophy was basically a reversal of the 85–15 formula. Instead of having quality control being primarily the responsibility of a few managers, or desk engineers isolated from the shop floor, the opposite should prevail. Quality control should be built into the structure of job tasks and worker management relations. All hierarchical levels – shop floor workers, foremen, middle mangers, top management – should be exposed to statistical quality control techniques. Continuous training and discussion should be the norm, based on seminars, study groups, and lectures.

The Japanese strategy is akin to the difference between preventive medicine and curative medicine. Focus the main effort on preventing defects from oc-

Exhibit 7/4: Quality Control Approach

Cost $

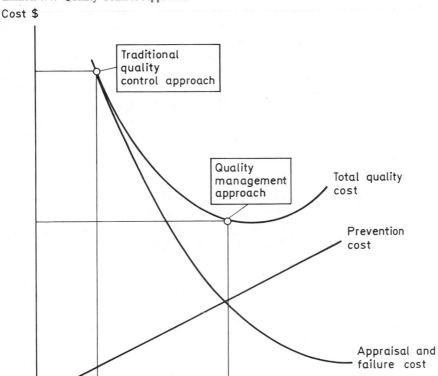

Worse ◄─────────── Quality ───────────► Better

Source: Adapted from Urwick ORR and Partners

curring in the first place. As shown in Exhibit 7/4, the preventive approach can actually cost less than the traditional approach. This latter view is based on a principle of minimum overall cost, i.e., one above the costs of zero defects. The basic reason is that it is extremely difficult to rectify mistakes once they are made. One survey in Britain, for example, found that an astonishing 87 per cent of costs for quality control was spent on product failures, e.g., wasteful rejects, rectifying faults, and servicing goods returned by customers.[9] Only three per cent was spent on preventing faults.

In Japan, the enormous interest in the past twenty-five years of quality management had taken on a country-wide dimension. At the national level, a major focal point for quality control, education and training is JUSE – the Japanese

[9] *The Economist* (October 31, 1981), p. 97.

Union of Scientists and Engineers. This organization acts as a forum for developing methods and techniques and for spreading awareness of quality control management. At the level of plants and factories, literally hundreds of thousands of quality control circles (QCC) have sprung up, involving millions of workers. Today QC circles are active not simply in the management of quality control, or defects, but also in cost savings, safety improvement, pollution control, employee education and energy savings. Through magazines and pamphlets, such programs are widely propagated. The Deming Prize begun in 1951 is awarded on nation-wide TV to competing firms as the major achievement for innovation in quality control. Even if a conservative estimate is made, perhaps one in eight Japanese workers is engaged in QC circle activities.

QC Circles in Practice

A quality control circle can be defined as a small group of workers carrying out voluntarily analysis of job related quality problems. Such a work group involves the active participation of all members and, by forming part of a broad company strategy to quality control, promotes worker self-development, skills development, leadership skills and teamwork.

In practice, QC circles consist of groups of six to ten workers engaged in the same type of work and usually at the same hierarchical level. (Groups as large as fifteen or twenty can occur, although the norm is around ten.) The groups are very problem focussed, meeting about once a week, often outside company work hours (but meetings during company time are not unusual). Each group has a leader or spokesman, who coordinates the team's efforts and often reports back to management on the solutions developed. In many instances, the quality control circles include foremen as integral members of the work group, and many serve as circle leaders. What is critical to the QC circle concept as a

Exhibit 7/5: An Ishikawa Cause/Effect Diagram for Quality Control Analysis

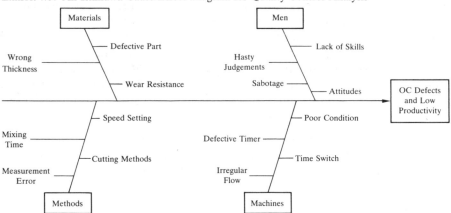

practical tool is the set of techniques available for analysis, discussion and feedback.

Among the techniques used are a variety of charts and diagrams which display statistical results of actual production. The mathematics involved is not terribly sophisticated, although the impact of the statistical analysis can be quite pronounced. The tools used to display the statistics range from vertical bar charts, histograms, graphs, scatter diagrams, and control charts. Other techniques include cause and effect diagrams or Ishikawa charts. An example of the latter serves to illustrate the point that quality control circles operate with data rich agendas. They are not theory seminars or general discussion groups.

A cause and effect diagram is a tool to define problems as an effect or outcome and to reduce it to the underlying causes. One such approach is an Ishikawa chart, developed by Kaora Ishikawa, director general of the Japanese quality control group and former President of The Editorial Board of the magazine, *Foreman Quality Control*.[10] The Ishikawa cause and effect diagram is a fish-boned frame to analyze the four M's – materials, manpower, methods, and machines. For each problem or effect, e.g., low productivity or number of defects per units produced, examination is made of the statistical results of each area. For manpower, for example, the underlying causes may be poor skills. This problem may be related to lack of training, job turnover due to absenteeism, or age of the worker. Instead of a problem in worker skills, the basic cause may be in worker attitudes, which relate to problems in supervision, pay, or motivation.

Although many QC circles operate as voluntary groups, and often meet outside company time, management plays an important supportive role. Initially this role may involve training for foremen and QC leaders: for example, in activities related to record keeping, managing group discussion and task assignments, and report writing. Although QC leaders are usually rotated, and often are chosen by a vote of the group, they serve as an important linkage between the ideas of lower skilled workers and the more highly motivated managerial group.

An umbrella term used in Japan to describe the various activities of QC circles and ZD campaigns is the system of *Jishu Kanri* – usually known as "JK" and loosely meaning "voluntary management". JK activities started with the Japanese Iron and Steel Foundation in May 1969, and has expanded to include over thirty-thousand work groups, with hundreds of thousands of workers. Human relations, individual development, leadership, and work satisfaction through creativity are major goals for JK groups, over and above those of quality

[10] See Ishikawa (1981).

improvement and error elimination. One survey of managers, for example, found that of the top seven reasons for valuing JK activities, thirty-six per cent indicated improved awareness of problems (improvement in observation), twenty-two per cent cited strengthened team work (improved participation), and twenty per cent noted improved willingness to work (responsibility) (Sugisawa and Heros, 1977).

7.6 Organizational Design Issues

Quality management impacts on the structure and climate of the total organization. As such, imitation of the Japanese approach to quality control without changes in hierarchical control, information flow, and lines of responsibility is likely to end in failure. As noted, the Japanese approach has involved a long range effort at developing employee responsibility and job enlargement. Trust is an important element here, with foremen, supervisors, and managers trained to accept individual worker responsibility, without an elaborate review system of peers checking peers. Work counseling and employee guidance are valued practices of Japanese managers and they are reflected in the close contact between supervisors and employees. For example, in one study of U.S. owned and Japanese owned firms in the U.S. there was twice the ratio of employees reporting to first line supervisors in the American firms compared to Japanese – 30:1 and 15:1.

In terms of organization structure, this point has several implications. In the first place, the typical Japanese organization has fewer staff resources isolated from line managers. Not only do foremen typically report directly to plant managers, the staff functions normally seen as desk jobs in Western companies are fully integrated into line management. The best example of this design issue is the engineering function, but there are parallels with other tasks such as cost accounting and materials purchasing.

Cole (1979), for example, cites the case of engineering design in the U.S. and Japanese car industry. In the U.S. design engineering is a relatively autonomous function, with integration and coordination with manufacturing and marketing relatively weak. "Accustomed to a relative monopoly on product specifications, the design department tends to produce drawings with exact manufacturing details even though it is not necessarily best qualified to set parameters on reliability, maintenance and users' cost."

In Japan, by contrast, engineering is a fully integrated function not only with marketing and production, but also with workers and consumers. Japan's high utilization of engineers in industry reinforces this strong production emphasis, but so do training programs covering elementary subjects on plant layout, production scheduling, inventory analysis, and equipment maintenance. Matsushita Electric, for example, requires its first year engineers to rotate between appliance stores where customer queries and complaints are heard, and the plants where the products are made.

Almost all Japanese companies treat engineers as blue collar workers, despite their higher pay. Company uniforms are usually identical, salaries are paid monthly with semiannual bonuses, and wages are linked to company seniority. Engineers work hand in hand with blue collar assembly workers, and industrial and design engineers as well as cost accountants are available for specialized assistance to QC circles. In some cases, the workers may request special lectures or seminars in particular topics, such as job analysis, metallurgy, or computers.

The strong engineering orientation of Japanese companies reinforces a competitive strategy carefully cultivated over the past thirty years, namely the development of process technology, rather than new products per se. In some cases, such as steel, the changes in process technology to continuous casting, for example, are quite dramatic. In many fields, the process technology improvements are less spectacular but still significant in productivity or cost reduction. One reason for this emphasis is the well cultivated system of promoting employee suggestions as part of QC circle activities.

Again, however, the Japanese approach to suggestions differs from most Western practice. In Japan, the emphasis is on maximizing the number of suggestions, not their importance. Because quantity is the objective, not quality, the rewards for usuable suggestions is quite low, from a few dollars to under five hundred dollars. Despite this, the number of usuable suggestions is much higher in Japan than the U.S. According to one study, General Motors of Detroit received an average of 0.84 suggestions per eligible employee per year, and adopted 23 per cent. In 1980, Toyota received 17.9 suggestions per employee, and adopted close to 90 per cent (*Focus Japan*, 1981).

Japanese managers see suggestion schemes as much more than a special bonus for good ideas. Suggestion schemes are part of a general organizational climate to develop trust and communications across departments and between workers and managers. Norms are cultivated to offer creative ideas but also to accept improvements. Training programs are conducted to improve the way suggestions are made. The Japanese Association of Suggestion Systems (JASS) and The Japan Human Relations Association are two of the major vehicles for conferences, company visits, and field trips to develop and improve employee suggestion systems. A survey of these two associations found that in fiscal 1980, of the more than 25 million suggestions made (12.8 per capita of rank and file employees), total benefits to the companies amounted to about ten billion dollars, while the monetary rewards for the workers were about four billion.

7.7 Summary and Conclusions

The role of organization has been cited two decades ago as a main reason for American productivity success; today the argument is turned on its head and now explains American productivity difficulties. Is there a reconciliation of these positions? What role does organizational form really play?

The argument set out in this chapter is that organizational strategy and structure must be placed in both historic and cultural context. The rise of the American divisional structure was an organizational innovation which allowed great flexibility in the face of changing technology and markets. Administrative coordination costs were lowered, communication and performance control were superior and strategic response was quicker. However, the competitive advantage of this organizational form was greatly diluted as other countries adopted similar or improved structures (e.g., project management, matrix structures, etc.) so the differences in organizational effectiveness were much greater in the underlying decision processes, where cultural and individual style differences are more central. In this respect, the European and Japanese forms contrast with the impersonal bureaucratic, short term horizons of the American corporation.

In all of this, Japanese management combines many structural features of the American corporation, but incorporates a management philosophy nurturing individual commitment and corporate integration. This kind of philosophy is not inherently Japanese – witness the same approach among Jesuits in the Catholic Church, the R.C.M.P. in Canada, and Marks and Spencer in Britain, to cite three diverse examples. What is Japanese is how widespread the approach is among big and small firms alike and how particular Japanese cultural norms serve to reinforce it. For example, Hofstede (1980) finds that on measures of power distance and individualism/collectivism, Japan was higher on the first (53 vs. 39 on a scale of 11–94) and substantially above the U.S. on the second (91 vs. 45).

Macro organizational characteristics can take many forms and industry norms and hardware technologies cannot be ignored. What is impressive about Japanese management is how organizational form and hardware technology have been combined to promote employee and individual commitment by basic human resource policies. Organizational processes of leadership, communications, and decision-making stress a constant managerial awareness of understanding the individual who works in the organization and his world of values and aspirations. The successful Japanese organization may be viewed abroad as the prototype Theory Y organization, but beneath the veneer of individual participation and involvement is a highly formalized system of financial controls and excellent information systems. Even QC circles, so envied and misunderstood in the West, are a vast organizational <u>web of suggestions and ideas</u> <u>mobilized around detailed information gathering and analysis</u>. The ideas and suggestions provide a constant check on the status quo and the accepted way of doing things. <u>Through QC circles, Japanese companies build bottom-up sys-</u> <u>tems of experimentation, constant improvement, innovation, and above all,</u> <u>quality and pride</u>. Japan's most profound innovation has been the quality con- trol circle. <u>QC circles serve many purposes but their common characteristic is</u> <u>to mobilize group norms and social cohesion for work norms.</u> The growing application of this concept in North America and Europe is testimony to the essentially non-cultural features of this human resource approach, and the likelihood that quite different macro structures – from co-determination and socio technical systems – are quite consistent with the Japanese approach to organization. However, <u>QC circles don't operate in a vacuum. Japanese com-</u> <u>panies operate with rather developed human resource policies for training,</u> <u>socialization, careers, job rotation and the like: the essential point is to under-</u> <u>stand not only how these various policies are fully integrated around a corpo-</u> <u>rate culture and the goals of individual members, but also how human resource</u> <u>policies are integrated with other functions such as marketing, production, and</u> <u>finance</u>. This subject is taken up in the next chapter.

Chapter 8
Human Resource Strategies and Work

"Increasingly, business and labour are realizing that solving 'people problems' is as important as generating capital and introducing new technology."

Business Week

8.1 Introduction

Industrial relations is probably the one area receiving the most academic interest among observers of Japanese management. At first glance, the reasons are obvious. Japan has enjoyed the lowest unemployment, the lowest strike levels, the most enviable pattern of technological change, and the most successful record of labour productivity. A great number of Western commentators has viewed the Japanese system as agreeably different and culturally eccentric, but one not amenable to Western emulation. Traditionalism, paternalism, and cultural uniqueness have been code words to describe the Japanese system, especially in contrast to American practice. More comprehensive analysis of the total picture of Japan's human resource practices – the emphasis on software systems and the internal labour market – have shown that the cultural explanation is greatly limited and even confusing. At the other extreme, some analysts have gone so far to suggest that the Japanese model of permanent employment and emphasis on internal markets are not only highly functional but actually represents the direction of high technology organizations in North America and Western Europe (Dore, 1973). In this vein a cover story in *Business Week* makes the point that "quietly, almost without notice, a new industrial relations system with a fundamentally different way of managing people is taking shape in the U.S. Its goal is to end the adversarial relationship which has grown between management and labour and that now threatens the competitiveness of many industries."[1]

The cultural argument for Japanese industrial relations usually centers on the idea of extended family or kinship. The bonds between worker and manager reflect the national character stemming from the need for cooperative production in wet rice cultivation prior to industrialization. James Abegglen (1973) sets out this argument as follows:

[1] The article concludes: "clearly, a changed social and economic environment in the U.S. demands that labour and management create a new relationship . . . The U.S. industrial relations

Factory organization and its leaders are directly and closely tied to a non-urban pre-war traditional Japanese experience and outlook . . . tracing their origins directly to feudal merchant families. The tradition and outlook of these families remain an active and real force in the management practices of the companies.

Until recently, this interpretation has largely held sway in matters concerning Japanese industrial relations. The shift in emphasis is partly explainable by the economics of success – the better something works, the more it should be copied. In this respect, more serious study of the Japanese industrial relations system has focused not just on permanent employment security or the reward structure, but more fundamental issues. These include the nature and skills of the labour force, the underlying technology of the firm, the institutional patterns of hierarchy and communications, and the tradeoffs in authority control by management and technological innovation. In short, contemporary explanation of Japanese industrial relations should center not so much on the actual existence of certain Japanese characteristics of social organization, including lifetime commitment (*Shushin Koyo*), or familiastic management (*Keiei Kazoku Shugi*) or the firm as one family *(Kigyo-ikkei)*. Rather, the difference is one of seeing the costs and benefits of particular policies. For one thing, what seemed to be explained by cultural values – permanent employment – was developed rather recently, after the Second World War. For another, what was said to be particularistically Japanese was found in one or more guises in Europe and the U.S. And thirdly, what was allegedly a sociological and cultural argument was soon recognized to have a major economic dimension, involving calculated managerial choice. This aspect, the deliberate and calculated choice of providing job security to cope with technological change, has not been generally recognized. These issues form the basis of this chapter.

8.2 Two Models of Labour-Management

The theoretical analysis of Japan's industrial relations rests on three converging approaches to human resource management derived from economics, industrial relations and organization theory.[2]

The first approach is the investment in human capital literature, which involves the study of the income and economic growth implications of investments in people (Becker, 1962). Such investment has been shown in the now voluminous literature to be widely defined to include the health, skills, discipline and

system, so long arrested at primitive levels of development, can now evolve into a third stage – a participative stage." *Business Week* (May 11, 1981).
[2] For a good compendium of sources, see M. Blaug (1968), Nishikawa (1980), and Okochi et al. (1973).

education of human beings as workers and employees. The fundamental welfare questions concern terms of the net beneficiaries of such investments. In other words, who wins: those who make the investment (e.g. employers) or those who consume them (e.g., employees)? The theoretical issues concern the economic implications of the motivations to make human capital investments, and the consequences such investments yield both for managers and employees. The latter issue is critical in understanding the Japanese approach, in that the motivation to make investments in human capital will be conditioned by the likelihood of a net economic return (e.g., high productivity) offsetting the cost of the training, and the risk that the training recipient would seek work elsewhere, i.e., move to other firms. The strategy is that once having trained workers, management will want to keep them in an organizational career structure.

An important implication for this strategy is that individual mobility will be low. Firms under highly competitive external labour markets would not invest in general training (because of the risk workers would leave) but would pay trained persons market wages (because of the competitive labour market). Firms can influence the conditions of "perfect" labour markets by paying high wages or by "specific", as distinct from "general", training since the additional skills are tied to the firm in question, rather than to the industry or market at large. Experience on the part of an employee, in short, is a premium from the firm to discourage job turnover, since the cost of inexperience is additional specific training (Bell, 1962; Williamson, 1975).

The second theoretical analysis related to Japan draws from the economics/industrial relations literature on the institutional factors which influence the labour market for firms. The basic distinction here is between "internal" labour markets and "external" labour markets. Internal refers to the rules and hierarchies governing employer-employee relations within a plant or corporation, as distinct from the job allocation mechanisms involving the external labour market and the firm (Dunlop, 1958). The internal labour market is guided by rules of administration and differs from the external labour market, which is governed by supply/demand conditions in the economy at large.

All organizations face many functional imperatives such as recruitment, selection, training and integration of employees; in many, attention to these policies may be minimal or prefunctory. The basic question is whether the optimal size and skill profile (work force composition) can best be bought from the external labour market or developed internally by corporate training policies. In internal labour markets, there are few institutional constraints such as information, search and selection costs, and barriers to entry. The nature of the labour market (e.g., surplus supply conditions) influences the impact of institutional barriers.

In many situations there may well be human obstacles in the organization environment, such as union resistence, barriers to entry (e.g., by professional associations) as well as labour market conditions, such as labour shortages of special skills. Such issues may greatly increase the "transaction" costs of hiring workers such that specific "ports of entry" into the firm are governed by firm specific rules (e.g., selection procedures) and the internal career hierarchy is governed by internal conditions (e.g., promotion from within of existing employees) rather than by external labour force conditions (Doeringer and Piore, 1971).

In structured internal labour markets, job allocation mechanisms develop from internally generated rules governing training for job specific and firm specific skills, and turnover and absenteeism are viewed as costly due to the high transaction costs of worker selection and training. The focus is on the retention of skilled and experienced employees because of the work requirements of the individual job and the human capital attached to it.

The third theoretical approach involves the concept of organizational commitment, which refers to the relative strength of an employee's involvement in and identification with a firm (Argyris, 1973). Traditional models of the firm conceptualize the employee-employer relationship in an exchange framework, whereby employers provide "inducements", in the form of economic incentives and wages for "contributions" in the form of work behaviours prescribed within managerial policies. Behavioural models of the firm challenge the purely economic basis of this exchange, and advance arguments in terms of the psychological contract between the employee and the organization (Levinson, 1972). The nature of this contract[3] is governed by such variables as the particular vs. general job characteristics (task identity and performance feedback), personal characteristics (education, values, need for achievement) and work experience (e.g., individual vs. group attitudes). Recent studies have examined the antecedents of organizational commitment, and its relationship to such issues as turnover, absenteeism, and job performance (Porter et al. 1975). In brief, there may be worker-management relations based on explicit formalized contracts where wage and other economic features are carefully spelled out to establish responsibilities and delimit misuse of authority. Other employment systems may go much beyond this approach, with psychological factors being part of the system, including investments in worker commitment to effect performance outcomes in a high trust environment (Galbraith, 1977).

These three approaches combine from their distinct vantage points to offer a view of the firm where employment allocation mechanisms can be made either

---

[3] Levinson (1972) defines the psychological contract as "a series of mutual expectations of which the parties to the relationship may not themselves be even dimly aware but which nonetheless govern their relationship to each other."

with reference to external competitive and environmental conditions on the one hand, or with reference to the ways management can create buffers to those external conditions by internally developed incentives for training, commitment and turnover. Both policy approaches have costs/benefits. Together the three approaches suggest two ideal types which describe the employment relationship.

In the Type A model depicted in Exhibit 8/1, the major influence is on the external reference to the firm's adaptation to change. Type B, by contrast, incorporates the major change mechanisms to internal allocation procedures, not the external. Conceptually, these ideal types lead to two dynamic approaches to human resource management under conditions of change, namely those shown in Exhibit 8/2 and Exhibit 8/3, which show the relationship among the conditions to stay in the employment relationship to the likely outcomes, based on the theoretical models. The two ideal types, incorporating the features of the three theoretical approaches, correspond to North America and Japan labour practices and are examined in the next section.

Exhibit 8/1: Models of Human Resource Management

	Type A	Type B
Human Capital Approach	Low Training Investment Job Specific Training Formalized Evaluation	High Training Investment General Training Informal Evaluation
Labour Market Approach	External Reference Points Short Term Employment Specialized Career Hierarchies	Internal References Points Long Term Employment Non-Specialized Hierarchies
Organization Commitment Approach	Explicit Employment Contracts Extrinsic Incentives Individualized Jobs	Implicit Contracts Intrinsic Incentives Group Oriented Work

8.3 Type A: North America

The North American system of human resource management is not entirely homogeneous across industries, or between the public and private sector. Nonetheless, three general features of the U.S. (and Canada's) system can be outlined when making comparisons with other countries such as Japan (Kassalow, 1969; Adams, 1982, and Jamieson, 1973). The first point is that North American industrial relations have traditionally been based on strong adversarial principles. In contrast to Japan, for example, where the famous 1947 Doyukai Declaration recognized the firm as a coalition of three equals-

Exhibit 8/2: The Labour Market Model

	External		
Environmental Demands			
		Market Trends Social Values Business Cycle	Social Consequences
Internal			

	Open Entry, Ease of Entry and Exit: Labour Cost Flexibility	
Labour Force Policies	Hiring, Firing of Workers Mobility Influenced by Labour Market Wages	High Employee Turnover High Tardiness
	Low Training	Low Job Satisfaction Employee Commitment
Adoption of Technology	Onus on Management To Apply Knowledge	Low Labour Commitment to Technological Change
	Probability of Labour Substitution Strategy Worker-Technology Conflict	Limited Premium on Learning Skills High Costs of Innovation

Exhibit 8/3: The Human Capital Model

	External		
Environmental Demands			
		Market Trends Social Values Business Cycle	Social Consequences
Internal			

	Closed Entry-Exit: High Fixed Labour Costs	
Labour Force Policies	Careful Screening Processes High Worker Training Limited Labour Mobility	Low Turnover Low Absenteeism High Employee Commitment
Adoption of Technology	Limited Worker – Management Conflict Emphasis on Learning Skills, Bottom Up Decision-Making Premium on Timing of Changes	Low Costs of Innovation High Commitment to Organizational Learning

managers, workers, and shareholders (Yoshino, 1968), there has been a prevailing employer ideology which is at once rigid and defiantly "free enterprise". Such an ideology has produced what Professor Jamieson calls "protracted and at times violent resistance of many influential employer groups, frequently supported by governments, to recognizing unions or engaging in meaningful collective bargaining" (Jamieson, 1975: 343). Management's desire for control over many key operating decisions, the incentive schemes such as management by objectives for first line supervisors, and many symbolic differences between workers and managers have all reinforced a basic conflict model of the workplace. An additional and complementary result has been the high union militancy, violence, and strike activity. The legal and public policy framework in North America reinforces this adverserial relationship.[4]

Secondly, the evidence on wage determination in North America shows that the level of wages is primarily related to general economic conditions, including relative wages and general unemployment. Such issues as strikes and degree of unionization or even the role of profits are considerably less important. Unlike in Japan, where the dual labour structure has persisted, it is difficult to relate wage determination for particular "commanding industries" like automobiles to industry conditions, or to relate strike activity to business cycles. The major difference between union and non union wage differentials stems primarily from labour quality differences, and resulting work conditions (e.g., long hours, shift work, or unsocial work schedules).

Thirdly, contrary to the general impression, the U.S., Canadian, and British labour movements are highly diverse and fractionated. In fact, about two thirds of all wage agreements are negotiated between local unions and individual companies or plants – industry wide, market wide, or nation wide bargaining are rare and exceptional. Union resources to study the wider picture of economic relations of employers and employees are thus diminished and a consequence is a tendency for short term gains versus long term advantages. Among Western countries, other than Japan, only Sweden has a systematic, nationwide employer-union bargaining structure for all major sectors for settlement on a common timetable.[5]

---

[4] Adams (1982: 463) makes the following point: "The American Wagner Act of the 1930's initially encouraged employer recognition of trade unions. It was formally supportive of collective bargaining: it made illegal many employer unfair labour practices designed to penalize employers for union sympathies, and it compelled intransigent employers to negotiate once unionized. However, the Taft-Hartley Act of 1947 gave approval to employer attempts to convince employees to reject trade unions and collective bargaining. Subsequently few employers recognized unions voluntarily, and union organizing campaigns continued to be an open struggle for the loyalty of workers involved. Unionization came to be thought of as punishment for management failure."

[5] For an excellent overview of Sweden, and other European countries, see Schmidt (1972) in Aaron and Wedderburn (1972).

The general picture of human resource management can be made with reference to Exhibit 8/2. Western managers have at their command two major tools to adapt to general environmental demands, such as the state of the economy, demand for particular goods, and the international business cycle. These two tools are manpower policy and technology. Manpower policy includes the adjustment in the size of the workforce (adding workers, laying off workers) and the composition of the workforce, in terms of skills, experience, norms and attitudes of particular groups of workers. Adaption by technology implies changes in the state of knowledge of the production process (e.g. manual typewriter vs. electric IBM) inducing higher productivity or the replacement of human capital with machine capital (i.e. automation). For North American managers, the advantages of the labour markets systems should not be underestimated, at least in the past.

For one thing, faced with a generally unrestrictive immigration policy and high unemployment, employers have had a large pool of labour to draw on when new workers were needed, and favourable government social security programs to cushion workers when they were laid off. The open entry/exit policies have meant that selection and screening policies did not have to be too sophisticated[6], since a worker could be laid off (or might move) if the economic contract turned out to be unfavourable. A recent study of Canadian firms, for example, found that contrary to expectations, both large and small firms had underdeveloped manpower and personnel practices as compared to best practice usage elsewhere (Dimick and Murray, 1979). Traditionally, the industrial structure of countries like Canada and U.S., with the heavy emphasis on raw materials in the primary sector and growth in the service sector, meant that the adoption of new technology could be planned by managers without much direct employee feedback on performance. Even in manufacturing, the high level of capital intensity, the capacity of engineers to reduce or limit the impact of human skills, and the relative stability of real technological change – all these factors gave management an incentive to use this labour market approach to human resources. Finally, the education level of workers (and managers) has been such that the expectation of workers was largely economic rather than social.

In Herzberg's (1964) terminology, these economic or hygiene factors lead to human resource policies limited to such factors as salaries, supervision, and work conditions. There is substantially less emphasis on motivation or social factors including job design policies for worker responsibility, recognition, initiative and achievement. Competitive success was largely a function of in-

---

[6] The standard approach in the U.S. is the personal interview. Dunnette and Bass (1963) write: "The personal interview continues to be the most widely used method for selecting employees, despite the fact that it is a costly, inefficient and usually invalid procedure."

fluences under management's control (e.g., major marketing decisions) and human resources issues were largely subordinate to other corporate policies.

The consequences of the Western system probably were (and are) perceived in net benefit terms, at least by managers. With the availability of low skill workers, jobs could be designed with very low training needs, and management hierarchy was essentially enhanced since management controlled the uncertainties in the jobs – the pacing of machines, the flow of operations, the determination of tools and techniques, the establishment of priorities and standards. Production became essentially a closed system[7], and managers and staff specialists, not the workers, coped with the uncertainties of technological change and market disruption. This traditional approach had the predictable result that its adversarial features were reinforced, not only by an ideological framework of "we" and "them" but also by a legalistic structure of grievance and arbitration. Collective bargaining encouraged the adversarial approach during the negotiations leading up to a wage contract, and a legalistic grievance procedure prolonged and reinforced it during the life of the agreement.

Despite the differences among major industries, the patterns of collective bargaining and adversarial industrial relations have generated predictable and common results: enormously large and legalistic bureaucracies. In the U.S., where norms of individualism and free enterprise are strongest, this broad trend exists at the level of the corporation and only to a much lesser extent at the level of government. In Canada, Britain, and Europe, the lower levels of individualist orientation and lower levels of corporate legitimacy have prompted workers and trade unions to lobby for universal legal measures to restrain management prerogatives and widen welfare benefits. Continental Europe has gone the furthest in government legislated frameworks for management-worker relationships. The net effect has been to diminish and even remove management discretion over many fundamental workplace policies.

Ironically, it is the countries like the U.S., Canada, and Britain, where Anglo-Saxon norms of collective bargaining are strongest, that worker management conflict is greatest. Notwithstanding problems of data methods, if strikes are examined cross-nationally, many countries stand well above Japanese levels percent in man days lost per thousand employees, as shown in Exhibit 8/4. However, in North America, strikes tend not to occur significantly more frequently than Europe or Japan, but they do tend to be of much longer duration. In Britain, the evidence shows that the incidence of strike activity is greater in large plants (which other things being equal should also be the most productive).

---

[7] According to Thompson (1967), rational organizations should buffer their production core from environmental influences.

Exhibit 8/4: Days Lost per Thousand Employees

	August 1960–70	August 1971–76	1977
Japan	144	172	41
Germany	14	52	1
France	176	251	222
Britain	187	521	448
Canada	547	1002	387
Sweden	20	49	n.a.
U.S.A.	495	493	444

Source: U.S. Department of Labour

In summary, the labour market approach to human resource management has provided employers with a great deal of flexibility and control over staffing and manning levels, despite the adversarial management-worker features inherent in it. The cost of technological change has not been prohibitive, the competition for skilled workers has been manageable, and the social costs of absenteeism, turnover, and resistance to technological change have been acceptable if not directly confronted. The key question has become: do any of these assumptions still apply in the face of new technology and Japanese competition.

8.4 Type B: Japan

Despite appearances to the contrary, the Japanese employment situation is not homogeneous and shows differences by industry, size of firm, and geographic regions (Galanson and Odaka, 1976). Yet there are certain characteristics which are of sufficient importance to warrant some generalization. The first is that since Japan was much slower to industrialize than most Western countries (i.e., to shift the economy from primary sectors like agriculture to secondary manufacturing), there has been an historic shortage of skilled workers. Unlike West Germany or France, with millions of immigrant "guest workers" for many low skilled jobs, Japan's population dynamics have created labour supply problems – even today 11.0 per cent of workers are engaged in agriculture, forestry and fisheries, compared to seven per cent in Canada and only 4 per cent in the United States (see Exhibit 8/5). The second issue is that education and work careers in Japan are tied together. The emphasis in the past has been on middle school leavers (aged 15) progressing up to high school, junior colleges, and universities. The gradation of company jobs (and thus salaries) was directly related to educational attainment. And thirdly, there is the lifetime commitment feature, whereby the employer-employee contract has a long term (i.e., from job entry to retirement at 55) feature which implies a social as well as an economic aspect (Cole, 1972; Ichiro, 1975).

Exhibit 8/5: Per Cent of Civilian Employment by Economic Activities (1977)

Country	Primary Sector	Manufacturing	Service Sector
Britain	2.7	41.1	56.2
Canada	7.0	27.0	65.0
France	10.8	26.5	52.7
West Germany*	6.4	34.8	58.8
Japan	11.9	34.8	53.3
United States	3.7	30.5	65.8

* 1976

Sources: I.L.O.; U.N. Statistics

These three characteristics apply to the larger firms more than the small ones (i.e., the persistence of the dual sector economy), to technologically advanced more than technologically mature (e.g., electronics vs. stainless steel cutlery), and to male more than female workers and to males over 30 more than under 30 (Azumi and McMillan, 1976). Moreover, there is flexibility within the corporate groups structure. Firms use subcontracted workers as an additional compliment to the regular work force where production by demand increases, and senior workers are often shifted to smaller firms. In periods of falling demand, production cutbacks are managed by letting temporary workers go (Ballon, 1973).

The foreign perception of Japanese unions and individual workers as docile and submissive is largely misplaced, since it ignores the basis of strength in the union structure derived by the post-war legal reforms carried out by the American authorities. Under various legislated reforms, such as The Labour Conciliation Law, The Labour Standards Law, and the Labour Relations Adjustment Law – reforms so profound even by U.S. labour norms they amounted to what Ronald Dore has called a "social democratic revolution" – unions gained for their members not only basic pay and work conditions similar to management but the legal right to direct involvement in all management committees making decisions relating to labour conditions.[8] Firms, for example, above ten workers must submit their work rules to the Labour Standards office and clauses involving quick employee dismissal are not permitted.

The Japanese system can be analyzed with reference to Exhibit 8/3. As in the labour market model, managers have only two basic tools to adapt to environ-

---

[8] As Dore (1973) notes, there was "the unquestioning acceptance of the union as a legitimate bargaining agent in matters of wages and the protection of persons with rights to full facilities within the factory to do its legitimate job." Few managers, academics or consultants in North America or Europe who look fondly at Japanese productivity levels dwell on this basic point in labour-management relations.

mental conditions, namely the work force and technology. However, in contrast to the situation in North America, the workforce manpower strategy is asymmetrical such that managers can meet expansion/growth demand by hiring workers but cannot face contractions in production output by firing or laying off workers. In short, labour is not a variable cost but a fixed cost. Given the protracted post-war labour shortages and the resulting necessity of retaining workers in the firm, ports of entry (selection) are relatively closed and personnel screening is a critical function, hence the use of education and university ranking (with Tokyo at the top of a clear hierarchy) as the main employee selection mechanisms in the Japanese firm (Marsh and Mannari, 1978). As noted in previous chapters, even young students recognize the clear role of educational credentials in future career patterns. Firms and government departments also recognize the relationship between their own reputation and attracting the best students.

The management of Japanese organization thus takes a different turn from Western companies faced with a high mobility labour market approach. First, Japanese workers are viewed as a resource no different from any other high cost capital item – hence the best use must be made of them. Continuous training, job rotation and even foreign postings are used as vehicles for manpower planning. Second, given the population structure of most Japanese companies, wherein younger workers receive less pay than older workers, the *Nenko* system of wages tied to age and length of service provides Japanese management with a real incentive both to improve labour productivity and to attain market growth. Internally generated growth from increased production in turn lowers average wage costs when new workers are hired. Studies have generally shown that growth, market share, and productivity are valued more in Japanese companies, while profitability, paid in capital and net earnings per share are more valued in U.S. companies (Kamiryo, 1978). The U.S. picture seems to be equally true of Canada and Britain.

A third consideration is that in Japan, worker and technology are not viewed as being in conflict, such that new products or production processes are seen by workers as adding to their job security, not threatening it. As outlined in Chapter 5, Japan has often been described as an innovator, not an inventor, a copier rather than originator (Abegglen, 1970). The reason for this charge is that Japan has consistently been able to make often spectacular improvements in existing products or production processes, even where the technology has not been proprietary or particularly unavailable in other countries. Behind this imitative image of Japanese technology, however, is a basic shopfloor level process of consultation and two way communications flow which make constant technological change possible.

Quality control circles increase the knowledge level of shopfloor workers and the use of task assignments to groups rather than individuals encourages joint learning.[9] Even small or technologically less advanced plants can make process innovations or product improvements where security and incentive come from the large firms. The less adversarial nature of Japanese industrial relations has meant that the technology developed internally, or even the specialized technology held by foreign firms but given to Japan under license, is quickly diffused throughout the company and even an industry. Job rotation within the departments, and open communications and easy interchange across levels, together with traditional Japanese values of curiosity and self-improvement, all add to this process. However, the climate of cooperation and job security are seen as basic building blocks to the Type B model used by Japanese managers.

As noted in the last chapter, a major characteristic of labour-management relations in Japan is the enterprise union, and the legal framework which distinguishes union practices between the public and private sector. The enterprise union is the basic unit of employee organization in contrast to the industrial union in North America. Members of the enterprise union are the employees involved in the permanent employment system. About a third of all employees are so unionized, and this figure hasn't changed much in a decade. But in firms with more than 500 employees, the union percentage is about 64 per cent, compared to only 9 per cent with firms of 100 employees and less than 5 in firms of less than 30 employees (JIL, 1974).

About three quarters of all union members are in the private sector (12 million workers). There are four major National labour organizations (Exhibit 8/6), and some unions may belong to more than one organization. The *Shunto* or

Exhibit 8/6: National Labour Organizations in Japan

Organization	Membership	%
Sohyo – General Council of Trade Unions of Japan	4,525,237	36.5
Domei – Japanese Confederation of Labour	2,181,810	17.6
Churit su Roren – Federation of Independent Unions	1,320,798	10.7
Shin sanbetsu – National Federation of Industrial Organizations	61,270	0.5
Others	4,679,367	37.8
Total	12,382,829	100.0

Source: Ministry of Labour

---

[9] An additional issue is the physical design of the typical Japanese office or shopfloor. Unlike traditional practice in the West, senior managers are not isolated in private offices and, in fact, spend considerable time on the line. The typical office has no partitioned spaces except for conference rooms and meeting places for visitors.

Spring Labour offensive sets the going rate for labour generally, even though only a minority of workers actually participate. Because the enterprise union consists of a 'stew pot' of different occupations, bargaining concentrates on the wage increment each year and occupational and skill classification differences are not as important as in North America (or Europe), hence intra-firm mobility is facilitated.

It may be argued that enterprise unions actually decrease the power of workers as compared to the industrial unions in the U.S. In fact, this view is a misreading of worker management relations in Japan. Collective bargaining and the nation wide spring wage offensive focus on the company level or, for bigger companies, at the plant level. Despite the different goals of workers and managers, the emphasis is not an adversarial one against the company.[10] This point means that the enterprise unions must recognize the particular circumstances of the company's performance. Not only are the worker's skills likely to be company specific, i.e. more valuable to their own firm than to others in the industry in the event of bankruptcy, the wage structure promotes company loyalty by tying benefits to length of service.

It is no accident that in sectors with common problems, e.g. poor markets, surplus capacity, technological threats, enterprise unions will band together with their industry federation to negotiate common issues. For example, the metal workers have developed a common federation for the metal industries, and common federations may become a norm among Japanese enterprise unions, not unlike the confederate structures of West Germany's DGB.[11] Overall, however, the point remains that the collective bargaining process is not one intended to weaken the individual firm. Jamieson (1980) argues that industry wide bargaining in Britain represents a protection for the marginal firm and the retention of jobs while in the U.S., aggressive bargaining with the most profitable firm in an industry forces spillover effects across the industry forces spillover effects across the industry, even at the expense of marginal firms.

The organization consequences for the Japanese companies seem entirely predicable from the theoretical analysis summarized in Exhibit 8.1. A different set of tradeoffs is involved between the Labour Market and the Human Capital models. The starting premise is the premium on technology adaptiveness for the severe constraints on labour force changes. Labour costs are fixed in that workers cannot be easily laid off and they must be continually trained to make their contribution meaningful in economic and social terms (Oi, 1962).

---

[10] For an elaboration of this point, see Drucker (1981).
[11] Germany's DGB, The German Federation of Trade Unions, is largely apolitical and consists entirely of industrial unions the largest affiliate being 16 Metall, The Metalworker's Union. For an analysis see Gunter and Leminsky (1978).

Yet the emphasis on the retention of high skill labour force composition, together with the premium placed on managerial personnel policies of continuous learning, manpower training, and job mobility, is not without certain costs, given the overall emphasis on flexibility in the adoption of new technologies. In this model, the firm is able to meet the demands of change in the environment only by long run adaptation to technology; the emphasis on short run adjustments of the labour force is conceded to long run technological change. Workers cannot easily be laid off and employees facing "burn out" or low productivity are a severe drain on the organization. On the one hand, this cost inflexibility has important compensating implications for personnel policies. First, turnover of personnel is likely to be low, in the sense that workers will receive the incentives to stay in the organization for both intrinsic and extrinsic rewards, as well as in the sense that management can ill afford the high costs of selection and training. In Japan, the separation rates for the larger, more technologically advanced manufacturing firms employing 500 or more employees, averaged less than 2 percent from 1963–1973, compared to about 2.8 percent for 30–99 size firms (JIL, 1974). Second management will have an important commitment to develop an overall strategy of employee participation, commitment to consensus, decision, and employee, as distinct from managerial, commitment to innovation and change. And third, employees, desirous of an "adult" climate of organizational functioning, and immune from the "market" model of labour force layoffs, have no institutionalized reason for challenging the introduction of new technologies, in the sense that the new technologies will not lead to labour substitution, loss of jobs, or a commitment to managerial fiat.

In short, trust is a major lubricant to the total dynamics of man and machine, worker and manager. Increasingly in Canada, as in Britain and the United States, interpersonal trust is suspended for the formal, prescribed legal contract, where ambiguity, authority and discretion give way to detailed union clauses. Put differently, the contractual system is changed from one of implicit relations to explicit relations, and the organization climate or atmosphere changes. As Arrow has noted, "international productivity differences between countries with, or having access to, common technologies are partly to be explained by trust differences which impair or facilitate exchange (Williamson, 1975: 39). With reference to Japan, Professor Sumiya states, "the permanent employment system allows technological innovation without serious social difficulties" (Sumiya, 1969).

8.5 Applying Software Techniques

The shifting industrial structure of Japan to high growth, high value added sections parallels the enormous increase in investment in human capital through the educational system at large and through corporate level training programs. Because the relationship between the industrial needs of highly qualified manpower and high skilled jobs is so widely understood, most large firms and bureaucracies have developed highly sophisticated software systems of human resource management. The fact that most elements of these software systems are not in and by themselves particularly unique to Japan reduces the merits of any cultural arguments to explain Japan's productivity success. As Hatvany and Pucik (1982) point out, in summarizing Japanese policies, "the strategies and techniques we have reviewed constitute a remarkably well-integrated system. The management policies are highly congruent with the way tasks are structured, with the goals of individual members, and with the goals of individual members and with the climate of the organization. Such good fit is expected to result in a high degree of organizational effectiveness or productivity."

As noted in Chapter 6, part of the explanation for the success of particular techniques in Japan relates to the relatively high importance given to the human resource function in the overall scheme of the management hierarchy. This emphasis in turn reflects the competitive requirements prevalent among the large companies in each sector to attract and retain the best qualified workforce. The human capital model employed by Japanese firms reflects many software systems suitable for employees at each stage of the organizational career. What are these systems and how are they applied?

Exhibit 8/7 outlines a series of policies used by many Japanese organizations. The permanent employment system provides a powerful incentive for most firms to devise detailed policies not simply for white collar workers but for blue

Exhibit 8/7: Software Management Systems

New Recruits	Career Workers	Seniority Workers
Corporate communications (letters, magazines, letters to parents)	Career Planning	Mid-Career Retraining
	Employee Counseling	Wage only Payment Schemes
	Job Ranking	Retraining of Employees
Company Meetings	Job Rotation	Reployment to Subcontractor
Factory visits	Salary Bonuses	Sideways Promotion
Executive Speeches	Workshop University	Sponsoring Young workers
Union Introduction	Foremen Training Programs	Early retirement
Lectures/Orientation	Slow Promotion	Contracts as Consultants
Work Rotation	QC Circles	Retirement allowances
Live-in Training	Company Welfare Systems	

collar workers at each stage of their careers. The particular requirements of both the employee and the organization are quite different at each stage – recruitment, work careers, and approaching retirement. Because wages are tied directly to seniority, with wages varying from sixty to one hundred per cent of compensation depending on economic and profit conditions, various personal practices are recognized as critical elements of maintaining a corporate culture and adapting policies to external conditions. In general, the more advanced the state of technology employed in the company, the more sophisticated are the human resource techniques practiced for all employees at each stage of the career cycle.

Throughout Japan, new recruits typically join the organization in April each year, but actual socialization and education into the company starts as much as six months in advance, when the hiring decisions are made. Company visitations and various forms of direct communications are standard practice: the aim is to ease the shift from school or university to the workplace. Visits to the company typically involve informal meetings with executives from the same university, exhibits of company products, and lectures on the firm's structure. The actual hiring date starts with an initiating ceremony involving speeches by key executives, meetings with the labour union, instructions on the training program, and social activities such as sports and cultural clubs. Employee training usually includes a basic orientation program, on the job training, and a residency. In the past, orientation programs consists of lectures over one or two weeks by executives from various levels and departments. However, many of the larger firms like Sony, Hitachi and Kawasaki Steel have extended these training sessions to one to six months or more: a survey reported by Tanaka (1980) illustrates the quite detailed topics and issues covered for Japanese trainees.

An important feature of these early sessions is the use of the mentor system.[12] Mentors are middle level and senior managers who serve as role models, teachers, and informal helpers to employees in a formal organization. Research on mentors is rather sparse in North America (Burke, 1982) but there is some

---

[12] Daniel Levinson (1978) describes the mentor functions as follows: "He may act as a *teacher* to enhance the young man's skills and intellectual development. Serving as *sponsor,* he may use his influence to facilitate the young man's entry and advancement. He may be *host* and *guide,* welcoming the initiated into a new occupational and social world and acquainting him with its values, customs, resources and cast of characters. Through his own virtues, achievements and way of living, the mentor can be an *exemplar* that the protege can admire and seek to emulate. He may provide counsel and moral support in times of stress.
The mentor has another function and this is developmentally the most crucial one: to support and facilitate *The Realization of the Dream.* The true mentor . . . fosters the young adult's development by believing in him, sharing the youthful dream and giving it his blessing, helping to define the newly emerging self in its newly discovered world, and creating a space in which the young man can work on a reasonably satisfactory life structure that contains the dream."

Exhibit 8/8: Typical New-Employee Orientation Topics and their Content

Topics	Contents
Company Background	■ Background information ■ Organizational structure, occupational hierarchy ■ Long-range plans ■ Operating budget and financial situation ■ Employee-employer relations, labor unions ■ Working conditions and regulations ■ Salary structure ■ Employee welfare and fringe benefits
Products	■ Introduction to the range of company's products ■ Physical structure, working principles, price and users of company's main products and their value as merchandise in relation to competitive products
Production	■ Variation, flow, preparation of operational directives ■ Interpretation of production charts, blue prints ■ Principles of production processes ■ Product management and cost accounting
Sales	■ Performance and market share ■ Future perspective and trends of competitors ■ Dealer and agent relations ■ Sales techniques
Basic Business Skills	■ Exercises to increase proficiency with abacus, slide rule, business machines and computers ■ Business etiquette, including telephone manners, use of business cards, use of deferential language and posture, seating order in social space (restaurants, public and private transportation, meetings) ■ Instruction in business letter writing, format and expression ■ Fundamental statistical knowledge pertaining to such areas as marketing research and financial statements

Source: Tanaka (1980)

evidence that mentors can play a valuable role in sharing and transferring knowledge from experienced to new employees (Roche, 1979).

On-the-job training schemes are standard practice in larger Japanese firms and the focus is on practical knowledge of many functional areas, even those which won't be directly related to the future career job. Firms like Bridgestone Tire, Matsushita, and Mitsubishi provide on-the-job training for manufacturing tasks but also for jobs related to service and distribution. Familiarization of the workings of different departments in the organization and ease of communications by people of different backgrounds are two of the subordinate goals of these on-the-job programs and they help to translate the general knowledge learned in university and the orientation lectures to practical workings of the company. In this way, the style of training employed by Japanese firms is seen as a continuing investment in career development and, because it is oriented to learning general skills, it is focused on performance and objectives rather than promotion or career ladders.

As noted in Chapter 5, the religious cult of the Samurai ethic has remained strong in Japan and this influence has become a fixture in many residential training programs away from the company premises. Zen temples are popular places for *zazen* (literally seated Zen), which teach a code of diligence, with spartan life styles, physical exercise, and experience in living together. Some companies have programs with the self-defense training center, where military discipline, physical endurance, and team work are carefully nurtured in future managers.

In almost all companies, workers are required to keep diaries and records of their own training. In addition, companies keep quite detailed guidance notebooks on individual achievement and these form the basis of individual career planning. As Cole (1979:171) notes: "it is apparent from this detailed apparatus of data collection and record keeping that a cornerstone of company personnel policy is a very individualized treatment of workers *(Kobetsu Romu Kanri)*, which involves the constant monitoring of individual plans and the actions designed to shape and produce the desired outcomes. In particular, the focus on education is quite notable. Secondly, there is clearly an attempt to build into these plans individual hopes and aspirations."[13]

The emphasis placed on early career training and socialization extends in a detailed way to becoming institutionalized, integrated manpower and human resources policies for both managers and blue collar workers at the later stages of employment. Obviously there is great variation across companies and industries, and many firms have particular policies which represent the philosophy and culture of the organization. Firms like Matsushita and Sony are examples in electronics, for instance, where the personal stamp of Matsushita and Morita stand out in the Japanese corporate landscape.

Nor should the practices in Japanese companies be seen as total success stories. There are numerous instances where young workers do not accept the discipline and low emphasis on individual merit, and there are many instances where middle level executives experience "burn out" and low productivity. Even here, however, the policy of *mado giwa zoku,* i.e. giving a desk in the

---

[13] Cole's analysis is based on the car industry in Japan, but his points typify the approach of other manufacturing and service sectors. On the U.S. approach, he adds: "It is difficult even to imagine a major American company devoting the resources to compiling and utilizing the information necessary for blue-collar career guidance. The automobile industry in the United States would be the last place one would even think of looking for career development and guidance programs, given our image of the impact of technology on skill distribution and training requirements and the cyclical character of the industry." (pp. 171–172).

office near a window, represents an attempt to give a sideways movement to an employee who is low on performance but should not be fired.

Notwithstanding these costs, the basic question of the merits of the Human Capital approach remains highly contentious in scholarly circles. Many writers feel the system must give way to severe change, usually because of such factors as the rise in the educational levels and individualistic values of young people, and also a certain occupation consciousness where professional roles compete with enterprise loyalties (Cole and Tominago, 1976). Finally, there is the increasing levels of interfirm mobility, wherein employees shift from one firm to another (but almost never to a competitor), with a rising percentage of mobility from big to medium or small sized firms as starting wages for such organizations tend to be less and less unequal. It is often speculated that on such issues, the permanent employment features of the Human Capital model will disappear. Moreover, the high mobility features of the Labour Market model are much prized by economists in general and by individualist foreigners, particularly Americans.[14] Against these types of arguments stand the more sociological issues, such as industrial democracy of work and quality of work life. In this vein, it is worthwhile repeating Dore's (1973) belief that the Japanese approach will become the model for other industrialized countries to follow, mainly because of the efficient and humane approach to human resource management.

Still another approach is to see the Human Capital or Labour Market approach in the face of technological innovation. In many industrial circles it is almost a cliche that technological innovation stems from individual creativity and that technological advance stems from internal manpower policies promoting a high level of individual autonomy to employees. In fact, however, most technologically innovative firms are successful primarily because they have a strong technological organization, not only across various departments (R & D, Production and Marketing) but across hierarchical levels (Lawrence and Lorsch, 1969).

From a technological perspective, the Japanese emphasis on The Human Capital approach can be evaluated in the desire for a high level of workforce stability and a high level of constant incremental improvements, rather than intermittent major organizational change. As Richard Casement (1982) has

---

[14] Even in the U.S., the benefits of high mobility are now being reconsidered. According to one report (Deutsch, 1982), "A belated awareness is surfacing among American managers that it is counterproductive to recruit and train people and fit them into a company only to lose them, their services, and their company acquired knowledge to a competitor and then have to begin the costly cycle all over again . . . Until they recognize turnover's bottom-line importance for the 1980's, during which U.S. industry is struggling to maintain its competitive edge, double digit turnover will continue to weaken corporate and national productivity and raise the cost of doing business."

argued, "The evidence of past innovations is that the commercial winners are persistent tortoises (with conventional Japanese skills) rather than creative hares."

The implications of this point can be seen in reference to Japanese competition against America's Silicon Valley. California is the center of the U.S. microchip technology and numerous firms have developed as offshoots of other firms, largely as individual entrepreneurs attempt to exploit their individual inventions in microchip technology. So great has been the competitive recruitment of highly trained individuals that, as *Fortune* (1981) noted, employees could change jobs without changing parking lots. The Japanese firms, by contrast, had experienced very low job turnover and this stability of manpower allowed each firm to apply the lessons and ideas of one stage of the technological developments to the next stage in a logical and orderly fashion.[15] The result was that in the development of the 64K Rom chips, the Japanese firms cornered about 70 percent of the global market.

The real issue, however, is not the question of the Japanese or the American approach to human resource management because so many other national factors are involved. The issue is which approach, the labour market model or the human resource model, is most suitable to technological innovation and a highly educated labour force. There is still another issue which needs to be addressed, namely the question of population dynamics and organizational demographics.

8.6 Organizational Demographics

In a society where work, productivity, and pay are so closely related to age, questions of organizational demographics reflect national priorities for the next few decades. Japan has the most rapidly aging society in the world, and on present trends will have the highest ratio of population over 65, from under ten percent in 1982 to more than fifteen percent in two decades (Exhibit 8/9). The greying of Japan, from a country with one of the youngest mean ages to one of the oldest, has profound affects for society at large, but no where more critical than in the workplace arena for jobs, promotions, and labour costs.

---

[15] The advantages of mobility have often been cited as "cross fertilizing." As *Fortune* notes, firms like Texas Instruments and Motorola have located plants in isolated areas to retain workforce stability: "The development of the 64K demanded continuity in teamwork, which was lacking at the great majority of the Silicon Valley companies . . . the key was to keep those backup masterminds in their jobs. This was easier for Motorola and Texas Instruments to do. Both companies have located their memory divisions in the relative isolation of Texas – Motorola in Austin, T.I. in Lubock. Neither town is especially conducive to job hopping" (December 14, 1981)

Exhibit 8/9: Component Ratio of Elderly Population (65 years old and over)

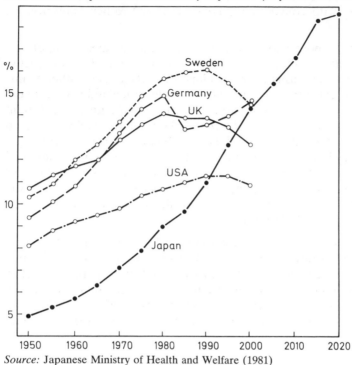

Source: Japanese Ministry of Health and Welfare (1981)

Various factors have combined to bring about these notable demographic changes. Population dynamics reflect a general situation which is stark: the country has gone from a state of many births and many deaths to one of few births and few deaths. From 1920–1950, the birthrate was about constant at 30 births per 1,000 population: it dropped to 14.9 in 1978. In addition, births per mother have dropped, from an average of 5.23 in 1920 to 2.37 in 1955, to 1.91 in 1975. In 1980, when only 1.5 million babies were born, Japan experienced the lowest birthrate since the end of World War II.

In 1920, there were 25.4 deaths per 1,000 of population; the rate in 1978 was only 6.1. Where life expectancy at birth was 50 years before the war, in 1981 Japan had male and female longevity records second only to Iceland: 73.32 years for men, 78.83 years for women. General economic growth, medical science and treatment, improved sanitation facilities, and better dietary standards are main factors accounting for Japan's considerable progress in raising health indicators to a very high level and contributing to an aging society.

The changing composition of the Japanese population, that is the distribution of the age structure, is now combining with a mixture of related issues such as higher female participation rates and increased education levels to impose a fundamental reordering of public policy priorities and human resources strategies practiced by the public and private sector alike. The changing age profile can be analyzed with reference to three groups: ages 15–29, 30–44, and 45–64.

As shown in Exhibit 8/10, the youngest age sector has gone in two decades, from 1960 to 1980, from being the largest to the smallest. Whereas in 1961, about 46 percent of all manufacturing workers were under 24, by 1975 this had decreased to 16.8 percent. At the same time, the aging trend of the 30–44 group went from a third in 1960 to 41.4 percent two decades later, while the 45–64 group increased by more than seven percent in only a decade.

These changes in the labour force stem from the larger population dynamics of aging Japan: only seven percent of the population were over 65 in 1970 (five percent between 1920 and 1955) compared to nine percent in 1982, and 19 percent expected in another forty years. Put differently, it took France 126 years to have a population percentage of elderly people from 7.9 to 14.3, Sweden 80 years, England 46 and Germany 36. Japan's transition to equivalent levels is taking place at rates two to five times as fast, or in only a generation span of 25 years. A direct corollary is that Japan's dependency ratios are being put upside down, from a state where there were 7–8 adult Japanese employed for every citizen over 65, to one where there will be only three in the year 2015.

Exhibit 8/10: Age Structure of Japan's Labour Force

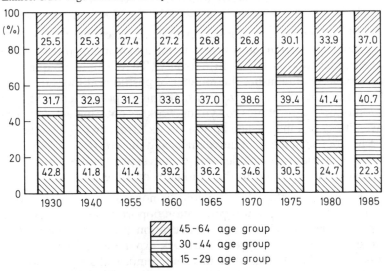

Source: Hirohide (1980)

The trend of these demographic statistics has a direct bearing on human resource policies. The biggest debate in Japan has focused on the issue of the age limit for retirement at 55. By 1980, for the first time, firms which had extended their age limit to 60 exceeded those with the 55 age limit (*Japan Times,* October 21, 1981). The Ministry of Labour has adopted 60 as the retirement target for all enterprises by 1985. There are important differences, however, by size of firm, and between men and women. About 95 percent of firms with more than 100 employees and eighty percent with between 30 and 99 employees have an age limit policy. Although the Supreme Court invalidated the discriminatory age limit system, a recent survey showed that 49.4 percent of firms set 60 as the retirement age for men, 12.1 percent set 57, and 22.8 set 55, while 31.4 percent set 55 for women and 28.7 percent 50 (Ministry of Labour, 1981).

Changes in wage policies as a result of organizational demographics already began in the last decade and have accelerated in the 1980's. The Nenko System of seniority based wages has been modified even in very large firms for employees over 50, as found in a Ministry of Labour Survey conducted in 1980: indeed, for employees in firms with less than 100 workers, peak earnings come between the ages of 40–44 (Exhibit 8/11). This trend means that many firms are introducing a variable wage component in addition to the seniority based system to provide greater flexibility to meet conditions of changing technology and lower growth. Already the work week is being shortened, from an annual average of about 2146 to 2000 hours (i.e., a 40 hour week with two weeks holidays annually), compared to 1934 in the U.S., 1799 in France, and only 1728 in West Germany. Again, however, there are major differences by size of firms and industrial sector: a union study found in a survey conducted in 1981 that companies in high technology areas averaged only 1706 hours per year.

All of these trends influence future human resources policies. Do they add up to a profound change not only in internal promotion and manning practices but in the general attitudes to work and to firm loyalty? There can be no question that the aging population diminishes the number of positions at the senior and middle levels of medium and large size firms. In this respect, there will be a shortage of promotion opportunities for young workers entering employment from the universities; this may usher an era of, as Drucker (1981) reports, "loosening the link between the right universities and the prestige employment under which careers in major companies, major universities and practically all government agencies are reserved to the graduates of a few schools."

Some analysts have argued that the changing demographics will cause employee resentment with work, as fewer promotion opportunities arise, and the mix of low skilled jobs and high levels of education increases conflict and discontent – in short, a decrease in work and work experience as a central life interest (Dubin, et al., 1981). This view has some empirical support: studies have consistently found a loosening of individual loyalty to the employer (Cole,

Exhibit 8/11: Age and Wage Profile

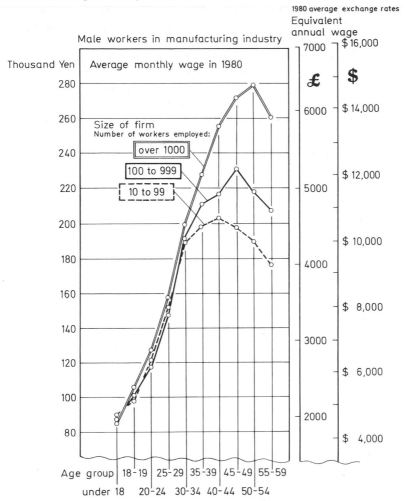

1976: 205; Odaka, 1975: 128–129). Intrafirm mobility will likely increase as a general phenomenon in the labour force, despite persistence of permanent employment among larger and more technology intensive firms. Japan's knowledge intensification strategies, together with the adjustments to the 1973 and 1979 oil shocks, have opened up the productivity gaps and wage levels between large and small firms. In many such sectors as steel, chemicals, and smelting, there are limits placed on small firms acting as subcontractors and suppliers, and these place that group at a competitive disadvantage, where low growth, rising wage rates and low productivity leads to a vicious downward spiral.

An optimistic scenario for Japan's aging workforce focuses on Japan's emphasis on high technology in electronics and new materials. In these sectors, barriers to entry are substantially reduced and new firm formation can be substantially higher. In this case, small and medium sized firms will have access to the very highly educated manpower from the universities and they will also have available new process technologies such as robotics which can make them more productive.[16] In other words, the greater mobility of Japanese workers, and even the retirement of older employees at still productive ages around 60 or 65, may plausibly increase, not decrease, Japan's productivity potential, technology diffusion, and employment opportunities.

Of course, non-work related activities may equally absorb some of this creative potential since fewer hours are spent on leisure in Japan than in the U.S., at least in the past. As shown in Exhibit 8.12, personal commitment to leisure is

Exhibit 8/12: Time Allocation in Japan and the U.S.A. (hour/minute)

	Men		Women	
	Japan	U.S.A.	Japan	U.S.A.
Time required for gratifying physical needs	10.33	9.42	10.24	10.12
Sleeping	8.04	7.30	7.39	7.49
Eating	1.31	1.12	1.44	1.18
Others	0.58	1.00	1.01	1.12
Work time	9.10	8.42	9.12	7.00
Job	7.54	6.18	1.12	0.60
Teabreaks	–	0.36	–	0.00
Housework	0.28	1.06	7.57	6.54
Commuting	0.41	0.42	0.02	0.00
Free time	5.09	5.36	7.24	6.48
Education and culture	0.07	0.12	0.13	0.12
Social activities	0.13	0.12	0.10	0.24
Spectator amusement	0.02	0.06	0.03	0.06
Sports and outings	0.13	0.12	0.08	0.06
Travel	0.08	0.48	0.11	0.54
Reading	0.40	0.36	0.27	0.36
Radio	0.35	0.06	0.26	0.00
Television	2.47	1.24	4.30	1.30
Others	0.24	2.00	1.16	3.00

Notes: 1. Japan = 1970 statistics; U.S.A. = 1965 statistics.
2. Japanese total exceeds 24 hours as the time spent in concurrent activities is included.
Source: Leisure Development Centre, Leisure Handbook

[16] According to the *White Paper on Small and Medium Enterprises 1980,* the trend to new technologies has progressed rapidly: "Nearly 80 percent of small and medium subcontracting enterprises have developed new technology either independently or under the guidance of client firms. Business firms, in turn, have actively supported subcontractors technology development

lower in Japan than in the U.S. and where leisure activities are pursued, they tend to be of passive pastimes like watching television. Although the data are more than a decade old, the pattern appears not to have changed: a survey by NHK television found that on Sundays both men and women in Japan spent far more time watching T.V. (over four hours) than any single activity except sleep and personal chores.

8.7 Summary and Conclusions

This chapter has focused on the human resource strategies practiced by Japanese corporations. Various explanations have been provided to explain the evolution of employment strategies, from broad cultural interpretations to calculated choices based on specific constraints and conditions. Broadly speaking, the two basic models or approaches – the labour market model and the human capital model – provide an efficient interpretation of strategic responses to organizational environments, and involve quite different tradeoffs on cost and benefits.

Larger Japanese enterprises have adopted the human capital approach, wherein young employees are hired through a careful screening process largely based on educational achievement, wages are a function of seniority rather than individual merit, and long term training programs provide a continuing investment in new skills and learning. Because wages are essentially a fixed cost, topped up by productivity bonuses for group merit and individual performance, Japanese managers must take a long term view of organizational strategies, since failure to integrate policies towards innovation and productivity can have disastrous financial consequences.

Despite the vast range of company policies, depending for instance on such issues as size of company, technological intensity, or relation to larger organizational groups, Japanese managers have developed a remarkable consistency towards human resource work policies. Indeed, while quality circles have been the prototype model discussed in the West, the longer term impact of Japanese human resource management may well be in the integration of hardware and software technologies for continuous technological change and innovation. Work groups are an important aspect of these techniques, but more fundamental practices such as organizational socialization, career planning, use of mentors, and concern for the individual employee reflect a commitment by top management to human resources which is striking by comparison to Western practice in many areas.

by loaning machinery and offering technical guidance. Many small and medium subcontracting enterprises that have made such efforts have reported remarkable improvements in their technology level, as well as increased order-acceptance" (p. 29).

The human capital approach is neither universal in Japan nor based on partic-ularistic cultural characteristics. Contrary to foreign perceptions, these non-cultural features of Japanese labour practices, while extensive in their applica-tion throughout most sectors and well understood by junior and senior em-ployees alike, do not easily fit into the category of "borrowed from the U.S.A." In fact, the experience of Japanese firms abroad, in the U.S.A., in Canada, in France, in Britain, has brought home to many Japanese managers just how limited is the Western approach to human resources.

Whether U.S. practice, for instance, has been in the "primitive" stage, to cite the word used by *Business Week*, is perhaps debatable. What should cause at least some reflection in U.S. management circles, however, is the fact that most of the truly innovative human resource techniques have come from Europe and Japan. Quality of work life programs are now pervasive in many U.S. sectors, and these have more parallels to Japanese techniques in their focus on plant level and job level practices, in contrast to corporate level and societal level approaches of European models of co-determination and industrial demo-cracy.

The larger issue is not, as already noted, the merits or demerits of one societal approach or the other, but what specific corporate human resource policies are most conducive to technological change, productivity, and individual learning. Japanese managers are faced with the same basic constraints as their Western counterparts, with perhaps even higher levels of employee expectations be-cause of two decades of unparalleled growth and very high levels of education. In the future evolution of the Japanese industrial structure, the Japanese may have an advantage over managers abroad – a well developed human resource philosophy developed at home, and a willingness to learn and adopt from abroad.

Chapter 9
Production and Operations Management

> "To cross at a ford means to attack the enemy's weak point, and to put yourself in an advantageous position. This is how to win in large scale strategy. You must research this well."
>
> *Miyamoto Mushashi,*
> A Book of Five Rings

9.1 Introduction

The popular image of the Japanese factory runs the gamut from a low paid sweatshop to the glistening rhythm of the automated factory manned by industrial robots. Despite the stereotypes related to Japanese processes, there can be little doubt about the production focus of Japanese management and the powerful influence of modern forms of scientific management originating in the ideas of Frederick Taylor. The production emphasis is clear in the tactical policies of Japanese factories. Products exported to the world market now have earned unrivaled reputation for quality and reliability. Comparative studies show that plant and equipment in Japan are replaced twice as rapidly as in Britain, and faster than the United States. Statistics show that stock turn, that is inventory turnover, is substantially higher in Japan than other Western countries. Waste reduction policies and energy efficiency are unrivalled. Are these results simply a function of resource scarcity? Are there cultural issues at work here, especially the receptivity to new ideas? Or is the issue of production emphasis more fundamental to Japan's entire strategy to new industries and technologies?

The emphasis on production in Japanese manufacturing, while influenced by American practice since the Second World War, has to be understood as part of the country's obsession to catch up with the West by adopting and improving Western technology. From the time of Meiji to the present, Japanese government and industrial leaders have recognized the country's backward state of technology and the constraints of living without raw materials. As a resource poor and technologically dependent country, Japan has had the most to gain from improving its production processes, even by borrowing from the West. Moreover, the costs of many of the inputs for Japanese industry have been much higher than in Europe and certainly the United States. For example, Japan has always been a crowded country, short of arable land, energy and food. Even when coal mining was transformed at the turn of the century to more capital-intensive processes, the output was substantially below equivalent mines in Europe or North America (Murakushi, 1979). The shortage of labour during the rapid growth years since the Korean War, and the cost of imported technology, have prompted Japanese managers to examine alternative production approaches.

Until OPEC changed the world energy situation in 1973, North American managers have never faced up to these same constraints and even now, understand them only imperfectly. Japan's advantages now involve a century of managing resource scarcity. Despite this point, Japanese management is influenced by the dynamics of internal organization. When employees are recruited from rural villages or the best universities, they bring to the organization a desire for security and long term career. The permanent employment system, while reducing managerial flexibility by making wages essentially a fixed cost, serves to promote experimentation and novelty with technology. As already noted, the relative absence of a basic conflict between worker and machine reduces the social backlash of technological change or even disputes about job demarcation. The diffuse decision-making pattern in Japanese companies and the relative absence of rational norms to "control" future events in the long term, make operational decisions supportive of long term strategy. Wheelwright (1981) makes the point as follows:

In Japan, the integrity of the production system and strategic purpose comes first. But Japanese manufacturers also realize that decisions at the level of operations can, if handled in a wise and consistant manner, have a useful cumulative effect at the level of strategy. Experience has taught the Japanese the value of placing even short term manufacturing decisions at the service of long term strategy – a lesson that American companies have learned only imperfectly.

This chapter focuses on production and operations management in Japan, starting with the historical roots of scientific management. Three contemporary issues are examinded – the dynamics of product experience curves and product design, the revolutionary system of process inventory and just-in-time scheduling, and the emergence of robotization and flexible manufacturing. The chapter concludes with speculations on the future of Japan's production emphasis and its impact on Western management.

9.2 Origins of Production Strategy

The phenomenal success of Japanese manufacturing in industrial products like motors and ships and consumer goods like electronics of every description is usually dated from the Second World War. Moreover, the familiar influence of

U.S. managerial theoriests in industrial engineering, statistics, and quality control is often credited with shaping Japanese managerial practices. Obviously, there is a strong element of truth in these assertions. However, in the area of production, much more than in marketing, historical factors come into play. Certainly, the desire to learn from Western technology has placed production – especially issues of process technology – at the forefront of post war redevelopment.

In many aspects, Japan has historically been ahead of technological developments compared to the U.S. and Europe. In iron and steel, for example, techniques for the heat treatment of metals had been developed in Japan before Europe, even though the scientific development of theories in chemistry and physics was more advanced in Europe. In cotton textiles, entrepreneurs like Sakichi Toyoda invented low cost power looms which rivaled the best in Europe at the turn of the century. Even before the Second World War, the leading cotton frames and looms were Japanese designed, and licensed abroad through Platt Brothers. Before and during the war, the Japanese had pioneered aspects of navy shipbuilding and aircraft production which was the equal or superior to foreign techniques.[1] The high cost of imported materials, the need to adapt to local geographical conditions, and Japan's education system with its emphasis on practical subjects have all impacted on production-related skills.

Notwithstanding these points, foreign theorists have had a lasting impact on Japanese management. Fifty years separate the two waves of foreign intellectual ideas. The first was inspired by the time and motion studies developed by Frederick Taylor and his disciples, like Henry Gantt. The second came with the statistical quality control theories of W. Edwards Deming and W. Juran. Both eras involve the core activities of industrial engineering or, to use its historical name, scientific management. As a field of study and practice, scientific management has become vastly more developed in Japan than even in the U.S. because of the more central role of engineers in management strategies, and because with electronics and robotics, the core topics of Taylor's early studies are seen as critical to global marketing success.

Although now a maligned figure in U.S. management theory, Taylor (1856–1915) pioneered the study of work and brought to his scientific research a concern with the social aspects of job design as well as engineering and cost considerations. The major criticism of Taylor in a contemporary perspective is his simplistic view of motivation. As noted by Ivancevich (1977), Taylor addressed this issue with the following premises about the individual worker:

---

[1] For excellent case studies of these and other examples, see "Technology Transfer and Adaptation: The Japanese Experience," *The Developing Economies*, Vol. XVII (December 1979).

1. The problem of inefficiency is a problem of management, not the worker.

2. Workers have false impression that if they work too rapidly, they will become unemployed.

3. Workers have a natural tendency to work at less than their capacities.

4. It is management's responsibility to find suitable individuals for a particular job and then train them in the most efficient methods for their work.

5. Employee performance should be tied directly to the pay system, or an early incentive or piece-rate wage system.

Taylor's interest covered numerous aspects of job tasks, including human development through scientific selection, on the job training, fatigue reduction, incentive systems, and cooperation. Notwithstanding the criticisms directed at his views related to motivation, he did develop a science of time and motion to study work, based on measurement rather than intuitive or rule of thumb methods. He is the father of modern selection and training methods, and he promoted cooperation between management and worker, who, he felt, both shared responsibility for work methods.

Taylor, of course, must be understood in the proper context of his time and industrial setting. From the 1880's when he carried out his studies of manual shovelling in a steel mill to the First World War, the United States was in a process of introducing large scale factory organization. The vast majority of workers were poorly educated immigrants. During this period, some of the most influential U.S. industrialists like Andrew Carnegie attempted to break the backs of craft unions, and Taylor has been criticized as being party to this effort. Taylor's effort at developing rationalized production processes has been interpreted as a means of using at best semi-skilled workers, with substantially smaller wage differentials across job positions.[2]

Taylor's influence in Japan came about with the translation of *Principles of Scientific Management,* published in the U.S. in 1911. The Japanese version had the title *The Secret of Saving Lost Motion* and sold almost two million copies. Contrary to Cole's (1979) assertion, railways and textiles was not the first industry where Taylor's ideas on standard motions were implemented. True, Sanji Muto of Kanebo Co. conducted surveys of standard motions in spinning – five years later, Toyobo completed the establishment of standard

---

[2] As Charles Perrow notes, "The owners 'expropriated' the craft skills and craft system, and put the label of company property upon the ingenuity, experience and creativity of the workers. Only now are we beginning to painfully rediscover and recommend giving back to the workers a small part of what had been their own property, in the form of such schemes as job enlargement, workers' participations, workers' autonomy, or group incentives." *Complex Organizations* (Glenview, Ill.: Scott, Foresmen and Company, 1979), p. 21.

motions involving operations and safety for work processes in spinning and weaving. In fact, as early as 1908, Junihoko Iwatare of Nippon Electric, Japan's first joint venture, studied scientific management at Western Electric and subsequently introduced it to his company. During 1913–1914, Daigoro Yasukawa visited Westinghouse Electric in the U.S. and introduced the bonus system at Yasukawa Electric Equipment in 1915. By 1919, the government subsidized the Kyocho Kai (Labour Management Cooperation Society), which had a section on scientific management, the Industrial Efficiency Institute (Nakase, 1979).

In Japan then, scientific management gained an immediate and impressive foothold and has influenced management thinking for generations. In Britain, by contrast, Taylorism was totally ignored until the First World War. Once it had become known, Taylorism was greeted by universal hostility, by management and by unions alike. Why was this so, and what lessons does the introduction of scientific management ideas say about management in these two countries?

The first aspect of Taylor's research work in Britain was that it involved scientific study, or ideas and theory. British management was (and is) guided by pragmatism and the cult of the amateur. There was a pervasive disrespect not only for the factory worker but for work conditions.[3] The large satanic mills were "grimly utilitarian, and if some were light and well ventilated this was as likely as not because of the requirements of the productive process rather than the human needs of the workforce." Despite the defense of Taylorism by such as C. Bertrand Thompson, criticism of Taylorism was as much managerial as it was unionist. The latter position was put forward by The Trade Union Congress, through its Committee of Engineering. In its view, the Committee was

of the opinion that the premium bonus system by encouraging individual selfishness, is demoralizing to the workman. That, by destroying craftmanship and encouraging specialization, it is harmful to the (engineering) industry, which moreover is burdened by a horde of supervising officials, whose maintenance as non producers imposes a considerable tax upon its profits; and further, the system is a menace to the community at large, owing to the abnormal and continuous increase in unemployment which is directly due to its working and which is bound to become intensified as the system extends.

---

[3] In a perceptive column, Francois Duchene writes that "the usual comment abroad is that the British are lazy. There is obviously a grain of truth in this . . . It only requires a little first hand experience to sense straight away his bitter assumption that the profit from work is not for him but for 'them' . . . The Ruhr may not be everyone's idea of the city beautiful, but the Ruhr barons practiced a careful and autocratic paternalism and Bismarck pioneered social insurance. Dickens is British, not German." "The British Worker: Is He Just Lazy?" *Newsweek* (March 26, 1973), p. 41.

The typical perspective of the British manager was perhaps best summed up by an anecdote of Robert Owen's visit to a Leeds factory. John Marshall, the factory manager, complained to Owen, "If my people were to be careful and avoid waste, they might save me £ 4,000 a year." Owen replied, "Well, why don't you give them £ 2,000 to do it? And then you yourself would be the richer by £ 2,000 a year."

By contrast to the hostility of Taylorism in Britain, the Japanese reception was open and widespread. The major reason for this was Japanese management. General economic conditions obviously favoured this reception. There was the fear in Japan of strong labour-management conflict, a perception of inefficient business and government practices relating to imperialist conflict, the establishment of the Zaibatsu holding companies, a felt need to reform personnel practices. It was left to Japanese managers to take the initiative. Two books on Taylor were published, one by Yukinori Hoshino, who was in the U.S. when Taylor brought out his *Principles of Scientific Management,* published in Japan in 1912 as *Kengaku Yoroku* (A Report on Observations). The second book was by Toshiro Ikeda, entitled *Secrets For Eliminating Futile Work and Increasing Production.* This book sold over a million copies through the decade. The President of Mitsubishi Goshi Kaisha distributed twenty thousand copies to his employees, and the head of Kawaska Shipbuilding Yard gave fifty thousand to his workers. Numerous articles were printed on various aspects of Taylorism, and books appeared on Taylor's theories of differential piece rates and the bonus system developed by Taylor's colleague, Henry Gantt.

This legacy of Taylorism and scientific management must be recognized in Japan, because the historical roots of the strong production orientation of Japanese management explain the patterns of contemporary production strategy. Inventory management, reduction of waste, quality circles, robots, and automated factories have become today's agenda for industrial engineering, but their practice is more advanced in Japan than anywhere, even the U.S.

Consider some anecdotal evidence on Japanese manufacturing. A Harvard professor's observations after a factory tour in Japan (Hayes, 1981):

Everywhere I saw evidence of Japanese manager's determination to prevent Murphy's law ("If something can go wrong, it will go wrong") from taking effect and to make sure that problems which do arise are resolved before they get to the plant floor.

The Japanese (manufacturing) cost and quality advantage originates in painstaking strategic management of people, materials and equipment – that is – in superior manufacturing performance.

Dore's (1973) comparative study of English and Japanese plants noted, "The impression of greater neatness and disciplined formality at Hitachi: a looser even sloppy informality at English Electric." There were even differences in dress: Hitachi workers wore safety helmets issued by the company in every shop where there were cranes: assembly line girls had uniform head scarves; English Electric workers wore a variety of clothes; they were urged to buy protective boots and they were offered for sale at a cut rate, but they were not compulsory. A foreman in Hitachi was addressed by his title – 'Foreman!' He addressed his subordinates by their names plus the polite suffix appropriate to this addressee's age. In English Electric foreman and their workers mostly used Christian names, occasionally for the foreman a "Mister' but there was generally greater informality." Further,

Work at Hitachi was more minutely organized. The bureaucratic procedures of formal regulation and recording penetrated further down the system. There was more use of pencil and paper, of written rather than verbal communication. Workmen erecting machines at Bradford had blueprints to which they referred only when they struck something which was unfamiliar. Their opposite numbers at Hitachi had not only blueprints but also a detailed work book specifying the operations and the order in which they should be done. They also had a log book in which they recorded each operation as they did it, noting for instance, that a hole had been wrongly drilled in a flange and had to be redrilled.

This contemporary emphasis on manufacturing and production management is reinforced by the prodigious output of engineering courses in the educational system. For example, at the undergraduate level, annual enrollment in Japan of students in engineering subjects is over three hundred thousand during the 1970's, compared to fifty thousand in the U.S. and about thirty thousand in Britain. While the U.S. has far and away the most number of graduates in all fields, Japan produces three times more engineers of all types – a fact noted a decade ago by Herman Kahn (1970). According to one report, this problem has led to not only a shortage of industrial engineering in the U.S. but a problem of quality:

The IE graduates we are getting are seemingly much more heavily into business systems and less involved with conventional engineering; so they are losing ground in their ability to be an offsetting balance on the design engineers – so when they take a new product from the processing standpoint and they attempt to duplicate it for production, they lack the necessary fundamentals – we have paid the penalty of these students not being the engineers that they would have been five or ten years ago (Mulroy, 1980).

The significant emphasis on scientific management in Japan has led to a variety of widely used production tools in industry. These hardware systems are not so well known in the West, although companies in the U.S. and Europe are adopting them in whole or in part. The tools are not novel in themselves – it is their extensive application and relationship to other strategic areas like marketing and personnel which makes them so significant. The three areas are progress cost curves, Kanban inventory techniques, and robotization. They are major production tactics which reinforce company level marketing strategies, and form part of the broad mosaic of Japan's societal strategies to gain technological superiority.

9.3 Progress Cost Curves

Progress cost curves have a variety of names – learning curves, experience curves, progress functions – and a long history. The first English literature reference dates to 1938 (Yelle, 1979) when Wright reported his observations on aircraft manufacturing. He noted that as the quantity of units manufactured doubles, the number of direct labour hours it takes to produce an individual unit decreases at a uniform rate. Today, the progress cost curve or experience curve is a staple diet in all textbooks on organization strategy and books on strategic marketing (Thompson, et al. 1980; Abell and Hammond, 1979).

Experience curve phenomena are related to but distinct from economies of scale and technological advances. Moreover, they tend to vary by product and sector. For example, U.S. research revealed that the experience effect was about twice as great in assembly (26%) as in machining (14%), because assembly work involved greater complexity and uniqueness (Hirsch, 1956). Studies carried out on a number of Japanese industries point to the fact that various firms in such industries as color television, motorcycles, jewelled watches, cameras, small cars, and steel have superior records of accumulating experience and gaining lower cost. The actual rate of decline is product specific, from about 12% in automobiles, 15% in color television to as much as 40–50% in semi conductors and integrated circuits.

As shown in the Exhibit 9/1 for integrated circuits, experience curves are plotted with cumulative output in physical volume on the horizontal axis and cost or price per unit of a product on the vertical axis. If the data are plotted on a linear scale, there is a logarithmic decline, and if the relationship is plotted on a double logarithmic scale (indicating percentage change as a constant distance on either axis) there is a straight line, constant relationship between experience and cost. As a management tool, the experience curve is not an automatic or purely engineering phenomenon: experience effects must be planned. For one thing there is a learning by doing effect wherein tasks carried out the first time take longer than with experience, such that unskilled labour takes more time than skilled and experienced workers. Feedback and scientific work study are part of this process. There must be a major managerial effort to reduce costs by work layout improvements, better supervision, product design simplification and more rationalized purchasing, inventory control, and scheduling. There also must be a recognition that experience curve effects may not apply to all products in the same way (e.g., semiconductors versus T.V. assembly), in all situations, e.g., when raw materials account for a significant percentage of

Exhibit 9/1: World Shipments of Integrated Circuits Learning Curve

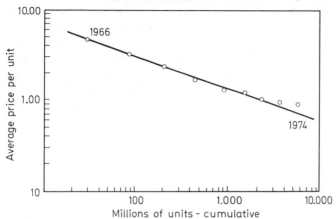

Millions of units - cumulative

Source: Texas Instruments

Exhibit 9/2: Alternative Pricing Strategies

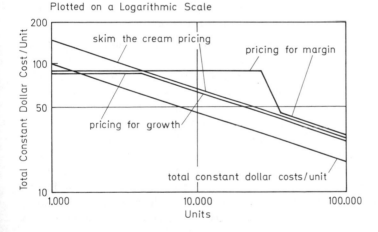

value added, or where technology changes, as when transistors replaced vacuum tubes, or, or when micro circuits replaced mechanical parts in adding machines and calculators.

The implications of experience curve analysis for management are many. In the first place, management must recognize its use in planning, and this means that good engineering data are essential. As noted below, the use of experience curves in "design to cost" is meaningless without a solid data basis. In terms of competitive strategy, the experience curve provides a very effective means of linking production strategy to R & D and marketing. Consider the case of pricing. Cost conscious producers may develop a strategy of using different pricing levels depending on the degree of competition and stage of the product life cycle. As shown in Exhibit 9/2, a firm can adopt a strategy of price exploitation in order to build profit levels but not necessarily to gain market share (assuming competitive conditions). Pricing for market share, by contrast, suggests a strategy of sacrificing profits (and medium term cash flow) to gain longer term market share and improved cash flow. When competition intensifies as a result of the attraction of new entrants due to price exploitation, higher cumulative production can allow for a shift to production based on lowest cost performance.

This analysis corresponds precisely with Japanese manufacturers in scores of products. However, there are other factors which need to be considered. For one thing, a high growth rate requires increases in capital investment for the newest, best practice equipment and processes. Without them, a firm may drop off the experience curve. (Japanese firms making 64K chips are using fourth and fifth generation equipment in the U.S..)[4] Another related issue is the strategic time horizon. Firms emphasizing short time horizons and quick payback periods are likely to forego long term market share and cumulative learning. Such cumulative learning may well mean that barring some technological breakthrough, a firm which falls behind can never catch up.

Do the Japanese have particular advantages in experience curve application? In theory, the answer must be no. In practice, the answer may be positive, because managerial practice has turned its use into a well defined science. The clear product focus of most Japanese manufacturers and the encouragement through tax incentives of the government have combined with singular attention to world class economies of scale. Plant and equipment, thanks to particular taxation and depreciation laws, are newer in Japan than in the U.S. by a significant margin (Exhibit 9/3). Japanese firms like Seiko in watches, Matsushita in televisions, and Kawasaki in motorcycles have effectively used global marketing strategies to develop cumulative experience by shrewd timing of market penetration for new products. Even in a mature industry like cars, Japanese producers have increased production experience at an annual rate of 28%, which allows cumulative experience to double within three years, so that real costs drop seven per cent per year. The comparable U.S. rate is 3.7% for

---

[4] *Business Week* made an assessment of Japanese trends and noted as follows: "A team of researchers from Stanford University recently made a comparative study of U.S. and Japanese semiconductor industries and found that in at least one of the cruicial stages in semiconductor assembly known as automatic bonding, the Japanese are typically using fourth or fifth generation equipment, whereas U.S. companies are using first- or second-generation machines that operate only two-thirds as fast. Japanese use of automated bonding equipment was far more widespread, too, than in U.S. industry, according to the research them." (December 14, 1981, p. 62).

Exhibit 9/3: Age of Plant and Equipment

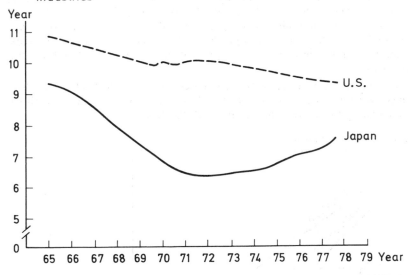

1 Comparison by industry

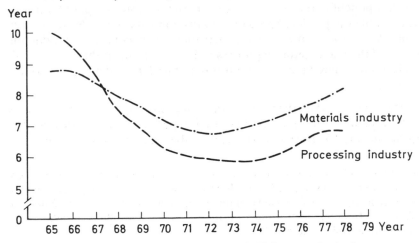

2 Comparison between Japanese and U.S. manufacturing industries

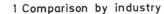

growth, doubling experience every 18 years, and a real decline in costs of only .6% annually.

The effectiveness of Japanese experience curve practice is indicated in a well known technique of "design to cost". The particular approach of design to cost is aided by another technique, namely reverse engineering. Instead of designing a product on paper with engineering specifications laid out in blueprints, take an existing product foreign to the firm (e.g., a competitor's), and break it down into component parts and processes. Learn the basic design but improve on it. Reassemble the product based on creative improvements. Reverse engineering and design to cost mean that a particular cost becomes the production constraint, and the manufacturing process is designed to meet that target. This approach is not uniquely Japanese, but it is better understood and more widely practiced there.

Texas Instruments, an American firm whose organizational culture has many parallels to Japanese corporations, has used experience curves for decades. T.I.'s president, Fred J. Bucy (1978) has described the emphasis on the Japanese approach as follows:

TI is competing head on with the Japanese in several major markets, among them semiconductors (where they have a $ 300 million government sponsored programme for very-large-scale integration (VLSI) development), calculators, and watches. What is to stop the Japanese from taking over these businesses as they have done in radios, stereos, T.V. sets, motorbikes and steel?

I think the big difference is that TI is the first major non-Japanese company they have run into that understands and uses the learning curve. . . . The key to using the learning curve is "design-to-cost", where you determine the cost required for the product and the system to manufacture it to hit that cost goal. The effect here is not just spreading overhead over a larger volume of product produced. It also involves constantly forcing manufacturing costs down through design improvements of the product and the production processes.

In Japan, both the government and industries understand this. Most other industries don't. TI has used this concept informally and formally for many years, and this is absolutely mandatory to compete successfully with the Japanese.

Exhibit 9/4: Value of Market Share

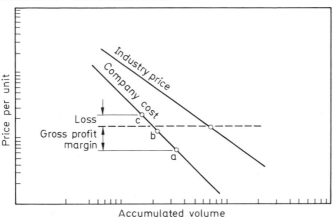

Source: Texas Instruments

To illustrate the impact of successful experience curve application, TI shows three firms in an industry, with current industry price indicated by the horizontal dashed line in Exhibit 9/4. The three firms have three cost positions depending on accumulated production. Company A has larger market share and higher profit margin, Company C operates at a loss, and Company B is marginal. According to TI's former chairman, "a company participating in a world market has an advantage over a company that builds its production base on a national market, but this advantage can exist only if cost reduction is accepted as the responsibility of the entire organization".

9.4 Kanban Inventory Systems

The experience curve is a technique which relates to the design and technology of a particular product. Another widely used production technique, virtually unknown in Western countries until recently and even less widely practiced, is the system of inventory control and production system called Kanban. Kanban is an inventory, parts delivery approach which combines just-in-time delivery to a rigid scheduling flow to reduce waste and inventory costs – incoming parts, work in process, and finished product.

The origins of the approach date from the post-war environment of parts shortages and delivery problems. When the Toyota Motor Company branched off from Toyota Automatic Weaving Machine Works and Toyota Automatic Loom Works in 1933 and was established as a separate company in 1937, parts delivery and volume increases were major problems. Production was only 1,000–2,000 cars per month, and the company felt that demand existed for increased volume.

At Toyota, one manager who considered such issues was Tai-ichi Ohno, the Vice President at Toyota and formerly in charge of Toyota's mechanical engineering section. The production concept which had a strong impact on Ohno was the American Supermarket. A supermarket is not only a vast storehouse of numerous products – it is a point where the customer is directly confronted, the last link in the distribution chain. As such, the supermarket is the point where buyers confront any product damages, shortages, and perishables. Empty shelf space or gaps become the trigger mechanism for staff to replace products. Additionally, large factories usually mean high rents which place a premium on store layout. The ideal is some optional space available for large inventories (warehousing) and adaptable for quick stock turnover and easy stock replacement.

These issues in "supermarket" management impressed Ohno and the management group at Toyota. The question was, could the production system applicable to a service institution like the American supermarket have any relevance to the mass production style typical of the car industry? After all the car industry is extremely complex: it consists of thousands of individual parts assembled in a stepwise sequential fashion. There are several different models and permutations for specific components. The models themselves change every four to five years. Moreover, the car industry is both labour-intensive industry involving workers (skilled and semi-skilled) and capital-intensive (involving high investment in land, plant equipment and distribution).

Conventional productional planning combines a sales forecast projected over a given time period and a production schedule for each stage of the workflow, in an ordered sequence. Managerial flexibility in coordination and information is achieved by holding buffer stocks (inventory) where potential bottlenecks in delivery can occur, or where small lot production of components is uneconomical. As shown in Exhibit 9/5, standard production planning is a critical aspect of organization design, where information on demand scheduling leads to "uncoupling" of production scheduling and product delivery decisions by inventory. Benefits of such an approach stem from the reduction of uncertainty caused by fluctuating demand for products (Galbraith, 1977). In essence, Toyota and other manufacturers have switched from a system of estimated production based on final demand to job order production based on minimum inventory of finished product. The key to this approach is flexible and short set-up times for assembly line machinery.

Exhibit 9/5: Buffer Stocks as a Design Strategy

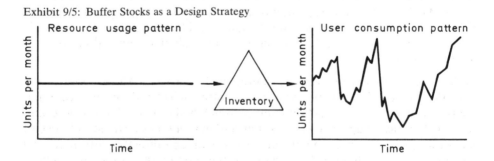

The advantages of the conventional system are well known, quite aside from any specific economies derived from large lot parts procurement. Management control over operations is enhanced be eliminating uncertainty arising from stockout or small lot production. There is more flexibility to increase or decrease output by changing the level of buffer stocks. Finally, by "decoupling" the various work stages, management can use less skilled workers, since supervisory personnel can localize specific knowledge requirements. Like the hull of a tanker ship, the aim is to increase the level of compartmentalization to lower the level of interdependence. In the language of organization design, the various parts are loosely coupled (Weick, 1976).

Most precepts of organization design are consistent with this classic approach to production. The basic aim is one of managerial control, even if inefficiencies or trade offs are not explicitly stated. Many costs, for example, are not known or even calculated. Imbalances between stocks which have high turnover and those with low turnover (dead stocks) are often not corrected. Managers may prefer to cushion the risks of their own errors by adding to their buffer stocks, usually to reduce exposure to disruption, e. g. worker absenteeism, machine breakdown, forecasting error, or worse, to pinpointing directly the production line fault. Additionally, increased management control and the desire for flexibility decrease the need to rely on direct labour for anything short of the physical job requirements of the worker (Argyris, 1973; Miller, 1981).

The Toyota system has recognized the costs and benefits of conventional product planning. The particular Japanese environmental need to husband raw materials and to eliminate factory waste led to Toyota's first principle – namely, to abandon or eliminate waste by supplying only the necessary parts when they are needed. The key to this principle was to define, control, and reduce the lead time from initial entry of parts and raw materials to their actual use. As much as possible, in-process stocks would be eliminated or reduced to the absolute minimum. Both inventory costs and labour time on materials handling are considered as surplus and thus waste.

As a means to implement this policy, the Toyota team turned to the idea recognized in the American supermarket concept: supply parts as they are needed, just-in-time. Instead of projecting materials requirements from the beginning stage of production to each subsequent stage – do the reverse. Start from the final stage of output and work backwards; instead of "push out", use "pull out." Information flows in a reverse order, with workers in the final stage dictating the flow of parts needed from the prior stage, right through to the initial production point. In this way, each step in production is carefully synchronized and parts flow from one step to the next just in time. Elimination of buffer stocks and tight coupling of the line increase the inflexibility of the process. Stockouts or interruptions in the flow of parts of any one stage breaks the continuity of the whole line. The needs for stable flows and close integration of the whole line depend both on internal coordination of production stages and orderly delivery of supply and parts. Such needs relate both to worker job design and supplier relations.

As it turns out, the Toyota system has theoretical origins in scientific management. More than fifty years ago, Taylor's student and assistant, Henry Gannt, developed planning tools which today look at the total production sequence in an attempt to develop assembly balancing techniques. The Kanban system requires higher levels of fixed costs for additional tooling, materials handling, and factory layout, but operating costs are substantially lowered.

9.5 Kanban in Practice

Toyota operates with an annual production plan, which is then broken down into a two step monthly plan. The first step consists of production estimates for all types and models. The second step is an actual plan for production which is the key operational plan. Both are provided to the subcontractors to determine their requirements. It is at this stage where production smoothing takes place, that is, the translation of the monthly schedule into a daily schedule outlining production by shift and by model. By tying the average cycle time needed to produce one unit of any model, the overall daily production schedule can be determined and with it, the daily parts required. This overall scheduling is assisted by a sophisticated computer program, which has features of the U.S. originated MRP (Material Requirement Planning).[5]

On the assembly line itself is a computer tape readout listing the requirements for each model as it moves along the line. The tape indicates the cycle time, information on parts, accessories, color and the like. The availability of this information allows the worker to operate the Kanban to control excess inventory.

The word "Kanban" refers to a small plastic plate, originally paper (about 3½" × 9") which provides the information to workers at each production station. There are, in fact, two types of Kanban cards, each worker takes from the parts container of existing stock to the stock point of the previous stage. The production-Kanban is then left at the stock point as a dispatch signal to replace the inventory used. The two Kanban cards act as a real-time information system indicating production capacity, stock usage, and manpower utilization.

In the early years at Toyota, Kanban operated in only specific areas of the production system, and it took over three years to introduce the system company-wide. Today Kanban operates not only system-wide in Toyota factories but extends to its numerous major suppliers. In this sense, the internal operations of a Toyota plant operate as an integrated, synchronized conveyor system linked to an "invisible conveyor" extending to supplier lines. A similar system, modified for particular companies or sectors, operates in other companies. Nissan Motor, for instance, Japan's second largest producer (the name Datsun comes from the original company, DAT Automobile Manufacturing) calls its system APM – the Action Plate Method.

---

[5] For elaboration of MRP, see Orlicky (1975).

To balance out production across all stages, such that no surplus stocks are building up or no production stage is short of components, Toyota and other manufacturers have succeeded in reducing the averate lot size, usually by shortening set-up time from hours to minutes. (A corollary, however, is that equipment maintenance must be very effective.) Set-ups average one per day in the United States, fewer in Sweden and West Germany, but three per day at Toyota in 1976 and took only one minute by 1983. For some operations like pressing, set-up time is only three minutes. Flexibility in production output is assisted in several ways. Because most workers operate several machines, reduced job rotation and hiring of temporary workers can increase production output. Shifting the work shift time by early attendance and overtime, or by changing the cycle time also allows flexibility in demand output. Temporary workers are the first to go if demand slackens. Regular workers are not laid off, but may be shifted to other work, such as maintenance, training for set up activities, or marking parts normally purchased from suppliers.

A critical element in the operation and practice of the Toyota system is the human relationships among managers, workers, and supervisors, such as Japan's software management systems of quality control, and *Jishu Kanri* (voluntary worker groups contributing to managerial functions.) Japan's system of using work groups as the basic structure of the labour force is well suited for Kanban scheduling. Quality control circles are assisted by specialized staff groups on call (e.g. engineering, accounting, production control) to help work groups solve problems. Perhaps the area of greatest success has been in set up time for particular processes, since short set up times makes feasible short lot production and thereby greatly reduces the lead times for production planning. Moreover, unlike most Western practice in organization design, Japanese companies use engineers directly with bluecollar workers. Indeed they often wear the same clothing and participate in the semi-annual bonuses (McMillan, 1981).

The difference in attitudes towards the relative autonomy of the worker is seen in Toyota's control of the assembly line – the *Jidoka*. In the conventional assembly line, only an extreme cause would merit stopping the entire line, and indeed, any unwarranted stoppage would potentially lead to worker dismissal. Toyota and other Japanese companies have challenged the need for a constantly moving assembly line. At Toyota, a red cord runs the length of the assembly line and any worker can stop the entire line. The usual causes for stoppage are equipment problems, shortage of parts, or discovery of defects. In the center of the line in a Toyota factory is an enormous number board, something like a stadium score board. This board indicates the specific spot where the line has been stopped, the area of the problem, and the time involved. In this way the system reinforces the basic aims of eliminating waste and reducing inventory.

The Jidoka system of allowing workers to stop the line serves as a method of pinpointing the source of errors and directing resources to the exact trouble spot. All workers and foremen are fully aware of the impact of a line stoppage, so that the possibility of such a clear detection system acts as a deterrence to slipshod work or careless behaviour. The origins of the idea are clearly traceable to the textile weaving equipment at Toyota Automatic Loom Works. In the same way that the loom stops when wool runs out from a spindle, the line stops when a defect is discovered or an excess or shortage of parts occurs.

The managerial consequences of this system should not be misunderstood. Where the conventional production system with its buffer stocks and decoupled production stages gives a premium to managerial flexibility and control, the Japanese system makes different trade offs (see Exhibit 9/6). The line is almost totally inflexible, with minimal buffer stocks and greater reliance on workers for inspection and quality control. Yet the high risk which at first glance appears to be a feature of the Japanese system also raises the awareness level of individual workers and the need to perform to standards. Even though one line at Toyota moves more slowly than some US plants (60 cars per hour, compared to 100 at GM's Lordstown Plant,) there are also lower defects and lower injury rates (and lower in-process inventories).

Exhibit 9/6: Trade Offs in Production Systems

	Kanban	Conventional
Basic Architecture	Inflexible	Flexible
Production Runs	Small Lots	Long Runs
Inventory	Stocks Seen as Waste	Stock Adds Flexibility
Planning Flow	Last Stage First	First Stage First
Information Costs	Low	High
Set Up Times	Frequent	Infrequent
Operating Control	Decentralized	Centralized

The capacity of the Kanban system for its internal operations is greatly fostered by its open consultation across functions, its decentralized planning among work groups, and top management's willingness to challenge conventional assumptions of hierarchical control. In this respect, the Kanban system's general application is limited only to management's willingness to make it work. Japanese companies investing abroad have the advantage of designing their factories and floor layout with Kanban principles in mind. U.S. firms like Westinghouse, Ford and G.M. are implementing Kanban tactics in American and Canadian plants, but only in limited areas.

The more extensive form of Kanban, however, involves the application of inventory control and delivery to the parts supplier. Here the principles of Kanban are applicable to any country but, in practice, there are important

Exhibit 9/7: Group Structure of Japanese Auto Manufacturers

Group	Group Affiliates	Number Listed on Stock Exchange	1979 Market Share
Toyota	32	14	30.6
Nissan	35	17	25.0
Honda	25	4	10.3
Mitsubishi	9	0	10.0
Toyo Kogyo	10	2	8.1
Isuzu	18	8	4.2
Hino	16	2	3.5
Fuji Heavy Industries	4	1	3.7
Suzuki	10	0	3.4
Daihatsu	6	0	0.8
Nissan Diesel	6	0	0.4

obstacles. As *outlined previously*, in Japan, the linkages between suppliers and the parent company goes far beyond a simple buyer – seller relationship common in North America and Europe. The parent company is not just a buyer of parts and components: it provides credit, equipment, machinery, technological know-how and managerial experience (often by transferring "retired" senior managers as board directors of supplier firms.) More directly, parent firms also hold shares in the suppliers, even when the suppliers are also quoted separately on the stock exchange. As shown in Exhibit 9/7, all of Japan's auto manufacturers have a number of such "captive" suppliers in the group, and the linkage extends to product planning and process developments in long range strategy.[6]

In North America, competition among large enterprises in a sector like automobiles is confined to the legal corporate entities. In Japan, by contrast, such subcontracting relations adds to the complexity of the corporate planning process and means ologopoly competition is severe. This informal corporate planning linkage extends to major and minor suppliers, and to trading firms and banks. Not only does this system strengthen the competitive edge of Japanese manufacturers, by providing the parent firms with virtually guaranteed delivery schedules and assured product quality, it acts as a clear barrier to supplier firms, such as those from overseas, who want to break into the close family circle. It also goes a long way to explaining the almost defiant reluctance of the Japanese manufacturers to enter North American markets via direct foreign investment. The reason is simple: their family group structure would be diffi-

---

[6] This kind of organization explains why Toyota, for example, can contract out about 70 percent of its components while General Motors makes about 77 percent of components internally. In the Spring of 1982, GM announced that it was loosening its ties with steel suppliers by requiring competitive bidding.

cult to replicate on foreign soil. The forward planning systems of the manufacturers includes close cooperation with the major and minor suppliers – Toyota alone, for example, has over two hundred – and this planning relationship is nurtured by close personal ties, consultative committees, and information exchange. Technology, production techniques, and productivity improvements are the main areas of cooperative effort, especially since the car industry is facing so many challenges. In the area of engines, for example, Toyota and Datsun have pursued the substitution of metals for ceramics, and all car makers are forging new links with electronics suppliers to provide the new components, gadgets, and back up systems (digital indicators for speed control and fuel availability) which will account for as much as a fifth of a car's total cost by 1990.

What is the net effect of the Kanban system of smoothed production? At the simplest, Kanban can be weighed in net inventory savings per unit for output.[7] Estimates vary, but amount may be as high as $ 500–$ 700 per car, depending on how various factors are aggregated. A more fundamental assessment of Kanban suggests that shopfloor production tactics and their behavioural impact get more attention in Japan than in other countries; as well the implications of hardware and software technological change are more fully appreciated by workers and managers alike. The Kanban system, for example, not only turns certain accepted canons of inventory control and production scheduling on their head, it drastically alters the accepted notions of workforce management in assembly line manufacturing. An equally fundamental point is that Kanban, by radically changing set-up times and lead-times for production scheduling, vastly alters the flexibility of mass assembly to meet market demands, even for small lot sizes. Coupled with the newest trend in Japanese production – robotization – this trend has the potential for revolutionary changes in traditional assembly line technology and in concepts of product definition.

9.6 Robotics

A visitor to Japan can recognize robots in the most unlikely places. On highways and in construction zones, robots are used to direct traffic. Robots perform the physical movements of beautifully decorated and life-like animals on display in department stores. Robots are increasingly used in hospitals, old age

---

[7] A study carried out by Booze Allen and Hamilton (1981) showed significantly higher inventory turnover between 1970 and 1978 in Japanese firms than European and U.S. firms – from 190 percent in toiletries and cosmetics and auto parts to 16 and 9 percent for electrical equipment and machine tools. When high inventory levels are related to cost of capital (which in recent years has been much lower in Japan) Japanese manufacturers are gaining a double productivity

homes, and nursing wards to perform basic tasks for sick and disabled patients. Even children are at home with robots, with a bewildering range of robotic toys and a comic literature which made "Star Wars" standard fare in Japan. Television programs depict the use of robots in a wide variety of non-manufacturing uses which the average citizen can relate to. Spraying of insecticides and fertilizers on farms; inspecting and packing of eggs; cutting trees in forests, instead of by manual chain saws; submarine robots for fish farms – such are the examples shown on T.V. to educate people about the positive use of robots. Surveys of robot manufacturers claim that there will be robots to look after handicapped patients, sweep streets, guide blind people and feed bedridden patients. In other words, even though 98 per cent of robots used are in manufacturing, the population gets educated to their general use in society at large.

Kawazaki Heavy Industries Ltd. produced Japan's first industrial robot in 1968 under license from the U.S. firm, Unimation Inc.[8] Since then, Japan has become the robot capital of the world, with as many as 150 companies engaged in robot production and the largest number of robots in industrial use. Machine tool makers have become major players in robotics because of the close technological link with numerically controlled machine tools. Originally designed in the U.S., the first robots in Japan were imported in small numbers. Production engineers studied their use and make up, and applied them to domestic production in specific tasks like welding and paint spraying.

After a decade of study, improvement, testing and innovative application, robotics in Japan was converted into a growth sector, not only in the domestic market but world-wide. The term flexible manufacturing systems (FMS) has become the code word for the transformation of traditional assembly lines using electronics to substitute mechanical systems and robots to take over many human functions. This general trend to more robotics is usually analyzed in human terms, such as the number of displaced workers and the threat of unemployment. In point of fact, the behavioural issues are relevant, but mostly in the context of doing away with the most boring and unsafe jobs and the need for upgrading worker skills and retraining. In this respect, robotics represents no greater threat than any other kind of technological change in past industrial society (see Lawless, 1977).

The real impact of robotics, and the issue of most concern to the Japanese, is the revolutionary change in assembly line production. In big firms, robotics has

---

advantage – much greater stockturn and much lower carrying cost of tied up capital in inventory charges. Most firms in North America or Europe don't set targets for optimal inventory levels and carrying costs. See Foster (1977).

[8] An overview of this development and brief case studies of robot applications are given in *Industrial Robots* (Tokyo: JETRO, 1981).

the potential to introduce mass assembly production cost savings to small lot production runs. For small firms, robotics offers some of the flexibility in production traditionally characteristic of very capital intensive large corporations. What does this mean in simple language? Consider the progress cost curve discussed earlier applied to a particular product, say videorecorders.

Traditional production engineering applied to assembly line industries – cars, watches, radios, cameras, refrigerators – has favoured economies of scale, long production runs, and product specialization. Economies of scale accrue because of the declines in unit costs of production as absolute volume increases over a period of time. Long production runs decrease costs because of learning and improving as a consequence of cumulative volume. Production specialization adds to productivity because of the decreased need to change equipment and incur setup costs as a result of product diversity. When Henry Ford was willing to offer any color for the Model T, as long as it was black, he may not have expressed the accepted canons of modern marketing but he was aware of traditional engineering cost principles. Robotics offers the chance to change them.

For large firms, robotics may bring the opportunity to introduce enormous flexibility in production scheduling for very diverse products on the same assembly line even for small batches (small lot production accounts for an estimated 60 percent of U.S. manufacturing). Downtimes for equipment during changeovers will be substantially reduced, since robots can be programmed to accept detailed instructions of changes on the line. Toyota, Nissan and other car manufacturers have already introduced elements of this through computerized scheduling and Kanban inventory techniques, such that the same line can produce not only numerous variations on similar car models but also different models on the same shift. Robotics will speed up this process as their program software increases in sophistication. For large firms, the likelihood of an infinite range of extras and special features means that mass assembly can produce truly unique final outputs.

The impact of robotics for small firms is no less revolutionary. The small firm will have the opportunity of entering many market segments normally reserved for large firms because within certain volume ranges, robotics will equalize costs for big and small firms alike. Programmable robotics can handle multiple functions – e. g., drilling, burring, and polishing – and with superior productivity and quality. Small firms will not be faced with the cost disadvantages of better work skills and staff support of big firms, but will still be able to cope with the small lot production and flexibility characteristic of the small business sector. It ist for this reason that the use and development of robots in small business in Japan is so widespread, and has received special government support.

An accurate interpretation of Japan's lead in robotics – both in production and in use – must take into account traditional emphasis on production, and the potential to rationalize operations in the face of specific challenges, like labour shortages, an aging workforce, and behavioural problems in job design. Additionally, robots are a natural outgrowth of the country's obsession with best practice manufacturing technology, because of the commitment to quality control and productivity. It is these domestic production issues which have induced Japan's leading manufacturers to transform traditional assembly systems to more highly automated ones, and to aspire to flexible manufacturing systems (FMS) and possibly, totally automated factories.[9]

Data on robot use and production are inconsistent, mainly because of different definitions of what constitutes a robot. One estimate by *Business Week* indicates that Japan has more robots in use than all Western countries combined. An estimate of U.S. delegates to the International Symposium on industrial robots showed that on the wide definition of robots – i.e. sequence machines – Japan had eight times as many robots as West Germany, the second largest user, and fourteen times the number in the U.S. Even on the narrower definition of playback robots, Japan still had a vast lead, 6.7 times that of West Germany and 1.4 times that of the U.S. In manufacturing, the Japanese industry has a lead of a similar magnitude, which the Japan Industrial Robot Association estimates at the end of 1980 to be 14,000 robots in Japan compared to 3255 in the U.S., 850 in West Germany, 600 in Sweden and 500 in Italy. A survey in 1979 of 444 nonmanufacturing companies and robot users predicted that overall production of robots will total $5 billion by the end of this decade.

The predictions of rapid development of robots and the potential for the automated factory raise a host of practical issues concerning displaced workers, new forms of organization, and new systems of production. In one sense, the huge literature on the subject – mostly in journalistic sources – is reminescent over the concerns with automation in manufacturing only a decade or two ago (Simon, 1976).[10] The parallel is that there are many statements and predictions which have very little empirical data to support them, and even less strong theoretical grounds to make any realistic assessments.

At the level of work and work systems, robots can be viewed as an outgrowth of mechanization in industry, and then to automation. Mechanization refers not only to the work tools used by workers – hammers, typewriters, computers – but the change of energy sources from human (or animal) power to mechanical energy. Automation is a related but quite different aspect of the man-machine

[9] "The Next Step In Factory Automation" *The Economist* (December 19, 1981), 79–80.
[10] In a rhetorical question "Will The Corporation Be Managed By Machines?" Simon (1976:23) wrote: "Within the very near future – much less than twenty-five years – we shall have the technical capability of substituting machines for any and all human functions in organizations." The prediction was made in 1960.

relationship. Automation refers to the use of self controlled machines to accomplish work. Modern factories in all societies engage in both processes, but the implications both for the analysis of job design and the meaning of work are imperfectly understood.

Historically, much of the introduction of mechanical equipment has served to eliminate the purely physical tasks performed by human effort. Increasingly, the comparative advantage of human work is in three areas, according to Simon: (1) The use of the brain as a flexible, general purpose problem solving device; (2) The flexible use of human sensory organs and hands; and (3) The use of legs, on rough terrain as well as smooth, to make this general purpose sensing – thinking – manipulating system available whenever it is needed. Man's capacity for flexibility is not an absolute advantage against machines: in some areas, production engineering can change tasks based on principles of flexibility to relative inflexibility so that machines gain a cost advantage. Moreover, there are also inherent costs to using humans – motivation costs, physical weaknesses (fatigue, boredom, bathroom relief) and sensory limitations (hearing low noise, eyesight precision, touch sensitivity). Much of these issues are at the background to job design issues, of course, but they are also now germane to having robots match human sensory and brain skills.

Far more attention has been paid to the first area, namely, designing workflows to let machines substitute for human physical and sensory movement. The growing literature on quality of worklife and "blue collar blues" is a reflection of the social costs of this traditional engineering approach to job design. The basic aim is to remove worker discretion and to make the machine "idiot proof," or "sabotage-proof".

Indeed, industrialization itself has been a historical process whereby the individual has less and less control over the content of his own job contribution, as represented by the quality of skills and the nature of the finished product. Mass production, of course, has largely obliterated craft skills in most industries, and have greatly altered the nature of work relationships involving the individual employee, machines, and other workers. Robots represent a major force in this broad trend and Japanese management may be more successful in recognizing the deleterious aspects of robotization, just as they have in the past in assembly industries. Why is this so?

A number of forces are converging in Japan to support more widespread use of robots in production. From the labour force perspective, there is a double trend-namely an aging of workers in manufacturing, especially of employees in the 30–49 year cohort, and a recruitment of more educated cohort of new employees 29 years or younger. Younger workers are increasingly unwilling to man the jobs which tend to be boring and repetitive (traditional car assembly) or which are dangerous, dirty or unpleasant (painting and welding). Like their older counterparts, younger workers aspire to white collar jobs which involve greater task variety, intellectual challenge, and continuous learning. Both age and higher skills content add to wage costs which, in the absence of off-setting productivity gains, threatens the firm's competitive position. Robots are an accepted response.[11]

Labour market conditions reinforce this acceptance, since permanent employment in the larger companies makes job layoffs less likely. The shortage of up to 800,000 workers in heavy duty skilled jobs means that the broader demographic manpower issues are recognized by workers and managers alike, particularly for the most tedious or dangerous jobs. Japan's automobile industry and its celebrated success against Detroit have done much to educate workers in other industrial sectors and in firms of all sizes how productivity is central to industrial performance internationally. Seen in this light robotics is simply an extension of broader technological and production trends, such as the shift of mechanical systems to electronics (mechatronics) or the applications of computers and on-line information systems into everyday fields as diverse as banking, shopping, and television games.

In the short period of a little more than a decade, Japan has moved from being an importer to the major user and potentially the largest exporter of robotics. One reason why precise figures are difficult to gather is that, as in the United States, many of the larger users of robots have designed machines for their own purposes and have not yet begun sales to other firms. The largest user is the automobile industry, followed by the electrical machinery, plastic molding and metal working industry. Specific tasks required of robots are material handling in machinery, spot welding, assembly arc welding, material handling, painting and inspection (see Exhibit 9/8 for projections).

The range of robots available is depicted in Exhibit 9/9, which shows two dimensions of robotics – their programming and their task variety. The most basic and traditional robot is simply an extension of mechanization. This fixed sequence robot is essentially a single purpose machine whose tasks are programmed to particular specifications. An example is a mechanical arm to transfer materials from one point to another on a line, or to pack small parts into packages. Other applications include plastic molding, spot welding, or paint spraying. While easily the most simple of robots, fixed sequence machines have the advantage of being cheap and thus widely accessible to even very small companies. They can be programmed to operate on a continuous basis, even on an overnight shift when few other workers are on duty. Over eighty per cent of Japan's robots are fixed sequence robots, or about twenty-five per cent of current production. A slightly more complex type of robotics extends this ap-

---

[11] In April 1982, The Japanese Labour Ministry announced a two year study on the employment impact of robots.

Exhibit 9/8: Forecast of Future Japanese Demand for Industrial Robots by Use

(Unit: *1 Billion)

	1980			1985				1990		
Machining	14.0	(22.8%)	25	29.0	(15.0	13.6)	44	48.0	(14.7	12.0)
Spot Welding	7.0	(11.4%)	18	18.5	(10.8	8.6)	26	26.5	(8.7	6.6)
Assembly	6.0	(9.8%)	21	43.5	(12.6	20.3)	50	102	(16.7	25.5)
Arc Welding	4.5	(7.3%)	20	21.5	(12.0	10.0)	35	37.0	(11.7	9.3)
Plastic Moulding	4.5	(7.3%)	8	9.0	(4.8	4.2)	11	12.0	(3.7	3.0)
Metal Press and Shearing										
Painting	3.0	(4.9%)	10	11.0	(6.0	5.1)	15	16.5	(5.0	4.1)
Inspection Measuring	3.0	(4.9%)	9	9.5	(5.4	4.4)	17	17.5	(5.7	4.4)
Casting	3.0	(4.9%)	10	20.0	(6.0	9.4)	20	50.0	(6.7	12.5)
Die Casting	2.0	(3.3%)	3	4.0	(1.8	1.9)	7	8.5	(2.3	2.1)
Metal Heat Treatment	2.0	(3.3%)	3	3.5	(1.8	1.6)	4	4.5	(1.3	1.1)
Forging	1.0	(1.6%)	5	5.5	(3.0	2.6)	8	9.0	(2.7	2.3)
Plating	1.0	(1.6%)	3	3.5	(1.8	1.6)	4	5.0	(1.3	1.2)
Other Uses	0.5	(0.8%)	2	2.5	(1.2	1.2)	4	4.5	(1.3	1.1)
	10.0	(16.1%)	30	33.0	(17.8	15.5)	55	59.0	(18.2	14.8)

Total										
Domestic Demand	64.0		200	250			370	500		
Exports	1.0		40	50			80	110		

N.B. Numbers in Parentheses Denote Percentage Shares in Total Domestic Demand.

Source: Nomura Research Institute

Exhibit 9/9: A Typology of Robot Machines

Tasks Performed

		SINGLE	MULTIPLE
P R O G R A M M I N G	Simple	Fixed Sequence Robots	Numeric Control Robots
	Complex	Machining Center Robots	Sensor Aided Robots

proach to sets of tasks. Companies such as Nissan Motor and Kawasaki Heavy Industries operate what amounts to a machining center or building block system which combines a number of operations around a single control system. The tasks themselves are fairly simple and repetitive, but the more sophisticated control systems allow great flexibility to combine tasks of varying speeds and uniformity. These machine center robots provide greater flexibility in production scheduling and also reduces floor space of conventional equipment.

Major advances in control programming with micro processors have provided new opportunities to automate very simple tasks at fairly low costs.

The more sophisticated line of robots involve advances in the range of movements and skills built into the robot machines. The skill factor represents the more basic aspects of task design, such as dexterity, precision, and flexible speeds. Numeric controlled robots have revolutionary potential in these areas, and are best exemplified in industrial assembly such as automobiles. Numeric control robots are capable of driving screws, tightening bolts and nuts, welding seams, inspecting joints and measuring lengths.

The more advanced intelligence robots are sensor aided machines capable of visual, touch or audial feedback. Japan's strengths in cameras and electronics are contributing to the development of electronic sensing systems in robots which have made some headway in truly smart machines. Matsushita, for example, has a sensor robot capable of recognizing different colored parts (e.g., red, white, and blue balls in a container). However, robots which can interpret complex visual data, respond to many different surface touch, or listen to a variety of sounds are in the very early stages of development and offer only long term possibilities of improvement. Sensory robots are expensive – more than $100,000 – and become cost effective only in particular conditions. Example tasks of sensory robots presently in use include robot removal of foreign matter in bulk drug powders, grouping fruit products by grade, and checking the proper positioning of labels on bottles. Yamanouchi Pharmaceuticals Ltd., for instance, has introduced a robot costing over $200.000 which uses laser beams and video cameras to inspect liquid medicine in ampules. Working four to five hours a day, the robot can inspect 90,000 ampules, ten times the volume of human inspectors who require a minimum of six months training.

Japan's widespread diffusion of robots not only to many industries but to even very small firms parallels the general propensity to invest in new plant and equipment and to adopt best practice production technology. An innovative policy to promote robotics in Japan was a government leasing scheme designed to entice small companies to adopt robotics in production. Called Japan Robot Lease, the program involved twenty-four robot manufacturers, ten insurance companies and The Japanese Development Bank. Machines lease for as little as ninety dollars a month and can be traded in for better machines as they come on the market. The Japanese government has also promoted robot manufacturers with fast depreciation schedules and tax writeoffs, and MITI has formulated as seven year $150 million program to develop better intelligent robots for such ideals as the automated factory and flexible manufacturing systems.

9.7 Summary and Conclusions

The Japanese emphasis placed on industrial engineering, basic production principles and the organization of work has received only scant attention in Western countries. The overwhelming academic explanation of Japanese productivity success has been given to issues of behavioural processes such as slow promotion and consensual decision-making, or organizational issues such as sophisticated human resource policies, emphasis on line management, and long term strategy horizons. These software management elements are important but they too readily ignore the underlying emphasis on hardware technology at both the societal and corporate level.

In Japan engineers have a much more prominent role in management thinking than most Western countries (but no more so, for example, than in the aerospace industry of the U.S. or Europe). What is striking about the Japanese approach, as contrasted for instance in France where engineering is a high status profession, is the extent to which industrial engineering practices have been linked to human resource policies and marketing needs. In the automobile industry and the steel industry, Japanese manufacturers have introduced innovative engineering design policies which have turned their productivity standard into the world's best. From 1969 to 1979, the car industry has been able to increase productivity by 400 percent.

The three areas stressed in this chapter – progress cost curves, just in time inventory management, and robotics, all focus on techniques widely practiced in Japan, and are increasingly being copied by some Western companies. The wider issue is that in their application and diffusion, Japanese managers have put the lie to the argument that they are copiers rather than innovators. These engineering issues related to hardware technology also demonstrate that much of the productivity issues in Japan are not culturally determined or established by some mystical treatise on national values.

In this regard, it is no accident that quality control circles, so widely touted as a panacea for many productivity problems, grew out of an emphasis on statistical analysis of production, not on human resource policies. QC Circles, in short, are a direct descendant of scientific management and Frederick Taylor, not human relations and Elton Mayo! Shop floor work in Japan, as well as operations management, reflect many of the philosophical concerns expounded by Taylorism, including scientific decision-making and management-labour co-operation.[12] Stereotypes of Japan's human relations practices have for the most part ignored the underlying production emphasis on work simplification, product standardization, design to cost, reverse engineering, and elimination of waste.

[12] For a spirited defense of Taylor, see Locke (1982).

Fortunately, detailed comparisons with Japanese management practices and productivity, especially of particular industries like cars, steel, machine tools, or consumer electronics, have started to highlight the weaknesses in business practices in North America and Europe. Curiously, the alleged management triumph of the U.S. in the 1960's – so readily copied in Canada, Britain, and Western Europe – namely the academic business school – has been found seriously deficient in the very area of Japanese strength – production management. As Miller and Graham (1980) point out, "Many prominent graduate schools of business were eliminating production courses from their curicula because of the course's unpopularity among students. Enrollments in remaining programs were small and declining. Nationwide POM (production/operations management) departments either disbanded or merged with other departments." As noted in earlier chapters, Japan is making a national commitment to high technology sectors and has plans to spend up to four percent of GNP on research and development as part of an ongoing industrial strategy. Changes in electronics, machine tooling, and other areas of hardware technology are making fundamental – indeed revolutionary – advances in production techniques.[13] Robotics is the best known, but state of the art in new technologies such as computer aided design, computer aided manufacturing, flexible manufacturing systems and automated service bays is at the forefront of this evolving industrial change. The education system, the supply of highly qualified professional manpower,[14] and the ongoing system of continuous training all reinforce this broad trend. Moreover, they are being extended to areas where Japanese productivity has been relatively poor – government departments, trading firms, distribution, and other areas of the service sector. As the next chapter indicates, not all of Japan's management practices have been a total success story.

[13] Ayres and Miller (1982a, b) provide a cogent analysis from a U.S. perspective.
[14] According to one report by The American Electronics Association, U.S. colleges will produce by 1985, 15,000 new electrical and computer engineers for a market need of 51,000. See Main (1982).

Chapter 10
Japanese Marketing: From Sogoshosha to Big Mac

> "The trading firm means, in effect, that the responsibility for production and marketing is divorced . . . paradoxically this probably makes the Japanese industrialist more marketing conscious than his western counterpart."
>
> *Peter Drucker*

10.1 Introduction

Of the many enigmas concerning Japan, marketing must stand out in a prominent way. Japanese products flood the foreign markets of world, often at prices which seem lower than those in Tokyo or Osaka. In foreign markets, Japanese business prowess appears the model of success; at home, Japanese distribution appears the model of byzantine inefficiency. And aside from foreign suspicions of pervasive nontariff barriers, the Japanese market is bewilderingly complex, as when soya sauces come in several brands from the same producer and foreign manufacturers find consumer demands more exacting then virtually any other country. The public understanding of Japanese marketing abroad is usually linked to the large trading firms, the *Sogoshosha*. In one sense, this perception is accurate. Japanese general trading firms control such a significant portion of total imports and exports – around fifty percent – that they influence almost every facet of economic life, from the sourcing of raw fish to the supply of equipment for commuter trains. Internationally, the *Sogoshosha* are among the world's largest commercial enterprises anywhere. Firms such as Mitsui, Mitsubishi, and Sumotomo are at the apex of Japanese industrial groupings, controlling not only huge foreign subsidiaries but shaping the domestic marketing distribution network, from large department stores to new shopping centers.[1]

Yet any understanding of Japan's marketing system, while incomplete without an analysis of the role of the trading firm concept and philosophy, must include a recognition of two other issues. The first is the trend away from the trading firm channel by the major manufacturers, which are now developing their own marketing organization. Indeed, for most products usually associated with high

---

[1] The Japanese literature on trading firms in Japan is huge. A good review of these sources can be found in Daito (1975) and Yamamato (1980). For analyses in English, see Lifson (1978), McMillan (1981), Young (1977), and Roehl (1982).

quality and price competitiveness – cars, watches, televisions, video recorders, stereos, consumer appliances – it is the sales arm of the manufacturers which are the marketing stars, not the trading firms. These manufacturers have been incredibly successful because they have developed marketing niches, that is, segments of the market either ignored or abandoned by foreign competition. Examples abound. When North American television workers gave up on black and white television, Japanese makers produced small black and whites for kitchens, dens, and playrooms. When large photocopier and office equipment makers left a gap in small machines, for limited use and low budgets, the Japanese manufacturers moved in with a vengeance.[2]

For the Japanese, an important influence on marketing strategies has been the foreign retailers. Japanese manufacturers have arranged to sell product lines to foreign retail channels often using the retailer's brand name. For example, in television and stereos, giant retailers such as Montgomery Ward and Sears Roebuck, which have traditionally had links with U.S. manufacturers, now sell Japanese products and brands. By developing these different distribution channels, the Japanese manufacturers have taken advantage of local consumer tastes and buying habits. Similar trends are now found in Europe.

Curiously, this marketing prowess abroad is severely hindered at home by the antiquated Japanese distribution system, the second major aspect of the total marketing approach. It consists of the thousands of neighbourhood retailers and wholesalers which handle three quarters of consumer spending. It is this presence of super modern manufacturing efficiency matched with corner shopkeepers which at once define and shape marketing in Japan. Where the one is a model of technical prowess, the other is a model of village welfare and social integration. This chapter addresses these issues in the context of Japan's overall competitive strategies. In this respect, to see trends or interpret past practices, the starting point is the rise of the trading house system and its contemporary role as the engine for world-wide communications and information scanning in the global shopping center.

10.2 Trading Firms: Concepts and Definitions

Historically the modern concept of the trading firm dates from the joint stock companies of the mercantile period in Britain and Europe. The main engine of economic growth was imperialist expansion, such that the organizational strategy of the trading concerns involved the control of end-markets. In Japan, by contrast, foreign threats and geographical isolation led to the strategy of *So-*

---

[2] Baranson (1980) notes that in some products, entry of Japanese producers led to segment relinquishment. For a detailed case study, see Canadian Television Industry, York University (1982).

goshosha control of manufacturers in order to compete freely in international markets, usually with government support (*Sogo* – "all around," *Shosha*, companies in foreign trade). As noted already in previous chapters, Japan's attempts at industrialization in the last century involved extensive learning from foreign models, especially European trading firms of various descriptions – The Dutch and British East India Company, Hudson's Bay Company, and Denmark's East Asiatic Company were prominent foreign examples. More to the point, Japanese skills in specific trading functions – insurance, warehousing, financial services – were severely underdeveloped. It should not got unnoticed that in many fundamental ways, the Japanese domestic environment of the last decades of the 19th century closely paralleled that following World War II. In both periods, the role of the large trading firms in domestic and foreign trade was central to Japan's entire economic development (Daito, 1975).

There is no precise definition of a trading house, since the manufacturing and marketing functions can vary tremendously, particularly when sales cross national borders, political jurisdictions, legal systems, cultural and organizational archetypes and the like. Lancaster (1980) adopts the following definition: "A trading house is a non-manufacturing business entity conducting an international commercial activity, exporting, importing or a combination of both between two or more countries." Ozawa (1979), by contrast, defines trading firms as "industrial organizations unique to Japan, organizations whose existence is almost unparalleled elsewhere. There are literally thousands of trading companies in Japan (anywhere from 3,000 to 8,000, depending on the criteria used for classification)".

In the simplest sense, a trading firm markets goods and services produced in one country to one or more other countries. Intermediary functions can be of a generalized or a specific type. For example, general functions can include the handling of paperwork for importing and exporting, obtaining foreign exchange, advising on transport modes, arranging insurance, providing storage arrangements and the like. Specific types of functions include obtaining and providing market research for clients, arranging financial credit, and linking clients to special agencies and new customers.

An important additional role for trading firms is to act as a facilitator of trade. Developing or actually creating trade flows can come about by identifying markets through specialized product scanning and organization unattainable by the producer at an acceptable cost. A trading firm, in short, is supply-demand oriented rather than user- or maker-oriented (Anderson, 1979). In this respect, there are various possibilities. Trading houses can act for the producer as principal but on a contractual basis. For some products and markets, the trading house may itself become the principal, assuming the risks of selling to foreign markets. As will be seen below, this is the major strength of the large Japanese trading house, although other forms exist; for example, a trading house may serve as agents for foreign buyers seeking producers in the local market (Emori, 1971; Young, 1977).

Of course, most marketing systems involve complex interactions of intermediaries, including agents, brokers, warehouses, advertising agencies and similar bodies. The real question is to what extent does the marketing function dominate other functions in the total organization? In most North American firms, particularly those in manufacturing, the "modern" organizational design gives primacy, not equality, to marketing, as compared to production, research and development, or finance. Kotler (1976: 406) outlines the perspective as follows:

A company can have a modern marketing department and yet not operate as a modern marketing company. Whether it is the latter depends upon how the officers of the company view the marketing function. If they view marketing as one of the several equal functions in the organization, the company is probably not a modern marketing company. If they view marketing as the hub of the enterprise, and not just one of its spokes, the company has achieved modern marketing stature.

From an organizational viewpoint, there are two general perspectives of the linkage between the manufacturer and the customer. In the first case, and the one prevailing in North America, the linkage should be direct with no, or at least minimal, intermediaries. Manufacturers thus desire direct access to customers and their feedback, and with it, prefer to avoid any loss of marketing control and perceived isolation. This argument for integration usually involves the range of incentives for scale economies of distribution, inventory management, and customer servicing. In short, there are high transaction costs for these functions and the typical response is to internalize them through forward integration (Williamson, 1975).

In the second case, the manufacturing organization specializes in the production function and "contracts" out the marketing function to an external organization, the trading firm. Conceptually, the main argument for this approach is the economies of scale in the total marketing function of many products and specialized services. For the trading firm, the major financial obstacles are high start-up costs in personnel, market research, and distribution channel information and control. Once developed, however, incremental costs of volume expansion are quite low, since the main transaction costs are informational. Properly organized for bridging information linkages between many manufacturers and many consumers, the trading firm can afford to work on high volumes and low margins, even for low value-added, standardized products. Japan historically has been the best case study of this approach.

The powerful information base of the trading firms in Japan has to be recognized both in terms of their historical evolution and relationships to the group structure of Japanese big business, as well as in terms of their product market strategies. In the first instance, the trading firms, while historically concentrating on bulk commodities, minerals and other highly standardized imports, as well as undifferentiated exports, have had close relationship to manufacturing companies in the various major groups – the pre-war Zaibatsus and the post war groupings. The trading firms have operated for these groups as an information scanning and exchange arena – indeed, it is not too far fetched to interpret their role in this informational sense rather than in their pure trading role.

This perspective is reinforced by the strategic evolution of the trading firms in recent years. It has been the trading firms which have been in the vanguard of Japanese direct foreign investment, rather than the manufacturing firms, as in Britain or the United States. In terms of gathering and interpreting data on foreign market developments, both after the war and in recent years, few Japanese manufacturing firms could afford the substantial investments in informational infrastructure, least of all to match that of the European and American multinationals. The fact that Japan had ten major Sogoshosha to develop this information system, and an efficient means of digesting and using it in the domestic market via the large corporate groupings, added to the efficiency and speed with which corporate strategies could develop. That is why, for instance, in recent years the trading firms have been the key organizational linkage in export consortia where "turnkey" projects and sales of entire projects, from subway systems to petrochemical complexes, require a major firm to act as prime organizer to many separate manufacturers, suppliers and subcontractors.[3]

For the trading firm operating on an international basis of even minimal scale, the key operating asset is thus informational: the range and quality of trading contacts; the human capital of skills and experience in particular products, markets, functions, or services; and the hardware system of on-line communication flows, ranging from personal meetings, telephone calls and computer systems to the ubiquitous telex.[4] In Japan, where these informational linkages

[3] A recent Swedish study indicates the scale of these projects. In 1977, 13% of Japan's total exports were carried out by consortia structures. Germany's exports with consortia structures grew 25% per year between 1970 and 1976, from 700 million DM to ver 3,000 million DM. French exports via consortia grew by 41% between 1970 and 1977, reaching 15 billion francs. Many European governments cover front end costs (often via government procurement policies) for systems marketing (Industridepartementet, 1978:39).

[4] Japan's White paper on International Trade (1981) shows the following 1980 data on overseas business offices of the Japanese and other countries. Foreign business office include those of Japanese trading firms which are more than 50 percent foreign owned:

| | Japanese Abroad | | Foreigners in Japan | | C/A | D/B |
	A) Offices	B) Employees	C) Offices	D) Employees	%	%
U.S.	931	21,644	167	1628	17.9	7.5
Europe	597	13,223	97	852	16.2	6.4
S.E. Asia	1263	26,705	156	1423	12.4	5.3
Other	1302	23,937	124	2248	9.5	9.4

easily rival most countries' diplomatic network, overseas personnel of firms like Mitsui, Mitsubishi, and Marubeni are coupled directly to their offices in Tokyo and Osaka from more than 100 countries. According to one trading firm "our company has 130 bases in the world connected by telex. The total length of our communications network is 400,000 kilometers – equivalent to four circumnavigations of the earth. There are 20,000 messages everyday. On the basis of information coming in from all over the world, many factors, such as commodies, freight charges, and foreign exchange rates, are brought together in order to conduct transactions and to analyze the possibilities for long term projects." (Marubeni, 1978). The largest trading firms allocate about ten percent of their operating expenses on international communications. Information is gathered on the competitive tactics of foreign companies, weather patterns worldwide, political trends, and foreign price movements. In some circles, it is said that the *Sogoshosha* have only two intelligence rivals worldwide, the Pentagon and the Vatican.

This huge informational base and communication system are somewhat akin to what MacRae (1976) calls the organizational confederation of entrepreneurs, since in practice, trading firms operate with a very high element of entrepreneurial decentralization. This system operates as an unparalleled early warning system for new products, technologies, and markets and makes the trading firm a key player in the corporate strategies of business groups. To function as such, however, trading firms need not only informational resources, but a financial asset base to provide credit, absorb foreign exchange rate risks and costs, and act as financial agent for producer firms, particularly small businesses. The sheer size of the largest trading firms, and their pivotal role in the major business groupings, make their financial dealings part and parcel of the total banking system. The *Sogoshosha* stand as the main intermediaries between separate manufacturing companies and small business groups and the major banks (Exibit 10/1). In some cases, the financial role of the trading firms may go beyond these functions to include equity investment, direct loans, or guarantee for loans, although this approach has developed only recently (Jetro, 1980).

10.3 Sogoshosha in Practice

The recurrent problems of low productivity growth in North America and the dynamism and technological sophistication of Japan have prompted the search for lessons in export trade there. Academic interest in the *Sogoshosha* has been minimal, although Young's (1977) study has partly filled a void, at least from a U.S. perspective. In Canada, Tsurumi (1980) provides an overview of the *Sogoshosha* and tries to make a case for their establishment there. A parliamentary committee recommended the setting up of a national trading house

Exhibit 10/1: Major Business Groups Formed around GTCs

GTC	Main bank	Business group	Main members
Mitsubishi Corporation	Mitsubishi Bank	Mitsubishi Group	Mitsubishi Group
Mitsui Bussan	Fuji Bank (Mitsui Bank)	Mitsui Group	Mitsui Group
Sumitomo Corporation	Sumitomo Bank	Sumitomo Group	Sumitomo Group
Marubeni Corporation	Fuji Bank	Fuyo Group	Yasuda Group Shoden Group Nissan Group Hitachi Manufactures Group
C. Itoh	Sumitomo Bank	Dai-ichi Kangin Group	Furukawa Kawasaki Group Seibu Group
Nissho-Iwai	Sanwa Bank	Sanwa Group	Obyashi Gumi Hitachi Shipbuilding Teijin Ube Kosan Han Kyu Group Sekisui Chemical
Tomen	Tokai Bank	Tokai Group	Toyota Group Meitetsu Group Chiyoda Group
Kanematsu Gosho	Tokyo Bank (Dai-ichi Kangyo Bank)	Kanematsu Gosho Group Dai-ichi Kangin Group	Shosha Group

Source: Company Records

and the Trudeau government has followed with a trading firm model called Canagrex to export agricultural products. In April 1981, the U.S. Senate unanimously passed a resolution permitting bank investments in export trading companies and providing for certification of trading firms as immune from antitrust laws. For both countries, Japan is clearly the reference point for a new form of marketing organization.

In fact, Japanese trading firms trace their modern structures and policies to the early days of the Meiji Revolution in 1868. In Europe, trading firms by this time had two centuries of experience: The Dutch East India Company, Britain's Hudson Bay Company, and mercantile houses in Liverpool, Rotterdam, and Hamburg. In terms of management structure, such organizations had relatively simple arrangements. The key linkages were personal, between top personnel in the home country and carefully trained administrators in the co-

lonial territories. Aside from military or political staff, the main personnel in
the subsidiaries were men of finance and communications were very much a
problem of geographical distance. In such circumstances, personal relations
formed the basis of trusted bonds and shared goals in the organizational network.

This framework lasted for centuries in the European case, and competition for
scarce resources was relatively weak. The descriptive term "mother –
daughter" relationship is particularly apt – it connotes a comfortable and re-
laxed commercial relationship which lasted until decades after the Second
World War (Franko, 1979). Today many of the European firms having colonial
histories have survived, such as East Asiatic Company, France's Cie Française
de l'Afrique Occidentale and Société Commerciale de l'Ouest African, and
Britain's United Africa Company. UAC, for instance, has joint ventures in
Africa, owns department stores, shipping companies, and sells products for
more than 200 foreign firms.

When Japan first opened the doors to international commerce, companies like
Mitsui and Mitsubishi established trading houses with government support to
cope with the specialized needs of both exports and imports (Morikawa, 1970).
Various government measures introduced by the post-Meiji government attempted to develop Japanese commercial practices, including policies not uncommon today. For example, Japan participated in various international ex-
positions, such as Vienna in 1873 and Philadelphia in 1876; trade consuls were
used as commercial intelligence networks; there were subsidies for Japanese
shipping firms, assistance for marine insurance companies, and facilities for
converting yen-denominated bank cheques. Despite such measures the existence of foreign merchant houses, or *shokan,* with their superior skills in
international trade compared to the evident inexperience of the Japanese,
prompted a new approach. Led by Kaoru Inoue, a leading political and commercial figure, the Japanese government attempted to mobilize domestic organizational strengths. The vehicle was the House of Mitsui.[5]

Inoue had joined with a group of merchants to organize Senshusha in 1872.
This firm imported foreign goods, mainly on procurement orders from the
government. The main products were guns, woolen textiles, and chemicals. As
a major fund raiser for Inoue, Mitsui was offered the chance to buy Senshusha,
which it soon merged with its branch offices throughout Japan as Mitsui Bussan
Kaisha (Mitsui Trading Company). The close nexus of government, business,
and control of Japan's import channels was thus established. These and other
trading firms were an integral part of the pre-war industrial groups, the *Zaibatsu* (Yamamura, 1976), although their present size, success, and prominence
clearly date from the post-war era.

---

[5] For a detailed historical case study on Mitsui see Roberts (1973).

Actually there are three kinds of trading firms in Japan and each serves quite different needs. The first kind is the best known, namely the *Sogoshosha,* the huge firms, nine in number, which dominate Japan's export and import trade. As shown in Exhibit 10/2 and 10/3, the *Sogoshosha* are not only giant firms in themselves, with total sales turnover in excess of $350 billion, they are huge in any comparison of international corporations. Just to keep their scale in perspective, in 1981, they were larger by $90 billion in sales than the top ten U.S. multinational firms combined, and larger by $40 billion in sales than the top ten non-U.S. multinationals, which of course, include such giant oil firms as Shell, British Petroleum, Total, and Kuwait Petroleum (*Forbes,* July 5, 1982). The *Sogoshosha* are the central institutions in Japan's total international trade stra-

Exhibit 10/2: Breakdown of Top Nine General Trading Houses' Turnover in by 1978 (Value ¥ 1,000 million)

		Breakdown			
	Turnover	Exports	Imports	Domestic	Overseas
1) Mitsubishi Corp.	8,837 (100%) 19%	1,700 (19%) 18%	2,251 (26%) 26%	4,350 (49%) 19%	536 (6%) 12%
2) Mitsui & Co.	8,361 (100%) 18%	1,590 (19%) 17%	1,648 (20%) 19%	4,462 (53%) 19%	661 (8%) 15%
3) C. Itoh & Co.	6,561 (100%) 14%	1,327 (20%) 14%	994 (15%) 11%	3,456 (53%) 15%	784 (12%) 18%
4) Marubeni Corp.	6,271 (100%) 14%	1,636 (26%) 17%	962 (15%) 11%	2,837 (45%) 12%	836 (13%) 19%
5) Sumitomo Corp.	5,849 (100%) 13%	1,234 (21%) 13%	809 (14%) 9%	3,502 (60%) 15%	304 (5%) 7%
6) Nissho-Iwai	4,177 (100%) 9%	846 (20%) 9%	834 (20%) 10%	2,085 (50%) 9%	412 (10%) 10%
7) Toyo Menka	2,136 (100%) 5%	479 (22%) 5%	418 (20%) 5%	888 (42%) 4%	351 (16%) 8%
8) Kanematsu-Gosho	2,040 (100%) 4%	313 (15%) 3%	469 (23%) 5%	1,093 (54%) 5%	165 (8%) 4%
9) Nichimen Co.	1,789 (100%) 4%	479 (27%) 5%	346 (19%) 4%	694 (39%) 3%	270 (15%) 6%
Total	46,021 (100%)	9,604 (21%) 100%	8,731 (19%) 100%	23,367 (51%) 100%	4,319 (9%) 100%

Source: Dodwell's

Exhibit 10/3: Financial Profile of Japan's Sogoshosha (1981)

Firm	Revenue (millions)	Net Income (millions)	Assets (millions)	Market Value (millions)	Employees (thousands)
Mitsui & Co. Ltd.	68,709	84	23,403	1,539	13.0
Mitsubishi Corp.	58,271	189	23,258	3,698	14.2
C. Itoh & Co. Ltd.	51,502	58	16,409	1,355	10.0
Marubeni Corp.	47,404	31	16,245	1,295	14.0
Sumitomo Corp.	44,931	98	11,190	1,422	10.0
Nissho-Iwai Co. Ltd.	32,124	−14	9,811	635	8.0
Toyo Menka Kaisha Ltd.	15,912	12	5,336	293	4.6
Kanematsu-Gosho Ltd.	14,676	2	5,639	168	3.7
Nichimen Co. Ltd.	13,534	18	4,971	232	3.4

Source: Forbes (July 5, 1982)

tegies. By combining the economies of information flows and their enormous bargaining leverage in commodity and raw materials markets (where there are usually few sellers) these firms have provided the Japanese economy with a steady flow of competitively priced imports for downstream processing. Further, through their logistical systems for imports and exports they have reduced the transportation costs of global distribution in markets relatively isolated from Japan. Their activities are not just the buying and selling of goods, services and commodities; they serve as bankers in lending credit and finance; they act as principals and coordinators in exporting turnkey projects and plants, establishing overseas joint-ventures, and serving as a linking agency for third country trade. The key is their enormous global information systems. As such these firms are enormously diverse and operate on huge sales volume and low profit margins. Mitsui, for example, had total sales in 1981 of U.S. 68.7 billion, but a net income of $84 million, or a fraction of one percent of sales. The small net profit also applies to the other *Sogoshosha,* usually less than a quarter of one percent, but varying by size of firm, product range, markets, and general economic conditions.

The extreme diversity and large size of the *Sogoshosha* contrast with the second type of Japanese trading firm, the specialized traders or *Senman Shosha.* These firms number in the thousands and limit their operations to quite specialized and focused strategies. Some firms may handle only particular product lines in a large number of markets. Some specialize by product and market, or even a region of Japan. For example, one small trading firm concentrates only on hospital supplies manufactured in southern Japan for Asian markets. Another medium-sized firm concentrates on motors and pumps, and focuses on the markets of the middle east and Francophone Africa, mainly from an office in Tokyo and an agency in Paris. Almost all these specialized trading houses handle the full range of trading functions, from transport and freight to customs and credit (Tsurumi, 1980).

The third type of trading firm in Japan and one of the fastest growing, is the captive sales arms of manufacturing firms, such as those in electronics, automobiles, office equipment and precision machinery. In this category are the sales arms of the automobile firms (e.g. Toyota Motor Sales) and the electronic firms (e.g., Matsushita Electric). The main reason for the development of these trading firms is the need of the manufacturer to establish direct customer contact, to handle after-sales servicing, and to establish a brand name image and dealer network. Most of the largest electrical manufacturers – Matsushita, Sanyo, Toshiba and Sharp – have an extensive domestic network of stores, many of which deal only with their own products. Matsushita alone, for example, has 60,000 stores, of which about 25,000 are exclusive brand outlets. It is for this reason that the wholesale distribution system in Japan acts as an import impediment for foreign products. As it turns out, many of these same firms are branching out to other products, as well as participating in foreign ventures via direct investment.

Despite the variety of size, type, and function, the Japanese trading firms are extremely competitive, even within product groups. For example, while the *Sogoshosha* are spread throughout Japan and around the world in a bewildering array of products, markets, services, and third nation trade flows, within specific market segments in Japan, competition for trade is fierce. For instance, there are one thousand small trading firms importing food products, 900 handling textiles, 500 dealing in logs and lumber, another thousand in machinery (Jetro, 1980). Another indication of competition is the pattern of wholesale prices in Japan. Despite rising wage costs, wholesale prices for such sectors as chemicals, petroleum, coal, iron and steel, electrical products, auto parts, and transportation equipment declined in the 1960's and early 1970's.[6] In 1980 there were more than 30,000 Japanese employed in the overseas operations of Japan's trading houses – the nine *Sogoshosha* alone had 908 overseas offices.

To understand the real scope and operations of the Japanese trading house sector, three points are critical. First, there must be a recognition that the entire economy runs on the basis of the trading firm model, domestic sales as well as imports and exports. This means that the corporate strategies of individual producers are predicated on the presence of the trading firms, with their provision of business credit, loans and payment guarantees, and secured market outlets. It follows, therefore, that any transfer of the trading house concept to another country, especially for a single firm, must take this cumulative impact of thousands of specialized trading firms into account.[7]

---

[6] From 1955 to 1980, the consumer price index has increased faster than the wholesale price index. The inefficiency of this distribution system partly explain this phenomena.

[7] Countries active in adopting the trading house model for export promotion include Korea, Malaysia, Mexico, and Brazil. See McMillan (1983) and Tsurumi (1980).

A second fundamental consideration is the style of management and commercial expertise which is so highly developed in the trading house sector. Operating with huge volumes but very low margins, the trading firms are, in fact, collections of individual brokers and traders linked to contacts, agents, producers, and customers in international markets. Like most Japanese corporations, the trading firms recruit from the best universities, but the formal education is typically general – specialized training takes place within the firm. European or even American business school education is not terribly relevant for the trading firm system of management, where the emphasis is almost exclusively on marketing, distribution, and finance. Further, the Japanese companies have centuries of traditions and practices to draw on, and these are not easily copied or transferred abroad. It remains unlikely that this organizational entrepreneurship in trading houses is easily exported, as compared to management practice in manufacturing (McMillan, 1980).

The third basic point is that in their trading functions, the Japanese firms are not only exporters but also importers (often providing the first export sales of foreign firms). The *Sogoshosha* account for about half of all Japanese imports (Exhibit 10/4) and in some cases, eighty or ninety percent of the imports of particular commodities. The *Sogoshosha* are responsible for about one fifth of Japan's domestic trade, which itself accounts for about half of each company's sales. As noted below, the *Sogoshosha* are major players in reshaping Japan's total distribution system, which has relatively low productivity by international

Exhibit 10/4: Top Nine General Trading Houses' Shares in Japan's Total Exports and Imports (Value ¥ 1,000 million)

		Japan's		Top 9 General Trading Houses				Ratios	
	GNP (A)	Total Exports (B)	Total Imports (C)	Turnover (D)	Exports (E)	Imports (F)	D/A	E/B	F/C
FY 1969	64,514	6,047	5,761	16,706	2,857	3,599	25.9%	47.2%	62.5%
1970	75,524	7,290	6,967	20,565	3,509	4,365	27.2%	48.1%	62.7%
1971	83,166	8,474	6,824	22,499	4,314	4,140	27.0%	50.9%	60.7%
1972	96,884	9,071	7,659	26,618	4,555	4,797	27.5%	50.2%	62.6%
1973	117,258	10,877	12,369	38,320	5,767	8,004	32.7%	53.0%	64.7%
1974	139,219	17,080	18,276	46,841	9,577	10,462	33.7%	56.1%	57.2%
1975	153,126	17,026	17,396	45,321	9,453	9,550	29.6%	55.5%	54.9%
1976	171,736	20,669	19,713	49,914	10,636	10,408	29.1%	51.5%	52.8%
1977	191,426	21,790	18,509	47,009	10,860	9,204	24.6%	49.8%	49.7%
1978	210,636	19,990	17,057	46,021	9,604	8,730	21.9%	48.0%	51.2%
Annual Growth (1969–1978)	14.1%	14.2%	12.8%	11.9%	14.4%	10.4%	–	–	–

Note: Figures of Ataka & Co., which was absorbed by C. Itoh & Co. in 1977, are included in (D), (E) and (F) for FY 1969–76.

Source: MITI: Economic Planning Agency. Japan's total imports and exports: Ministry of Finance.

standards (in Japan, on average, there are twice as many wholesalers in the distribution chain as in the U.S.). In terms of imports and exports, the *Sogoshosha* have been in the forefront of Japan's highly efficient transportation and communications networks, and have pioneered innovations in air cargo, electronic systems, and shipping. They have also invested in novel shipping and distribution methods, from palletization, containerization, and air-conditioned warehousing, to automated loading systems, and refrigeration.

Obviously Japan's position as a resource-poor, "throughput" economy, contributes to the concentration of the import functions of the trading firms. Such imports tend to be unprocessed, standardized commodities whose selling price is set in world markets. Dealing in high import volumes tends to cushion the financial risks of export trade, since costs of global information and distribution systems, currency flunctuations, and buffer inventories can be spread across both imports and exports. It follows that in recent years the *Sogoshosha* have led the way in Japanese direct overseas investment, often with domestic manufacturers participating in equity along with host country firms. By the end of 1978, foreign investment by the *Sogoshosha* amounted to U.S. $4 billion, an increase of 33 percent since 1974. Mitsui and Co. led the way with almost thirty percent of the *Sogoshosha's* total investment.

The linking pin role of the trading firms within large industrial groups serves to coordinate the trading functions to the financial and manufacturing strategies which, in total, has a more competitive impact than the U.S. multinational form. This result stems from the sheer diversity and scope of the trading firms operations and their capacity to link products to many markets via national subsidiaries. This coordination role of Japanese trading firms is improved only in part by the interlocking ownership patterns of organizations in the industrial groups. A more direct linkage in terms of shared goals and policies is the system of Presidents Club involving the Presidents of each company in the group voting as an individual and equal partner.

These clubs are usually held once a month, although Mitsui's *Nimoku Kai* (Second Thursday Club) is a more exclusive exception. It has 23 member companies and dates from October 1961. The largest Presidents Council, that of the DKB group, the *Sankin-Kai*, started in 1977, has 45 member companies. For the Mitsui group, the Monday Club *(Getsuyo-Kai)* is the norm; at Mitsubishi, there is the Friday Club *(Kinyo-Kai)* and at Sumitomo, there is the White Water Club *(Hakusui-Kai)*. Through general discussions and information exchange, these meetings provide the basis for a continual readjustment of group strategies and investment patterns. For example, topics beyond general economic, financial, technological and political trends touch on joint investments, problems of troubled sectors, intra-group brands and trademarks, declining and growth industries and the like. While each group brings an enormous concentration of economic assets, within the group the various roles are diffused in ways quite different from the largest U.S. firms. Unlike the situation in U.S. conglomerates, there is a strong incentive in the Japanese groups to share and exchange information, since what may have very limited value to one company may be invaluable to another member of the group. It is the effect for the total group which is paramount and the trading firm is the main nexus of information coordination. That partly explains the enormous diversity of products and services of Japanese trading firms, since even small volumes and a narrow range of some products can still be handled economically: the overheads are spread over everything from *Ramen* (Japanese noodles) to missiles. There is thus enormous concentration of economic power and potential for harmful corporate behaviour from the perspective of the consumer.

10.4 Trading Firms and Japanese Distribution

The influential role of all trading firms in imports, exports, and the domestic market is central to modernizing the country's inefficient distribution system. Foreigners have often argued that Japan's distribution system forms part of an effective system of non-tariff barriers, which include government regulations, technical barriers (e.g., auto emission standards) and Japanese consumer psychology against foreign goods. Unfortunately, foreigners not only place unwarranted credence on such shibboleths, they often attempt to enter the Japanese market with domestic trading firms as local partners. In so doing, they fall into the trap of not recognizing the basic differences between industrial products and consumer products, where distribution channels and often sales service requirements are quite different. In point of fact, such problems are largely misunderstood, and show the need to recognize the cultural and institutional factors explaining Japan's total marketing system.

When Napoleon derided Britain as a nation of shopkeepers, he could easily have said the same thing about Japan. Japan's vast distribution system is rooted culturally in the life of its agricultural past and small villages. Even Japan's bigger cities are no more than an assemblage of villages and neighbourhoods. What is so striking is the extent to which this village structure has persisted in distribution, despite the vast modernization in manufacturing. Actually, the number of "mama papa" stores has increased in the past decade. The net result, as shown in Exhibit 10/5, is a diverse and complicated distribution network different for each product and variant by the size of the producer and end retailer or user.

The data in Exhibit 10/6 show the persistence of small retail outlets, which even today, account for about three quarters of all consumer shopping. While international comparisons are flawed by differences in the definitions used and

Exhibit 10/5: Typical Distribution Channels in Japan

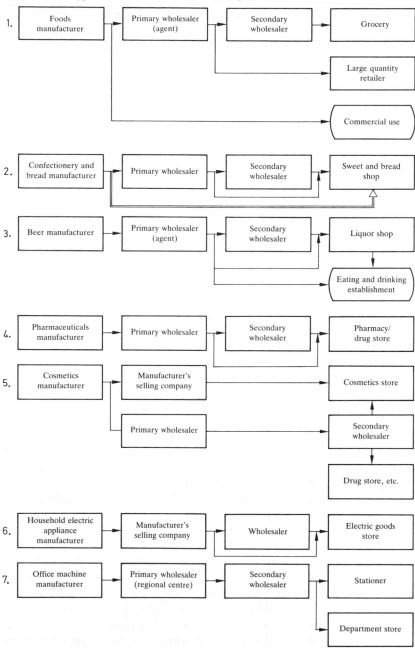

Source: JETRO

Exhibit 10/6: International Comparisons of Wholesalers and Retailers

	Japan (1979)	Britain (1974)	France (1975)	W. Germany (1978)	U.S.A. (1977)
Number of Wholesalers	369,000	51,000	97,000	113,000	383,000
Employees per Wholesaler	10	14.8	6.4	9.9	9.4
Population per Wholesaler	315	1,095	1,095	540	542
Number of Retailers	1,673,000	351,000	533,000	340,500	1,855,000
Employees Per Retailer	3.6	6.9	2.6	6.1	8.1
Population Per Retailer	69	160	99	180	117
Retailers/ Wholesalers	4.5	6.9	5.5	3	4.8

Source: Dodwell's

dates of statistical gathering, the clear picture is that Japan has a larger number of retailers and wholesalers than any other major country on a per capita basis. For example, there are only 3.6 employees per retailer in Japan, less than half the average in the U.S. and about half that in Britain. Only France has a lower rate, and since 1975, the year of the French statistics, prominent French chains, such as Au Printemps and Carrefour, have developed large retail stores through France. In Japan, there are only 69 people per store, compared to 99 in France, 117 in the U.S., 160 in Britain, and 180 in West Germany. The same pattern exists in wholesaling. In this respect, trading firms are only minor players in the total distribution chain.

Behind these statistics are a variety of social, economic and political factors which explain the persistence of Japan's distribution system. The three are interrelated. For example, there is the price of land which, at a cost of about 35,000 yen per square meter, is ten times the equivalent price in the U.S.. Where consumer prices have increased four fold between 1955 and 1978, land prices went up by a factor of twenty-eight. For small "mama papa" retailers and wholesalers *(tonya)* which typically combine a business and a house in the same premises, there is a clear incentive to have one member of the family earn a salary from government or a large manufacturer and to run the business with the family. As a political lobby, such merchants have been effective in requiring department stores and supermarkets to get regulatory approval from local authorities. Since 1979, stores larger than 500 square meters have required approval from local chambers of commerce, whose membership usually consists of small retailers and wholesalers. The key legislative regulation is the *Daiten-Ho* (Large Scale Retailing Establishment Law) that stipulates that any large store can be created only when neighbouring small merchants approve its size, days open, and hours of business. High land costs and legislative restrictions provide cost advantages to small retailers, which in turn favour neighbourhood shopping – even for high ticket items like electronic appliances and automobiles. Since supermarkets in Japan average 2050 square meters of floor space and department stores 17, 100, small stores still accounted for 83.3 percent of the country's 73.6 trillion yen retail market. In some of the newer suburbs, supermarkets have been in the vanguard of urban development by buying huge tracts of land and building stores linked to housing and new shopping districts.

The implications of this vast distribution system in Japan are many. In the most obvious instance, it means that consumer prices in Japan are higher because of the profit margins associated with the many layers in the distribution channel. Wholesalers operate strictly on a margin basis, but the rate varies according to such factors as competition, capacity utilization and the degree of *giri,* or mutual interdependence existing between two firms. Price coordination is pervasive in Japan, meaning that the level of industrial cooperation achieved by small firms through trade associations is extraordinarily high. With generally uniform prices for most goods, consumers have no incentive to favour large stores over small stores, since even discount prices will be similar. Similarily price coordination is an effective means of eliminating "excessive competition" at the retail end and instead, pricing and marketing strategies really amount to managing the relationships within the distribution channels (Elimelech, 1980). Rebate schemes are widely used. Foreign products in a channel are often subject to fixed prices, fixed margins. The irony is that many Japanese goods sold abroad are actually cheaper than in Japan, expecially in countries like the U.S., Canada, and Britain which have relatively efficient distribution systems. To foreigners, the alleged issue of "dumping" is really one of distribution, and Japanese consumer groups and many businessmen are no happier about it than foreigners. As Ross (1980: 281) has noted, "To expect Japan to significantly alter its system overnight may not only be unrealistic but also somewhat unreasonable. For the foreign manufacturer, then, the main issue is not the introduction of change. Rather learning how to work within the operational parameters which the system has established constitutes the problem at hand."

10.5 Modernizing Distribution

Various pressures have been developing for changing the distribution system, some of it external to Japan, such as foreign exporters. Limited change has also come from marketing innovations by manufacturers on the one side, and by modern retailers on the other.[8] There is no question about the complexity of distribution, but it applies equally to Japanese and foreigners alike. In recent years more rapid penetration of products from South East Asia, compared to the U.S., lies in their greater understanding and effective use of the Japanese system (Gregory, 1979). Some Japanese companies have attempted to assist Western importers to cope with the Japanese market. Sony, for example, imports refrigerators from Whirlpool, cleaners from Hoover, and food equipment from Oster. However, the major threats to the cumbersome distribution system is not coming from the trading firms but rather the department stores, the supermarket chains, and the manufacturers. As is usual for Japan, each sector is also a competitive threat to the other.

The department stores actually lost market share in the 1970's and held less than six percent of retail sales in 1980. As a result, they have tended to develop links with foreign companies to handle exclusive rights for particular goods, in exchange for agreed levels of purchases, regardless of sales. The department stores operate only in the large cities – the largest, Mitsukoshi, for instance, has only 14 stores throughout the entire country. They cater to consumers for more expensive items, especially high fashion apparel which account for 49 percent of sales. The department stores also handle the vast market for presents during the gift and bonus seasons (July and December). The large retailers have also established private brand manufacturers at home and abroad to circumvent the wholesaler channels. Wholesalers have responded in kind by equity investments in their own outlets, and some have even established private brand manufacturing.

However, it is the supermarket chains which have grown the fastest, averaging 10–12 percent in the 1970's to capture about 25 percent of total retail sales. In many ways, the supermarket chains have succeeded by introducing into Japan retail practices well developed in the U.S. and Europe. Daiei, for example, which increased its sales in 1980 to $4.9 billion to become the largest retailer in Japan (1957 sales were $75,000), has been the most aggressive. It has developed about a fifth of its sales through in-house brands and acquired foreign expertise from Lawson's of the U.S. In an attempt to get into the department stores segment, it tried to acquire one of the major chains, Takashimaya. Daiei has developed links with Au Printemps of France, and markets goods from Marks and Spencer of Britain and J. C. Penny of the U.S.. Saibu retails merchandise supplied by Sears Roebuck of the U.S.

Perhaps not surprisingly, it is the chain stores which are introducing the fast food outlets of Japan. This development follows from the practice of *Shohin Teikai* or licensing goods for sales. In retailing, well known brands like Cardin,

---

[8] For a background analysis of these trends up to 1971 in Japan, see Tamura (1971).

Yves St. Laurent and the like are prominent examples. In the same way, the chains have sought out licensing arrangements for fast foods. Ito Yokodo operates Denny's Inc. of California under license, Daiei is the franchisee for Wendy's hamburger and the Victoria Station restaurant chain, Nichii operates Arby's roast beef sandwiches. By contrast, two of the best known U.S. fast food companies, Kentucky Fried Chicken and McDonalds, are joint venture arrangements. Mainly as a result of U.S. influences (thirty one percent of all U.S. retail sales come from franchises), Japanese marketing is adapting to franchise outlets in areas as diverse as hairstyling, sporting centers, and convenience stores. However, while there were almost three thousand franchise outlets in Japan by 1980, they have largely been in new areas of retailing rather than changing traditional distribution outlets to any significant degree. Shopping and buyer habits remain deeply ingrained despite more cars, bigger malls, and more automated service bays, characteristic of U.S. and European cities.

External pressures for change have come from foreign imports, which have increased in importance as a result of growing consumer awareness and high disposable incomes. The term *hakurai-hia* – literally meaning borne by ships – refers to foreign made products and they often command premium prices in the domestic market. The key challenge for foreign importers is to gain excess to existing distribution channels. In some cases, new channels may have to be created, but the very high cost of land, and the enormous expense of media advertising, inhibit this approach.[9]

Case studies undertaken by MITI (Exhibit 10/7) tend to confirm this approach. Among examples of firms which have gone alone in the Japanese market are major enterprises like IBM and Xerox, or firms with special competitive advantages such as U.S. phonograph companies (price) and French clothes designers (style and brand name). The more likely possibility is a tie up with Japanese firms. General Foods, for instance, attempted to crack the Japanese market alone; after developing links with Ajinomoto, the company gained 17 percent of Japan's market share for instant coffee. The leader is Nestle from Switzerland with 63 percent. Another contrast is in safety razors, where Warner Lambert, with ties to Hattori Watch Co., has outpaced Gillette, which uses an American approach of bypassing wholesalers.

Despite the enormous complexity of the distribution system, there are some basic features which help to simplify the underlying logic across the channels. In principle, the factors which largely guide just who influences the distribution channel is a function of a) the level of industrial concentration at the manufacturing level or b) the retail needs for assembly of a wide range of products,

---

[9] Detailed analysis is provided in Ross (1980), pp. 298–304.

Exhibit 10/7: Foreign Products with Large Market Shares in Japan

Items	Producers (Brands)	Nationalities	(%)
Carbonated beverages	Coca-Cola Co.	U.S.A.	60
	Pepsi Co., Inc.	U.S.A.	5
Instant coffee	Nestlé Alimentana S.A.	Switzerland	63
	General Foods Corp.	U.S.A.	17
Black tea	Unilever Ltd. (Lipton)	Britain	27
	R. Twining & Co., Ltd.	Britain	23
	Brooke Bond Liebig Ltd.	Britain	11
Dry soup	CPC International Inc. (Knorr)	U.S.A.	84
	Nestle Alimentana S.A.	Switzerland	8
Canned soup	CPC International Inc. (Knorr)	U.S.A.	21
	Campbell Soup Co.	U.S.A.	39
	Heinz (H. J.) Co.	U.S.A.	8
Sportswear	Adidas	West Germany	
	Hauser	France	} 60
	Lacoste, etc.	France	
Ropes for mountain	Mammoth	Switzerland	
climbing	Beal	France	} 88
	Edelrid, etc.	Switzerland	
Disposable diapers	The Procter & Gamble Co.	U.S.A.	50
Plastic foam products	Dow Chemical Co.	U.S.A.	30
	BASF A.G.	West Germany	30
Plasticizer (BBP)	Monsanto Chemical Co.	U.S.A.	100
Butyl rubber	Esso Eastern Chemicals Inc.	U.S.A.	100
Deodorizers	American Drug	U.S.A.	59
Turbo-chargers	Garrett Corp.	U.S.A.	64
Panel heaters	Dimplex	Britain	40
	Koehring	U.S.A.	
	Hosty Corp.	U.S.A.	} 50
	Balkan Australia	Australia	3
Computers (of more than	I.B.M. Corp.	U.S.A.	40
500 million yen/unit)	Sperry Rand Corp. (Univac)	U.S.A.	12
Instant cameras	Eastman Kodak Co.	U.S.A.	45
	Polaroid Overseas Corp.	U.S.A.	45
Golf balls	Dunlop	Britain	55
	Wilson	U.S.A.	
	Top Flite	U.S.A.	} 7
	Titleist	U.S.A.	
Safety razor blades	Warner-Lambert Co.	U.S.A.	70
	Gillette Co.	U.S.A.	10
Chemical admixtures for concrete	Martin Marietta Corp.	U.S.A.	50
Camping stoves	Application Des Gaz	France	67
	EPI Gas Ltd.	Britain	29
Stem wine glasses	Owens Illinois Inc.	U.S.A.	60
	T.G. Durand	France	} 20
	Schott Zwiesel	West Germany	

Source: To Miti

Exhibit 10/8: Determinants of the Distribution Entities Taking Organizing Initiative

High	a. Manufacturer Takes Major Role	b. Manufacturer Takes Some Initiative	c. Wholesaler Takes Initiative	
	Automobiles Musical Instruments (Pianos) Electrical Appliances	Film Cosmetics Detergents Cameras	Mayonnaise, Butter, Cheese, Seasonings, Chewing Gum, Chocolate, Whisky, Toothpaste, Home Pharma- ceuticals	Requirement for Assembling a Range of Products and Brands at the Retail Level →
	d. Wholesaler or Retailer Takes Initiative		e. Smaller Wholesaler Takes Initiative	
Low	Furniture Women's Apparel Men's Apparel Eyeglasses Shoes		Local Food Products Men's Socks Miscellaneous Household Goods	

Industrial Concentration

Source: JETRO

where the latter takes precedence over the former in importance (i.e., when assembling and coordination of products is important, despite industrial concentration), the distribution channels are very long. Exhibit 10/8 illustrates this relationship and with specific product examples.

10.6 Summary and Conclusions

This chapter has examined the major features of Japan's marketing and distribution system. In the domestic market manufacturers and service firms alike are faced with a basic fact of life, namely a complicated and fragmented distribution system reflecting Japan's village structure, family run outlets, and neighbourhood shopping. No aspect of Japanese business so closely displays the cultural and historical features of the country's evolution from an agricultural to an industrialized society. At the same time, these same features pose the greatest challenges to both modernization and to smooth economic relations with foreign importers.

At the center of Japan's marketing strategies have been the trading firms and the dominant organizations are the large *Sogoshosha,* which rank among the largest commercial enterprises anywhere. The power and competitive advantage of the *Sogoshosha* have probably peaked, as manufacturers reach out to manage their own marketing functions and as retailers undertake direct import functions themselves. The trading house sector itself acts as a competitor to the *Sogoshosha,* which have started to focus on new trade strategies ranging from consortia exports and service contracts, to direct foreign investment, and third country counter trade.

The opening up of Japan's market to import penetration goes hand in hand with the country's evolving industrial structure and emergence as a mass consumption society. The protracted arguments about modernizing the distribution system to make Japan more open for foreign imports will probably continue, especially in North America, where distribution is considerably less complex. Just how much of an impact this debate will have in practice is rather questionable. The trading house sector will still control a very significant percentage of all imports and exports, because of their global scale and specialized information systems. The department stores will concentrate on higher priced items with lower sales turnover, while the supermarket chains will gain greater control over wholesale channels along North American lines. The trend to encompass the marketing function by manufacturers will continue, but mostly for the products requiring after sales service or exclusive outlets. The examples of cars, consumer electronics, cameras and cosmetics stand out. Tokyo and Osaka dominate big store sales with 60 percent, but this still leaves a vast market of retail sales in smaller cities and communities. For the foreign importer, these trends mean that the Japanese market will remain a great challenge, requiring long term horizon and investment.

Moreover, the Japanese consumer is also changing, and this requires a clear focus on what to sell, as well as how to sell. The trading firms have played an extremely significant role in bringing the world's best products to Japan, so today the typical Japanese consumer is more demanding than probably any in the world. Salary levels and spending patterns have played a part, but so has education, travel, and voracious Japanese reading. Since housing is so expensive in Japan, there are differences in household budgets. The Japanese spend more on food, clothing, and household fixtures, but less on housing as such, compared to most Western countries. The aging of the population is also another factor, as is the trend to working mothers and an education pattern where forty percent of the age cohort 18–24 will go to university; by 1985, eighteen percent of the population will have a university or college degree.

What all of this means for Japanese and foreign competitors alike is that both consumer and industrial marketing will require new levels of sophistication and adaptability. As Japan's domestic market evolves, it may well set a standard for quality, price and reliability such that foreign competitors and Japanese producers alike will face new ground rules and new challenges. An indication of just how significant is this change is the emergence of Japanese multinational firms and increased direct foreign investment – the subject of the next chapter.

Chapter 11
The Acid Test: Japanese Management Abroad

"In the automobile industry, given the product, it is impossible for us to think only in terms of the Japanese market . . . We are more interested in what percentage of the global market we can get than what percentage of the Japanese market we may or may not have."

Takashi Ishihara, President, Nissan Motor Co., Ltd.

11.1 Introduction

From Amsterdam to Boston, Calcutta to Dakar, the neon lights reflect the blazing brand names of Japanese corporations – Canon, Seiko, Toyota, Kirin and Toshiba. The new tourist hordes in the ski resorts of France, Austria, the U.S. and Canada wear the finest European sports clothes and equipment – and usually a Sony walkman. Japanese restaurants have sprung up in the major culinary cities of the world – an appreciation of the merits of Japanese food, to be sure – but also a reflection of the growing presence of Japanese nationals abroad. The economic consulting firms compete to work with governments on their bids for Japanese investment – while public officials join the trek to Tokyo and Osaka in an auction to woo new jobs. At the same time, the undervalued yen, huge trade surpluses, fundamental shifts in energy economics, and new confidence in techniques and management methods have all combined to make Japan the new player in the multinational corporate chess game.

Unlike Western countries, Japan's manufacturers have channelled foreign investment money in a very specific geographical sequence, namely in Southeast Asia, then to third world countries, and more recently to North America.[1] In contrast to the American model of multinationals, Japan's overseas investments have not been at the cutting edge in technology of the manufacturing sector. Rather the investment has often been in areas where domestic production began to lose competitiveness – from rising wages, resource costs, or uneconomic transportation. Put differently, overseas investment by Japanese firms has been focused in sunset industries, leaving exports to develop in domestic sunrise sectors. Japan has deliberately (and in a fundamental way,

---

[1] For studies on Japanese foreign investment, see Tsurumi (1976), Yoshino (1976), Yoshihara (1978) and Ozawa (1979).

quite rationally) focused the penetration of foreign markets in the high value added, advanced products by exports rather than by overseas investment.

Japan's distinctiveness in the multinational corporate arena has another added feature – namely the key role of trading firms in sourcing, and more recently, investing in primary goods. North American and for the most part European multinationals have been resource firms (mining, pulp and paper, petroleum) and manufacturing establishments. While both Western and Japanese investment has followed similar paths in emerging global sectors like finance and banking, Japan has been unique in the leadership role played by the trading house sector in both export and direct foreign investment strategies. As noted in the last chapter, Japan's trading sector is led by the *Sogoshosha,* whose corporate tentacles reach out to every corner of the world. The trading firms have been at the vanguard of penetrating foreign markets in manufactured goods but recent strategic shifts by Japan's producer firms means that they themselves want to reach directly to serve foreign markets. What do these conflicting trends mean for Japanese management strategies? Does the move by Japanese manufacturers into direct marketing mean the demise of the traditional trading sector? Does the rise of large overseas manufacturers from Japan auger in a new era of Japanese multinational corporation? Do Japan's managerial practices transfer to foreign cultures, alien political systems, and less cooperative union environments? These are the issues addressed in this chapter.

11.2 Japanese Investment: Past Trends

Any interpretation of Japan's industrial evolution as a major economic power must come to grips with certain political and management challenges in the years ahead. During the past two decades or more, Japanese industry has made progressively successful forays into the five continents of the world. For the most part, this growing involvement in the global economy has taken three broad paths – each related, but each sufficiently different to form, in the decade ahead, a rather different strategy to Japan's emerging role as the undisputed leader in the Pacific Rim.

What have these three traditional paths been? The first path has involved the trading firms. To service Japan's import needs for basic raw materials, food, and energy, the *Sogoshosha* have developed global scanning, huge information banks and transportation and logistical networks to establish and service long term supply contracts. Although their basic thrust has been and remains bulk goods and commodities selling in high volumes, the *Sogoshosha,* plus hundreds of specialized trading firms, have added "piggy back" fashion a host of manufactured and service goods to their import lines. Additionally, they have served as the front line conduit for domestic manufacturing firms wishing to penetrate foreign markets, especially when only small volumes or specialized orders have been involved. As argued in the previous chapter, because of a weak trading sector in many Western countries, the Japanese trading houses have gained a leading edge in Europe and North America in the latter's overseas export trade flows.[2] About twenty-five percent of total world trade is in trading or barter, also known as counter trade with the largest percentage concentrated in Soviet Block and Third World countries (McMillan, 1983). In the area of energy and raw materials sourcing, where the international environment is typically characterized by fluctuating international demand, political instability, or war, the trading firms have been on the vanguard of post-war of managing Japan's security of supply challenges, in part through direct foreign investment (Tsurumi, 1976; Young, 1979).

The second path has been in labour intensive, low-tech manufacturing. The clear picture which emerges is a two stage investment pattern, at first in Southeast Asia, and more recently in Europe and North America. Product life cycle factors have been the guiding strategic model – the key success factors have been the skills in shifting functional strategies based on production and cost to those based on scale economies, international brand names and quality. The trend in Southeast Asia, starting in the 1950's but rising rapidly in the 1960's, and steadying off in the 1970's, has been one of transferring offshore the production sectors which involve Japan's domestic comparative disadvantage, i.e., areas where low cost labour, more land space, or cheaper raw materials and energy sourcing provided offshore production sites in Asia with a competitive edge. Textiles, electronic machines and appliances, timber and pulp were the first growth sectors dominating Japanese foreign direct investment, followed in the late 1970's by chemicals, food processing, heavy machines, and other manufacturers. In most cases, technology transfer to these Asian sites has been involved, especially with joint venture forms of organization (Ozawa, 1974; Kojima, 1977).

The second stage of manufacturing investment strategies has focused on Europe and North America. In a fundamental way, this stage has really been a continuation of the same objective, albeit in different forms, of the investment patterns adopted in Southeast Asia. While the trading firms have spearheaded the initial Japanese export penetration of manufactured products in foreign markets, the shift has been to the establishment of overseas beachheads by establishing local distribution/warehousing/service branches after import vo-

---

[2] Mitsubishi's U.S. subsidiary, Mitsubishi International Corp., had 1980 sales of $13 billion, or 22 percent of the total of the Japanese parent. A large portion was third country trade.

lume reaches minimum production levels. In scores of sectors, from color TV's to zippers, cars, ball bearings and consumer electronics, the deliberate aim has been to postpone overseas production until a sufficient import threshold had been reached via exports. Once the minimum volumes became developed, aggressive overseas marketing from offshore sites often provide the death knell to local companies. Exhibit 11/1 outlines the basic functional strengths developed by Japanese firms as they conquered overseas markets.

The third path of Japan's overseas thrust has been in export plant sales and offshore turnkey projects. These forms of overseas investment have relatively recent origins in the world economy. The rapid industrialization in Middle East OPEC countries, development in third world markets, and growth in Asia have opened up an entirely new branch of global trade quickly exploited by the Japanese (and also South Korean firms, especially in the area of civil engineering and construction). Whether the project was the construction of an entire university or telecommunications facility in Saudi Arabia, a new urban transit system in Caracas or Hong Kong, an integrated pulp and paper mill in Brazil, the basic structure incorporates large scale contracts involving hundreds and even thousands of subcontractors and suppliers organized around a lead firm in a consortia arrangement. By no means have Japanese firms been the only players engaged in international plant sales and turnkey export consortia. (The U.S. and West Germany still do more plant sales than Japan's $16 billion annual trade.) However the Japanese have enjoyed two distinctive advantages in the growth over the past two decades. For one thing, Japanese foreign aid has been largely oriented to bilateral assistance to developing countries. Almost twice as much aid from Japan compared to major European countries, and five times that of the U.S., went to "project aid" tied to infrastructure development – roads, harbours and seaports, railways and power plants, and major heavy industry investments – hydro, cement steel, fertilizer.[3] In many of these projects, major Japanese firms developed overseas turnkey skills which have been used for competitive success in other markets, including Western countries. Secondly, the large industrial groups in Japan, lead by trading firms and the major banks, have been quick off the mark to recognize the organizational and managerial competences required to mobilize competitive consortia bidding and implementation strategies. While there have been major and notable failures – Mitsui's petrochemical complex in Iran and the giant steel combine in China – they must be seen in the total context of Japan's overseas consortia and plant sales strategies.

For a variety of reasons, the basic direction of these three paths to overseas investments is changing. In the first place, there are the long term structural

---

[3] See Japanese Economic Cooperation (1981).

Exhibit 11/1: Life Cycle Trends in Japanese Growth
Basic strategy: Enter low end

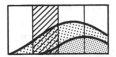

Strategic emphases
- Market analysis
- Production technology
- Southeast Asia (experimentally, US)
- Trading firms

Representative products
- Computers
- Gas turbines
- Compressors
- Construction equipment
- Large-scale integrated circuits
- Color film

Basic strategy: Expand to medium and high ends

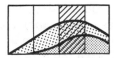

Strategic emphases
- Economies of scale
- World market
- "High class" image orientation
- OEM or own brands

Representative products
- Turbines/generators
- Plain paper copiers
- Pianos
- Automobiles
- Telecommunication equipment

Basic strategy: "Win the world"

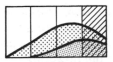

Strategic emphases
- Global brands (more than two companies)
- Non-price competitiveness
- Overseas production
- Continued innovation (prolong life cycle)

Representative products
- Cameras
- Stereo equipment
- Tape decks
- Personal calculators
- Motorcycles
- Watches
- Steel

Past the peak (shift to NICs)
- Radios   • Shipbuilding
- TV   • Plywood
- Textiles

Create new market
- VLSR
- VTR

Source: Ohmae (1982: 113)

shifts in the domestic economy away from heavy industry to more technologically advanced sectors. As Japan relocates its declining or sunset sectors offshore, new source countries are emerging, including Asian countries but also
African and Latin American markets. A variety of economic forces – energy
costs, import competition, and tariff barriers – are fundamentally altering the
competitive productivity of Japan's entire postwar heavy industry infrastructure. Steel from Korea, petrochemicals from Saudi Arabia, and shipbuilding
from Brazil are three cases in point.

Secondly, the ground rules of the global economy are themselves changing.
Many industrial sectors have grown up around national markets because of
country-specific factors like government intervention or country specific tastes
and industry structures. As international forces gain ascendency, many industries are evolving into structures where worldwide visions and strategies are
becoming the critical competitive weapons. The automobile industry is the
classic case, but many areas of consumer electronics, banking and financial
services, construction and large scale computers are probable contenders experiencing the same trends. What this means for Japanese industry is a need to
shift from an essentially ethnocentric, domestically based production focus
with global marketing to a geocentric, internationally based production focus
with tightly integrated marketing strategies.[4] For Japan, the critical challange
may rest more with management capabilities involving familiarity with foreign
languages and cultures than with any inherent difficulties or challenges in production and marketing.

Thirdly, Japan, with its huge domestic savings and rapidly evolving financial
and informational services networks, stands at the threshold of enormous challenges as the geographical centre of Asia's new investment and trade patterns.
In the next two decades the full flowering of the Southeast Asia market will be
reached, together with major competitive challenges of new countries on the
world stage such as India, Pakistan and at a distance, China. The economic and
trade trends are obviously more predictable than the highly volatile political
trends. In either case, Japan stands in the centre of this maturing Pacific Rim,
with consequences for all corners of the world. This chapter picks up these
issues in the context of Japanese foreign investment and the emergence of
Japanese multinational corporations. The next chapter addresses the issue of
Tokyo as the leading financial centre of Asia.

---

[4] Perlmutter (1969) classified firms in terms of their headquarters orientation to national subsidiaries as ethnocentric (national ownership), polycentric (nationality of host country), and geocentric (truly international).

11.3 Overseas Investment: New Directions

Throughout the 1950's and 1960's, the Japanese government severely restricted domestic firms from investing abroad. This policy underwent extensive changes in 1972, when the surveillance apparatus of the Ministry of Finance was changed. Prior to that change, the vast amount of Japanese foreign investment was concentrated in supplies of raw materials and natural resources, as well as in relatively small scale manufacturing ventures, mostly in sectors like textiles, shoes, cutlery and the like where Japan had lost cost competitiveness to other Asian countries.

In a world where foreign investment and the rise of multinational firms have raised the spectre of the demise of the nation state, Japan's pattern of overseas

Exhibit 11/2: European, Japanese, and U.S. Foreign Investment Profiles

	Europe-Based[+]	Japan-Based[*]	U.S.-Based[**]
Size of Parent Firm:	(1) Traditionally In Former Colonies by Large Firms (2) Large Firms Invest In European Continent and non-U.S. markets	(1) 40 percent of investments by small, medium size firms (2) Large R & D firms go abroad often with small subcontractors	(1) Large R & D intensive firms dominate overseas investments (2) Small to medium size firms may have subcontracting relations with foreign manufactures
Stock of DFI[++] 1971	$ 57.2 billion $ 98.8 billion	$ 4.4 billion $ 19.4 billion	$ 82.3 billion $ 137.2 billion
Ratio of FDI to Manufacturing Exports**	34%	30%	177%
Where Invested	Global Markets, Shared Between Developed/ Developing Countries	Developing Nations 75% in Asia	Two-thirds in Developed Countries
Sectors*** Primary Manufacturing Tertiary	5.6 72.6 21.8	32.0 31.8 36.2	34.5 42.7 22.8
Organization of Subsidiaries	Many Joint Ventures Majority Owner	Joint Venture Dominant Many Minority Interests	Fully Owned or Majority Controlled
Partner if Any, of Subsidiaries	Local Partners and Governments	1. Local Partners and Trading Firms 2. Japanese Firms in Some Industrial Group	On Its Own or Local Partners
Parents Control Over Subsidiary	Loose	Loose	Close
Parent Subsidiary Relationship	Local Market Oriented	Local Oriented	Globally Integrated

   * Adapted from Tsurumi (1976)
  ** U.S. Department of Commerce (1980)
 *** MITI, *White Paper on International Trade*
   + Dyas and Thanheiser (1976), Franco (1979), Hymer and Rowthorne (1970)
  ++ U.N. Center on Transational Corporation

investment differs remarkably from other leading Western economies with substantial multinationals: the U.S., Britain, West Germany and France. By geography, Japan has invested more in developing countries than in the rich industrialized countries of the West, especially Europe. By type of investment, Japan has typically used joint venture arrangement, often with minority control – U.S. firms, in particular, have preferred unambiguous 100 percent ownership and control (Stopford and Wells, 1972). By size of firm, small companies in Japan have been major players in overseas investment–accounting for about half the number of companies active in foreign investment (White Paper on SME, 1980). As shown in Exhibit 11/2, the contrast between the U.S., European, and the Japanese approach up to the early 1970's was quite notable not just in geographical emphasis but in organizational strategy, technological sophistication, and managerial control.

To be sure, long established historical patterns are reflected in these patterns – such as the well documented capacity of U.S. firms to pioneer technical innovations in the growing home market and then exploit the resulting monopoly advantages as the driving force for foreign investment in protected overseas markets; the European linkages between home markets and overseas colonies and dependencies; and the largely regional economic base of Japan in the regions of the prewar "Greater Prosperity Sphere" of Asia. After the initial quick buildup of cases after the 1972 liberalization, there has been a regular

Exhibit 11/3: Japan's Recent Investment Abroad (reported-and-approved basis) (unit: million dollars)

	Acquisition of Securities		Acquisition of Claims		Acquisition of Real Estate & Overseas Direct Work Projects		Establishment of Branches		Total	
	Number of Cases	Value	Number of Cases	Value	Number of Cases	Value	Number of Cases	Value	Number of Cases	Value
FY 1951–68	1,675	802	428	882	43	301	314	22	2,460	2,007
FY 1969	439	223	73	404	3	36	29	2	544	665
FY 1970	556	296	135	570	11	32	27	6	729	904
FY 1971	648	471	147	333	53	38	56	17	904	858
FY 1972	1,206	1,781	223	252	293	62	52	243	1,774	2,338
FY 1973	1,926	2,177	581	1,100	504	120	82	96	3,093	3,494
FY 1974	1,137	1,262	514	1,098	214	18	46	18	1,911	2,395
FY 1975	833	1,652	580	1,485	137	11	41	132	1,591	3,280
FY 1976	882	1,487	577	1,882	135	15	58	78	1,652	3,462
FY 1977	830	1,319	708	1,388	164	35	59	65	1,761	2,806
FY 1978	889	2,038	1,124	2,383	334	98	48	80	2,395	4,598
FY 1979	990	1,833	1,255	2,994	398	105	51	63	2,694	4,995
Comulative Total	12,011	15,339	6,345	14,771	2,289	871	863	823	21,508	31,804

Note: 1. Only newly reported-and-approved investments are registered in the category of "Number of Cases."
2. Figures of "Value" are rounded.

Source: Look Japan, July 10, 1980

and steady increase in the value of foreign investment abroad, for securities acquisition, real estate and projects, and investment in plants. (Not entirely coincidently, Japan faced in 1971 Nixon shock – the effective devaluation of the dollar changed the yen exchange from Y360=U.S. 1 by more than 16 per cent.) In all, Japan's cumulative overseas investment amounted to $31,804 million – about a seventh of that for the United States.

Japan's foreign investment is carefully balanced by both region and by industry sector. Since the late 1970's, the United States has emerged as the largest host country to Japanese investment, although South East Asia is the largest area – 27.2 percent, down from a third at the beginning of the decade. In North America, where there is more than $8 billion of direct foreign investment and an estimated 125,000 employees working for Japanese affiliates, recent investment patterns have typically been of a defensive nature – protecting market share derived from successful exports penetration, as distinct from market entry investment strategies. Year to year trends have to be treated with caution as exchange rate considerations, domestic balance of payments, and political factors all influence annual capital flows. In Asia, by contrast, and increasingly in South America where the value of investment abroad almost matched overseas investment in Europe and the Middle East combined, the patterns reflect long range committments, such as oil, coal, mining, and petrochemicals (Exhibit 11/4).

The third way of seeing Japanese direct foreign investment is to consider overseas trends by industry categories. In this respect, there are important implications of special significance in the Japanese case, because of the important role played in domestic and overseas trade by the trading firms. The key features include not just the shift from one sector to another such as from manufacturing to raw materials, towards banking or real estate. The long term impact of these shifts suggests an evolution toward the development of true Japanese multinational firms. Multinationalism of Japanese companies has been confined mainly to the trading firms, although the rise of major Japanese banking and service firms has raised the spectre of a new area of overseas competitive threat, as the next chapter argues.

As shown in Exhibit 11/4, manufacturing investment has fluctuated throughout the seventies from a low of 22.4 of all investment to a high of 44.3 percent, ending at the end of 1979 for a total of $10,867, compared to $525 million in 1972. Chemicals, iron and steel and nonferrous metals and the traditional textile sector represent the significant investments, reflecting the importance of major investments in Iran, Iraq, Indonesia and more recently in Australia. Notably absent from the manufacturing sector compared to U.S. and European firms are investments in automobiles, pharmaceuticals and office equipment. As will be explained below, there has been a very clear preference on the part of capital intensive, high value added companies in Japan to consider

Exhibit 11/4: Japan's Direct Investment Abroad by Industry (unit: million dollars, %)

	FY 1972	FY 1973	FY 1974	FY 1975	FY 1976	FY 1977	FY 1978	FY 1979	Cumulative Total
Manufacturing Industries									
Foodstuff	29	68	64	58	25	48	67	103 (2.1)	532 (1.7)
Textile	163	326	175	98	112	158	172	89 (1.8)	1,564 (4.9)
Lumber & Pulp	35	64	61	89	63	52	23	33 (0.7)	680 (2.1)
Chemical	66	394	97	151	270	325	705	238 (4.8)	2,312 (7.3)
Iron & Steel, & Non-ferrous Metal	53	245	149	148	171	99	498	578 (11.6)	2,127 (6.7)
Machinery	37	85	89	98	53	61	119	160 (3.2)	792 (2.5)
Electric	69	156	99	96	164	161	243	180 (3.6)	1,270 (4.0)
Transportation Machinery	42	80	38	100	93	86	114	150 (3.0)	803 (2.5)
Others	31	79	103	87	74	85	99	161 (3.2)	805 (2.5)
	525	1,496	874	924	1,025	1,074	2,038	1,693	10,867
Subtotal	(22.4)	(42.8)	(36.5)	(28.2)	(29.6)	(38.3)	(44.3)	(33.9)	(34.2)
Other Industries									
Agricultural & Forestry	16	70	27	36	46	136	90	83 (1.7)	570 (1.8)
Fisheries	12	28	25	28	18	14	33	72 (1.4)	267 (.8)
Mining	911	511	742	707	995	452	338	857	6,506
	(39.0)	(14.6)	(31.0)	(21.6)	(28.7)	(16.1)	(7.4)	(17.2)	(20.5)
Construction	7	16	18	32	51	39	72	85 (1.7)	359 (1.3)
Commercial	225	436	348	668	404	344	823	834	4,612
	(9.6)	(12.3)	(14.5)	(20.4)	(11.7)	(12.3)	(17.9)	(16.7)	(14.5)
Financial & Insurance	171	305	143	310	219	176	154	198 (4.0)	2,046 (6.4)
Others	165	416	183	432	610	472	871	1,006 (20.1)	4,883 (15.3)
Real Estate	62	120	18	11	15	35	98	105 (2.1)	871 (2.7)
Branches	243	96	18	132	78	65	80	63 (1.3)	823 (2.5)
Total	2,338	3,494	2,395	3,280	3,462	2,806	4,598	4,995	31,804
	(100)	(100)	(100)	(100)	(100)	(100)	(100)	(100)	(100)

Note: Figures in parentheses indicate percentage shares of the total.

Source: Look Japan, July 10, 1980

overseas investment as a last resort, with preference for serving foreign markets via exports. Even when domestic cost advantages have disappeared (despite the fact that raw materials are imported) and when intangibles may still remain – such as the tight control of supply arrangements with subcontrators and related firms – Japanese firms still prefer market penetration via exports rather than foreign investment.

Already, however, the outlines of the basic changes are clearly emerging. In raw materials and food, there will be the traditional ABC policy of diversifying sources and resorting to local lending, and reducing the total level of direct investment to small percentage of total investments. This is the importance of the growing increase, shown in Exhibit 11/3, of the acquisition of claims, as compared to the acquisition of securities. Japanese firms lent capital to their foreign subsidiaries to increase and expand local capacity. Exchange rates and differential interest rates, plus local government regulations for local content, and export restrictions of a processed products, will largely determine this trend in the years ahead.

Clearly the trading house sector will be the center pin for this raw materials expansion. Since Japan's trade in raw materials already accounts for 25 percent of the world's total (for a population amounting to only three percent), the *Sogoshosha* are the major candidates to lead this overseas investment assault. To date, some of the lessons abroad in investments have been painful. Ataka, one of the big ten *Sogoshosha* in the 1970's, invested heavily into the Come-by-Change oil refinery in Newfoundland and lost a quarter of a billion dollars, bringing the entire company down in the process. The Mitsui Group invested over one billion dollars in the Japan-Iran joint petrochemical complex, only to be tangled in the Iranian Revolution and the subsequent Iran-Iraq war.

The timing of the strategy shift of the trading firms towards direct overseas investment has entailed a high degree of risk, but the timing is not altogether a disadvantage for the Japanese groups. On the risk side, there is the growing element of nationalism and protectionism among the resource rich countries. These factors promote the desire for local ownership, increased value added for basic materials, and export sales offshore. The Japanese propensity to use joint venture forms of organization has an appealing feature for countries like Australia, Canada and Brazil, among the developed countries, as well as in third world countries which often take their cue from this ABC group. Despite

Exhibit 11/5: Japan's Direct Investment Abroad by Region (unit: million dollars, %)

	FY 1977			FY 1978			FY1979			Cumulative Total FY 1951–79		
	Number of Cases	Value	Percentage Share	Number of Cases	Value	Percentage Share	Number of Cases	Value	Percentage Share	Number of Cases	Value	Percentage Share
North America	692	735	26.2	1,055	1,364	29.7	1,228	1,438	28.8	7,717	8,202	25.8
U.S.	656	686	24.4	1,016	1,282	27.9	1,171	1,345	26.9	7,275	7,394	23.2
Canada	36	48	1.7	39	82	1.8	57	93	1.9	442	808	2.5
Latin America	213	456	16.3	245	616	13.4	208	1,207	24.4	2,458	5,580	17.5
Brazil	84	263	9.5	86	258	5.5	55	409	8.2	1,093	2,738	8.6
Mexico	10	10	0.4	16	37	0.8	22	516	10.3	159	733	2.3
Asia	511	865	30.8	669	1,340	29.1	759	976	19.5	7,318	8,643	27.2
Hong Kong	110	109	3.9	136	159	3.5	225	225	4.5	1,506	939	3.0
Indonesia	83	425	15.1	84	610	13.3	65	150	3.0	877	3,888	12.2
South Korea	33	95	3.4	51	222	4.8	45	95	1.9	1,023	1,102	3.5
Philippines	58	27	1.0	44	53	1.2	43	102	2.0	500	537	1.7
Singapore	89	66	2.4	161	174	3.8	166	255	5.1	924	800	2.5
Taiwan	54	18	0.6	102	10	0.9	92	39	0.8	987	323	1.0
Middle East	25	225	8.0	18	492	10.7	18	130	2.6	222	2,101	6.6
Iran	12	172	6.1	7	390	8.5	2	76	1.5	108	931	2.9
Saudi Arabia	—	49	1.7	5	17	0.4	9	19	0.4	40	108	0.3
Europe	163	220	7.8	251	323	7.0	301	495	9.9	2,158	3,893	12.2
U.K.	43	50	1.8	87	66	1.4	100	67	1.3	589	1,823	5.7
Africa	58	140	5.0	59	225	4.9	67	168	3.4	659	1,306	4.1
Oceania	99	165	5.9	98	239	5.2	113	582	11.6	976	2,078	6.5
Australia	64	146	5.2	58	204	4.4	84	566	11.3	655	1,734	5.5
Total	1,761	2,806	100.0	2,395	4,598	100.0	2,694	4,995	100.0	21,508	31,804	100.0
(Total of Investment in Industrialized Countries)	928	1,106	39.4	1,371	1,893	41.2	1,619	2,499	50.0	10,613	13,947	43.9

Source: Look Japan, July 10, 1980

this advantage, the Japanese companies have often had to adapt to an alien environment which often includes dealing with a foreign government whose outlook to investment is at variance to what Japanese managers experience at home. It is for this reason that the trading firms usually seek out the involvement of such agencies as the Japanese Export-Import Bank for concessionary financing and the Overseas Economic Cooperation Fund loans to developing country governments.

There are two reasons why the timing of the trading firms' investment strategy is more favourable in the 1980's. In the first instance, the relationship between the trading firms and the Japanese manufacturing sector is undergoing profound changes. Since the manufacturers have moved into high value added, high growth sectors, there is a basic requirement to establish direct contract with the customer through sales and distribution networks. As the product line itself expands and becomes more complex, the need for add ons and after-sales services increases – in short, the transaction costs of these relationships increase the obligation for direct organizational coordination by the manufacturer, without the need of the trading firm (Roehl, 1981). The vast distribution networks developed by Japanese manufacturers in Europe and North America, first in automobiles and motorcycles, followed by televisions, videorecorders and microwave ovens, and more recently by computer and photocopy equipment illustrate this emerging strategy of the manufacturing sector. In this respect, the traditional three step pattern of production growth – export through trading firms – build volume for overseas production – integrate production/marketing – has reached a new stage both for manufacturers and for the trading firms. First, what does this imply for the trading sector?

For the trading firms, this manufacturing shift change means two things. Except for small and specialized niches, the large trading firms will continue to lose their intermediary role in the export function for the big manufacturers. As regards energy, raw materials, and food, their import/export role also undertakes a shift in direction primarily due to external prices. This factor involves the changing locational advantages of production due to energy sourcing. In the past three decades, the Japanese have built up a huge infrastructure of heavy industry (iron and steel, ship building, petrochemicals) where the primary domestic considerations were transport and logistical policies for importing raw materials and energy (Exhibit 4/6, Chapter 4). The changing economies of bulk transport, and the comparative advantages of importing energy for globally efficient heavy industry on-shore, provided Japan with enormous productivity advantages during the 1950's and the 1960's: the fundamental economics of energy in the aftermath of OPEC have begun a basic shift out of downstream investments. This change means that global energy economics favour the location of downstream investments – ethylene for chemicals being the primary example – towards the source of feed stock, which means in Saudi

Arabia primarily, Mexico and Canada to a certain extent. For Japan, the obvious investors are the major industrial groups, led by the *Sogoshosha*. In Saudi Arabia, the so-called Seven Sister firms – the integrated oil majors like Mobil, Exxon, and Shell – and the Japanese groups led by Mitsubishi have linked up with Sabic (Saudi Basic Industries Corporation) to build petrochemical complexes capable of providing two-thirds or more of the world's supply (Forbes, 1982). The sheer size and complexity of these kinds of ventures – aluminum in Indonesia, mining of all sorts in Australia, urban transit in Hong Kong, construction projects in the Middle East, to cite some major foreign examples – point to a new element in world trade – export and investment consortia.

Overseas involvement in the management of Japan's supply dependence relates to the emergence of the second area of development for the trading groups – the export of entire plants. Starting from a very small base of a few hundred million a year in 1966, Japan's plant export sectors has become a $15–16 billion dollar industry. These plant exports involve integrated engineering and construction projects built in Japan and transplanted by ocean to in site locations around the world. Example projects include pulp and power plants to Brazil, turbine power generation plants to Bangladesh, petrochemical plants to Argentina, or desalination plants in Saudi Arabia, Asia, the Middle East, Afria, and Latin America. The scale of the projects themselves have required close working relationships between the trading house sector, the engineering and construction sector, and the major banks. In most cases, plant exports involves a degree of technology transfer and government to government linkage not found in traditional export packages. Some areas of export plant sales build volume and value added to manufacturing sectors such as machinery, specialty steel, and metal casting. However, the main thrust of Japan's multinational corporate development will come from mainstream manufacturing – a subject treated in the next section.

11.4 Japanese Multinationals

The corporate evolution of Japanese foreign investment strategies in manufacturing have evidently followed a path guided by life cycle penetration of particular produce niches. Conceptually this path may be depicted with reference to Exhibit 11/6. In the first stage, foreign market penetration has been achieved by exports from Japan, mainly in selected product areas where there are cost advantages in production and where local competitors have left open a gap in the market – black and white television, small cars, sporty motorcycles and the like. In some cases, the producing firm in Japan handled the overseas sales penetration – Honda in cars and motorcycles, for instance; in others, a trading firm was the main vehicle for foreign marketing – Toyota in automobiles is a

Exhibit 11/6: The Evolution of Japanese Manufacturing

		Strategic Advantage	
		National	International
Production Location	Home Market	*Stage 1* Exports	*Stage 2* Sales and Distribution
	Overseas	*Stage 3* National Subsidiaries	*Stage 4* Global Firms

case in point. Ironically, the export pull for many Japanese companies was not an overseas strategy at all – it was the major department stores in the U.S. which wished to add lines not provided by the major American manufacturers but which Japanese firms willingly made under a foreign brand name. The lesson did not go unnoticed in Japan, as when television manufacturers and later office equipment producers altered the U.S. practice of a two tiered distribution system to a single tier chain of independent dealers.

In all three cases, the Japanese firms gradually shifted market development strategies from penetration directly by export to one of local sales and distribution networks. During the past two decades, the production and sales of increasingly sophisticated products have required greater awareness of consumer trends and market structure which a trading arm could not itself provide. As a result, most manufacturers reached out to foreign markets by building local sales and distribution outlets. While a trading firm may have been involved in the initial phase, the Japanese production firms used the sales and distribution outlet as much more than a service arm of the basic marketing strategy. In fact, these sales arms became an important source of information flowing back to production sites in Japan about local market trends and prospects. (A Japanese firm selling weigh scales in Canada saw the trends away from imperial measurement to the metric system. By developing excellent use of publicly available government statistics, this sales company initiated alterations to the basic product made in Japan: an electronic control which allowed the machines to weigh in both metric and imperial. In three years, the company gained a 40 percent market share.) In a similar fashion, Honda penetrated the U.S. market mainly by relying on direct sales service, first in the Los Angeles and other California markets, only later by developing the most extensive dealer network in the U.S. – an estimated 2000 outlets compared to the only local U.S. manufacturer, Harley Davidson, with 500 dealers (Leontiades, 1982:306).

As a general rule of market development, however, Japanese firms have been most reluctant to shift to an overseas investment strategy until a high level of sales penetration has been achieved. It is this shift from a stage two to a stage three strategy where the most difficult decisions are made for Japanese firms, but for reasons quite different from the usual explanation offered in overseas countries. The fundamental driving force of Japanese firms has not been marketing but production – cost leadership and volume production, process engineering, quality control, product design and packaging. Japan's strategic advantages in production have overwhelmingly originated in the home market where years of process technology refinement have led to a high value, low cost production position. The challenge for Japanese firms has been a balancing act of learning foreign market requirements while maintaining production advantages at home. To play this balancing game, Japanese firms have faced two conflicting sets of forces – one favouring export penetration strategies characteristic of Stage 1 and Stage 2, and the other favouring an investment strategy in foreign markets. For the past ten to fifteen years, Japan has been spectacularly successful with this carefully weighed approach. The big question is, can it continue? The general answer seems to be negative, but for reasons which are more complex than sometimes even the Japanese appreciate. On a more general scale, Japanese export penetration has coincided, not necessarily by accident, with a variety of factors contributing to a favourable export environment. In no fixed order, these factors include:

- exploiting production scale economies

- ease of global communications

- revolution in low transport costs

- homogeneity of consumer tastes

- reduction of trade barriers

- equalization of factor inputs, e.g., labour, materials, energy

- internationalization of knowledge

Many of these items are the result of what Drucker (1968:81) called the "global shopping center" and with it the emergence of common consumer tastes and values in all corners of the world:

Today the whole world, whatever its actual economic condition – and whatever the political system in force in a given area – has one common demand schedule, one set of common values and preferences. The whole world, in other words, has become one economy in its expectations, in its responses, in its behaviour.

The overwhelming thrust of Japan's export penetration has been on the sale of relatively undifferentiated products – i.e. products serving global tastes based either on demand developed in the export market (color television in the U.S.) or on tastes and styles highly suitable to the Japanese market but increasingly accepted abroad (35 mm cameras, small cars, radial tires). Because Japan has

been a follower nation in the past century of industrial development, manufacturers have had little opportunity to lead in tastes and styles – Japan had to
accept those foreign tastes and develop a flexible production system to serve
them.[5]

Theoretically, Japan's strategy, if that's what it can be termed, fits well with a
little known trade model advanced by a Belgian economist, Jacques Dreze
(1960, 1961). According to Dreze, smaller and less developed countries should
concentrate on internationally standardized products. Because their markets
are small, there is limited opportunity to influence the consumer tastes of
foreign markets. Tariffs and quotas, as well as "psychological distance," impose market barriers to developing volume production through scale economies. The important relationship is between the length of production runs and
product differentiation. Dreze (1960) develops what he calls the "hypothesis of
standardization" – a view that a country should concentrate on products made
to international standards, and thereby reap scale economies and real cost
efficiencies.

Dreze (1960, 1961) cites the example of Belgium, which concentrates exports
on standardized products like semifinished iron and steel, flat glass, and automobile components which don't vary among producers and models; examples
include batteries, tires, windows, seat fabrics and radiators. Even in ceramics,
Belgium focuses on white china rather than colored or decorated which has
qualities subject to taste (e.g. Royal Doulton in Britain, Lemoge in France, and
Rosenthal in West Germany). The contrast is not just with taste and style-
setting countries like these larger European countries, but with the smaller
European countries noted for national brand names. Where Belgium concentrates in standardized leather goods and plywood to gain volume, other coun-
tries concentrated in low volume differentiated products like fashion shoes
(Britain or Italy) furniture (Sweden and Denmark), and clothes (France and
Italy).

The hypothesis of standardization adequately explains Japan's enormous concentration on all aspects of production, and until recently, limited development
of differentiated products. Like watches, TV's, cars, and motorcycles in the
consumer field, or steel, ships, and machinery in the industrial sector, the
production emphasis has been on undifferentiated segments where scale economies, volume output, and superb capacity management and quality produc-

---

[5] This approach explains Japan's very high export elasticity, which shows the extent to which a
country's exports increase or decrease as global exports rise or fall by a given unit, denominated
as 1. A high elasticity means that a country's exports will increase at a faster rate than average
global increases. According to MITI's White Paper on International Trade, Japan's export
elasticity was 2.03 in the years 1960–1965, 1.71 in 1965–1970, and 1.75 in 1970–1976. Comparable figures for the U.S. were 0.70, 0.86, and 1.15.

tion have led to marketing prowess overseas. In the 1980's, various factors are forcing Japanese managers to change this approach.

In the first place, countries which specialized in focused segments can find that their products have become accepted as the international standard. This happened to Sweden in telephone equipment and some areas of machinery, Danish home goods and furniture, and Swiss pharmaceuticals. In many product lines in the 1980's – VCR's, cameras, small cars, consumer electronics of all sorts – Japan's standards are the globally accepted standards. A second issue is that many high value added products are inherently more complex and subject to differing consumer tastes and shopping habits, which themselves are subject to variation by national boundaries and culture. The third factor is more general, and refers to the kinds of country specific environmental forces requiring a local presence to serve foreign markets. Some of these issues include the following:

– local factor endowments

– need for local sourcing

– complexity in logistics

– exploiting intangible assets (brand names)

– diversity in market channels

– local languages, laws, tastes

– market imperfections

– economies of internal organization

The overseas investment approach of Japanese firms portends a strong impetus towards national subsidiaries to serve local markets, but which themselves can export (more than three quarters of Japanese firms in Europe export to third country markets). Japan is a very long way from developing truly global companies on the American or European model, where home country influences become secondary to global corporate strategies. For example, of the 100 largest world enterprises, Japan had only eight, compared to the American's 48, or Europe's 33 (Britain 7, Italy 3, France 11, Germany 12).

11.5 Exports vs. FDI: U.S.-Japan Comparisons

In the area of secondary manufacturing, Japan has served foreign markets primarily by exports, not direct foreign investment. American firms, by contrast, have eagerly penetrated foreign markets by direct foreign investment (often by acquisition of locally owned firms). Are these tactical alternatives to serve foreign markets merely cultural differences between U.S. and Japanese management? Do they represent more fundamental questions concerning the nature of multinational enterprises and their corporate evolution in global markets? Are there theoretical issues which these conflicting approaches suggest clarification?

In the past decade, research on the multinational firm and foreign investment has been a growth industry, with various competing schools of argument vying for prominence. Unlike international trade theory, which is built around a premise of the free mobility of goods in factor markets, modern foreign investment theory is based on the absence of a free global market. As Rugman (1980:366) notes "foreign direct investment is the converse of the pure theory of international trade. If the world were characterized by a model of free trade, there would be no need for the MNE."

Market imperfections derive from many government imposed instruments such as tariffs, quotas, subsidies, taxation and local sourcing. They also derive from firm specific factors as technology, size, financial control, access to raw materials, distribution systems and the like.

In a dynamic world, therefore, direct investment often occurs from a defensive posture intended to forego entry by competitors to a captive market. Size, technology, and even initial entry are strategic weapons to gain competitive advantage over any rival firm. Direct investment does provide a certain amount of risk in that, once established, withdrawal is very costly for the firm and for the host country. From the perspective of uncertainty and unpredictability, multinational firms in oligopolistic markets must weigh the danger of remaining in existing markets, even when they are very profitable as against the risk of entering new markets not necessarily as profitable, in order to forestall competitive entry and possible future barriers to entry.

This motivation for direct investment demonstrates a very subtle but central issue in the analysis of foreign investment and the multinational firm. The subtlety rests in the fact that it is the barrier to trade through export, not the removal of barriers which is the raison d'etre of the multinational corporation. As noted, there are obstacles presented by the location of one or more MNE's in a foreign market to the competitive detriment of any rival multinational which motivate entry by direct investment of additional firms. A further factor, however, is the action of host governments, most notably in the case of tariff barriers, but also in the case of differential monetary and fiscal policies and a battery of industrial policies (e.g. tax advantages, subsidies to investment, etc.) which can provide a motivation for multinational firms to exploit local opportunities by entry into the host market. In other words, in a world of very high factor mobility, multinational firms are capable of moving from one jurisdiction to another, and if economies of scale are great enough (as they usually are), they can exploit the differentials created by national policy to their own profitable advantage.

In a provocative analysis, Kioshi Kojima (1973, 1977) has conceptualized the difference between Japanese style, foreign investment and U.S. style foreign investment. In the U.S. case, most foreign investment in manufacturing has been concentrated in those industries where U.S. companies tend to have superior technologies or marketing advantages, and it was the presence of foreign trade barriers – real or potential – which largely motivated domestic firms to cross the threshold of trade by exports to trade by direct investment. As Raymond Vernon (1966) describes it, "the U.S. trade position in manufactured goods is based heavily on a comparative advantage in the generation of innovations, rather than on the more conventional notion of relatively cheap capital. The big post-war increases in U.S. overseas investment in manufacturing subsidiaries has come about mainly in the kind of industries that would have expected to have participated in such a process: industries associated with innovation and with oligopoly. It explains why so much of the investment is found in the chemical industries, the machinery industries, the transportation industries, and the scientific instrument industries."

This "technological gap, product cycle" theory of foreign investment has two basic consequences for the United States. In the first place, such investment patterns prove to the profitable for U.S. companies only so long as they can continue a stream of technological innovations and face foreign trade barriers. Also U.S. companies undermine via some foreign investment America's comparative advantage against lower wages and rising productivity. Increasingly, in the mature industries, third world countries will use their cheaper labour to challenge U.S. products. The U.S. will (like Canada) be squeezed both ways.

Kojima (1973) calls this U.S. form of foreign direct investment anti-trade oriented because it conflicts with the fundamental dynamics of international trade based on national comparative advantage.

The genuine product cycles and foreign direct investment takes place successively only within the innovative and oligopolistic industry group. Foreign direct investments from these new industries which ranked at the top of American comparative advantage are "anti-trade oriented" or involve foreign direct investments which work against the structure of comparative advantage. Those new industries should strengthen exports of their products if they were conscious of national economic interests, but actually they set up foreign subsidiaries, cutting off their own comparative advantage and inducing increased imports of those products from abroad where they invest. Both the loss of foreign markets and reverse imports later on result in balance of payments difficulties and the "export of job opportunities".

Kojima describes Japanese investment as trade oriented because the inward investment complements host country policies aimed at exploiting domestic comparative advantage for trade. Japanese foreign investment in manufacturing is basically in the sunset or "throw away industries" where Japan can no longer compete or where host country factor markets work to the advantage of overseas investments.

Japan's trade-oriented foreign investment strategies complement national policies aimed at improving domestic comparative advantage for trade. According to Professor Kojima (1973), "the major part of investment was directed towards natural resource development in which the Japanese economy is comparatively disadvantaged. Even investment in manufacturing has been confined either to such traditional industries as textiles, clothing, and processing of steel, in which Japan has been losing its comparative advantage, or the assembly of motor vehicles, production of parts and components of radios and other electronic machines, in which cheaper labour costs in Southeast Asian countries are achieved an the Japanese firms can increase exports, substituting for exports of final products, exports of machinery and equipment for the factory and technological knowhow."

The contrast between Japanese foreign investment on the one hand and American on the other has led to a need for reassessment of strategies in the U.S., owing in part to balance of payments problems, continued resentment against the U.S. practice of 100 per cent, especially in industries susceptible to strong nationalist pressures (Stopford and Wells, 1972), domestic unemployment and rising wage costs abroad. Many American firms, which invested abroad partly to escape the demands of unions for higher wages, have recently discovered that foreign wage rates are as high as or are reaching U.S. wage levels. Further, the steady buildup of overseas productivity now means that foreign subsidiaries and foreign firms can compete with U.S. domestic firms, including the American parent – Ford West Germany or ITT Europe being good examples. Small wonder then that many American multinationals would like to divest themselves of some of their foreign subsidiaries (e.g. Chrysler, U.K.), return production location to the United States, and export from the home market. The whole basis of U.S. foreign investment strategies of the past two decades may well be undergoing fundamental change – investment back in the U.S. The irony is that the opposite trend – Japanese investment abroad, is accelerating at unprecedented levels.

On the other hand, U.S. firms have unparalleled advantages in the strategic positioning of multinational corporations. Market factors have been the driving force for U.S. companies, not production, and in recent years there has been an attempt at the corporate level to rationalize production and marketing towards long term trends. In areas like Canada, Europe, and Asia, where national tariffs and other trade barriers have been reduced through GATT and the Tokyo round of trade negotiations, U.S. companies have redefined their overseas mandate in terms of such factors as market size, domestic and foreign competition, and the local environment. The profile of evolving U.S. firms is depicted in Exhibit 11/6a.

Exhibit 11/6a: The Evolution of US Multinationals

Strategic Advantage

	Narrow	Wide
National Market Horizon	Exports or Sales/Distribution	National Subsidiary
International	World Product Mandates	Global Firms

Where market horizons are essentially domestic, because of government, country size, or local conditions and the U.S. firm's strategic advantage is relatively narrow, the best approach is to serve that market directly via exports or a local sales/distribution system. Where the same market conditions exist but the U.S. form enjoys a wide strategic advantage across functions, the best strategy is a national subsidiary with only loose links to the parent's decision control system. Much of the recent divesture of subsidiaries by U.S. firms in the past decade can be explained by these policies.

In the mature multinational firm where U.S. firms lead the world, there has been a further stage. For some firms such as Westinghouse and General Electric, there has been a shift to a world product mandate, i.e., an international product mandate to a particular national subsidiary based on a narrowly defined strategic advantage. The alternative in the case of an international market horizon and a widely based strategic advantage is the fully integrated global corporation.

11.6 Transferring Japanese Software Management

Permanent employment, seniority-based reward systems, bonus payment systems and quality control circles are the familiar features of Japanese software management. As the growth of Japanese investment increases in Europe and North America, research studies have begun to emerge that the essential aspects of Japanese managerial practices do indeed transfer well to foreign settings. The positive examples of Japanese management transfer are easy to identify and document.

- Mitsubishi Australia took over the operations of Chrysler Australia, which in 1977 took 60 hours to make a car. By 1980, it took only 23 hours and while the workforce was reduced from 6,700 to 4,000, output per worker went up 80 percent (*The Economist*, January 30, 1982).

- YKK entered the French market in zippers where the typical delivery time for orders was 8–10 days. YKK developed its quick order delivery system to differentiate a basically standardized product to provide merchandise from order time to delivery in 24 hours (Yoshimari, 1980).

- Kyoto Ceramic installed a factory in the U.S. with a transfer of technology and managers from Japan. Despite complications in equipment and worker experience, the U.S. plant operated along Japanese approaches to organization and communications, with similar levels of productivity.

It would be a mistake, however, to assume either that all Japanese management transfers are successful, or when they are, success is due solely to software management systems. Two examples illustrate this point.

The first concerns an investment in textiles in Eastern Canada. The Japanese wanted to establish a quality enterprise in the textile center of central Canada, but after a series of complicated negotiations involving the Federal and Provincial governments, agreed to invest in one of the small eastern provinces in a remote fishing community. The Japanese installed some of the finest equipment available anywhere in the world, workers were trained in Japan, and some workers visited sites in Britain and Germany as well as Japan. Although production output was actually ahead of financial projections after four months in 1974, when the plant opened, a thirteen month strike against the company followed. The Japanese partners, Mitsubishi Rayon and Ataka Trading Corporation, withdrew from the venture and wrote off their investment at a rumoured loss of $9 million. In this instance, despite the excellent hardware in place, the Japanese had difficulty managing the software elements developed for their overseas investment, including their understanding of government decision making.[6]

The second example involves a detailed case study of two Japanese factories in Britain, matched with a U.S. owned plant and a British plant. All four plants were similar (the British was much larger in size), operated large batch, mass production technologies in colour T.V. sets. A cursory glance at the data in Exhibit 11/7 shows that while labour productivity, quality, and absenteeism are better in the Japanese than the American or British, the explanation hardly rests in the notion of employee satisfaction, better work conditions, or more holidays. Moreover, there was no evidence that Japanese productivity success was due to superior equipment or more automated production. According to Makota Takamiya (1981), the difference in the Japanese level of productivity could be accounted for by three factors: production management, interdepartmental communication, and industrial relations. In more detail, what were these factors?

In production management, the Japanese firms emphasized different techniques than the British or the American. In the area of quality, where the British

---

[6] See Cirtex Knitting case, York University, 1980.

Exhibit 11/7: Productivity and Performance in Four British Factories

	Japan A	Japan B	United States	Great Britain
Number of Employees	700	300	700	2,000
Labour Productivity*	0.83	1.07	0.71	0.56
Quality Record+	4–5%	10%	14–15%	85%
Employee Satisfaction**	15.6	12.71	13.20	11.32
Labour Turnover	30%	25–30%	30%	30%
Absenteeism	4%	5%	8%	8%
Sick Pay – Hourly Employees	nil	nil	2–28 wks.	8–40 wks.
Holidays – Hourly	1 yr.–17 days	1 yr.–17 days	20 days	20–25 days
Unionization Rate	98%	98%	–	100%
No. of Unions	1–Operators 1–Technicians	1–Operators 1–Technicians	–	7

* Sets produced per day
+ Rejection rate of printed circuit boards assembled
** Employee Survey index

Source: Adopted from Takamiya (1981)

firm relies on a very sophisticated test machine, the Japanese emphasize three worker teams, two inserting components and one worker visually checking and correcting, and supervisors constantly feeding back to workers performance checks through graphs and tables, regular morning meetings, and attention to shopfloor tidiness. In the area of work practices, demarcation of jobs is much less visible in the Japanese firms, both across departments and among levels. Recruitment, training, and job rotation reinforce this flexible rostering of employees. In contrast to both the American and British firm, strict discipline was apparent in the Japanese firms, including forbidding of eating, drinking and smoking on the shop floor during breaks.

The Japanese and American firms produced only a few models – 4 to 8 in the former, six in the latter. The British produced 60, each with different components, chassis, and cabinets! The powerful influence of the finance and sales function in the British firm often meant that customers were promised new models with no prior discussion with production. Communications between engineering design and production were poorly managed, with coordination left to chance and costly duplication.

The "hands on" approach to coordination in the Japanese plants, such as job rotation, cross departmental communications, and meticulous reporting systems similar to "Ringi" in Japan were characteristic of a working through people philosophy. The U.S. firms relied on highly developed formal manuals and standard operating procedures and methods. As many studies have shown (Hickson and McMillan, 1980), U.S. firms tend to develop a formal, impersonal structure within which personalities and workforces fit their behaviour according to standard controls; the Japanese firms personalize the coordination methods around shared norms developed through training, job rotation, managerial guidance, and corporate culture.

Detailed research on managerial practices in Japanese foreign plants is rare, but the work by Takamiya (1981) demonstrates the Japanese emphasis on software-hardware linkages developed in plants and factories in the home market. In terms of management, the organizational elements are hardly earth shattering – more employee involvement, more and better utilization of information, more "hands on" management by actual participation in the shop floor. The presence of many Japanese factories in relatively educated and affluent areas such as Wisconsin or California in the U.S. or Ontario in Canada do not provide reliable evidence that the Japanese approach to management is transferable.[7] It is areas such as the T.V. sector in strikebound Britain, where domestic productivity has been so low, which provide a better guage to this transferability problem. Another piece of evidence is more direct: in the several factories located in the class conscious, strike ridden valleys of the Welsh coal fields, the Japanese have established plants abroad similar to those in the home market: in ten years, with productivity equal to plants elsewhere, they have yet to experience a major strike.

11.7 Japan's Joint Venture Alternative

In recent years, the decision of foreign firms to invest in the Japanese market has opened up a general debate on the merits of direct foreign investment, technology agreements and licencing, or joint ventures. Traditional reasons for inward investment in Japan, such as protection of scarce knowhow and technology processes, tariff and non-tariff barriers, or shipping and logistical costs, have remained important, but other factors come into play. Some firms have found the local cultural and language complications, and the distribution system, formidable entry barriers. As a result, firms from the U.S. or Europe have developed joint ventures with Japanes firms to develop market presence – Dow Chemicals with Otsuka, or Merck and Company with Banyu Pharmaceuticals. Some firms such as Texas Instruments, and more recently, Motorola, have found that a presence in the Japanese market has provided a window to quality control and production methods. Some foreign firms have developed various technology agreements (Taisei and Bechtel in construction; Matsushita and Phillips in electronics).

The evolution of Japanese technology developments has opened up a new respect by foreigners for a linkup with Japanese companies. The public perception of various types of international agreements, such as General Motor's

---

[7] See JETRO (1981) and Freedman (1982).

Exhibit 11/8: Investment and Business Tie-Ups of Japanese Auto Makers with Foreign Auto Makers (Passenger Cars)

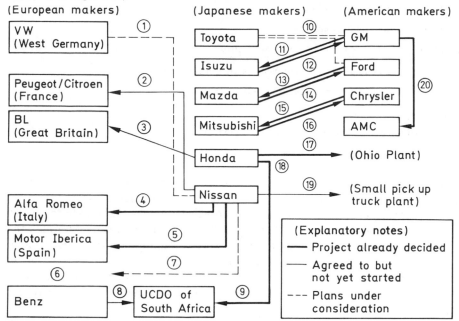

1 Business tie-up

2 Technologiy license on exhaust gas purification device

3 License for the production of Honda designed cars (Production to commence in the summer of 1981 for distribution in EC countries)

4 Signed an agreement for launching a joint venture for the production of subcompacts. (Nissan's equity 50% and Alfa's equity 50%)

5 Acquisition of 36% of the outstanding shares of Iberica. Decided to participate directly in the management of the company.

6 Great Britain (Plans to build a passenger car plant)

7 Published a feasibility study in January 1981 for local production

8 Contribution of 27% of equity

9 License of production knowhow of subcompacts

10 Business Tie-ups

11 Contribution of 34.2% of equity

12 Plans for the supply of principal parts (transmission and axles, etc.)

13 Contribution of 25.0% of equity

⑭ Plans for the supply of principal parts (transmission and axles, etc.)

⑮ Contribution of 15.0% of equity

⑯ Rans for the supply of engines

⑰ Started assemblying motorcycles in Sept. 1979

⑱ Decided to build an assemblying plant for cars in Jan. 1980

⑲ Decided to produce cars locally (Oct. 1980)

⑳ Supply of engines

Source: MITI, White Paper on International Trade, 1981

linkage with Fijitsu Fancuc Ltd. in robots, suggests a basic recognition of Japan's production and technology skills. The more fundamental point, however, is the generally creative and outward approach Japan has taken to both inward foreign investment and external linkages through joint ventures. Although the Japanese government has traditionally exercised many controls over foreign ownership and technology, most of which have been gradually loosened in recent years (Henderson, 1975), the overall approach has been one of maximizing Japanese learning of foreign technology and foreign markets. In recent years, this approach has taken on new meaning.

Japanese firms in each sector where growth has been a goal have attempted to build international linkages for technology, market development, and third country joint ventures. The automobile is perhaps the most dramatic example of this broad approach. The three largest Japanese firms have developed ties with major foreign firms in international markets, largely on a case to case basis. Three of the eleven car firms have substantial foreign equity (by G.M., Ford and Chrysler). In an emerging global industry like automobiles, where national traditions and government restrictions are still the norm, such arrangements play a role well beyond technology and production. For one thing, agreements between a major Japanese firm like Nissan, which is evolving a production tie-up with Volkswagen among other firms, helps to neutralize certain protectionist pressures vis-a-vis local production companies and their own governments. (It was no accident, for instance, that Japanese penetration of the European car market started in countries with no domestic car industry.) At the same time, Japanese firms are subject to strong bidding tactics among different countries hoping to attract foreign investment.

The propensity of Japanese firms to develop joint ventures has other implications. In some cases, it allows the Japanese firms to utilize their own extensive distribution system in Japan for foreign licensed products – Eli Lilly's tie-up with Shiongi in drugs or Merck and Company's joint venture with Banyu Pharmaceuticals are two cases in point.[8] Japanese agreements for outward production arrangements may spring from joint ventures developed in the Japanese market – SmithKline of the U.S. has both a joint venture with Fujisawa in Japan and both have developed a venture in the U.S. market.

The importance that the Japanese attach to joint ventures in overseas markets is well illustrated in the case of consumer electronics. For years there has been talk of an integration of European firms to match the scale of Japanese consumer electronics firms like Sony and Matsushita. One view of this kind of pan-European alliance was a tie-up between Grundig, Bosch, and Telefunken of West Germany, Thorn E.M.I. of Britain, Phillips of Holland (owning 25% of Grundig) and France's Thompson-Brandt. The complication was not just in the domestic rivalries in the European family. Japan's Matsushita has a production agreement both with Bosch and Thompson-Brandt, and Matsushita's subsidiary, J.V.C., has a link with Thorn and Telefunken. In other words, these forms of technological and production agreements provide the Japanese with a strong blocking strategy to retain market share and overall cost competitiveness in foreign markets against local firms.[9]

11.8 Summary and Conclusions

The 1970's and early 1980's have witnessed a startling increase in awareness of Japanese production and technological capabilities, largely as a result of export penetration to the four corners of the world. The 1980's and 1990's may see Japan move to the commanding heights of the multinational corporate chess game, implying a significant shift from export led growth to investment induced penetration.

The issues involved are complex, dynamic, and riddled with surface contradictions. They are complex, because they encompass so many policy and institutional relationships. In no order of importance, there is the difference between Western "production" firms and Japanese trading firms; there is the contrast in the role of small firms which are export oriented and big firms; there is the investment location, whether developed country or developing; there is the importance of 100 percent ownership of foreign subsidiaries often acquired through takeover versus joint ventures through start up by new investment; there is the question of global corporations as a portfolio of national subsid-

---

[8] Merck and Company sought to expond its investment in Japan from a joint venture to an acquisition of majority control in Banyu Pharmacentical and Toxii Pharmacentical, at a cost of $350 million. The Japanese Government was expected to provide immediate approval.

[9] The strategy of countering foreign competition in their own market is explored in Watson (1982).

iaries or an integrated international company optimizing world profits; there is, finally, the most fundamental question of the rationale for foreign investment as compared to exports.

The foreign view of Japanese corporate performance and strategies for the 1980's may well fall between two extremes: a highly rational one of deliberate planning and maximization of Japanese interests abroad, or one of incremental adaptation to foreign conditions based on complex national strategies. Japan's external investment strategies go well beyond these two positions. MITI has initiated the macro framework of industrial sectors – steel, housing, automobiles, computers are important examples – which are subject to internationalization either through foreign competition as in steel or shipbuilding or through outward Japanese investment as in housing construction or automobiles.

What is distinctive about the historical pattern of Japanese investment has been two factors, namely the role of trading firms in both raw materials and in manufacturing; and the flow of foreign investment from Japan's comparatively disadvantaged industries combined with the emphasis on servicing foreign markets by exports. It is the nature of the sectors involved and the impact of the underlying technologies which have shaped the internal structures and coordination mechanisms in Japanese firms, not the feature of Japanese culture per se. Japanese managers have transferred many aspects of organizational practices cultivated in the home market. Generally, however, the kinds of problems besetting U.S. and to a certain extent, European multinationals, have not been faced by Japanese firms.

For one thing, Japanese investment abroad has often consisted of relatively small plants for export substitution and penetration of nearby markets. In this way, Japanese firms have built up systems of national subsidiaries but they are a long way from the fully integrated production and marketing systems characteristic of large U.S. multinationals. Indeed the Japanese are so new to the global multinational arena that they have yet to develop a large cadre of truly international managers capable of operating abroad in many foreign languages and in different legal and political jurisdictions.

To be sure, the Americans in particular, as well as the British among the Europeans, have a long (and controversial) history of developing global corporations. Not only has their own language been the *lingua franca* of international trade, as nationals they have not had the insecurity of military defeat or the burden of racial minorities. In a larger context, the Japanese have been more than aware of these points, and they have been clearly sensitive to placing strong controls on foreign subsidiaries which can raise the sensitivities of host governments. For instance, American firms abroad have consistently been subject to various U.S. laws, even when the U.S. laws conflict with host country legislation. This practice is called extraterritoriality and extends not only to

U.S. companies and managers abroad (French, British, and Germany subsidiaries blocked, for instance, in supplying machinery and parts for the Soviet pipeline) but to non-American subsidiaries – as when Abitibi Paper and Price Corporation, two Canadian paper companies, were investigated by the U.S. justice department.

The evolution then of U.S., European, and Japanese multinationals follows not simply the logic only of markets and technology, but the larger geopolitical system, where Japan's role is relatively limited. Ironically, this point may not be a sign of economic weakness but a source of competitive strength. Japanese firms have exploited commercial advantages in Francophone Africa against the French car industry, in South America against European and U.S. firms, and in third world countries not aggressively pursued by non-Japanese firms.

In this emerging role of international economic superpower, there is one area not yet addressed – the role of Japanese finance and banking. This subject is taken up in the next chapter.

Chapter 12
Asian Wall Street: Japanese Banking

> "Japan is the second most important economy in the free world – industry wise – but not necessarily finance wise."
>
> *Alfred Brittain III,* Chairman and CEO, Bankers Trust

12.1 Introduction

When foreign bankers convened in Tokyo in October 1982 to join the celebrations for the Bank of Japan's one hundredth birthday, they were able to see at first hand the paradoxes and contradictions of Japanese industrial success. In one sense, the central bank prides itself as the staid, conservative, elitist, and ever so orthodox pillar of the country's financial system. In another sense, as expressed both in its geographical setting of beautiful willow trees along the Kanda river or its earthquake-proof building equipped with elevators, antifire window shutters, and flush water toilets, the Bank illustrates so well the Japanese capacity to reach outward and learn from abroad – the building structure itself dates from 1896 and was made entirely from foreign materials.

The Japanese banking system represents a microcosm of the cross currents of change facing not only the corporate sector but indeed the society at large. Since Meiji, the banking and financial system has been directly controlled by the government with a view to channeling money directly into the growth centers, usually with amazing success. Consensus politics has triumphed over deregulation and the use of market forces such that Japan's banking system has been considerably underdeveloped both at home and abroad. The contemporary challenge is to adapt the system to the needs of an advanced industrial and service economy tightly linked to international trade and financial flows.

To be sure, there can be little doubt as to the banking sector's leading role in the economy and the vast size of the city banks in the international pecking order.[1] The main financial institutions form the center of a vast web of inter-

---

[1] According to *Fortune's* 1982 ranking of non-U.S. banks listed by assets, three of the top ten, ten of the top 25, sixteen of the top 50, and 24 of the top 100 banks in the world were Japanese (August 23, 1983:54). Ranked by assets against all banks, including American, the top five Japanese banks – Dai Ichi Kango, Mitsubishi, Fuji, Sumitomo, and Sanwa stand eighth, eleventh, thirteenth, fourteenth, and fifteenth in the world.

locking corporate connections – almost half the listed companies on the Tokyo Stock Exchange belong to only fifteen major industrial groups: they account for almost three quarters of corporate income and sales and half the bank loans. Despite this commanding presence, the financial institutions stand before mounting pressures to change the basic ground rules both for how banking is run and more broadly, for what is Japan's basic role in the world's financial system. Is, for instance, Tokyo to become a world financial center on the order of London or New York? Is the yen to become a fully convertable currency like the dollar? What do the increasing level of Japanese foreign investment and the evolution of Japanese multinational firms mean for MITI's traditional role in planning the future direction of the economy?

Even within the banking system, the winds of change are creating enormous pressures to reduce the level of centralized bureaucratic control and to subject the competing elements to direct market forces: political pressures abroad may be the catalyst for such changes, but technological and economic forces are imposing some inexorable influences to bring the financial system in line with the manufacturing sector's superstar sophistication.

The Japanese financial system consists of a combination of large city banks, regional banks, long term credit, trust banks, insurance companies, securities houses, postal savings, mutual loans and savings (Sogo) banks, and even the *Sarakin* – or loan shark companies catering to salaried employees. Like the economy itself, the financial system has become huge by any standard – the banks alone do most of the financing for Japan's $200 billion international trade and the Tokyo stock market is second only to New York – $151 billion in market capitalization in 1983, compared to New York's $1595 billion. Yet the signs of change point to a new challenge, namely from a financial structure oriented primarily inwardly around specialized institutions to one oriented internationally around integrated financial services.

The trend towards large scale outward foreign investment is but one symptom of a much larger set of forces thrusting Japan into the role as the leading economic and financial country of Asia and a real economic superpower on the world stage. To date the government has been rather selective in the areas where foreign banks can operate in the Japanese system, and the Japanese banks have been restrained in the roles they have played in the international market place. In one sense this represents an example of the inherent conservatism of the Japanese business and industrial elite, but it also illustrates the differences in the way the Japanese have interpreted the rise of OPEC, the recycling of petrodollars into countries like Brazil, Mexico, and Poland, and the use of government aid or bank lending as substitutes for foreign investment in economic development.

For the banking sector, competition and the general maturity of the economy, together with issues like the emerging Pacific Rim, and Tokyo as a leading international money market, are tearing down the decades of forced regulation and bureaucratic controls. In terms of technology, the Japanese financial system is experiencing the same revolution in banking as other countries (Crane and Hayes, 1982). The powerful information processing capabilities of large computers, the widespread linkages to on-line terminal facilities, and sophisticated software systems have all combined to derail the traditional boundaries around such sectors as banking, insurance, securities, and trust firms. Credit cards and automated tellers may be the visible indicators of this new technology, but underneath them are global telecommunications and instantaneous access to boardrooms anywhere in the world (Fraser and Vittas, 1982). This internationalization of banking into an integrated financial services industry involves syndicated loans, consortia financing, samurai bonds, Eurodollar-Euroyen issues and the like (Sampson, 1980).

For Japan, this new technology propels new forms of competition, from foreign banks entering the Japanese market to Japanese banks entering new agreements with international institutions, In either case, the long term impact is to change the balance between what the government wants to control and regulate, and what the financial system can do independently of the government. Similarly the banks' intimate connections to corporate groups in a period of very fast growth (when up to eighty per cent of financing has been through debt) can change dramatically when some of the larger groups are so liquid that they can literally act as bankers to their own suppliers and subcontractors.

This chapter proceeds in the following way. The next section provides an overview of the Japanese financial system and the key role of the Ministry of Finance. The next part analyses the impact of changes in the financial system for the corporate sector domestically and for Japanese multinational firms. What these issues imply for the development of Tokyo as an international financial center is then discussed, including the impact this change could mean for other financial centers in Asia.

12.2 Japan's Banking System: An Overview

The origins of Japanese banking date back to the rise of Osaka as the major business center of the country.[2] By the seventeenth century Osaka was the leading city in Japan and equal in size and influence to many of the leading centers of Europe. The merchant classes were expanding their business, traders were developing broadly based networks of customers and clients, and

---

[2] For a good overview of Japan's banking history, see Adams and Hoshii (1972). A contemporary profile is provided by Wallich and Wallich (1976) and Prindl (1981).

Exhibit 12/1: Financial Institutions in Japan

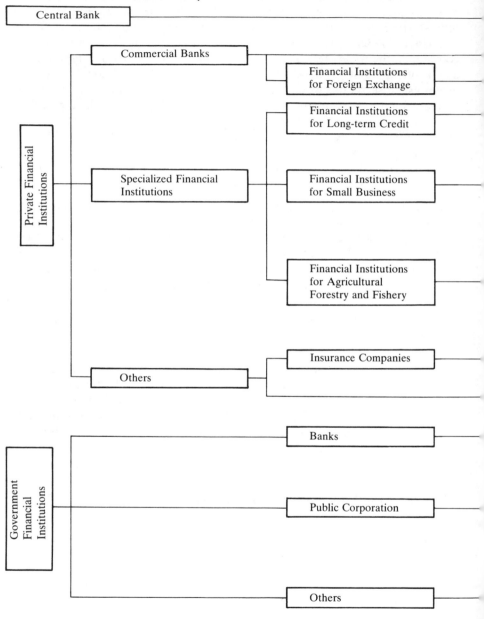

Note: Figures in parentheses denote the number at the end of December 1980.
Source: Bank of Japan

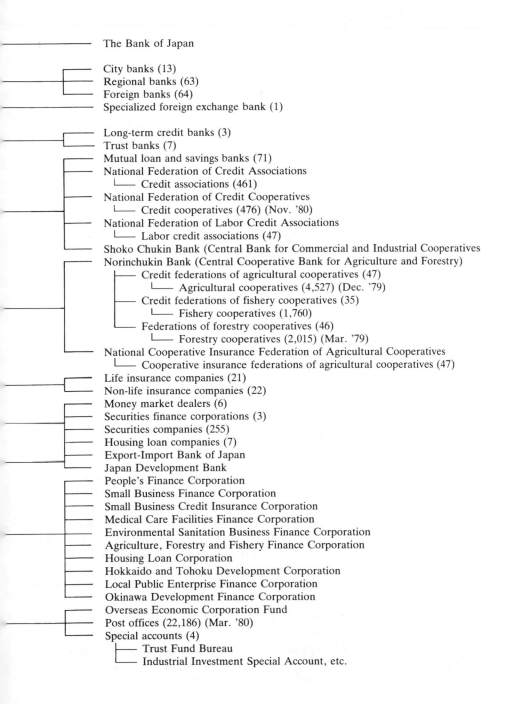

The Bank of Japan

City banks (13)
Regional banks (63)
Foreign banks (64)
Specialized foreign exchange bank (1)

Long-term credit banks (3)
Trust banks (7)
Mutual loan and savings banks (71)
National Federation of Credit Associations
└── Credit associations (461)
National Federation of Credit Cooperatives
└── Credit cooperatives (476) (Nov. '80)
National Federation of Labor Credit Associations
└── Labor credit associations (47)
Shoko Chukin Bank (Central Bank for Commercial and Industrial Cooperatives
Norinchukin Bank (Central Cooperative Bank for Agriculture and Forestry)
├── Credit federations of agricultural cooperatives (47)
│   └── Agricultural cooperatives (4,527) (Dec. '79)
├── Credit federations of fishery cooperatives (35)
│   └── Fishery cooperatives (1,760)
└── Federations of forestry cooperatives (46)
    └── Forestry cooperatives (2,015) (Mar. '79)
National Cooperative Insurance Federation of Agricultural Cooperatives
└── Cooperative insurance federations of agricultural cooperatives (47)
Life insurance companies (21)
Non-life insurance companies (22)
Money market dealers (6)
Securities finance corporations (3)
Securities companies (255)
Housing loan companies (7)
Export-Import Bank of Japan
Japan Development Bank
People's Finance Corporation
Small Business Finance Corporation
Small Business Credit Insurance Corporation
Medical Care Facilities Finance Corporation
Environmental Sanitation Business Finance Corporation
Agriculture, Forestry and Fishery Finance Corporation
Housing Loan Corporation
Hokkaido and Tohoku Development Corporation
Local Public Enterprise Finance Corporation
Okinawa Development Finance Corporation
Overseas Economic Corporation Fund
Post offices (22,186) (Mar. '80)
Special accounts (4)
├── Trust Fund Bureau
└── Industrial Investment Special Account, etc.

farmers were harvesting growing yields of rice for the villages and the urban classes. The need for credit to finance these diverse transactions required the services of such early banking intermediaries as merchant financiers, family lenders to the samurai leaders, and money lenders to the population.

By 1617, only ten years after tobacco entered into use as money in the Jamestown settlement of Virginia in the USA and six years before Pennsylvania became the first American state to issue paper money, the merchant financiers in Osaka issued paper notes backed by silver, and this same group evolved into a "Bankers Association" with responsibilities over the bank notes. Yet from these very early days, public authorities provided official sanction to the devolution of a real banking system, a sanction which became most pronounced in the Meiji era but which continues to this day.

With the gradual opening up of the Japanese economy to foreign influences in the middle of the last century, and especially after the changes in the economic structure during the Meiji period (1868–1912), the evolution of the banking system became a primary national concern. Unlike in Britain, for instance, where the banking system evolved prior to industrialization, mainly around the trading functions of the British Empire and sanctioned with special prerogatives by the Crown, Japan faced in the nineteenth century the challenge of developing a banking system as a complement to industrialization, not as an antecedent to it.

Two major developments during the Meiji period established the basic structure of Japanese banking for more than a century – indeed, today's challanges of removing the high level of government regulation of the banking sector and introducing greater use of market forces date from the initiatives introduced during the heyday of state intervention at the end of the last century.

The first arrangement was the decision to establish specialized banks focusing on particular lending requirements. Under the primary influence of Prince Masayoshi Matsukata, the government created the Bank of Japan in 1882 with the passage of the Banking Act. Two years earlier, the government also created the Yokohama Specie Bank, now the Bank of Tokyo, which served primarily as the financial arm of the Ministry of Finance (former Vice Ministers of Finance have served as the bank's President). Within a timespan of a generation, additional financial vehicles were created in the form of the Industrial Bank of Japan, developed in 1900 to finance capital for new industry, the Long Term Credit Bank, and the Agricultural Cooperative Banks to finance the needs of the agricultural sector. Despite their distinctive purposes and goals, each of the institutions had in common the pursuit of the primary economic objective – the development of the Japanese economy by channelling the limited capital accumulation to the sectors and companies most in need of it (Patrick, 1967).

At the same time, the banking sector evolved around another key decision, namely the development of the large commercial banks, a sector which today is dominated by the smaller core of thirteen large city banks. (The City Banks are further divided into the big seven, which are heavily involved in international business, and the small six, which are oriented to regional business and small and medium size companies.) The particular feature of these commercial banks is their style of lending of what might be called "indirect financing" but what some writers (Drucker, 1969) equate as equity capital. Unlike the United States, for instance, where the banking system is largely divorced from the equity market, the development of Japanese industry in the last century required a different model, because there was no equity market. Many Japanese writers commented on the distinctive Japanese requirements for industrialization, and realized that neither the banking system as developed in Britain, nor the capital market as developed in America, served as an adequate model for capital-poor Japan. In fact, the model which became the basis of the commercial banks in Japan was the European "universal bank".

Originally founded in France, the universal bank became the most widespread in Germany, a country which also lacked heavy industry but where the system of small guilds and workshops was widespread. An important feature of the universal bank was its expressed objective of investing in firms initially as a form of venture capital and later as a major voice in the operation of the enterprise. Under the leadership of financiers like Shibusawa Eiichi, who founded the Dai-Ichi Bank, Japan's private banking system took on the feature whereby the growth of major enterprises would be financed directly in tandem with the large city banks, as they became known in Japan, and where each major bank became the central organization for large industrial groups, known as *Zaibatsu* (*Zai* – business, *Batsu* – group). Before the Pacific war, the four large banks formed part of the four largest zaibatsu – Mitsubishi, Sumitomo, Mitsui, and Yasuda (the latter tied to Fuji Bank).

Although various reforms were introduced into the banking system with the post war reforms, including of course the zaibatsu dissolution and the loss of foreign branches, circumstances actually favoured the reorganized banks for the growth environment of the next three decades. Ironically, as with so many features of the American occupation, the banks were the unintended beneficiaries of many US imposed policies. By stripping the senior levels of management in the industrial concerns, the Americans unwittingly provided the banks with a more strategically central role in the affairs of the reorganized but diverse companies in the combine. By placing the entire country's direction on rebuilding the economy mainly through capital investment while holding back consumption, the reforms reinforced the basic tendencies for high personal savings, which in turn became the deposit base for the commercial banks to lend to their former zaibatsu family firms. Because of the strong government control over the financial system through the Ministry of Fiance, Japan actually operated with direct guidance over credit allocations for particular banks and through them for particular industrial sectors. Obviously this tightly run system of central control works best when the sectors chosen are in the high growth lane in an economy which itself is growing fast. The complications enter when the number and complexity of sectors change, when the degree of overseas involvement escalates, and when the overall economy is subject to major international shocks – hence the challanges to changing the current structure.

The overall framework of the banking system, outlined in Exhibit 12/1, shows the various private, public, and semi-public institutions. At the top of the structure of the structure is the Bank of Japan, governed by the Bank of Japan Law of 1942, and which serves as the financial arm of the government, regulates monetary policy, controls the country's bond issues, and manages the international value of the currency through exchange market stabilization policies. While none of these roles is particularly unique compared to other central banks, the institution derives a great deal of importance because of the central policy role played by the Ministry of Finance.

In Japan, the Ministry of Finance provides both the overall framework for the banking system and oversees its operation in considerable detail, often over and above any policies specified by legislation. Because the Finance Ministry plays such a central role in the operations of the entire government, responsible for the entire budget process and budget instruments, it has truly attracted the best and the brightest from the top universities. As one analysis put the matter:

Standing at the center of government activity, the Ministry of Finance and its Budget Bureau are legally responsible to the cabinet for preparing the annual budget; less formally, they are responsible to the nation for preserving Japan's financial solvency. If government spending is to be restrained, the job must be done here. Monopolization of the cutting role gives the ministry great power and appropriately high status; its officials are the elite of the elite, respected throughout the government (Campbell, 1977:43).

The overall importance of the Ministry of Finance in shaping the policies of the Bank of Japan, is greatly affected by the particular instruments used to shape domestic banking policy and regulation. All central banks are guided by the more universal kinds of policy instruments such as setting interest rates for the structure as a whole, providing bank financial credit, and establishing credit ceilings. These tools go hand in hand with particular practices in Japan which shape the unique environment of the banking system. For instance, in terms of bank credit, the Bank of Japan provides credit in the form of loans which allows the City banks to overlend (liabilities greater than assets) in a way which is impossible in Western countries.[3]

---

[3] Suzuki (1980) makes the point as follows: "In referring to overloan as a special characteristic of Japan's financial structure, one is concerned with the banking system as a whole being in debt to

However, central bank direction goes even beyond this low reserve credit allocation. Through a policy known as "window guidance" or *Madoguchi-shido,* the bank directs funds for lending towards particular sectors, usually in concert with MITI's analysis of emerging sunrise sectors, and through credit allocation, chokes off funds in sunset sectors. Window guidance is not a passive or docile instrument; it can be the vehicle to provide the necessary infusion of money for sectors about to take off – automobiles in the 1960's, consumer electronics in the 1970's, or computers in the 1980's; it is also the instrument to cut off credit in the throwaway industries as the industrial structure shifts to the new technologies and high growth markets.

In a managerial sense, this direct interventionist stance can be interpreted as a top down, central planning instrument of national policy. In one sense, of course, it definitely is. However, there is the other side of the coin to this planning exercise. Firstly, in each of the city banks, there is an enormous effort devoted to analysing the competitive position, productivity, and market potential of each major industrial sector on an international basis (i.e. Japan's relative standing vis a vis foreign competitors). In each of the banks, there is a strong element of individual specialization around particular industry or product groups – enough, for instance, to allow officials from Sumitomo Bank to assume top management direction of Toyo Kogyo (Mazda) when the car company almost went under in the mid-1970's.[4] This enormous planning exercise and detailed understanding of competitive dynamics gets translated down to the corporate level as well, a point which has special significance when it is recognized that in most of the commanding heights of the economy, there are several competing groups.

This detailed planning at the level of the bank and the large firm reinforces *Madoguchishido* (literally, bank teller guidance). It is the most important and direct feature of the central bank's control over the entire system. Under *Madoguchisho,* there is continuous and usually daily contact between the Bank of Japan and the city banks. Officials from the central bank review all features of commercial transactions, from aggregate lending practices by sectors, to detailed company transactions involving credit, deposits, and foreign currency. It is clear that enormous power can be wielded, as when credit to trading firms

the Bank of Japan, not with the condition of individual banks. Since overloan is a macro matter, it is intimately connected with the Bank of Japan's method of supplying money and hence the very real importance attached to overloan in monetary theory. For instance, Japan's overloan position as of December 1972 – deposits of financial institutions at the central bank minus central bank loans to them was – 1,748 billion yen for Japan, plus $26,579 for the U.S., plus £302 pounds for Britain, plus 26,210 million deutschmarks, and plus 37,187 francs for France."

[4] Seven years after Toyo Kogyo's crisis, Sumitomo Bank owned 3.7 percent of the company's stock and nine current or former bank officials held key positions, including Company Chairman (*Business Week:* January 25, 1982: 104).

was cut back during the oil crisis when there was an appearance of speculation, or when particular sectors are targeted as growth possibilities in the future.[5]

In a negative sense, the process is unbelievably complicated, time consuming, and expensive. It may also be an approach whose importance and effectiveness can be measured in the past. For one thing, most of the large industrial groups are so diversified and well entrenched in all the key technologies, that competitive forces can more efficiently accomplish the same goals than central fiat. Another factor is that the system evolved during a period when capital accumulation had to be horded and channeled in the most important areas, typically with government backing because of the enormous rate of leverage or over-borrowing. Senior executives within both the central bank and the Ministry of Finance are obviously aware of these problems. While there are often journalistic reports of major policy clashes between the proponents of the status quo and of change, the likelihood of a significant redirection originating within these institutions, as distinct from being thust on them from outside events, is somewhat remote, given the realities of their power structure and the entrenched positions of senior level bureaucrats (Suzuki, 1980).

Pressures for change are coming from within Japan and abroad. In recent years, the very success of the Japanese economy has prompted the major corporations to reorganize their balance sheets to increased equity levels, sometimes through large share purchases from foreign investors (Sony, for instance, has more than forty per cent of its shares in foreign hands). At the same time, many of the larger and more successful companies have become so liquid that they are for all intents and purposes debt free, and therefore outside the scrutiny of the very system oriented to help them. Firms in the highly successful export sectors are generating more cash than they can possibly use and corporate loans have been reduced as a result. For example, of 95 companies in the electrical and electronics industry recently surveyed by the Industrial Bank of Japan, 84 per cent reported that their capital needs of $3.45 billion was being met from internally generated funds (*Business Week,* December 14, 1981:50). Additionally there is the increasing shift of the economy towards internationalization and overseas investment, with which the regulated system is ill-equipped to cope. Finally there are the stresses and strains brought on by the changing nature of the banking system itself, reinforced by international banking to be sure, but one where the neat organizational boxes of specialized sectors are giving way to integrated financial services, a move which will finally push the banking system into the full gale of market forces.

---

[5] Kure (1973) argues that with interest rates subject to regulation, the Central Bank policies are effective because of competitive rivalry among the city banks where market share is of paramount importance.

12.3 From Competition within Japan . . .

To recognize the range of forces working to uproot the ground rules of Japan's banking system, it is necessary to understand how the banks stand in relationship to the larger companies, how the banks have become caught in a squeeze for deposits and customers, and what both factors mean in an international context. As noted above, the banking sector, and more specifically the City Banks, have been on the receiving end of the government's extensive powers of administrative guidance, channelling money into particular sectors and prescribing a wide range of performance requirements.

Some loosening of the system has occurred, but the changes have been largely cosmetic and the pace slow. Consider the case of interest rate setting. In a largely free banking market, as developed in New York, London, or Switzerland, there is relative freedom for interest rate setting to attract customers. Institutions compete to attract business by varying the interest rate paid, but also such features as the term, degree and timing of convertability, and related services. There is also in a developed market a range of services: commercial paper, bankers acceptance, treasury bills and the like which open up the range of opportunities for financing and refinancing. Because interest rate setting has been controlled in Japan, various anamolies have developed which have had a wide range of repercussions.

The most important one is the system of *Terigaku Yokin* or fixed time deposits in the Postal Savings Bank. This institution, administered by the Trust Fund Bureau, has over 22,000 branches throughout Japan, and about 200 million separate accounts. The reason is simple: the tax system. Under Japanese law, individuals can deposit up to three million yen without incurring tax on interest; the loophole is that there is no ceiling on the number of deposit accounts. The result is that the Postal Savings Bank now has assets amounting to about 400 billion dollars, or about a fifth of the nations savings. The nature of these accounts, i.e. motivated by tax avoidance, the sheer size of the totals involved, and the customers (farmers, fishermen, men and women in small towns, younger citizens) make the problem of changing interest rates a difficult political decision.[6] If the rates are lowered, this constituency is angered; if they are raised, the competition with the banking sector is greater and the cost to government is also increased, because the funds must be invested in government bonds or in bank debentures.

---

[6] The Ministry of Postal and Telecommunications enforces the Tax code on postal deposits, which means the enforcement is weak; the Ministry of Finance enforces the tax (35%) on time deposits in commercial banks, which means the enforcement is rigorous.

This massive influx of deposits into postal savings is but one side of the tensions within the banking system: the other is lending and the decisions over who – the city banks, the securities houses, the longterm credit banks, or the trust banks – can lend what. During the high growth period before the 1973 oil crisis, the lending practices of the financial institutions followed the familiar paths created by specialization: each sector stuck to its own area, meaning that the cream of the lending market was dominated by the big City banks lending out personal deposits to the large corporations. After the oil shocks, two changes occurred. First, to keep the economy on an even keel, the government slammed hard on the monetary brakes when inflation climbed above twenty-five per cent in 1974.

In normal circumstances, this restriction of the money supply should have meant interest rates would climb accordingly, as in North America in 1982. In fact, interest rates stayed around six per cent. However, because of the credit allocation restrictions, big firms decreased their lending from commercial banks and switched to the capital markets for bonds and equities. Bank lending accounted for only ten per cent of plant investment at the end of the 1970's compared to sixty per cent in 1974; since 1977, the capital markets have provided more financing for industry than the banks.

The second major change has been Japan's massive use of classical Keynesian pump priming to sustain capital spending and economic growth. Government bonds outstanding increased from about $70 billion in 1975 to $335 billion in 1980. Thus while companies once were heavy net borrowers, or almost ten per cent of GNP up to 1975, governments (central and prefectural) have taken on this pump priming task, spending over five per cent of GNP through deficit bonds. While government spending and budget deficits have become a familiar refrain in many countries – witness the US case with President Reagan – the Japanese situation differs in that the level of personal savings, at over a fifth of disposable income compared to less than six per cent in the United States or about 14 per cent in Germany or Britain, is quite sufficient to absorb the level of government debt. Moreoever, while the amounts seem large at Y80 trillion, or $365 billion, they are only 31.7 per cent of GNP, compared to the US level of 35.2 or Britain's 46.4 (*The Economist,* October 23, 1982:69).

What has been the impact of the huge government deficits and resulting borrowing requirements? The first impact has been a strategy of financing the deficit through very large bond syndicates with ten year terms and forcing the city banks to take a forty per cent share. (At about $70 billion, this share was much greater than the deposits taken in; put another way, these government bonds, paying relatively low yields, amounted to about a fifth of bank assets.) In a period of low interest rates, these terms were not overly serious; however, when the monetary breaks were again applied after the 1979 oil price increases, interest rates went up and bond prices collapsed (from about Y99.5 to Y72 in the secondary market) and bank profits fell in the billions, even after the Ministry of Finance repurchased a trillion yen worth of the lowest yielding bonds.

Various innovations have been introduced since 1980, such as introducing securities on more flexible maturity terms and authorizing Euroyen bonds. However, most of these changes have simply glossed over the more fundamental problems of cutting the government deficit, mainly by reducing subsidies on grossly inefficient sectors like agriculture (a move which would raise imports of agricultural products) and by cutting back on the larger and financially inefficient public corporations like the Japanese National Railway. Unfortunately, the budget cutbacks did not occur and when the Suzuki government fell in 1982, the strains of the domestic financing system exposed the underlying fiscal crisis.

The consequence of this financing problem is the liklihood of a pentup rivalry breaking out among the different sectors of the financial system, pitting the conservative forces within the Ministry of Finance and some of the weaker institutions like the Trust Banks, the Regional Banks and the Agricultural Cooperatives against the long-term Credit Banks, the City Banks, and the Securities Houses, with perhaps the foreign banks in Japan caught in the middle.

Already the outlines of the new competition are emerging. The Big Four securities houses – Nomura, Nikko, Daiwa, and Yaimichi – have not only developed overseas branches but two – Nomura and Daiwa – have applied for banking licensing overseas. Although the security houses are much smaller in asset terms than the banks, about Y3 trillion yen to the banks Y92 trillion, in profit terms the picture differs: in 1981, net profits of the security houses were about Y93 billion to the top four banks' Y100 billion.

The main competitive advantage of the securities houses is their traditional monopoly on corporate underwriting, which has increased dramatically as companies reduced their dependence on the city banks for long term credit. Moreover, the securities houses combine two functions, namely the merchant banking function of issuing shares, and the stockbroking function of selling them – a seeming contradiction but one which dates approximately to the post war period when they were the central vehicles for stock dispersals of the *Zaibatsu* and ensuing "share democratization movement" and elevation of the individual investor (individuals account for about a third of equity holdings on the Tokyo Stock Exchange, but half of sales turnover). For their part, the securities firms are moving into high yield mutual funds, more direct corporate lending, and US style commercial paper. Firms like Daiwa Securities and Yaimaichi Securities have formed venture capital companies, partly as a response to MITI's efforts to promote small business development in areas like microelectronics, biotechnology, new materials, and optical fibres.[7] In response, the banks want to enter areas dominated by the securities firms, namely brokerage operations, selling government bonds, and share underwriting.

Ironically the first serious direct rivalry between these two main areas of the banking system may occur where the Ministry of Finance can't control the industry boundaries, namely the offshore market. Their strong overseas presence (see Exhibit 12/2) implies that individual firms can link up with international institutions for syndicated loans, for certificate deposits in foreign currencies, and even for direct loans to foreign multinationals, governments, and international organizations. What these incremental steps imply for changes in the domestic market add up to the most fundamental question of all, namely the true internationalization of the Japanese banking system and the rise of Tokyo as a world banking center.

12.4 . . . to Tomorrow, the World

In a recent profile of Japan's financial institutions, Anthony Rowley (1981:68) summarized a long range view with both a rhetorical question and a calculated answer:

Do Japanese banks aim to conquer the world just as the country's vehicle makers and electronic companies have done, or are well on their way to doing? The anwer seems to be yes – in time. 'The Japanese want to dominate international banking eventually. For them it is a question of when, not if,' declares one American banker in Tokyo.

The emergence of Tokyo as an international financial center plus the importance of the Japanese banking system on the international stage are but another step in the continuing evolution of Japan's economy. In this sense, it represents a fairly clear continuum from agriculture to manufacturing, from manufacturing to services, from trade in services to trade in information and knowledge. Japan's economy has shifted from an agricultural based economy up to the Pacific War, to a heavy industry driven economy up to the 1960's, to a high technology driven economy into the 1980's. The development of a sophisticated and highly developed financial center can be seen as part of the change in the service economy, with a strong international focus in areas like fashion, culture, leisure, education, science, as well as banking. Moreover, Japan's

---

[7] Japan has only 150 companies trading shares in the over-the-counter equities market; the United States, by comparison, has 10,000. Grossman (1983) views the prospect of U.S. style venture capital business succeeding in Japan as unlikely, mainly because Japanese entrepreneurs want to pass a business to future generations, while U.S. entrepreneurs start a business with a view to selling it.

Exhibit 12/2: Japanese Banking: Branches Abroad, Competition at Home

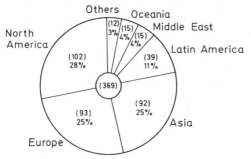

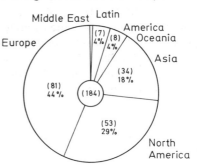

Japanese Branches Abroad

Foreign Branches in Japan

Source: Bank of Japan

Exhibit 12/3: A Comparison of International Banking Centers

Country	$ US Billion	Market Share
Britain	559	26.8
United States	214	10.2
France	165	7.9
Bahamas	155	7.4
Japan	149	7.1
Luxembourg	101	4.8
Swiss Trustee a/c	88	4.2
Singapore	78	3.7
Belgium	77	3.1
Netherlands	71	3.4
West Germany	66	3.2
Switzerland	63	3.0
Canada	59	2.8
Bahrain	46	2.2
Hong Kong	45	2.1
Italy	41	1.9
Cayman	39	1.8

Source: Financial Times (September 27, 1982:X)

relatively slow penetration into those growth sectors suggests a fairly thorough and comprehensive approach to this change, since it implies a rather fundamental reorientation of the domestic society in terms of language, customs, foreign regulations, and the like.

In terms of banking, where does Japan stand in the international pecking order? One index is to compare Tokyo with other financial centers in terms of money lent in the Eurocurrency market. As given in Exhibit 12/3, London is the leading banking sector with about twenty-seven per cent market share, compared to 10.2 per cent in the US and between 7.1 and 7.9 percent for Japan, the Bahamas, and France.

On other measures of banking performance, Japan's financial market has a long way to go to become as important as London, New York, or even Singapore and Hong Kong for the important offshore business. As indicated in Exhibit 12/4, Japanese banks are well behind competitors in major foreign countries; more tellingly, the holding of yen in foreign reserves is scarcely four per cent in 1980, but this figure has increased from less than one per cent in 1976.

Exhibit 12/4: Japan's Financial Market in Perspective (Billion U.S. Dollars)

	Japan	France	Britain	Germany	U.S.A.
Foreign Loans Outstanding By					
Banks*	149	165	559	66	2.4
Turnover of Bonds ('81)	725		322	228	3700 ('80)
Stockmarket Turnover	180	12.6	36.7	5.6	382 (NY)
Currency Held As Foreign**	3.7%	1.7%	3.0%	14.0%	73.1%
Reserves					
World Eurocurrency Markets+	64	120	408	24	63

 * Loans to Non Residents and Foreign Currency Loans to Residents
 + Size of Commercial Banks Foreign Currency Assets, 1981
 ** Percentage of World's Total Foreign Reserves Held By Monetary Authorities By Currency
Source: Ministry of Finance, Japan; Bank For International Settlements

However, the sheer volume of financial transactions in recent years gives a more realistic picture of the trends, especially now that the government has lifted the restrictions for foreigners in the Tokyo capital market. In 1981, for instance, foreign exchange trade amounted to $3 trillion. Capital flows amounted to $35.9 billion – $13.1 billion inflows, and $22.8 billion outflow. Foreign financial institutions issued $2.5 billion in yen-denominated bonds in the Tokyo market in 1981; Japanese banks abroad issued $2.6 billion in yen loans; portfolio investment in foreign markets reached $6.1 billion. By the end of 1981, the outstanding value of yen denominated assets held by foreigners both within Japan and abroad amounted to almost $100 billion.

Despite the magnitude of these figures, and the underlying trends behind them, there has been very little research on the relative standing of the Japanese banking system and of Tokyo as a leader financial center. Reed (1980:32) makes the point as follows: "Tokyo remains conspicuously absent from the writings on important international financial centers. Western writers and scholars tend to measure all financial centers by how closely they approximate the norms of London or New York".

Reed's (1980) own research traces the rise of Tokyo as an international center, which is seen by Kindleberger (1974:54) as an area possessing "the highly specialized functions of lending abroad and serving as a clearing house for payments among countries. Banks, brokers, security dealers, and the like establish branches in such centers." There is general agreement on the prerequisites for the development of a financial center:

First the country's currency system must be stable and sound. Second there must be a substantial and constant demand for and supply of the country's currency. Third, the balance of payments accounts should be reasonably well adjusted over a period of time to avoid sudden shifts in the supply and demand of the country's currency. Fourth the center must be the seat of domestic financial institutions capable of handling the business transacted in such a center. Fifth, the center must be the domocile of agencies or branches of foreign financial institutions which can perform their normal functions without being hampered by legal restrictions or discrimination. Sixth, there must be specialized institutions which supplement the commercial banking system in foreign financial transactions. And seventh, the center is usually the domicile of the principal office of the nation's central bank (Reed, 1980:21).

On these criteria, Tokyo is well advanced in developing the conditions for reaching full international banking status. On criteria one, and four through seven, Tokyo faces no domestic obstacles. On the second, the yen has been increasing in the international bond market, reaching seven percent in 1979, but that was before foreign exchange restrictions were removed in 1980. As explained below, the third criteria has caused problems in recent years with the yen fluctuating widely against the dollar, partly because of the very high interest rates in the US but also because interest rates have been extremely low because of such measures as the Temporary Interest Rates Adjustment Law of 1947, which effectively allocates credit by government fiat rather than unrestrained market forces.[8] Low interest rates are closely related to the sixth factor: Japan's soaring balance of payments surpluses are one of the main reasons for the rising foreign pressures for internationalization of the yen.

For Japan to build a real international presence as a financial center, there would have to develop an offshore market along the lines of the Eurocurrency market. Plans for offshore facilities in Tokyo have been discussed since the Asian version of the Eurocurrency market began in Singapore in 1968, when various public policies were introduced, such as low tax treatment and removal

---

[8] Sakakibara and Noguchi (1977) argue that Japan's postwar economic success is largely due to the fact that the institutional framework for financial control developed for wartime mobilization was retained after the war largely intact, despite expectations of changes: "Meant as a temporary measure, the law's primary purpose is to enable banks to agree on rates of interest under the government's administrative guidance. Of interest is the fact that both SCAP and the Japanese government at this point (1947) decided to make the proposed law a temporary measure, anticipating a total revision of the financial laws and decrees in the near future."

of the withholding tax. The Ministry of Finance and the Japanese central bank hold conflicting opinions on the offshore question, which means that plans for an offshore facility may come only in time.

Finance Ministry officials, plus the banking establishment, favour the offshore idea as a natural extension of the Asian financial market with Tokyo as the center, as a means of growing with the economic opportunities throughout the Pacific Basin, and as a strategy for reducing Japan's very large deficit in invisible earnings. Although some Finance Ministry officials have a certain trepidation concerning the impact of full liberalization, there is a recognition that the presence of offshore facilities in Japan is preferable to financial transactions conducted by Japanese institutions in the European market outside their control.

On the other side of the argument stands the Bank of Japan, which sees in offshore institutions the deregulation not only of the banking system but the basic industrial planning apparatus developed since the Second World War. For the banking sector, an open market would immediately challenge the industry boundaries of specialization – the City Banks lending short term, the Trust Banks lending middle term, and the Long Term Credit Banks lending long term. More to the point, the kinds of restrictions which prevented the City Banks from issuing debentures could be circumvented by them lending offshore; in the same way, the Trust Banks worry about the spillover effects of the offshore market leaking on the domestic market and threatening their competitive position.

The theoretical arguments for and against the emergence of Tokyo as a financial center of the first rank must be tempered against the practical expediencies of domestic politics, and the real costs of shifting the Japanese economy towards full internationalization.[9] The long term thrust of internationalization of Japanese banking clearly involves a changed role for the yen, from which there can be no retreat. If the Japanese government and the banks do go that route, there are formidable obstacles and challenges, but the Japanese aren't without advantages. Critics of Japanese economic success typically point to the allegedly unfair commercial practices followed in Japan. For example, the chorus of arguments against Japanese tariffs gave way to arguments on nontariff bar-

---

[9] In May 1982, the government announced new measures for foreigners to issue unsecured debt in Japan. For example, to gain access to the Samurai or public debt market, foreign companies must have about $625 million in shareholders equity, and meet stringent criteria relating to the ratio of long term debt to capitalization, the ratio of working income to total assets, interest coverage ratio, and ratio of long term debt to cash flow. The criteria are so strict that it has been estimated that only 70 companies in all the US or Europe could meet them. The number of corporate offerings are so few that in the Samurai public market, only one corporate issue for foreigners occurs per quarter; in the private "Shibosai" market, only three placements are allowed, with limits of only ten billion yen. For discussion, see Thomas (1982).

riers. Arguments against Japanese domestic financial controls have shifted to government reluctance to open up the banking sector to full internationalization. Not only is the historic evolution of this sector not well understood, the reality of events are well ahead of foreign perceptions, a situation which makes the Japanese uncomfortable in international forums, but which also masks the actual state of their competitive position.

Consider, for instance, the arguments of the recent past against Japan's official exchange rate of Y360 = $US1 up to 1971, which gave way with the introduction of a floating exchange rate to charges that the government had been rigging the exchange rate. As an article in *Fortune* put it, "the yen's disappointing reluctance to strengthen has renewed long-standing suspicions in the business community in this country (the US) and in Europe that the Japanese somehow cleverly manipulate the exchange market to hold down the value of their currency and maintain an unfair advantage over their hapless trading partners" (Kirkland, 1982:91).

To the uninitiated, the idea that the government through the central bank "intervenes" in exchange rate support implies a deliberate manipulation of the currency for domestic competitive advantage. In fact, all central banks intervene in the exchange market to some extent, in order to moderate disruptive fluctuations in currency valuations, especially in the face of potential speculation on the currency when multinational firms measure their liquid funds in the hundreds of billions of dollars. Cooper (1977:77) calls this intervention a strategy of "smoothing and braking" and notes that "we do not know what the equilibrium exchange rate over any time period is, but it allows for the likelihood that the 'market' does not know either".

The view that Japan has rigged the yen rate of exchange has received some empirical analysis, but the verdict seems decidedly negative. In a detailed analysis, Quirk (1977) set out to test whether foreign exchange intervention has been aimed at target setting (i.e. rigging the yen) or moderating the speed of exchange rate adjustment. The latter approach is called "leaning against the wind". Quirk (1977:662) summarizes his results as follows:

There is clear evidence that Japanese intervention behaviour has been consistent, both in direction and magnitude, with leaning against the wind. It has sought to moderate movement in the yen/dollar exchange rate in either direction by providing sustained support to either the dollar or the yen – in each case for periods exceeding two months and up to eight months (as in 1976). No evidence was obtained to support the view that intervention has been directed to a target level for the exchange rate, or that intervention has responded more closely to movements in the effective yen exchange rate.

The opposite argument to the undervalued yen is to blame the cause on the overvalued dollar, mainly through high interest rates in the US. While this

point is made in both Japan and the United States, a variation has been put
forward by McKinnon (1983). He argues that while US interest rates have been
extremely high, thereby exacerbating the severity of the recession and under-
mining American competitiveness, the real problem has been the narrow view
of looking at monetary targets purely in a domestic context, not an international one. While monetary targets in the US have been fairly stable for the US
(see Exhibit 12/5), the Federal Reserve has been following the wrong targets.
In other words, by adjusting the money supply accordingly, the severity of the
exchange rate gaps widened with consequent implications for the recession and
continued decline of US exports and competitiveness. As McKinnon (1983)
puts it, "in response to the surge in foreign demand for dollar assets that should
have cut American interest rates, they began to move in the wrong direction
because the dollar was allowed to appreciate too much. If, instead, the Fed had
been following a correct "internationalist" monetary policy, a stable exchange

Exhibit 12/5: Comparative Money suppy and Yen/Dollar Rates

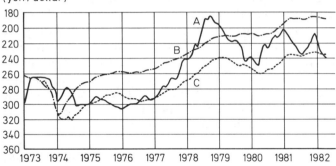

Source: Federal Reserve Bank of St. Louis

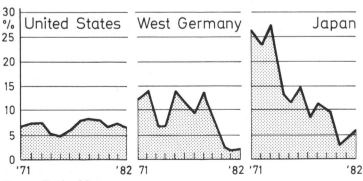

Source: Bank of Japan

rate would be an important monetary target. Then upward pressure on the dollar in the foreign exchanges would clearly signal that American monetary policy was too tight. In this country, money supply would automatically expand, allowing interest rates to fall and rebalance the international bond market without having the dollar overshoot in the foreign exchanges."

12.5 Summary and Conclusions

Internationalization of the banking system represents the complement to the spread of Japanese multinational enterprise and the shift of the domestic industrial structure to first class status in the global economy. For the country as a whole, the change in the banking structure represents a fundamental redirection of the economy. For the first seventy-five years of industrialization after Meiji, despite the growth of industry and the importance of entrepreneurs and large scale industrial organizations, the Japanese economy was structurally based around agriculture and traditional craft industries. Despite the outward appearance of secondary manufacturing, the country remained, and even today reflects, rural community values and small clan norms of behaviour. Even the political structure and voting patterns show the primacy of this rural legacy.

The march to industrialization, started in Meiji, accelerated at the turn of the century, warped by militarism in the thirties, and begun anew after the Pacific War, proceeded within a carefully constructed planning system fostering growth and international competitiveness, with the banking sector guiding through bureaucratic fiat the channeling of capital to the sunrise sectors and new technologies. As part of the process, industrialization brought about, but also was shaped by, urbanization, mass education, and internationalization. It was the trading sector, led by the *Sogoshosha*, which spearheaded the external thrust of Japan's economy, followed by the new industrial firms in such sectors as automobiles, consumer goods, and electronics, usually because they had long overreached the limited goals of the planning system. As success breeded more success, other large firms and many small firms followed suit and the basic financial problems began to emerge: how to channel the huge trade surpluses and high domestic savings into productive investment. While the underlying problems were clearly present when President Nixon devalued the dollar in 1971, international crises like the oil shocks, large and rising deficits by the government, and cautious and defensive government bureaucrats all combined in their own way to postpone the day of reckoning when the banking sector itself had to face internationalization like the trading firms and the manufacturing sectors had earlier.

Internationalization of the banking sector offers many opportunities-consider, for instance, just how anemic the British economy would look if the City in London, the home of some 600 banks from around the world, were to shift to Zurich or New York. The plus factors are mainly economic and technical. The negatives are social and political. Domestically, these negatives amount to questions of language, of confidence, and even of software management systems. Japanese banks have pushed the development of hardware technology about as far and as fast as any country, but the management requirements for the international money game are quite different from domestic manufacturing. Consensus decisions and long lead planning work well in production areas, but in the fast paced money markets, where exchange rates and bids can change in minutes, the Japanese approach is slow, cumbersome and, when yen-dollar exchange rates are seesawing, as in 1982, quite ineffective. As in technology and innovation, where the Japanese have performed better in groups than as individuals, these software management problems represent challenges to overcome, not real barriers to longer term success.

The more real problems are the social and political factors posed by internationalization. Clearly the center of growth in the world's financial markets is in the Far East, but unlike in trading and manufacturing, the Japanese must contend with rivals in Hong Kong and Singapore. Tokyo has the market depth which the other two financial centers presently lack, and the political stability and economic muscle as well. In the normal scheme of things, Tokyo appears as a natural counterpart to London in Europe and New York in North and South America. Politically, there are real problems.

Would, for instance, Hong Kong, faced with political uncertainty over its legal status, and Singapore, smaller and equally vulnerable, simply fall by the wayside if Tokyo developed offshore facilities as a fully developed international center? Will the natural economic nexus around Tokyo be counterbalanced by political and diplomatic pressures to diffuse economic and financial power in Asia, particularly if Tokyo begins to rival London and New York for both corporate and government financing?

As argued in the next chapter, the potential for internal rivalry within the Asian countries may well be tempered by increased rivalry of the Asian block countries vis a vis both Europe and North America, particularly when the income and technological gaps begin to close in another decade. In that respect, the development of Tokyo as the major international center may mean that Hong Kong and Singapore will grow as important complements in the Asian currency market. Already some Eurocurrency financing in Europe is shifting to Asia, and some specialization within the Asian market can be expected. For example, Singapore may continue to develop the Asian currency market, Hong Kong could focus on funds management and loan syndication, and Tokyo leading both the bond market and overall funds sourcing. In this way, specialization could lead to greater interregional efficiences and increased banking sophistication while the region continues as the fastest growing area of the world.

Chapter 13
Storm Clouds or Spring Rain?

> "If world economic growth remains slow, Japan will also experience growing difficulties in maintaining its strategy of permanent industrial deployment: the 'old' sectors will close up faster than new ones can develop."
>
> *Albert Bressand* in *Foreign Affairs*

13.1 Introduction

The literature on Japanese management usually ranges from the golden superlatives to the critical negatives. Books like Herman Kahn's (1970) *The Emerging Japanese Superstate* and Ezra Vogel's (1979) *Japan as Number 1* give a flavour of the generally optimistic thrust. Woronoff's (1979) *Japan: The Coming Economic Crisis* or Brzezinski's (1972) *The Fragile Blossom* reflect the more pessimistic perspective. From the point of view of management and organization, the thrust of this book occupies the middle ground. What the Japanese do well, they do superbly well, both in terms of software systems and technological hardware. From the stance of competitive analysis, there is only false deception in underestimating Japanese competences. Equally, however, there is little point in making overgeneralization: the Japanese have major weaknesses in many industries and sectors; indeed these very weaknesses are the testimony of the level of management prowess in the well run companies and growth sectors.

The aim of this chapter is to examine three of the broader issues which touch on potential Japanese problems, both in terms of the future direction of the economy and management capability at large, and the foreign reaction and competitive retaliation in global terms, especially by the US and Europe, but also by the new Japans attempting to overtake their former occupier and erstwhile teacher. The three questions examined in this chapter are as follows: are the Japanese becoming too efficient for their own good, mainly as a result of their laser beam approach to targeting future sunrise sectors? Is the Japanese emphasis on economic matters – what they themselves call their position as economic animals – risking a confrontation with their Western allies on other issues, such as defense spending and foreign aid to third world countries? Is the global shift stemming from the forces of technology and communications establishing a new institutional framework for the world economy around the Pacific Basin or Pacific Rim, with Japan at the center?

The operating environment for tomorrow's manager requires a global focus. For Japan, this focus is especially important at different levels. In the same way that management at the corporate level faces constraints and challenges arising out of industry and societal pressures, Japan's overall international standing in trade, defense, and alliances impacts the future pattern of investment, techno- logy, banking, and management learning. What these three questions or issues – the laser beam theory, the free rider theory, and the Pacific rim theory – point to is the future role of Japan in the world, both in terms of how the Japanese perceive their own position, and how others perceive it and establish con- straints for the Japanese. The answers offered are only tentative, but they give a better context of assessing the future of Japanese management practices and competitive capability.

13.2 Are the Japanese too Efficient?

The startling success of Japanese industry in a whole range of products has prompted not only a wide acceptance and perhaps reluctant admiration from consumers around the world, but a growing suspicion that the Japanese have become too efficient for their own good. Indeed, the feeling is sometimes expressed that the Japanese are targeting specific industries, market segments and product categories that have global market potential, even if the result is a long list of foreign casulties. Swiss watches, Scotch whiskey, American and British steel, European shipbuilding, American, Canadian and British televi- sion, German cameras, British and US machine tools, American and European small cars, British and US motorcycles – there is a long list of product areas where Japanese producers have entered at the low end of the market only to build up volume and cost economies and eventually become the market leader.

The competitive challenge of Japan is usually exacerbated by weak coordina- tion of trade policy by foreign countries. Automobiles are the prime example, but the history of recent cases from machine tools to motorcycles and television has many parallels. In automobiles, the Japanese manufacturers attained their first significant market penetration in countries without a car industry, such as Ireland, Norway, Belgium, and Switzerland. From this base, they built up volume in countries such as Britain and West Germany with a domestic man- ufacturing industry, often by competing directly, or by competing for their own export market. The Japanese, for instance, while held to a small per cent of the market share of the French market, simply went after the French export mar- ket in Switzerland, Germany, and Francophone Africa.

What is particularly problematic about this Japanese success is the overall magnitude of Japan's cost leadership position and the depth of Japan's competitiveness. In every circumstance where they have made deep in-roads in foreign markets, it is not just one Japanese company but often several at one and the same time. The competitive battlefield of Japan's domestic industry is thus transferred to the foreign markets, leaving local enterprises worn down with the onslaught of new products, technologies, and novel marketing vehicles (Kotler and Fahey, 1982).

To be sure, the Japanese do target particular sectors, as analyzed in Chapters 4 and 5. The aim is to seek out areas that provide longterm market growth based on domestic and international demand, to stage in value added production, and to apply both process and product engineering. What is not fully recognized is the technological base for this approach to planning. Companies like Canon in cameras and office equipment have succeeded primarily because of their underlying strength in lens technology and microelectronics. It was their capacity to mobilize this technology into commercial applications using superb marketing skills, rather than any government planning process, that accounts for the company's growth. Competition at home, from Nikon, Asahi Pentax, or Minolta, for instance, pushed Canon into new areas of lens technology such as photocopiers. Yet this product area opened up a new range of direct competitors in office equipment, such as Sharp, Matsushita, Toshiba, Hitachi, Sanyo and the like.[1]

This fierce competition within Japan is the accepted norm; there is no easy settlement of market shares or "competitive equilibria": the ultimate desire is to capture one hundred per cent market share. Unlike in Western sports where a tie is an accepted outcome, Japanese competition is like Japanese sports or martial arts: the result is a clear win or lose. Unfortunately, this leaves the Japanese open to the charge of singling out targeted sectors in a laser beam fashion where foreign competitors get wiped out over time. There are two related points to this argument. The first part is the level of government support in the form of tariff and non-tariff barriers, especially in the early stages of product development. The foreign perception is that companies cannot gain a foothold in the Japanese market to gain the threshold experience, volume and cashflow necessary to match Japanese producers. The inevitable result is that once the Japanese companies gain this volume and experience at home, it is simply too late for the foreign companies in their own market. The second side of the argument is that the Japanese government is providing a significant level of funding for new technologies – in housing and urban technology, in biotechnology, in fifth generation computers, in new energy and materials – that other governments either can't afford or don't provide on principle. The reality is shown in Exhibit 13/1, indicating the comparative support of government in R&D funding.

---

[1] For case studies on this point, see Baranson (1980).

Exhibit 13/1: Comparative Levels of Government R & D Support*

	(A) Gross R & D Expenditure	(B) Government Share	(C) Non-Defense Spending	B/A
United States (1980)	$ 53,460 B	$ 26.4 B	$ 14.4 B	48%
West Germany (1979)	$ 17,200 B	$ 7.6 B	$ 6.8 B	44%
France (1979)	$ 8,800 B	$ 5.2 B	$ 3.2 B	58%
Japan (1980)	$ 20,800 B	$ 5.84 B	$ 5.76 B	28%
Great Britain (1978)	$ 6,000 B	$ 2.8 B	$ 1.6 B	48%

* Calculated at 250 yen to U.S. Dollar

Source: Adapted from MITI

For Westerners, there is much self-serving nonsense in these arguments. The US government underwrites a great deal of its frontier technologies through the defense and space programs, and through university contract research.[2] The same approach is used in Britain, although there is less emphasis on the universities. Because Japan does not have a significant defense establishment, the use of front end support through MITI is more direct, but it doesn't obviate the fact that other countries also support, albeit indirectly, their high risk, frontier technology. What is different about Japan is how the government bureaucracy can marry public investment in new technology to commercial market needs, which thus translates as laser beam targeting of industries.

The foreign perception of Japan's trade structure has some validity, as the Japanese themselves have recognized. Exhibit 13/2 shows the export structure for three countries: Japan, the USA, and West Germany. These diagrams, revealing the horizontal division of labour among manufacturers of the same industry group, shows clearly that there are significant export targets in the Japanese case: cars, electronics, transportation equipment in general, and steel. Japan's exports have increased in a decade at a greater rate than Japanese imports. The trade surplus with both the United States and Europe has grown enormously. Without equal offsetting mechanisms such as major foreign investment flows, appreciation of the yen, or tourism and military spending abroad. Indeed the yen's value may serve to reinforce Japan's export specialization by making raw materials cheaper to import and making high value-added production more profitable in markets with over-priced currencies.

[2] In 1981 and 1982, the U.S. government spent $4,625 and $4,609 billion for research and development at American colleges and universities. The 1983 and 1984 estimates are $4,962 and $5,198 respectively. According to the American Association for the Advancement of Science, from which these figures are published, the largest agency providing grants is the National Institute of Health, with about 43 percent of the total. The National Science Foundation and the Department of Defense follow with about 17 percent of the total outlay (*The New York Times*, June 25, 1983).

Exhibit 13/2: Structure of Export and Import Specialization of the Manufacturing Industry (1979)

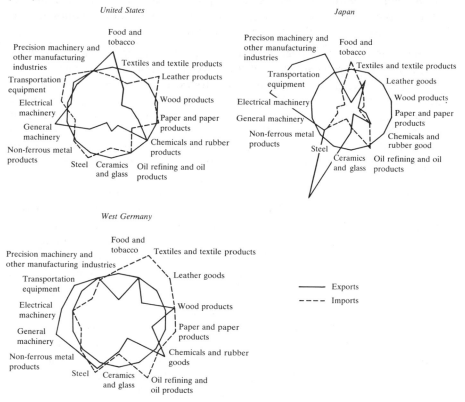

Notes: 1. Export (import) specialization coefficient (relative share)

$$= \frac{\text{Share of product group A in the total value of country's exports (imports)}}{\text{Share of product group A in the total value of OECD's exports (imports)}}$$

2. The central circle represents the average value of OECD (specialization coefficiency = 1)

Source: OECD, (B) Statistics

While the competitiveness of US and European companies in many sectors has fallen relative to Japan, there has also been a spiral-like movement in techno-logy and investment which has widened the gap in key sectors like steel, ma-chine tools, consumer electronics and, until recently, automobiles. Japan's drastic reaction to the first oil shock in 1973 forced most manufacturers to reexamine the technological processes and production systems, both on the hardware and the software side. The inevitable result was a basic revolution in all the major areas of production – the shift from mechanical to electronic, from energy-intensive to energy-savings, from labour intensive to capital intensive, from domestic-oriented to export-oriented. An obvious side effect has been the increasing reliance on the rich export markets of the West to finance the retooling and technological upgrading, while the cast off technology and equipment have gone to the third world countries.

To some extent, luck has been on the side of the Japanese. At a time when Japanese industry was faced with this massive reorientation following the 1973 and 1979 oil shocks, and the evident desire to more towards improved levels of technological sophistication, European and American firms themselves undertook mostly defensive and inward strategies of protectionism, sector abandonment, and government-imposed quotas. The result of this approach has been negative in two basic repects. First, not only has the foreign gap in productivity widened with the Japanese, the perception of foreign consumers has clearly become one of favouring Japan as better producers of quality goods. This self-reinforcing perception makes the position of many US and European companies doubly weaker because the timing of their adaption to the new circumstances comes when they can least afford it. The second negative has been to shift the onus of change on American and European producers, particularly in those sectors not competitive with equivalent Japanese producers, rather than to focus on those areas of Japanese protection where there are real competitive disadvantages.[3]

For their part, the Japanese are not unaware of the danger. They still import less than half per capita in manufactured goods than the Americans – $250 to $550, as against $800 for Europe. Various changes have been made to the country's non-tariff structure, including the system of testing foreign products, but the heavy and open protection for some of Japan's most uncompetitive sectors – agriculture, fishing, and some areas of financial services – raises doubts abroad about the country's open market. To complicate the situation, many European countries have imposed a variety of bilateral restrictions on Japanese products, and countries like Canada and the US are now applying Europe-style quota restrictions on sectors like cars and steel, which could form an unwelcome prelude to new growth sectors like computers and office equipment.

The difference in the future is that the seminal areas of Japanese development are at the core of the new technologies facing the industrial world in the next quarter century. Steel and automobiles are, after all, nineteenth century indus-

---

[3] As Diebold (1980:138) notes, "In the 1974 Trade Act, the U.S. Congress told American negotiators to assure themselves that any new agreements provided a balance of advantages for each American industry affected. This was a response to the fear of some industries that they would be "sold down the river" to benefit some politically more influential groups and the widespread feeling that past negotiations had left European and Japanese in a preferred position in a number of key industries."

Exhibit 13/3: Technological Development Capabilities of Japan and the United States

1. Strong Japanese fields	Cameras, watches, consumer electronic products, audiovisual equipment, office equipment, shipbuilding, steel
2. Strong U.S. fields	Space development, aircraft, nuclear power, medical equipment, oil production, foods, chemicals, aluminium, software, service industries
3. Fields of future Japan-U.S. competition	VLSls, sensors, computers, peripheral and terminal computer equipment, optical communications, office automation equipment, industrial robots, flexible-manufacturing systems, videodiscs, amorphous silicon, carbon fibers, fine ceramics
4. U.S.-led futuristic technologies	Genetic engineering and biotechnology, Josephson junction circuits and other new elements, nuclear fusion and other new energy sources

Source: Moritani Masanori, Nichi-Bei-Ō gijutsu kaihatsu senso (Japan, the United States, and Europe: Comparative Technology), Tokyo, Toyo Keizai Shinposha, 1981

tries. There are limits to how much any of the Western countries can maintain significant global market shares in the face of the large market, low wage competition from third world countries, not just for end products but parts, components, and add-on features. Japan's superior production technologies and global marketing capacities are ideally situated to enter the high end of sectors dominated by the US and Europe – aerospace, pharmaceuticals, and housing – and to develop new ground rules to compete in fundamentally new sectors – biotechnology, ceramic technology, commercial space technology, and fifth generation computers, with all the off shoots from artificial intelligence to machine translation equipment (Exhibit 13/3).

Japan's success in upgrading its technological base after the Pacific War occurred in an era of high economic growth. It was only when the recession after the second oil shock firmly took hold throughout the industrialized world that US and European policy makers started to take stock of Japanese success. As Japan enters new sectors and introduces new techniques, the possibility of applying the same formulas to their success could inevitably lead to more protection and more product quotas. Here the past success at separating as much as possible the economic sources of conflict from the political agenda will be far more difficult, not least because the new areas of Japanese growth converge on a field Japan has studiously avoided in its trading strategies – the area of defense.

13.3 Guns and Butter: Japanese Defense Issues

As the only country to suffer the blow of atomic weapons, Japan is in a unique position from the perspective of national defense. The basic points are well known. Japan's constitution, under the famous ARTICLE IX clause, pledges

the country to "forever renounce war" and never to "maintain any war potential". As an economic superpower Japan spends less than one per cent of GNP
on defense, an amount a prominent newspaper noted as equivalent to what the
Japanese spend each year on ice cream. As a player in one of the world's largest
industries – what Sampson (1979) calls the arms bazaar – Japan has only a
limited role which, at about $3 billion annually, is less than a single aircraft
carrier in the US. Japan's top five defense contractors – Mitsubishi Heavy
Industries, Kawasaki Heavy Industry, Mitsubishi Electric, Ishikawajima-Har-
ima, and Toshiba scarcely have the sales volume of any one of the top ten US
defense contractors.

In recent years, Japan's economic success has forced a reassessment of the
defense posture. Primarily because of strong anti-militarist feelings in the population at large, the long time ruling Liberal Democratic Party has kept defense
spending under the one per cent mark of GNP. While this measure is relatively
small, compared to 6.1 per cent in the US ($180 billion), or 4.3% in Germany,
5.4% in Britain, or 4.1% in France, Japan's very large economy means that the
absolute level of spending, at $12 billion, is very significant.

Japan's military history, its pacifist stance since the war, and its trade relationships with other countries all shape the conflicting currents in the defense
debate. The conflicts are not simply political but also raise questions of trade,
technology, and future corporate strategies. For the past forty years, Japan has
lived under the defense umbrella of the United States. Japan has had only a
limited military capability, mostly defensive in nature. Japan's quarter of a
million personnel in the Self-Defense Forces, plus weapons procurement from
the United States, form the backbone of the country's own military arsen-
nel.[4]

The US position regarding Japan's defense policy is on the surface quite
straight forward. The gap between US defense spending and Japanese spending is not only too great, but it coincides with continuing trade surpluses and
constant pressure on the yen/dollar exchange rate. Behind the general desire
for more defense spending, aside from the various military strategies and alliance committments, are some basic trade and technology considerations. The
simplistic approach to more defense spending by Japan is procurement of arms
from the US. Japan would upgrade its military capability, the balance of payments problem would be partly rectified, and the defense burden would be
more equitably shared.

Yet there are more fundamental issues at hand, again focusing on the trade and
technology issues only. From the American perspective, increased Japanese

---

[4] The historical and philosophical aspects of Japan's defense policy are reviewed in a set of essays
published in *Japan Echo* (Vol. 5, No. 4, 1978) under the title "The Defense Debate Flares
Up."

spending on defense, while desirable from a military perspective, is a mixed blessing, and one fraught with commercial complications. If the Japanese spend too much more on defense, there is the question of how the Americans can continue to make them dependent on US technology. Given the increasing importance of electronics in weaponry technology, there are real questions about how far behind the Japanese are in some crucial areas. Moreover, once the level of Japanese spending starts to mount in particular areas, what is the incentive – for longer production runs and economies of scale – to apply the same production capabilities to certain classes of weapons that were applied in steel, ship-building, and automobiles? (Nissan Motor Co. Ltd. has already diversified into the defense and aerospace fields.) Although the main defense contractors in Japan – Exhibit 13/4 – are large companies, their defense related work accounts for a very small per cent of their total sales.

Within Japan, the pressures for a greater manufacturing capability in weaponry have always existed – as far back as 1952, the Keidanren established its Defense Production Committee to lobby for arms and ammunitions sales. Government White Papers on Japan's defenses have continuously emphasized the role of research and development, and even the United States has now recognized the flow of technology transfer should go in both directions. Japan has already

Exhibit 13/4: Japanese Defense Companies

¥ million	Top 20 Companies, based on Amount of Defence Contracts	
	Fiscal 1980	Fiscal 1979
1. Mitsubishi Heavy Industries	234,540	96,930
2. Ishikawajima-Harima Heavy Industries	108,470	53,960
3. Kawasaki Heavy Industries	81,190	49,550
4. Mitsubishi Electric Machinery	72,380	39,900
5. Tokyo Shitaura electric	32,900	18,190
6. Japan Electric	22,310	16,640
7. Ito-Chu Aviation	14,040	16,580
8. Japan Petroleum	12,900	13,670
9. Japan Steel Works	12,270	10,290
10. Sumitomo Heavy Machine Industry	12,040	8,860
11. Komatsu Works	12,020	8,560
12. Hitachi Shipbuilding	11,410	8,150
13. Tokyo Instruments	9,390	7,660
14. Hitachi Works	8,920	7,300
15. Maruzen Petroleum	7,930	7,150
16. Oki Electric Industry	7,750	6,710
17. Shinmeiwa Industry	7,290	6,701
18. Mitsubishi Shoji Trading Co.	6,940	6,700
19. Daikin Industry	6,760	5,850
20. Shimazu Works	6,710	5,790
Total	¥ 688,160	¥ 395,501

produced a domestic industry for the production of tanks (Type-61, Type-74), armoured personnel carriers, anti-tank missiles and launchers, support fighter aircraft, transport planes, and anti-submarine flying boats. There are a wide variety of European and US weapons produced under license, including anti-aircraft guns, ground-to-air guided missiles, fighter interceptors helicopters. Japan also has its own indigenous space program which, while relying on US rocket launching technology, has been receiving increased levels of funding over a ten year time period. It is virtually impossible to predict what will be the outcome of the pressures put on Japan to increase defense spending – pressures from within Japan, mainly from businessmen and nationalists, from the US, worried about the global burdens of tis own defense responsibilities, and the actions of the Soviet Union in Southeast Asia. However, if past experience is a guide, increased defense spending in Japan will have two specific characteristics. First, Japan will avoid the kind of cost plus spending characteristic of most of American defense weaponry, where the level of technology has increased while production productivity has declined (Fallows, 1980). Japanese competition within the domestic market will be focused on productivity improvement around very similar products and technologies with a view to lowering unit costs as volume increases. A second feature of Japanese military technological development would be the complimentary relationship with the civilian economy. Part of the advantages Japan enjoys in civilian technology is the fact that highly trained manpower has not been diverted to high cost, low commercial payoff areas like space, certain classes of military weaponry, and exotic technologies. Japan currently spends a fraction of its total small defense budget on research and development, namely one per cent. The United States spends, at $20 billion, almost twice as much on research and development as Japan spends in total. The US rate of R&D commitment of 10.3 per cent is even lower than France's 12.5, or Britain's 13.5, but is double Germany's 5 per cent.

In terms of contrasting credos, the assumption has become widely accepted in US planning circles that commercial applications result from defense and space technologies. In Japan, the opposite premise holds. Strong commercial technologies and applications provide the best assurance of military and defense spinoffs. In the near term future, the domestic political constraints against sharply increased defense spending will coexist with the international pressures for a larger defense responsibility and manufacturing capability. By limiting defense spending in real terms to the one per cent or so of GNP, while other countries in the West are spending three to seven times that per cent, the Japanese cannot avoid having military and defense issues integrated with trade and technology matters. This balancing act – low defense spending and low aid – with surpluses in trade and technology – has become especially difficult, especially in Europe where the absence of a common position is the norm – and may well result in rising protectionism aimed at Japan.

The most obvious general alternative to increased defense spending for Japan lies in the area of foreign aid, particularly in aid which increases the technological base and competitiveness of recipient countries. Yet even in this less politically sensitive area, Japan's role is relatively small. Exhibit 13/5 reveals that net official development assistance from Japan has increased substantially since the early 1970's, from an average of $527 million to $3.3 billion in 1980 and $3.17 billion in 1981. However, as a per cent of GNP, Japan's contribution is even below the average of all Western governments and significantly below the amount contributed by several countries where defense spending is low. Japan, in other words, is low on both defense and aid.

Exhibit 13/5: Net Official Development Assistance from DAC Countries to Developing Countries and Multilateral Agencies: Net Disbursements (1970–1981)[a] (U.S. $ million, except as indicated)

	1970–72 Average	1977	1978	1979	1980	1981(P)[b]	% of GNP 1970–72	1980	1981	Share of Total (%) 1970–72	1980	1981
U.S.A.	3,408	4,682	5,664	4,684	7,138	5,760	0.32	0.27	0.20	43.1	26.7	22.6
France	1,122	2,267	2,705	3,370	4,053	4,022	0.67	0.62	0.71	14.2	15.1	15.8
Germany, F.R.	714	1,717	2,347	3,350	3,517	3,182	0.32	0.43	0.46	9.0	13.1	12.5
Japan	527	1,424	2,215	2,637	3,304	e3,170	0.21	0.32	0.28	6.7	12.3	12.5
U.K.	595	1,103	1,460	2,104	1,781	2,194	0.42	0.34	0.43	7.5	6.7	8.6
Netherlands	240	908	1,073	1,404	1,577	1,510	0.63	0.99	1.08	3.0	5.9	5.9
Canada	398	991	1,060	1,026	1,036	1,187	0.42	0.42	0.43	5.0	3.9	4.7
Sweden	158	779	783	956	923	916	0.44	0.76	0.83	2.0	3.4	3.6
Italy	144	198	376	273	672	670	0.14	0.17	0.19	1.8	2.5	2.6
Australia	236	400	588	620	657	649	0.60	0.48	0.41	3.0	2.5	2.5
DAC, total	7,903	15,722	19,986	22,413	26,776	25,461	0.35	0.37	0.35	100.0	100.0	100.0

[a] The Development Assistance Committee (DAC) is one of the specialized committees of the OECD. DAC members include Austria, Belgium, Denmark, Finland, New Zealand, Norway, Switzerland and the Commission of EEC, as well as countries shown above.
[b] Including previously unrecorded administrative costs.
Source: OECD, Development Co-operation, 1981, and Press Release. June 23. 1982

The pattern of Japanese aid allocation reveals that economic assistance to developing countries has some connection to overall economic and foreign policy considerations. Rix's (1979) study of the administrative structures within the Japanese bureaucracy points out that there are no overall 'rational' criteria for economic aid. However, there are in fact at least four principles underlying the aid programs. One has to do with Japan's access to raw materials, as Ozawa (1979) makes clear. Japan's closer relationship to the Middle East countries after 1973 is a case in point, as is the closer ties in recent years with China. A second issue relates to Japan's perceived role in Asia. Asian countries have been the main recipients of Japanese aid – the closer the country's economic ties to Japan, the more the aid. This point relates to the third, namely national security. Countries like South Korea and Indonesia are two examples of countries with close economic relations with Japan, but whose domestic military and foreign policy moves have a direct bearing with the Japanese government. The fourth factor is technology and trade. Because Japan has been a conduit for Western technology sales to Asian countries, large manufacturers and *Soga Shosha* have developed vested interests in maintaining a flow of knowledge and expertise into these fast growing countries, often through expatriate Japanese or through Japanese engineering consulting or construction firms undertaking feasibility projects in the regions. In other words, through an incremental approach, the Japanese bureaucracy has developed well worn channels for economic aid in the form of what Rix (1979:264) calls "a cumulative cycle of bilateral commitment".

Successive Japanese administrations have cited the problems of slower economic growth and the huge government deficits as the main reasons for going slow on more aid or defense spending. Underneath these issues, however, is a recognition that there are strong emotional sentiments towards pacifism at home and anti-Japanese sentiment. Because so few foreigners study in Japan when they are young, visit Japan as tourists when they are older, or emulate the Japanese in life style or social norms like people do Americans (and especially New Yorkers and Californians), there are few non-commercial sources of social bonding that creates good will and emotional attachment to the country. How Japanese politicians weigh these choices may prove ominous for both the country's economic future and for the definition of the new responsibilities in the emerging Pacific Century.

13.4 Pacific Rim and Pacific Century?

Early in 1975, Norman Macrae of *The Economist* heralded the dawn of a new era – Pacific Century 1975–2075, centered around Japan. This new epoch is seen as the replacement for the American Century 1875–1975, which in turn preceded the British Century 1775–1875. In each case, not only business but education, culture, politics and technology all become influenced by the apex of national power (Macrae, 1975:15–35). In terms of the fullest comprehension of Japanese industrial success, the Pacific Rim concept represents nothing less than a global reorientation away from the Atlantic nexus joining America and Europe, and the rise of the Pacific Rim, with Japan at the center.[5]

Already the Pacific is the leading ocean of marine transport, satellite communications, and data transmissions, and the site of the fastest growing countries.

---

[5] In the widest sense, the Pacific Rim is defined as including: Japan, People's Republic of China, Taiwan, South Korea, Hong Kong, Indonesia, Singapore, Malaysia, Thailand, Philippines, Australia, New Zealand, Chile, Colombia, Ecuador, Peru, Mexico, Guatemala, El Salvador, Honduras, Nicaragua, Panama, Costa Rica, Canada and the United States.

Historically, of course the Pacific has always been the source of fascination for the West, from Marco Polo's adventures in Cathay, the arrival of Portuguese pirates in the sixteenth century, and America's clipper trade with China in the last century, to the twentieth century fascination with China and the more recent interest in Japan.

The Nomura Institute, one of the strongest advocates of the Pacific Era, goes so far as to see a new destiny for Japan. The central idea is a new group of nations, "Japan, the United States, Australia, New Zealand and Canada" forming the central core of nations much like the Continental countries of Europe forming the old nucleus of the Atlantic basin. According to one view,

The Pacific economic basin has the edge over the Atlantic economic basin in growth potential. Moreover, this dynamism is sustained by the existence of ample food and energy resources and the increasingly close relations between the United States and Japan (Tokuyama, 1978:43).

Among the potential natural resources in the Pacific Basin area are the agricultural lands of North America, Australia and the Mekong Delta, oil reserves off Vietnam and the East China Sea; coal deposits, uranium, and petroleum throughout the region.

The Pacific Rim idea, based on either a political vision of common interests and shared values, or on an economic foundation of integrated trading arrangements and common tariff policies, is hardly novel. In fact, to many non-Japanese in Asia, the Pacific Rim or Pacific Basin concept is simply a thinly disguised revival of the Greater East Asian Co-prosperity Sphere of World War II. Despite the high level of interdependence with Japan, the countries of South East Asia are only too aware of their vulnerability to economic dependence. As Hofheinz and Calder (1982:11) correctly point out:

The striking fact is that, since World War II, Japan has essentially achieved its goals of growth to world power status and of dominance of western Pacific markets without firing a shot. Eastasia today is a zone of co-prosperity nearly as comfortable and extensive as the Japanese general staff of 1943 could have wished.

Since 1980 successive Japanese administrations have quietly promoted the Pacific basin idea, without taking the lead among the Asian countries. At the public level, there is a general recognition that the 1980's are different than the 1930's, especially in the relations between Japan and China, The USA and China, and the economic role played by the European powers in Indonesia, Singapore and Malaysia, and even Australia and New Zealand. The general principles being promoted for the Pacific Basin are regional development and cooperation, free trade and capital transfers, exchange of people through immigration and educational training, and joint research on economic and technical problems.[6]

At the heart of the problems facing the Pacific Basin or Pacific Rim vision are the fundamental divisions of geography, ideology and economy. In its expanded format, the Pacific Rim includes not only the island economies of Asia but also the economies of North America, Australia and New Zealand. Within this huge geographical spread are the ideological camps of the market-based economies of the Free World and the state planning systems of the communist countries. In this latter connection, the military lines are drawn essentially between the Soviet Union, a Pacific power in its own right, and the United States, with the uneasy relationship with China. Then there is the contrasting states of development among the countries in terms of technology, exploitation of raw materials, and educational levels.[7]

Each of these three issues would be sufficient to cause a slowdown in the rate of integration across the region. Taken together, and combined with Japan's reluctance to assume political leadership, they would indicate that any sudden and dramatic development of the Pacific Basin idea is very unlikely. By contrast, economic relations between sets of countries or regions within the Pacific Basin are proceeding at a much faster pace.

Perhaps the cornerstone of Japan's Pacific Rim foreign policy thrust starts with ASEAN – the Association of South East Asian Nations, formed in 1967 and consisting of Indonesia, the Phillipines, Malaysia, Singapore, and Thailand. Initially ASEAN focused on settlement of political disputes among the member countries, but following the ASEAN Declaration of Accord announced in 1976, the emphasis has been on economic cooperation based around complementary industrial projects, some preferential trade agreements, joint commodity planning, and in more recent years, pressuring Japan to provide more aid in technology, to import more goods from ASEAN countries, and to provide special assistance for large scale infrastructure and construction projects.

Building up an institutional basis for the Pacific Rim remains difficult, even within a framework of Japan and ASEAN countries. Policy initiatives in favour of the Pacific Rim have been limited, and serious acceptance of the idea in any concerted away among the political and bureaucratic elites exists only in Japan and Australia. Within the ASEAN countries, whose trade flows among the

---

[6] There are four subregional economic organizations: ASEAN, discussed below; LAIA – Latin American Integration Association; ANCOM – Andean Common Market; and CACM – Central American Common Market.

[7] For two anthologies examining trends in the Pacific Rim, see Boyd (1982) and PWPAJ (1979).

members averages only about 15 per cent, there is a general awareness of the growing dependence for exports on Japanese economic growth. For example, as seen in Exhibit 13/6, the level of Japan's exports to ASEAN countries has remained static as a total per cent, the level of imports has increased substantially, both absolutely and relatively. The extent of this growing trade has prompted various proposals for a Pacific Free Trade Area (Kojima, 1977); however, these same countries are also aware of the ideal of diversified sources of foreign investment, technology, and trade.

The emergence of the Pacific Rim tends to sharpen the delicate sets of diplomatic and trade relations which Japan's government and multinational managers must cope with in the 1980's. Essentially, Japan is balancing three broad categories of interaction – that with the United States, but indirectly Mexico and Canada; that with the Asian countries, and that with its communist neighbours – China, the Soviet Union, and their satellites. The complexity of managing these triangular relationships arises from the fact that it will become increasingly difficult to manage any one successfully without at least indirectly causing a measure of conflict with the others.

Exhibit 13/6: Japan's Trade with Selected Countries in the Pacific Basin (in millions of U.S. $ and %)

	Japan's Exports						Japan's Imports					
	1960		1970		1979		1960		1970		1979	
	$	%	$	%	$	%	$	%	$	%	$	%
Canada	119	2.9	563	2.9	1738	1.7	204	4.5	929	4.9	4105	3.7
U.S.	1083	26.7	5940	30.7	26403	25.6	1545	34.4	5560	29.4	20431	18.5
Australia	144	3.6	589	3.0	2607	2.5	344	7.7	1508	8.0	6298	5.7
New Zealand	24	0.6	114	0.6	584	0.6	32	0.7	158	0.8	805	0.7
Mexico	18	0.4	94	0.5	841	0.8	103	2.3	151	0.8	483	0.4
(East Asian market economies)	(358)	(8.8)	(2218)	(11.5)	(14263)	(13.8)	(106)	(2.4)	(572)	(3.0)	(6498)	(5.9)
Republic of Korea	100	2.5	818	4.2	6247	6.1	19	0.4	229	1.2	3359	3.0
Taiwan	102	2.5	700	3.6	4337	4.2	64	1.4	251	1.3	2476	2.2
Hong Kong	156	3.8	700	3.6	3679	3.6	23	0.5	92	0.5	663	0.6
(ASEAN)	(501)	(12.4)	(1808)	(9.4)	(9646)	(9.4)	(509)	(11.3)	(1866)	(9.9)	(16276)	(14.7)
Thailand	118	2.9	449	2.3	1714	1.7	72	1.6	190	1.0	1169	1.1
Singapore	87	2.1	423	2.2	2679	2.6	14	0.3	87	0.5	1473	1.3
Malaysia*	32	0.8	166	0.9	1507	1.5	194	4.3	419	2.2	3257	2.9
Philippines	154	3.8	454	2.4	1622	1.6	159	3.5	533	2.8	1583	1.4
Indonesia	110	2.7	316	1.6	2124	2.1	70	1.6	637	3.4	8794	7.9
(Centrally planning economies)	(124)	(2.1)	(1084)	(5.6)	(6562)	(6.4)	(113)	(2.5)	(780)	(4.1)	(5066)	(4.6)
China	3	0.1	569	2.9	3699	3.6	21	0.5	254	1.3	2955	2.7
USSR	60	1.5	341	1.8	2461	2.4	87	1.9	481	2.5	1911	1.7
Democratic People's Republic of Korea	NA	NA	23	0.1	284	0.3	NA	NA	34	0.2	152	0.1
Vietnam**	61	1.5	151	0.8	118	0.1	5	0.1	11	0.1	48	0.0
Subtotal	2371	58.5	12410	64.2	62689	60.8	2956	65.8	11524	61.0	59962	54.2
World Total	4055	100.0	19318	100.0	103032	100.0	4491	100.0	18881	100.0	110672	100.0

Note: Custom clearance statistics in calender year.
  * Total of North and South Vietnam.
** Figures for Malaysia 1960 are for Malaya.

Source: Japan Tariff Association, *Summary Report: Trade of Japan, December, 1979*

The United States and Japan, with over $60 billion dollars in bilateral trade, billions in foreign investment and technology flows, share many common interests, but in terms of defense and trade surpluses, there are important sources of fundamental conflict. Even though joint problems and challenges are also significant – together, for instance, they are the biggest consumers of imported oil and raw materials – there are fundamental imbalances in how they deal with one another. Where Japan's industrial policy is coherent and proactive, the US approach is disjointed and reactive. Where Japan takes enormous initiative to learn and use foreign languages, educate and foster young executive in the United States, and learn from and apply foreign management ideas at home, Americans have for a generation unconsciously slipped into a "Made in the US" mentality from grade school to the board room and the Oval Office. On defense policy, Japan may bend to some extent on US pressures, but on industrial, technological and trade matters, the sheer coherence and focused direction may well give Japanese managers the upper hand against US policy when measured in global terms.

The second piece of the triangle, that with the Asian countries, involves a rising level of trade and investment, with the Asian countries adopting Japanese-style industrial planning and technology strategies. From their point of view, there is a tradeoff between increased dependence on Japan or slower growth, but the only real source of diversification is North America, whose protectionist policies hurt them the most because they are generally less competitive on non-price considerations like quality and technology. Moreover, their own situation gives Japan certain advantages. As highly authoritarian states, they are dependent on economic growth for social peace. Not having collective strategies on investment, trade, and tariffs, they can lose collective bargaining leverage to the stronger Japanese. Even though the Japanese themselves may not be particularly liked, the lingering anti-Americanism among Asian elites, and basic resentment of the European colonial past, may also offset this disadvantage for Japan.

Despite then the major areas of conflict in these bilateral sets of relations, where the conflict and problem areas are primarily economic, there is a strong commonality in military and defense posture vis-a-vis the third side of the triangle, Japan's relations with the communist countries. Japanese and American cooperation remains the basic building block of Japan's entire foreign policy framework. However, within this general picture is a slowly developing set of independent Japanese initiatives in the Middle East, Vietnam and the Siberian region of the Soviet Union (mining, oil exploration, rail and port facilities). In each of these areas, Japanese strategic interests have guided the economic targets for cooperation, but they have in no way jeopardized the overall security relationship between the US and Japan.

Obviously there are limits as to how far the cooperative relations with China and the Soviet Union can go to the detriment of the United States. Moreover, Japan may well want to ease some of the trade frictions with the US by shifting the export and investment focus into East Asian countries such that they will carry the brunt of North American and European trade restrictions. If the US and Japan relations do become competitive beyond trade matters, such that the security framework was fundamentally changed, Japan may well seek a new accommadation either with China, or possibly within a broad Asian framework to include India.

In any case, the Pacific Rim idea is only in the dawning era, and with Japan's rising stock of capital, technology, and educated human resources, the questions that can be raised center on what all this means for what Japan can truly teach the world, and what that means for lessons for foreigners. That topic is taken up in the next chapter.

13.5 Summary and Conclusions

This chapter has reviewed some of the broader issues facing Japan over the next decade. The three issues examined were the targeting of industries for growth and technology, defense and the idea of Pacific Century. In each area there are important storm clouds on the horizon for Japan. They stem from the general definitions of Japan's future role in the global system, the country's capacity to adapt to rapidly changing circumstances, and an emerging consensus concerning Japan's enormous economic and technological power.

In the narrow sense, the issues converge on Japan's competitive strengths and the perceived foreign desire for Japan to change past strategies. In point of fact, any careful assessment of Japan's recent activities, whether on the government front or at the level of the corporation, suggests that Japanese officials have learned to live rather well within any set of rules either imposed on them, like the constitution and defense treaties, or those worked out by either bilateral or multilateral agreements like GATT. In either case, Japanese managers and government officials have had an amazing track record at putting together the winning combination of information and organization to mobilize resources into a coherent and proactive direction. This being so, Japan may well face a future of perpetual short term conflicts based on either sector by sector issues or, more challengingly, fundamental differences on currency valuations, trade rules, and the like. The diplomatic challenge may well be to stem the tide of latent anti-Japanese sentiment in many Western countries, but also with the neighbouring East Asian Pacific.

The rise of the Pacific Rim concept, and the importance of defense issues with the United States, raise the spectre of Japan's future as an independent player in the global chess game. On economic and industrial matters, Japan and the US are clearly competitors, but only on the narrow sense of corporate competition. In terms of fundamental economic welfare, American consumers gain by superior and cheaper Japanese products, in the same way that Japanese consumers gain by better American products. In this respect, the world economy is facing a watershed between mercantilist, nation-state conflict, and corporate level competition across international markets.

The danger is escalating corporate conflict to nation-state conflict and it is particular acute in the case of Japan and the United States, because it raises the possibility of Japan deviating from an almost forty year era of peaceful cooperation. Japan could pay an enormous burden for pursuing an independent defense line, but even this possibility opens up a box few Americans would wish to contemplate.

On the other hand, as the two most developed technological powers, Japan and the United States could develop an era of truly global cooperation to solve some of the most pressing problems facing the world. Already, Japan is undertaking some of the most interesting intellectual work on global problems. For instance, because Japan is so dependent on imports of energy, Japanese managers in companies, think tanks, and government have thought long and hard how electricity can be harnessed from the oceans, food grown in the desert, minerals mined from the sea, energy extracted from inhospitable climates. Japan's aging population poses social challenges in medicine, engineering, and technology which have global implications if the solutions sought in Japan can be applied elsewhere. Japan's experience of very rapid growth and economic development, from about one quarter Britain's per capita income in the early 1950's to about double it in three decades, raises abject lessons for other countries in similar states of development. The future of Japan thus holds potential for great achievement if the future is seized. Some ideas along those lines are outlined in the final chapter.

Chapter 14
Samurai Duel: Learning From Japan

> "It is always wise to look ahead, but difficult to look further than you can see."
>
> *Winston S. Churchill*

14.1 Introduction

For a hundred years and more, Japan has been the most prolific copier of things foreign. Whether in the bustling shopping districts of downtown Tokyo or in the remote villages of southern Kyushu, the foreign visitor cannot fail to be impressed with the perceived uniqueness of the ancient culture or the ubiquitous presence of foreign goods like fast food, cars, or clothing. Japan is not alone in learning from abroad, and this century is not unique in foreign learning – what is impressive is how Japan has turned foreign learning into a highly developed practice, and a profitable one too. Purchases of foreign technology have amounted since 1945 to only about $9 billion, or forty per cent of their current annual spending on research and development. The Japanese have perfected the art of foreign learning so well that many products are thought to be Japanese in origin. Even many Japanese tend to think that some of the ancient crafts like pottery and house construction, Japan's language, music and tea ceremony are indigenous to the country.

Other countries absorb and learn from abroad. England, after all, carries the proud lineage of the Romans, the Germans, and the French, not to mention the Scots, the Irish, the Welsh, or the Indians, the Pakistanis, and the White Commonwealth. The countries of North and South America are distinctly "immigrant" countries, which is to say they were peopled and developed by learning from abroad, not just in techniques and customs but by direct transfers of peoples.

Where Japan is different in foreign learning is in the systematic and economic husbanding of domestic resources – human, financial, and organizational – to learn and apply foreign knowledge for rapid economic growth and technological development. To be sure, Japan's success in this endeavour, as Johnson (1982) cogently argues, has to be understood in the context of the priorities on industrial development by the Japanese state, priorities which have openly been directed to "catching up with the West".

For fifty years or more, the Japanese have experimented with an impressive variety of institutional and organizational arrangements to improve this social learning from abroad. The mechanisms are evident. Students studying abroad. Learning foreign languages. The foreign offices of JETRO – Japan's External Trade Organization staffed by businessmen. Managers studying foreign markets. Trading firms and banks compiling statistics on trade, technology, and new products. Detailed competitive analyses. Worker visits abroad as a component of the productivity bonus. Government translation of foreign journals. Television and radio programs on foreign trade. Reading materials for wives and children on Japan's export-led economy. The list goes on. History and culture have a role to play in explaining Japan's gift in learning and the enormous propensity to respect learning. The waves of importing from abroad – the post-Meiji reforms, the turn of the century accession to military power, and the post-war reforms – all reinforced a set of forces wherein foreign ideas and techniques were widely accepted. By contrast, the economic superiority of Europe and later the United States imposed an intellectual snobbishness against ideas and influences Asian, let alone Japanese.

Language has a role as well. Paradoxically, it is an accepted axiom among many Japanese that their own facility in foreign languages is not a natural strength. The ambiguous gramatical rules of English, the complexity of declension and conjugation of latin languages like French and Italian create formidable obstacles for Japanese learning. By the same token, Japanese is also a formidable language for foreigners, both for speaking and for writing. Until recently at least, the Japanese have accepted that their language is not a lingua franca anywhere; Americans have taken for granted the status of their own language.

The issue of language typifies the educational challenges of young Japanese and the imposition of discipline and hard work on young people. With some 5000 basic Chinese ideographs, plus an alphabet to form foreign-based words by sounds, the Japanese language itself illustrates the learning qualities of the people. Where the French attempt at the official level to block out the new words of the lingua franca, the Japanese creatively absorb foreign and especially English words. As Passin (1980) notes, "English is in the process of being completely absorbed and, just as happened to Chinese in the past, its entire vocabulary is becoming available for use in Japanese. Nowadays, when new words have to be coined, they are more likely to be struck from the English mind than the Chinese one".

The emergence of Japan as an economic superpower has prompted a new sunrise industry, namely the learning from Japan movement. Much of what various writers have suggested involves specific techniques – quality control, just in time, permanent employment, consultative decision-making, competitive analysis, quick die changes, small business sub-contracting, and the like. The arguments presented in this book suggest that the emphasis on particular

techniques developed and refined by the Japanese is both dangerously misleading and short term in effect. The real message of the "Learn from Japan"
movement is not the adoption of new gadgets or quick fixes. It is not, in fact, a
message inherently Japanese. The real message is the shift in the world economy to one of truly global trade and competition, where management and
organizational skills – not raw materials and capital – are the key to developing
comparative advantage.

The Japanese have responded to the new international forces both out of need
but also out of vision and acumen. The competitive response has been at three
levels – government in the form of proactive industrial policy, industry in the
form of sector by sector analyses, and corporate in the form of technology and
competitive strategy. This chapter takes up this concluding point by addressing
the two issues: the Japanese impact on foreign country trade patterns and on
the style and practice of management.

14.2 New Trade Patterns

The recent trade conflicts in the global economy represent the cross currents of
trade organized around any one of three principles. The first represents the
framework of traditional national economies: Britain vs. France, or the U.S.
vs. Japan, for instance. The second principle is much more complex operating
within the framework of multinational corporations operating subsidiaries
across national boundaries. The third principle operates with the broader but
critical regional economic groupings – the European Economic Community,
Japan and ASEAN, the United States and Canada and Mexico as satellite economies for raw materials and cheap labour. Changes in institutional arrangements, the technology gap, exchange rates, terms of trade, and energy sourcing
have all combined in complex ways to accelerate changes in these three frameworks for organizing trade, with some countries more successful than others.

In terms of Japan, there can be little doubting the thrust of adapting to global
trends. It is impossible to trace empirically, but the argument presented in
previous chapters is that Japan has combined its hardware and software technologies at both the macro and the micro levels to meet this new global challenge. Organizationally, the Japanese address this challenge in unique and
impressive ways. Big business and small business work together through sub-
contracting and technology transfer to reap the advantages of scale with that of
flexibility. Banks and corporations work together to apply resources to the
growth sectors while revitalizing declining or mature sectors. Government and
business work together to share information and adopt policies to keep Japan
internationally competitive. Corporations in the manufacturing sector work

together with the trading firm sector to purchase raw materials, gather and exchange information, and initiate foreign sales and where necessary operate consortia structures in international projects.

In themselves, these organizational partnerships are not unique. In Germany, for instance, the equity stake held by banks in industrial corporations has parallels with Japan. In France, the relationship between government and business is very close like Japan. In the United States, there are many sectors where large firms contract sourcing with small firms. Only in Japan, however, are the organizational arrangements so well institutionalized and accepted for international trade. Japan's educational system helps to reinforce this kind of structure, since young people compete vigourously to find a role in it. Especially in contrast to Britain, Japan's best and brightest are attracted to industry and entrepreneurs are held in high social esteem. The acceptance of applying ideas and technology from abroad by bright people strengthens these bonds even further. Despite some changes in the value system of a minority of young people, there is very strong acceptance of the goals of industrialization and economic growth.

Fortunately for the Japanese, there is a much clearer understanding of the nature of the global economy than that held by many Western managers. The Japanese place the highest priority on technology, even technology that is imported and improved. There is also a clear recognition that the global economy consists of much more than trade in manufactured goods sold from one producer to the customer. The global economy consists as well in a large state to state component of trade, a huge and growing component in barter and counter trade, and the sector dominated by trading firms. Only the Japanese have developed organizational mechanisms to penetrate these sectors globally.

Speculatively, one can compare Japan's approach to American and European strength. The following exhibit shows two dimensions, namely technology and customer type. The technological dimension takes the form of closed systems or open system. The closed system technology implies a tight integration of components with little or no change across a particular time frame. By contrast, the open system is constantly changing and there is more decoupling of components. The customer dimension is either public or individual, with the public implying government purchasing, although there may be choices by country.

Typical sectors in the first category are defense industries, the space industry, satellite communications, and public transport (subway system). These sectors involve a high degree of engineering, public procurement, and an important political component in the buying decision. Some of these characteristics apply to the second category of industries, such as aerospace, petrochemicals, telecommunications, and defense weaponry. For some countries, the production is

Exhibit 14/1: A Comparative Model of Technology and Trade

TYPE OF CUSTOMER

		Public	Private
T E C **Closed**		I	II
H N O L O **Open**		III	IV
G Y			

carried out by privately-owned firms, while in others by privately-owned firms. Similarly, the end consumer of these sectors may be governments or individual corporations.

For open systems technology, characterized by rapid change and flexible adaptation, there are Type III and Type IV sectors. In the former, there are such areas as municipal government services (garbage collection, schooling, police and security), medical and health treatment, and leisure services. Type IV sectors are the fastest changing, as in such areas as consumer electronics, automobiles, energy exploration, and fast foods.

In terms of global trends and contrasts, one might speculate on the differences between Japan, the US and Europe in these different categories. In the US case, there is a strong and historically based preference for private sector production and service for the individual consumer. There is little emphasis by either political party in the US for government ownership, and even in areas like defense, airports, and highways, some Americans would prefer private rather than public ownership. Most of the business-government relationship is oriented to the sector of the economy in private hands. By contrast to European and Japanese experience, areas like municipal transportation, medical services, and public leisure facilities are less developed in the U.S.

By contrast, the emphasis in much of Europe is on some of the same private sector areas but with a much strong public sector involvement. France and Britain are the two best examples, where nationalization of key sectors and government ownership of many services is an accepted norm. Lack of competition is also a factor but the value system places a certain preference for public goods. (It has been said of Europe that the key areas of excellence are war and luxury – the Titanic, after all, was a triumph of Victorian engineering, and Rolls Royces don't suffer from competition from Hondas and Toyotas.) Both government industrial policy and the education system tend to favour sectors with closed technology, and the pattern of European overseas trade heavily favours this category, from defense and aerospace to subway systems and construction.

The Japanese are somewhat in between, with major emphasis in large scale systems engineering characteristic of closed technology, but also enormous capability in open technology. Consumer electronics and automobiles are the obvious past successes, but to them are coming such sectors as personal computers, office automation, cosmetics and personal luxery goods, and the like. In the public area, the Japanese are experimenting with novel urban designs and systems construction, including modular housing.

Whether the Europeans have particular propensities and skills in public sector activities, or whether the Americans have particular strengths in private sector individual marketing, is a speculative point. What is clear is that the global trends involve novel organizational skills and the Japanese have mobilized the linkages across type of organizations – big and small, manufacturing and trading, public and private – in their outward orientation. It is no accident that in Europe, companies and government officials are debating the need to strengthen the private sector and develop a presence in many sectors which are emerging (biotechnology, robotics, telecommunications, personal computers) and which are threatened (shipbuilding, steel, automobiles, textiles and consumer electronics). In the United States the key debate involves the other side of the coin, namely the need for a government industrial strategy to coordinate departments and mobilize resources into the sunrise sectors.

In both cases, the barometer is Japan. The lesson therefore is to understand how Japan has responded to the changing international environment, not to slavishly copy Japanese institutional practices which have been developed and perfected over a long time frame. Japanese economic success is a symptom of the changing global economy. The next section focuses on this point from the perspective of management.

14.3 Management Changes

In North America in particular, there has been a major emphasis on studying Japanese success in terms of particular functions or particular specialities, such as personnel and human resources, production management, marketing, or finance. Much is made of the practice of career specialization, where a young graduate joins a company and works up the corporate ladder through a particular function without spending time rotating across functions. Moreover, the lack of emphasis on such areas as production and personnel as a ticket to the top has resulted in an emphasis on what Reich (1982) calls paper entrepreneurship – buying and selling companies to gain share price value gains, rather than company growth through technological development and production-led growth.

The academic approach of business schools on the North American model perhaps reinforces this approach, but practicing managers are no less prone to take and accept this piecemeal view and search for gadgets and tricks to apply quick fix solutions. Abernathy et al (1980) make a case for the view that the over emphasis on short term operating results and reliance on financial models – what TIME magazine once called "paralysis by analysis" – has caused a basic deficiency in the way management is practiced in North America. The Japanese, by contrast, practice a more relevant "hands on" style based around such basic principles as continuous improvement and holistic integration, as shown in Exhibit 14/2.

Exhibit 14/2: Japanese Productivity: A Total System

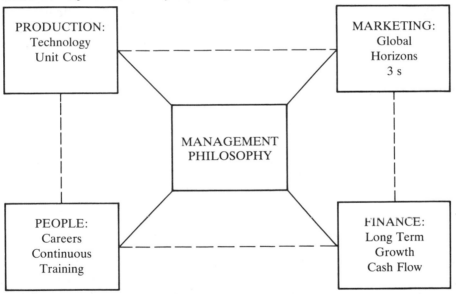

Books in North America such as Peters and Waterman's (1982) *In Search of Excellence* have pointed to the need for a consistent and holistic management philosophy, with the need to integrate various functional areas. Again, however, it is instructive to center on the educational system to see the contrasts between Japanese and Western practice. In Japan training of managers is overwhelming the role of companies – universities train and educate the individual. In North America, professional schools increasingly have become theoretical centers of scientific knowledge. Simon (1979:56) makes the point as follows:

Design . . . is the core of all professional training; it is the principal mark that distinguishes the professions from the sciences. Schools of engineering, as well as schools of architecture, business, education, law, and medicine, are all centrally concerned with the process of design.

In view of the key role of design in professional activity, it is ironic that in this century the natural sciences have almost driven the sciences of the artificial (i.e. the study of the man made artifacts of our environment) from professional school curricula. Engineering schools have become schools of physics and mathematics; medical schools have become schools of biological sciences; business schools have become schools of finite mathematics. The use of adjectives like 'applied' conceals but does not change the fact. It simply means that in the professional schools those topics are selected from mathematics and the natural sciences for emphasis which are thought to be most nearly relevent to professional practice. It does not mean that design is taught, as distinguished from analysis.

Japanese experience both in universities and in company work places a clear emphasis on design. The philosophy of management in the best run Japanese companies starts from a production emphasis. The point is not that US or European firms don't have good engineering – compare the technology and engineering emphasis of a French car company like Citroen, for example, or the fact that US firms like General Motors and Ford were two of the biggest investors in R & D just before the Japanese auto unslaught arrived in force – rather, the point is the need to integrate across functions.

Schematically the difference between Japan and Western companies can be shown in Exhibit 14/3. Companies plan at three levels, namely corporate, business, and functional levels. The corporate level determines the range and kinds of products, markets, and technologies in the firm's portfolio. Business level planning involves the long range profitability of any one particular product/market area, taking into account competitive cost advantage and life cycle considerations. Functional level planning concern the range of tactical questions and techniques within any one function, such as production, marketing, personnel or whatever.

Japanese practice places predominant emphasis on tactical and functional level strategies, i.e. the day to day operational issues which go into each product line. Top management devotes a high proportion of time directly involving

Exhibit 14/3: Japanese and Western Contrasts in Planning

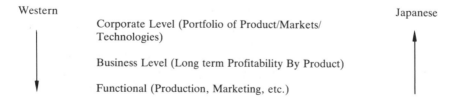

Western   Japanese

Corporate Level (Portfolio of Product/Markets/
Technologies)

Business Level (Long term Profitability By Product)

Functional (Production, Marketing, etc.)

itself in key operational areas – quality, inventories, scheduling, maintenance, plant design, and the like – because these go to the core of defining the success of the product around low cost and quality. Much of North American management time is devoted to portfolio planning, and to a certain extent, business level planning. The areas of functional planning are usually delegated entirely to operational management. These "design" activities, to use Simon's (1979) terminology, are relatively divorced from workers, whereas Japan's hardware and software systems are oriented to putting the most emphasis on the perfection of functional strategies.

14.4 A Final Word

The Japanese industrial system is complicated and complex; it is competitively developing new products, services, and technologies equal to the best available anywhere. This book has analysed the basic architecture of the industrial system, focusing on the national, industry, and organizational level. The historian of ideas will one day draw conclusions as to the relative merits or demerits of the Japanese system as compared to others. The Japanese have an enormous capacity to develop their own skills and capabilities, but they also are not so arrogant as to be unable to learn from others, technologically and managerially. Their competition in foreign markets has shaken many industries to their foundations, and that has provoked both fear and protection.

The Japanese have often been better marketers of products than of their own success story. The Japanese as a result have suffered the pale of both envy and racism. The future for both Japan and her competitors can be one of interdependence or of conflict. Any student of both history and management can only hope that the Japanese and her competitors will evolve a future to harness the enormous talent of this industrial system to the good of mankind everywhere.

References

Aaron, Benjamin, and K. W. Wederburn (Eds.) (1972): Industrial Conflict: A Comparative Legal Survey. London: Longmans.

Abegglen, James (1958): The Japanese Factory. Glencoe, Ill. Free Press.

Abegglen, James (1970): Business Strategies For Japan. Tokyo: Sophia University.

Abegglen, James, and Thomas Hout (1978): "Facing Up To the Trade Gap With Japan". Foreign Affairs (Fall), 146–168.

Abegglen, James, and Akio Etori (1982): "Japanese Technology Today". Scientific American, 247 (October): J1–J30.

Abell, Derek, and John Hammond (1979): Strategic Marketing Planning. Englewood Cliffs, N. J. Prentice-Hall.

Abernathy, William, J., et al. (1981): "The New Industrial Competition". Harvard Business Review (September–October), 68–81.

Ackerman, E. A. (1949): Japanese Natural Resources. Tokyo: Charles Tuttle.

Adams, Roy J. (1982): "Industrial Relations Systems in Europe and North America". In: John Anderson and Morley Gunderson, Union Management Relations In Canada. Toronto: Addison-Wesley.

Adams, T. F. M., and Hoshii Iwoo (1972): A Financial History of The New Japan. Tokyo: Kodansha.

Anderson, Arthur, and Co. (1979): "US Companies in International Markets – The Role of Trading Companies in Stimulating Exports". Brief Submitted To Committee on Banking, Housing and Urban Affairs, United States Senate.

Argyris, Chris (1973): "Personality and Organization". Administrative Science Quarterly, 14:1–22.

Argyris, Chris (1976): "Single-Loop and Double-Loop Models in Research On Decision Making". Administrative Science Quarterly, 21:363–375.

Aso, Makoto, and Amano Ikiu (1972): Education and Japan's Modernization. Tokyo: Ministry of Foreign Affairs.

Austin, Lewis (Ed.) (1976): Japan: The Paradox of Progress. New Haven: Yale University Press.

Ayres, Robert, and Steven Miller (1982a): "Robotics, CAM, and Industrial Productivity". National Productivity Review, Winter: 42–60.

Ayres, Robert, and Steven Miller (1982b): "Industrial Robots on the Line". Technology Review (May/June 1982), 35–45.

Azumi, Koya (1969): Higher Education and Business Recruitment In Japan. New York: Teachers College Press.

Azumi, Koya (1974): "Japanese Society: A Sociological View". In: Arthur Tiedemann (Ed.): An Introduction to Japanese Civilization. New York: Columbia University Press.

Azumi, Koya, and Charles McMillan (1975): "Culture and Organizational Structure". International Studies of Management and Organization, Vol. 5: 35–47.

Azumi, Koya, and Charles McMillan (1976): "Work Sentiment In the Japanese Factory: Its Organizational Determinants". In: Lewis Austin (1976).

Ballon, Robert (Ed.) (1973): The Japanese Employee. Tokyo: Charles Tuttle Company.

Baranson, Jack (1980): The Japanese Challenge. New York: Pergamon Press.

Becker, Gary (1962): "Investment in Human Capital: A Theoretical Analysis". Journal of Political Economy, 70:9–44.

Bell, Daniel (1974): The Coming of Post-Industrial Society. London: Heinemann.

Benedict, Ruth (1946): The Chrysanthemum and The Sword. Boston: Houghton Mifflin Company.

Blackmore, Russ (1981): "Human Software". Behaviour Research Methods and Instrumentation, 13:553–570.

Blauner, Robert (1964): Alienation and Freedom. Chicago: University of Chicago Press.

Blume, Marshall E. (1980): "The Financial Markets". In: Caves and Krause (1980).

Blumenthal, T. (1979): "A Note on The Relationship Between Domestic Research and Development and Imports of Technology". Economic Development and Cultural Chance, 27 (January).

Bolling, Richard, and John Bowles (1982): America's Competitive Edge. New York: McGraw-Hill.

Boulding, K., and Gleason (1972): "War As an Investment: The Strange Case of Japan". In: K. Boulding and Tapan Mukerjee (Eds.): Economic Imperialism. Ann Arbor: University of Michigan Press.

Boulding, Kenneth (1973): The Economics of Love and Fear. Belmont, California.

Bowles, S., and H. Gintis (1975): "The Problem With Human Capital Theory: A Marxian Critique". American Economic Review, 65:68–78.

Boyd, Gavin (Ed.) (1982): Region Building In the Pacific. New York: Pergamon Press.

Brzezinski, Zbigniew (1973): The Fragile Blossom: Crisis and Change In Japan. New York: Harper and Row.

Bucy, Fred J. (1980): "Presidential Address", Quoted in "Texas Instruments Inc.". In: John M. Stopford et al.: Strategic Management. London. John Wiley.

Burke, Ron (1983): "Mentors in Organizations". Journal of Canadian Petroleum Technology: 23, 10–13.

Business Week (1981): "One Country: Five Separate Economies" (June 1), 38–69.

Bylinsky, Gene (1980): "The Japanese Spies in Silicon Valley". Fortune (February 27), 74–79.

Calleo, David P. (1982): The Imperious Economy. Cambridge, Mass.: Harvard University Press.

Campbell, John (1977): Contemporary Japanese Budget Politics. Berkeley, Calif.: University of California Press.

Casement, Richard (1982): "Japanese Technology". The Economist (June 19).

Caves, Richard (1980): "Industrial Organization, Corporate Strategy and Structure". Journal of Economic Literature, XVIII: 64–92.

Caves, Richard, and Lawrence Krause (Eds.) (1980): Britain's Economic Performance. Washington: Brookings.

Caves, Richard, and Masu Uekusa (1976): Industrial Organization In Japan, Washington: The Brookings Institution.

Chandler, Alfred D. (1962): Strategy and Structure. Cambridge, Mass.: MIT Press.

Channon, Derek (1979): "Leadership and Corporate Performance In the Service Industries". Journal of Management Studies, 16: 185–201.

Chatov, Robert (1982): "Cooperation Between Government and Business". In: Paul Nystrom and William Starbuck (Eds.): Handbook of Organizational Design. London: Oxford University Press.

Cochran, Thomas C. (1972): Business In American Life. New York: McGraw Hill.

Cole, Robert (1971): Japanese Blue Collar: The Changing Tradition. Berkeley, Calif.: University of California Press.

Cole, Robert (1976): "Changing Labour Force Characteristics and Their Impact On Japanese Industrial Relations". In: L. Auston (1976).

Cole, Robert (1979): Work, Mobility and Participation. Berkeley, Calif.: University of California Press.

Cole, Robert (1981): "Technology and Organizational Innovation: A Review of the Literature". Unpublished Manuscript, University of Michigan.

Collins, Randall (1979): The Credentials Society. New York: Academic Press Inc.

Comptroller-General (1979): United States – Japan Trade: Issues and Problems. Washington: General Accounting Office.

Cook, Alice, and Hiroko Hayashi (1980): Working Women In Japan: Discrimination, Resistance, and Reform. Ithaca, N. Y.: Cornell University Press.

Cooper, Richard N. (1977): "IMF Surveillance Over Exchange Rates: A Wider View". In: Robert A. Mundell and Jacques J. Polak (Eds.): The New International Monetary System. New York: Columbia University Press.

Craig, Albert (1975): "Functional and Dysfunctional Aspects of Government Bureaucracy". In: Vogel (1975).

Crane Dwight B., and Samuel L. Hayes, III (1982): "The New Competition in World Banking". Harvard Business Review (July–August), 88–94.

Crozier, Michel (1964): The Bureaucratic Phenomenon. Chicago: University of Chicago Press.

Cummings, William K. (1976): "The Problems and Prospects for Japanese Higher Education". In: L. Austin (1976).

Curtis, Gerald L. (1971): Election Campaigning Japanese Style. New York: Columbia University Press.

Cyert, R. M., and J. G. March (1963): A Behavioural Theory Of the Firm. Englewood Cliffs, N. J.: Prentice-Hall.

Dahl, Robert, and Charles Lindblom (1953): Politics, Economics and Welfare. New York: Houghton Mifflin.

Dahlby, Tracy (1981): "The Bureaucrats: Sons of the Samurai". Far Eastern Economic Review (March 20), 34–40.

Daly, D. J. (1980): "Japanese Economic Developments, 1970–1976". In: S. Tsuru (Ed.): Economic Growth and Resources. London: MacMillan.

Daly, D. J. (1981): "Canada In an Uncertain World Economic Environment". Montreal: IRRP.

Dennison, Edward F. (1979): Accounting For Slower Growth: The United States In 1970's. Washington: The Brookings Institution.

Dennison, Edward F., and William K. Chung (1976): How Japan's Economy Grew So Fast. Washington, D. C.: The Brookings Institution.

Deutsch, Arnold (1982): "How Employee Retention Strategies Can Aid Productivity". The Journal of Business Strategy, 2.

Dewar, Margaret E. (Ed.) (1982): Industry Vitalization. New York: Pergamon Press.

Diebold, William Jr. (1980): Industrial Policy As an International Issue. New York: McGraw Hill.

Dimick, David, and V. V. Murray (1976): Personnel Administration In Large and Middlesized Canadian Businesses. Ottawa: Ministry of Supply and Services.

Doeringer, Peter, and Michael Piore (1971): Internal Labour Markets and Manpower Analysis. Lexington, Mass.: Heath.

Doi, Takeo (1973): The Anatomy of Dependence. Tokyo: Kodansha International.

Donnolly, Michael, and Keith A. J. Hay (1980): "Canadian-Japanese Agricultural Trade". In: Hay (1980).

Dore, Ronald (1973): British Factory, Japanese Factory. Los Angeles: University of California.

Dore, Ronald (1976): The Diploma Disease. London: George Allen and Unwin.

Dreze, Jacques (1960): "Les Exportations intra-CEE en 1958 et la position belge". Recherches Economique de Louvain.

Dreze, Jacques (1961): "Quelques Reflexions sereines sur l'adaptation de l'industrie belge au Marché Commun". Comptes Rendus des Travaux de la Societé Royale d'Economie Politique de Belgique, No. 275.

Drucker, Peter F. (1968): The Age of Discontinuity. New York: Harper and Row.

Drucker, Peter F. (1975): "Economic Realities and Enterprise Strategy". In: Ezra Vogel (1975).

Drucker, Peter F. (1978): "Japan: The Problems of Success". Foreign Affairs (April), 564–578.

Drucker, Peter F. (1981): "Behind Japan's Success". Harvard Business Review (January–February 1981), 83–90.

Dubin, Robert, et al. (1975): "Central Life Interests and Organizational Committment of Blue-Collar and Clerical Workers". Administrative Science Quarterly, 20:411–421.

Dunlop, John (1958): Industrial Relations Systems. New York: Holt, Rinehart, A and ·Winston.

Dunnette, Marvin, and Bernard M. Bass (1963): "Behavioural Scientists and Personnel Management". Industrial Relations, 2:125–131.

Dyas, Gareth, and Heinz Thanheiser (1976): The Emerging European Enterprise. London: MacMillan.

Economist Intelligence Unit (1981): Japanese Industry. Report No 110. London.

Emerson, John K. (1971): Arms, Yen, and Power: The Japanese Dilemma. Tokyo: Charles E. Tuttle Company.

Emery, F., and Eric Trist (1975): Towards a Social Ecology. New York: Plenum Publishing Corporation.

Emori, Markisa (1971): Japanese General Trading Firms. Tokyo.

Fallows, James (1980): "American Industry: What Ails It, How To Save It". The Atlantic, 246 (September).

Fallows, James (1981): National Defense. New York: Random House.

Forbes (1982): "The Hundred Largest Foreign Corporations" (July 5).

Fouquin, Michel, et al. (1981): Redeploiements Geographiques et Rapports de Force Industriels. Paris: Economie Prospective Internationale.

Frager, Robert, and Thomas P. Rohlen (1976): "The Future of a Tradition: Japanese Spirit in the 1980's". In: L. Austin (1976).

Franko, Lawrence (1979): The European Multinationals. London: MacMillan.

Fraser, Patrick, and Dimitri Vittas (1982): The Retail Banking Revolution. London: Michael Lafferty Publications.

Freedman, Audrey (1982): Japanese Management of American Workforces. New York: The Conference Board.

Galanson, Walter, and K. Odaka (1976): "The Japanese Labour Market". In: Patrick and Rosovsky (1976).

Galbraith, Jay (1977): Organization Design. Reading: Addison Wesley.

Galbraith, John Kenneth (1967): The New Industrial States. New York: Houghton and Mifflin.

George, Alexander L. (1972): "The Case For Multiple Advocacy In Making Foreign Policy". American Political Science Review, Vol. 66: 751–785.

Glaser, Nathan (1976): "Social and Cultural Factors In Japanese Economic Growth". In: Patrick and Rosovsky (1976), 813–896.

Gold, Bela (1981): "On Size, Scale, and Returns: A Survey". Journal of Economic Literature, XIX (March 1981), 5–33.

Gregory Gene, and Akio Etari (1981): "Japanese Technology Today". Scientific American.

Haitani, Kanji (1976): The Japanese Economic System: An Institutional Overview. Lexington, Mass.: D. C. Heath.

Hall, Edward T. (1970): The Silent Language. Greenwich, Conn.: Premier Books.

Hall, Edward T. (1977): Beyond Culture. New York: Double Day.

Hall, G. R., and R. E. Johnson (1970): "Transfers of United States Aerospace Technology to Japan". In: R. Vernon (Ed.) The Technology Factor In International Trade. New York: Columbia University Press.

Halliday, Jon, and Gavan McCormack (1973): Japanese Imperialism Today. Middlesex, England: Penquin.

Harrigan, Katheryn (1980): Strategies For Declining Industries. Lexington, Mass.: D. C. Heath and Company.

Hasegawa, Keitaro (1978): "Japanese Corporations and Crisis Survival". Japan Echo, V:85–93.

Hatvany, Nina G., and Vladimir Pucik (1982): "An Integrated Management System Focused On Human Resources: The Japanese Paradigm". Organizational Dynamics.

Hauser, Philip (1970): "The Chaotic Society: Product of Social Morphological Revolution". American Sociological Review, 34:1–18.

Hay, Keith (Ed.) (1980): Canada–Japan Economie Relation. Montreal: IRPP.

Hayes, Robert (1981): "Why Japanese Factories Work". Harvard Business Review (July–August).

Hayes, Robert H., and William Abernathy (1980): "Managing Our Way To Economic Decline". Harvard Business Review (July–August).

Henderson, Dan Fenno (1975): Foreign Enterprise In Japan. Tokyo: Charles Tuttle Company.

Herzberg, Frederick (1964): "The Motivation-Hygiene Concept and Problems of Manpower", Personnel Administration, 27:3–7.

Hickson, David, and Charles McMillan (Eds.) (1980): Organization and Nation: The International Aston Program, Vol. IV. London: Gower.

Hirsch, W. Z. (1956): "Firm Progress Ratios". Econometrica, 24.

Hofheinz, Roy Jr., and Kent E. Calder (1982): The Eastasia Edge. New York: Basic Books.

Horvath, Dezso, and Charles McMillan (1980): "Industrial Planning in Japan". California Management Review, Vol. XXII (Fall): 11–21.

Hoselitz, Bert (Ed.) (1968): The Role of Small Business In the Process of Economic Growth. Paris: Mouton.

Hout, Thomas, et al. (1982): "How Global Companies Win Out". Harvard Business Review (September–October), 98–108.

Hsu, F. L. (1975): Iemoto: The Heart of Japan. Cambridge, Mass.: John Wiley.

Hymer, Stephen, and Robert Rowthorne (1970): "Multinational Corporations and International Oligopoly: The Non-American Challenge". In: Charles Kindleberger (Ed.): The International Corporation. Cambridge, Mass: MIT Press.

Hyoe, Murakami, and Johannes Hirschmaier (Eds.) (1979): Politics and Economics In Contemporary Japan. Tokyo: Toppan Printing Co..

Ichiro, Nokayama (1978): Industrialization and Labour-Management Relations In Japan. Tokyo: Japanese Institute of Labour.

Ikedo, Masayoshi (1982): "Japanese Style Management in Britain". Japan Echo, IX (Spring).

Ivancevich, John M., et al. (1977): Organizational Behaviour and Performance. Santa Monica, Calif.: Goodyear Publishing.

Jamieson, Ian (1980): Capitalism and Culture: A Comparative Analysis of British and American Manufacturing Organizations. London: Gower.

Jamieson, Stuart (1973): Industrial Relations In Canada. Toronto: MacMillan.

Japan Cultural Institute (1979): "The Bureaucracy: Japan's Pool of Leadership". In: Hyoe and Hirschmaier (1979).

JETRO (1980): The Role of Trading Companies In International Commerce. Tokyo: Marketing Series No. 2.

JETRO (1981): Japanese Manufacturing Operations In the United States: Results of First Comprehensive Field Study, New York: Japan Trade Center.

JIL (1974): Japanese Labour Statistics. Tokyo.

Johnson, Chalmers (1982): Miti and the Japanese Miracle. Stanford: Stanford University Press.

Kahn, Herman (1970): The Emerging Japanese Superstate: Challenge and Response. Englewood Cliffs, N. J.: Prentice-Hall.

Kahn, Herman (1979): World Economic Development. Boulder, Colorado: Westview Press, 1979.

Kahn, Herman and Thomas Pepper (1980): The Japanese Challenge. Tokyo.

Kaplin, Eugene J. (1972): Japan: The Government-Business Relationship. Washington, D. C.: Department of Commerce.

Kassalow, Everett (1969): Trade Unions and Industrial Relations: An International Comparison. New York: Random House.

Kassem, M. S. (1974): "A Tale of Two Countries: Japan and Britain". Columbia Journal of World Business, IX:35–48.

Katz, Daniel, and Robert Kahn (1978): The Social Psychology of Organizations, New York: John Wiley and Sons.

Kendrick, J. (1980): "Survey of the Factors Contributing to the Decline in US Productivity Growth". Federal Reserve Bank of Boston: The Decline in Productivity Growth, Series No. 22:1–25.

Kiefer, Christie W. (1976): "The Danchi Zoku and the Evolution of Metropolitan Mind". In: L. Austin (1976).

Kindleberger, Charles (1978): Economic Response: Comparative Studies In Trade, Finance, and Growth. Cambridge, Mass.: Harvard University Press.

Kitamura, Kazuyuki (1979): "Mass Higher Education". In: W. Cummings et al. (Eds.): Changes in the Japanese University: A Comparative Perspective. New York: Praeger.

Kobayashi, N. (1969): "Management Differences". In: T. F. M. Adams and N. Kobayashi (Eds.): The World of Japanese Business. Tokyo: Kodansha International Ltd..

Kojima, Kioshi (1973): "International Impact of Foreign Direct Investment". The Oriental Economist (December).

Kojima, Kioshi (1977): Japan and a New World Economic Order. Tokyo: Charles Tuttle Company.

Komiryo, Hideyuki (1978): "Growth, Profitability, and Productivity". Management Japan, Vol. 11.

Komiya, Ryutaro (1975): "Economic Planning In Japan". Challenge (May–June).

Kotler, Philip (1976): Marketing Management: Analysis, Planning, and Control. Englewood Cliffs, N. J.: Prentice-Hall.

Kotler, Philip, and Liam Fahey (1982): "The World's Champion Marketers: The Japanese". Journal of Business Strategy, 3–13.

Krause, Lawrence B., and Sueo Sekiguchi (1976): "Japan and The World Economy". In: Patrick and Rosovsky (1976).

Lammers, Cor, and David J. Hickson (1979): Organizations Alike and Unlike. London: Routledge and Kegan Paul.

Lancaster, John (1980): "Sectoral Paper on Trading Houses in Canada". Ottawa: ITC.

Lawless, Edward W. (1977): Technology and Social Shock. New Brunswick, N. J.: Rutgers University Press.

Lawrence, Paul, and Jay Lorsch (1969): Organization and Environment. Homewood, Ill.: Richard D. Irwin.

Lefay G., and M. Fouquin (1980): "Specialisation et Adaption Face a la Crise". Economie Prospective Internationale (Janvier).

Leibenstein, Harvey (1966): "Allocative Efficiency Versus 'X-Efficiency'". American Economic Review, 56:392–415.

Leibenstein, Harvey (1976): Beyond Economic Man. Cambridge, Mass.: Harvard University Press.

Leontiades, Milton (1982): Management Policy, Strategy, and Plans. Boston: Little, Brown, and Company.

Leontief, Wassily (1982): "What Hope for the Economy?" New York Review (August 12).

Levinson, D. J., et al. (1980): The Season of a Man's Life. New York: A. A. Knopf.

Lind, Richard (1982): "IQ In Japan And The United States Shows A Growing Disparity". Bulletin of British Psychological Society.

Lipset, S. M. (1963): The First New Nation: Basic Books.

Locke, Edwin A. (1982): "The Ideas of Frederick W. Taylor: An Evaluation". Academy of Management Review, 7:7–24.

Macrae, Norman (1975): "Pacific Century, 1975–2075?" The Economist (January 4), 15–35.

Macrae, Norman (1976): "The Coming Entrepreneurial Revolution". The Economist (December 25).

Magaziner, Ira C., and Thomas Hout (1980): Japanese Industrial Policy. London: Policy Studies Institute.

Magaziner, Ira C., and Robert Reich (1982): Minding America's Business. New York: Harcourt Brace and Jovanovich.

Main, Jeremy (1982): "Work Won't Be The Same Again". Fortune (June 28), 58–65.

Mannari, Hiroshi (1974): The Japanese Business Leaders. Tokyo: University of Tokyo Press.

Mansfield, Edwin (1968): The Economics of Technological Change. New York: W. W. Norton.

Marsh, Robert, and Hiroshi Mannari (1976): Modernization and the Japanese Factory, Princeton: Princeton University Press.

Maruyama, Masao (1979): Thought and Behaviour In Modern Japanese Politics. London: Oxford University Press.

McKinnon, Ronald I. (1983): "An Internationalist Money Supply: How A Strong Dollar Threw The Fed". The New York Times (January 23, 30).

McMillan, C. J. (1978): "The Changing Competitive Environment of Canadian Business". Journal of Canadian Studies (Summer).

McMillan, C. J. (1980): "Is Japanese Management Really So Different?" The Business Quarterly (Autumn).

McMillan, C. J. (1983): "From Beaver Pelts to Steel Complexes: The Role of Barter and Countertrade In International Trade". Unpublished manuscript, York University.

MESC (1976): Course of Study For Upper Secondary Schools In Japan. Tokyo: Ministry of Education, Science, and Culture.

Miller, Jeffrey, and Margaret Graham (1981): "Production Operations Management: Agenda For the 1980's". Unpublished Manuscript, Harvard Business School.

Miller, Stanley S. (1981): "Make Your Plant Manager's Job Manageable". Harvard Business Review (January–February).

Ministry of International Trade and Investment (1980): White Paper On Small Business, Tokyo.

Ministry of International Trade and Investment (1981): White Paper On International Trade, Tokyo.

Mishan, E. J. (1969): Technology and Growth: The Price We Pay. New York: Praeger.

Morikawa, Hidemasa (1970): "The Organization Structures of Mitsubishi and Mitsui Zaibatsu, 1868–1922: A Comparative Study". Business History Review, 40.

Moynihan, Daniel (Jan. 16, 1983): "Centralize Trade Policy". The New York Times, EY 21.

Nagai, Michio (1971): Higher Education In Japan. Tokyo: University of Tokyo Press.

Nakagawa, Keiichiro (Ed.) (1976): Strategy and Structure of Big Business, Tokyo: University of Tokyo Press.
Nakagawa, Keiichiro (Ed.) (1977): Social Order and Entrepreneurship, Tokyo: University of Tokyo Press.
Nakagawa, Keiichiro (Ed.) (1979): Labour and Management, Tokyo: University of Tokyo Press.
Nakagawa, Keiichiro (Ed.) (1980): Government and Business. Tokyo: University of Tokyo Press.
Nakamura, Hideichiro (1979): "Plotting A New Economic Course". Japan Echo, VI.
Nakane, Chie (1973): Japanese Society, Hammersmith, U. K.: Penquin.
Nakase, T. (1979): "The Introduction of Scientific Management in Japan and Its Characteristics: Case Studies of Companies in the Sumitomo Zaibatsu". In: Nakagawa (1979).
Nelson, Richard R. (1981): "Research On Productivity Growth and Productivity Differences: Dead Ends and New Departures". Journal of Economic Literature (September), 1029–1064.
Odaka, Kunio (1975): Towards Industrial Democracy. Cambridge, Mass.: Harvard University Press.
Ohkawa, Kazushi, and Henry Rosovsky (1973): Japanese Economic Growth. Stanford: Stanford University Press.
Ohmae, Ken (1982): The Mind of the Strategist: The Art of Japanese Business. New York: McGraw-Hill.
Oi, Walter Y. (1962): "Labour as a Quasi-Fixed Factor". Journal of Political Economy, 70: 538–555.
Okita, Saburo (1980): The Developing Economies and Japan. Tokyo: University of Tokyo Press.
Okoci, Akio, and Hoshimi Uchida (Eds.) (1980): Development and Diffusion of Technology. Tokyo: University of Tokyo Press.
Okuchi, K., et al. (Eds.) (1974): Workers and Employers In Japan. Tokyo: University of Tokyo Press.
Olson, Mancur (1982): The Rise and Decline of Nations. New Haven: Yale University Press.
Orlicki, G. (1975): Material Requirements Planning. New York: McGraw-Hill.
Ouchi, W. G. (1980): "Markets Bureaucracies and Clans". Administrative Science Quarterly, 25:129–140.
Ouchi, W. G. (1980): Theory Z. New York: Addison Wesley.
Ozawa, Terutomo (1979): Multinationalism, Japanese Style: The Political Economy of Outward Dependency. Princeton, N. J.: Princeton University Press.
Page, Sheila (1982): "The Management of International Trade". London: National Institute of Economic and Social Research.
Pascale Richard, and Anthony G. Athos (1981): The Art of Japanese Management. New York: Simon & Schuster.
Passin, Herbert (1965): Society and Education In Japan. New York: Teachers College Press.
Patrick, Hugh (1967): "Japan, 1968–1914". In: Ronald Cameron (Ed.): Banking In the Early Stages of Industrialization, Oxford: Open University Press.

Patrick Hugh, and Rosovsky, Henry (Eds.) (1976): Asia's New Giant: How the Japanese Economy Works, Washington, D. C.: The Brookings Institution.

Pechman, Joseph, and Keimei Kaizuka (1976): "Taxation". In: Patrick and Rosovsky (1976).

Peck, Merton J., and Akiro Goto (1981): "Technology and Economic Growth: The Case of Japan". Research Policy, 10:222–243.

Peck, Merton J., and S. Tamura (1976): "Technology". In: Patrick and Rosovsky (1976).

Perlmutter, Howard V. (1969): "The Tortuous Evolution of the Multinational Corporation". Columbia Journal of World Business (January–February).

Perrow, Charles (1979): Complex Organizations: A Critical Essay, Glenview, Ill.: Scott Forseman.

Peters, Thomas, J., and Robert H. Waterman Jr. (1982): In Search of Excellence. New York: Harper and Row.

Pettigrew, A. M. (1979): "On Studying Organizational Cultures". Administrative Science Quarterly, 24: 570–581.

Pharr, Susan J. (1976): "The Japanese Woman: Evolving Views of Life and Role". In: L. Austin (1976).

Pollard, Sidney (1979): "Management and Labour in Britain During The Period of Industrialization". In: Nakagawa (1979).

Porter, L. W., et al. (1975): Behaviour In Organizations. New York: McGraw-Hill.

Porter, Michael (1980): Competitive Strategy, New York: The Free Press.

Potter, David (1953): People of Plenty. New York.

Prais, S. J. (1976): The Evolution of Giant Firms In Britain. Cambridge: Cambridge University Press.

Prindl, Andrea (1981): Japanese Finance: A Guide to Banking In Japan. New York: John Wiley and Sons.

Professors World Peace Academy of Japan (1978): The Pacific Era. Tokyo: Eighth International Conference on World Peace.

Quirk, Peter J. (1977): "Exchange Rate Policy in Japan: Leaning Against The Wind". IMF Staff Papers, Vol. XXIV:642–664.

Reed, Howard Curtis (1980): "The Ascent of Tokyo As An International Financial Center". Journal of International Business Studies (Winter), 19–35.

Reich, Robert (1982): Minding Americäs Business. Cambridge: Haward University, Press.

Rix, Alan (1979): Japan's Economic Aid: Policy-Making and Politics. New York: St. Martin's Press.

Roberts, John G. (1973): Mitsui. New York: Weatherhill.

Roche, Gerard R. (1979): "Much Ado About Mentors". Harvard Business Review, 57: 17–28.

Roden, Donald T. (1980): Schooldays In Imperial Japan. Berkeley: University of California.

Roehl, Thomas (1973): "Spiritual Training In A Japanese Bank". American Anthropologist, 5:1542–1562.

Ross, Randolf (1979): "Marketing Distribution Systems". In: Hay (1980).

Rugman, Alan (1980): "Internationalization As A General Theory of Foreign Direct Investment". Weltwirtschaftliches Archiv 16.

Sakakibara, Eisuke, and Yukio Noguchi (1977): "Dissecting the Finance Ministry – Bank of Japan Dynasty". Japan Echo, IV: 98–124.

Salter, Malcolm S. (1973): "Tailor Incentive Compensation To Strategy". Harvard Business Review (March–April), 94–102.

Sampson, Anthony (1980): The Money Lenders. New York.

Samuelson, Paul A. (1976): "American Economics". In: R. E. Freeman (Ed.): Postwar Economic Trends In the United States. New York.

Samuelson, Paul A. (1980): "The Public Role in the Modern American Economy". In: Martin Feldstein (Ed.): The American Economy In Transition. Chicago: University of Chicago Press.

Schwartz, Howard, and Stanley M. Davis (1981): "Matching Corporate Culture and Business Strategy". Organizational Dynamics (Summer).

Scott, Bruce (1982): "Can Industry Survive the Welfare State?". Harvard Business Review (September–October), 70–84.

Shimizu, Ryuei (1980): The Growth of Firms In Japan. Tokyo: Keio Tsushin Ltd..

Shinohara, Miyohei (1979): "The Rise and Fall of Economic Powers". Japan Echo, VI: 68–80.

Simon, Herbert A. (1976): The New Science of Management Decision. Revised Edition. Englewood Cliffs, N. J.: Prentice-Hall.

Simon, Herbert A. (1979): The Science of the Artificial. Cambridge: M.I.T. Press.

Stinchcombe, Arthur (1965): "Social Structure and Organizations". In: James G. March (Ed.): Handbook of Organizations. Chicago: Rand McNally.

Stoffaes, Christian (1978): La Grande Menace Industrielle. Paris: Calman-Levy.

Stopford, John, and T. Wells (1972): Managing the Multinational Enterprise – Organization of the Firm and Ownership of the Subsidiaries. New York: Basic Books.

Sumiya, Mikayo (1969): "The Impact of Technological Change on Industrial Relations In Japan". Developing Economies, 4:499–516.

Susuki, Y. (1980): "Strategy and Structure of Toponese Enterprise." Strategie Menogernent Tomnol, Vol. 2.

Suzuki, Yoshio (1980): Money and Banking In Contemporary Japan. New Haven: Yale University Press.

Takamiya, Makoto (1981): "Japanese Multinationals In Europe: Internal Operations and Their Public Policy Implications". Columbia Tournal of World Business XVI (Summer 1981), 5–17.

Takeuchi, Hiroshi (1978): "Keys To Corporate Resilience". Asahi Shibun Sho.

Tanaka, Hiroshi (1980): "The Japanese Method of Preparing Today's Graduate to Become Tomorrow's Manager". Personnel Journal (February), 109–112.

Tatom, John A. (1979): "The Productivity Problem". Federal Reserve Bank of St. Louis Review (September), 3–16.

Taylor, Frederick W. (1911): Principles of Scientific Management. New York: Harper and Row.

Thomas, Barbara S. (1982): "Easing Access To Japanese Capital". Business Week (August 30), 10–11.

Thompson, D. N. (1980): "Pricing and the Experience Curve Effect". In: D. N. Thompson et al.: Macromarketing: A Canadian Perspective. Chicago: American Marketing Association.

Thompson, James D. (1967): Organizations In Action. New York: McGraw-Hill.

Thurow, Lester (1981): "Where Management Fails". Newsweek (December 7):78.

Thurow, Lester (1982): "Trading Blows With Japan". Newsweek (January 10):62.

Tokuyama, J. (1978): "Japan's Role in the Pacific Era". Japan Echo, VI.

Trist, Eric (1981): The Evolution of Socio-Technical Systems. Toronto: Ontario Ministry of Labour.

Tsurumi, Yoshi (1976): The Japanese Are Coming. Cambridge, Mass.: Ballinger Publishing Co.

Tsurumi, Yoshi (1980): The Sogoshosha. Montreal: IRPP.

Twaalhoven, E. and T. Hattori (1982): The Supporting Role of Small Japanese Enterprises. Indivers Research. The Netherlands.

Useem, Michael (1982): 'Classwide Rationality in the Politics of Managers and Directors of Large Corporations in the United States and Great Britain". Administrative Science Quarterly, 27: 199–226.

Vernon, Raymond (1966): "International Investment and International Trade in the Product Cycle". Quarterly Journal of Economics (May).

Vernon, Raymond (1971): Sovereignty At Bay: The Multinational Spread of US Enterprises. New York: Basic Books.

Vernon, Raymond (1974): Big Business and the State: Changing Relations In Western Europe. New York. Praeger.

Vogel, Ezra (1975): Modern Japanese Organization and Decision-Making. Los Angeles: University of California Press.

Vogel, Ezra (1979): Japan As Number One. Cambridge: Harvard University Press.

Wallich, M. and S. Wallich (1976): "Banking". In: Patrick and Rosovsky (1976).

Watson, Craig M. (1982): "Counter Competition Abroad To Protect Home Markets". Harvard Business Review (January–February).

Weber, Max (1947): The Theory of Social and Economic Organization. New York: Oxford University Press.

Weick, Karl (1976): "Educational Organizations as Loosely Coupled Systems". Administrative Science Quarterly, 21 (March), 1–19.

Weidenbaum, Murray A., and Linda Rockwood (1977): "Corporate Planning versus Government Planning". In: The Public Interest, 46 (Winter), 59–72.

Wheelwright, Steven C. (1981): "Japan: Where Operations Are Really Strategic". Harvard Business Review (July–August).

Williamson, O. E. (1975): Markets and Hierarchies: Analysis and Antitrust Implications. New York: Free Press.

Woodward, Joan (1965): Industrial Organization: Theory and Practice. London: Oxford University Press.

Woronoff, Jon (1979): Japan: The Coming Economic Crisis. Tokyo: Lotus Press.

Yanamura, Kozo (1976): "General Trading Companies in Japan – Their Origins and Growth". In: Hugh Patrick (Ed.): Japanese Industrialization and Its Social Consequences. Berkeley: University of California Press.

Yelle, Louis E. (1979): "The Learning Curve: Historical Review and Comprehensive Survey". Decision Sciences, 10:302–328.

Yergin, D. (1982): "Beyond the Next Oil Shock". New York Times Magazine.

Yoshihara, Kunio (1978): Japanese Investment In Southeast Asia. Honolulu: University Press of Hawaii.

Yoshino, M. Y. (1968): Japan's Managerial System: Tradition and Innovation. Cambridge, Mass.: MIT Press.

Yoshino, M. Y. (1976): Japan's Multinational Enterprises. Cambridge, Mass.: Harvard University.

Young, Alexander (1979): The Sogoshosha: Japan's Multinational Trading Companies. Boulder, Col.: Westview Press.

Subject Index

Author Index

de Gruyter Studies in Organization

An international series by internationally known authors
presenting current research in organization.

Organizing and organizations are pre-requisites for the viability and future developments of society. Their study and comprehension are indispensable to the quality of human life.

Therefore, this series aims to:
- present to the specialist subject matter and information on significant problems, research methods and research results;
- give interested individuals access to different subject areas;
- aid decision-making on contemporary problems;
- stimulate ideas for future modes of behaviour and research.

The series will include monographs, collections of contributed papers, and handbooks.

Editorial Board:
Michael Aiken, USA (University of Wisconsin)
Franco Ferraresi, Italy (University Torino)
David J. Hickson, Great Britain (University Bradford)
Alfred Kieser, Federal Republic of Germany (University Mannheim)
Cornelis J. Lammers, The Netherlands (University Leiden)
Johan Olsen, Norway (University Bergen)
Jean-Claude Thoenig, France (INSEAD, Fontainebleau)

Forthcoming Titles:

Limits to Bureaucratic Growth
By *Marshall W. Meyer*
1984. 15,5 × 23 cm. Approx. 240 pages. Cloth approx. DM 78,–.
ISBN 3 11 009865 2

Political Management
By *Hall Thomas Wilson*
1984. 15,5 × 23 cm. Approx. 230 pages. Cloth approx. DM 76,–.
ISBN 3 11 009902 0

Management in China
By *Oiva Laaksonen*
1985. 15,5 × 23 cm. Approx. 290 pages. Cloth approx. DM 88,–.
ISBN 3 11 009958 6

Guidance, Control and Evaluation in the Public Sector
Edited by *F. X. Kaufmann, G. Majone, V. Ostrom*
1985. 15,5 × 23 cm. Approx. 650 pages. Cloth approx. DM 150,–.
ISBN 3 11 009707 9

Prices are subject to change without notice

WALTER DE GRUYTER · BERLIN · NEW YORK

ORGANIZATION STUDIES

An international multidisciplinary journal devoted to the study of organizations, organizing and the organized in, and between societies

Editor-in-chief: David J. Hickson, University of Bradford

Co-Editor: Alfred Kieser, Mannheim

Managing Editor: Gerard T. Moran

Contents

Subscription rates 1984

Per volume of four issues. Libraries and institutions **DM 98,–**/approx. US $44.75. Individuals (except FRG and Switzerland) **DM 49,–**/approx. US $22.50 (DM-prices are definitive, $-prices are approximate and subject to fluctuations in the exchange rate).

Published in collaboration with the European Group for Organizational Studies (EGOS) and the Maison des Sciences de l'Homme, Paris by

WALTER DE GRUYTER · BERLIN · NEW YORK

Verlag Walter de Gruyter & Co., Genthiner Straße 13, D-1000 Berlin 30, Tel.: (0 30) 2 60 05-0
Walter de Gruyter, Inc., 200 Saw Mill River Road, Hawthorne, N. Y. 10532, Tel.: (914) 747-0110